PATERNOSTER BIBLICAL MONOGRAPHS

The Characterisation of God in Acts

The Indirect Portrayal of an Invisible Character

PATERNOSTER BIBLICAL MONOGRAPHS

A full listing of all titles in this series
appears at the close of this book

PATERNOSTER BIBLICAL MONOGRAPHS

The Characterisation of God in Acts

The Indirect Portrayal of an Invisible Character

Ling Cheng

WIPF & STOCK · Eugene, Oregon

Wipf and Stock Publishers
199 W 8th Ave, Suite 3
Eugene, OR 97401

The Characterization of God in Acts
The Indirect Portrayal of an Invisible Character
By Cheng, Ling
Copyright©2011 Paternoster
ISBN 13: 978-1-62032-349-6
Publication date 2/10/2015
Previously published by Paternoster, 2011

PATERNOSTER BIBLICAL MONOGRAPHS

Series Preface

One of the major objectives of Paternoster is to serve biblical scholarship by providing a channel for the publication of theses and other monographs of high quality at affordable prices. Paternoster stands within the broad evangelical tradition of Christianity. Our authors would describe themselves as Christians who recognise the authority of the Bible, maintain the centrality of the gospel message and assent to the classical credal statements of Christian belief. There is diversity within this constituency; advances in scholarship are possible only if there is freedom for frank debate on controversial issues and for the publication of new and sometimes provocative proposals. What is offered in this series is the best of writing by committed Christians who are concerned to develop well-founded biblical scholarship in a spirit of loyalty to the historic faith.

Series Editors

I. Howard Marshall, Honorary Research Professor of New Testament, University of Aberdeen, Scotland, UK

Richard J. Bauckham, Professor of New Testament Studies and Bishop Wardlaw Professor, University of St Andrews, Scotland, UK

Craig Blomberg, Distinguished Professor of New Testament, Denver Seminary, Colorado, USA

Robert P. Gordon, Regius Professor of Hebrew, University of Cambridge, UK

Tremper Longman III, Robert H. Gundry Professor and Chair of the Department of Biblical Studies, Westmont College, Santa Barbara, California, USA

Stanley E. Porter, President and Professor of New Testament, McMaster Divinity College, Hamilton, Ontario, Canada

To my parents, who gave life to me
and
To God, who has given me the meaning of life

Contents

Preface	xiii
Acknowledgements	xv
Abbreviations	xvii

CHAPTER 1 INTRODUCTION	1
Statement of Purpose	1
Clarification of Terminology	2
The Narrator and the Implied Author	4
Character	5
Point of View	7
Plot	9
Characterisation	10
Methodology	12

PART I MIMETIC CHARACTERISATION OF GOD—SHOWING	17
CHAPTER 2	
THE CHARACTERISATION OF GOD BY HEAVENLY CHARACTERS	19
Conceptual Characterisation	20
Jesus	20
The Holy Spirit	24
Angels	26
Summary	29
Personal/Interpersonal Characterisation	30
Jesus	31
The Holy Spirit	36
Angels	40
Summary	41
Conclusion	42

CHAPTER 3	
THE CHARACTERISATION OF GOD BY MAJOR CHARACTERS (I) — PETER	44
Conceptual Characterisation	45
The Speech at Pentecost (2:14-40)	45
The Speech at the Healing of the Lame Man (3:12-26)	54
The Speeches before the Jewish Leaders (4:8-12, 19-20; 5:29-32)	63
The Speeches concerning the Cornelius Incident	67
The Speech to Cornelius' Household (10:34-43)	67
The Speech to the Jewish Believers (11:5-17)	71
The Speech at the Jerusalem Council (15:7-11)	74
Summary	77

Personal/Interpersonal Characterisation	78
Personal Characterisation—Divine Encounters	78
Interpersonal Characterisation—Interactions with Other Human Characters	81
Interactions with the Jewish Crowd	82
Interactions with the Jewish Leaders	84
Interactions with the Believers as a Whole in Jerusalem	86
Interactions with the Believers in Samaria and Judea and with Gentiles	88
Summary	91
Conclusion	91

CHAPTER 4
THE CHARACTERISATION OF GOD BY MAJOR CHARACTERS (II) — PAUL

	93
Conceptual Characterisation	93
The Speech at Pisidian Antioch (13:16-41)	94
The Speech at Lystra (14:15-17)	105
The Speech at Athens (17:22-31)	107
The Speech to the Ephesian Elders (20:18-35)	118
The Trial Speeches	123
The Speech to the Jerusalem Jews (22:3-21)	124
The Speech before Felix (24:10-21)	127
The Speech before Agrippa (26:2-23)	128
Summary	133
Personal/Interpersonal Characterisation	134
Personal Characterisation—Divine Encounters	134
Paul as the Object of Heavenly Instructions	135
Paul as the Intermediary of Miraculous Deeds	136
Interpersonal Characterisation—Interactions with Other Human Characters	144
Interactions with the churches in Jerusalem and Antioch	144
Interactions with the Jews	147
Interactions with the Gentiles	148
Interactions with the Roman Officials	149
Summary	150
Conclusion	150

CHAPTER 5
THE CHARACTERISATION OF GOD BY MINOR CHARACTERS

	153
The Believers: As a Whole, Stephen, Philip, Barnabas, James	153
Conceptual Characterisation	155
The Accordant Prayer of the Believers as a Whole (4:24-30)	155
Stephen's Speech (7:2-53)	159
James' Speech (15:13-21)	164
Personal/Interpersonal Characterisation	168
Interpersonal Witness of the Believers as a Whole	168
Personal Witness of Stephen	169

Contents   xi

Personal Witness of Philip	170
Personal Witness of Barnabas	172
Personal Witness of James	173
Summary	174
The God-Fearers: Cornelius, The Ethiopian Eunuch, Lydia	175
Conceptual Characterisation	176
Cornelius' Encounter with God's Angel	176
Cornelius' Encounter with Peter	177
Personal Characterisation	178
Personal Witness of Cornelius	179
Personal Witness of the Ethiopian Eunuch	179
Personal Witness of Lydia	181
Summary	182
The Opponents	182
Conceptual Characterisation—The Speech of Gamaliel (5:35-39)	183
Interpersonal Characterisation	184
Internal Opposition	184
Jewish Opposition	184
Gentile Opposition	185
Roman Opposition	186
Summary	186
Conclusion	187
PART II THEMATIC CHARACTERISATION OF GOD—TELLING AND PLOT	189
CHAPTER 6	
THE CHARACTERISATION OF GOD BY THE NARRATOR	**191**
Overt Narrator's Distinctive *Telling* of God	192
Exclusive Use of Epithet for God	193
Especial Indication of God's 'Interest'	195
Summary	198
Covert Narrator's Presentation of God in the Plot	199
The Role of God's 'Interest' in the Plot	199
Λόγος as a Direct Object	200
Λόγος as a Subject	201
God's Activities in Plot Devices	204
The Pattern of Divine Initiative in Promise-Fulfilment	205
The Pattern of Word-Miracle Ministry	207
The Pattern of Word-Suffering Ministry	208
Significance of the Word-Miracle-Suffering Ministry Pattern	210
God's Function in the Plot Progression	213
God's Working Pattern in the Plot Progression	214
God's Role in the Narrative Development	215
The Portrait of God along the Plot Progression	219
Summary	220
Conclusion	221

CHAPTER 7 CONCLUSION	**224**
Characteristics of the Characterisation of God	224
Double-Stratum Representation	224
Double-Orbit Presentation	225
Double-Track Characterisation	225
Double-Lens Characterisation	226
Distinctive Portrait of God	227
Invisible-yet-Perceivable	227
Dominant-yet-Cogent	227
Continuous-yet-Changing	228
Concluding Remark	228
Appendixes	**231**
Appendix 1: The Lukan Use of Πατήρ	231
Appendix 2: The Words Indicating God-Fearer	232
Appendix 3: References for the Narrative Voices	235
Appendix 4: The Epithets Applied to God	236
Appendix 5: The Referent of Κύριος	237
Appendix 6: Epithets Conveying God's Attributes	240
Appendix 7: Λόγος Compared with Ῥῆμα and Ὁδός	242
Appendix 8: Development of Narrative Units	244
Bibliography	**249**
Indexes	**273**
Author Index	273
Scripture Index	

Preface

To know more about God and to do his will have been my desire since I became a Christian. I often think about how to experience the living God more profoundly, and how this invisible God would reveal himself to those who seek to do his will. While reading the stories in the Bible (i.e. the revelation of God), I found that there were many angles of looking at a narrative, and wondered what would be the major points the author intended to communicate to the reader and ultimately what God wanted to disclose about himself and his will through these biblical authors. The Gospels and the Book of Acts are essential to the Christian faith. Acts, in particular, conveys God's works in the primitive church, which may shed light on how God may work today. How God is presented in the Acts narrative, thus, attracts my attention. This study concerns various characters' characterisation of God through their interactions with God's agents and plan. Having struggled to complete this study, I sensed that in the writing process my interactions with God, myself and others can also be an ongoing characterisation of God.

A peculiar feature of the book of Acts as a narrative is an empty spotlight: the one character around whom the whole story revolves—the ultimate cause which weaves together the whole narrative—is a character who never steps on the stage. That central character is God. This study adopts a literary/narrative approach to examine the characterisation of God in Acts, exploring how the author presents this invisible God so as to make the acts of the apostles the Acts of God.

The first part scrutinises the portrayal of God at the level of the narrative content, from which a mimetic portrait of God is drawn. It investigates the representations of God and his actions presented through divine and human characters in the narrative world. God's relationship with other heavenly characters is first elucidated in order to manifest that they act on behalf of the one God. Then God's relationship with human characters is brought into discussion which reveals an image of God who is actively at work through his agents. Through the speeches of the main characters God's redemptive plan is made known; these speeches are basically christocentric yet introduced in a theocentric framework. Through the interactions between characters God's will of universal salvation in Jesus is gradually unfolded as God's divine agents intervene in the lives of God's people and as God's human agents comply with his will and carry on the divine mission.

The second part of this study explores the characterisation of God in the level of the narrative plot, from which appears a thematic portrayal of God, that is, the narrator's core portrait of God. By examining God's role in the plot progression, the narrative emphasis on the portrayal of God is disclosed. The narrative summaries significant to the plot and the repeated patterns of God's activities convey that the Word of God plays a controlling role in the development of the narrative as well as of human salvation history. Throughout the narrative God is characterised as a supreme and sovereign Lord who authoritatively and powerfully brings salvation, in Jesus and through the Spirit, to his people.

Methodologically, in addition to the literary techniques of characterisation commonly examined by scholars, this study takes various characters' points of view into account, through which a full picture of God is presented. Furthermore, this study explores the narrator's fundamental image of God by investigating God's role in the overall deployment of characters and events. Hopefully, this research will enrich the understanding of God in Acts as well as the study of biblical characterisation.

Ling Cheng
August 2008

Acknowledgements

This book is a revision of my PhD thesis completed at London School of Theology in 2006. Without the guidance and support of my supervisor, Dr Conrad Gempf, this study would not have been completed. His encouragement in every possible way is a great blessing from God. My gratitude also goes to Dr Steve Walton for his scholarly input in the early stage of my research, and to the New Testament Conference of LST for their constructive critique. Additionally, I am grateful to my research colleagues who have supported me with their friendship and encouragement. Dr Sue Sainsbury, a friend close in spirit, and Dr Helen Wright, deserve special thanks for their proofreading. Particular thanks should be given to Dr Ronald Y.K. Fung, who greatly encouraged me to publish this study, and to Miss Jan Naas, who proofread the revision.

Without the faithful love and prayers of my closest friends and my family, I would not have gone through this demanding and, sometimes, lonely process of research. Enormous thanks go to Kuei-Hua Hsu, Kai-Chin Lin, Jan Naas, and Rosa Lin for their invaluable friendship and their thoughtful love for over 20 years. The unreserved love and support of my three brothers (Chung-Huey, Lin-Tsang and Ying-Huei) and sisters-in-law (Fei-I Chang, Chu-Ying Hsu and Shu-I Liang) are the greatest gifts from God in my life. Most of all, my highest gratitude goes to my mother, Yuh-Hua Pan, and my spiritual mother, Flora Chen, who love me more than themselves and who pray for me day and night. Finally, a sweet remembrance goes to my father, Wan-Lee Cheng, in heaven with God.

Ling Cheng
August 2008

Abbreviations

ANRW	Hildegard Temporini and Wolfgang Haase (eds.), *Aufstieg und Niedergang der römischen Welt: Geschichte und Kultur Roms im Spiegel der neueren Forschung*, Berlin: de Gruyter, 1972–.
AB	Analecta Biblica
BDAG	Walter Bauer, Frederick William Danker, William F. Arndt and F. Wilbur Gingrich, *A Greek-English Lexicon of the New Testament and Other Early Christian Literature*, 3rd edn., Frederick William Danker (revised and ed.); Chicago: University of Chicago Press, 2000.
BAR	*Biblical Archaeology Review*
Beg	F.J. Foakes Jackson and Kirsopp Lake (eds.), *The Beginnings of Christianity, Part I, The Acts of the Apostles*, 5 vols., London: Macmillan, 1922, 1926, 1933, 1942.
BETL	Bibliotheca Ephemeridum Theologicarum Lovaniensium
Bib	*Biblica*
BInt	*Biblical Interpretation*
BSac	*Bibliotheca Sacra*
BT	*Bible Translator (Technical Papers)*
BTB	*Biblical Theology Bulletin*
BZ	*Biblische Zeitschrift*
BZNW	Beihefte zur Zeitschrift für die neutestamentliche Wissenschaft
CBQ	*Catholic Biblical Quarterly*
EDNT	Horst Balz and Gerhard Schneider (eds.), *Exegetical Dictionary of the New Testament*, 3 vols., Grand Rapids: Eerdmans, 1990, 1991, 1993.
EQ	*The Evangelical Quarterly*
ExpT	*The Expository Times*
ETL	*Ephemerides Theologicae Lovanienses*
HTR	*Harvard Theological Review*
HUCA	*Hebrew Union College Annual*
Int	*Interpretation*
JBL	*Journal of Biblical Literature*
JETS	*Journal of the Evangelical Theological Society*
JLS	*Journal of Literary Semantics*
JSNT	*Journal for the Studies of the New Testament*
JPTSup	Journal of Pentecostal Theology Supplement Series
JSNTSup	Journal for the Study of the New Testament Supplement Series
JSOTSup	Journal for the Study of the Old Testament Supplement Series
L&N	Johannes P. Louw and Eugene A. Nida (eds.), *Greek-English Lexicon of the New Testament Based on Semantic Domains*, New York: United Bible Societies, 1989.
NAC	The New American Commentary
NICNT	The New International Commentary on the New Testament

NLH	*New Literary History*
NovT	*Novum Testamentum*
NTS	*New Testament Studies*
PT	*Poetics Today*
PTMS	Princeton Theological Monograph Series
RB	*Revue Biblique*
RE	*Review and Expositor*
SBL	Studies in Biblical Literature
SBLAB	Society of Biblical Literature Academia Biblica
SBLDS	Society of Biblical Literature Dissertation Series
SBLMS	Society of Biblical Literature Monograph Series
SBLSP	*Society of Biblical Literature Seminar Papers*
SBLSS	Society of Biblical Literature Symposium Series
SNTSMS	Society for New Testament Studies Monograph Series
SJOT	*Scandinavian Journal of the Old Testament*
SJT	*Scottish Journal of Theology*
TDNT	Gerhard Kittel and Gerhard Friedrich (eds.), *Theological Dictionary of the New Testament*, 10 vols., Geoffrey William Bromiley (trans.); Grand Rapids: Eerdmans, 1964-1976.
TynB	*Tyndale Bulletin*
VoxE	*Vox Evangelica*
VSQ	*St. Vladimir's Seminary Quarterly*
WTJ	*Westminster Theological Journal*
WUNT	Wissenschaftliche Untersuchungen zum Neuen Testament

CHAPTER 1

Introduction

God as character in Acts has drawn little scholarly attention. Most scholars, taking the traditional approach of historical criticism (which is author-centred), take a particular interest in the descriptive, educational, defensive, apologetic, theological or evangelical purpose of the author,[1] and focus their studies on the Spirit, Jesus, Peter, Paul, Stephen, Philip and so on. Although there are many important characters and many facets of interpretation, regarding Acts as a complete literary work[2] raises crucial questions, such as: Does the author simply want to tell the sagas of the apostles or the apostolic movement in the first century? While the works of the Holy Spirit are predominant, what is his relationship with human characters, with God and with Jesus? Does the author aim at presenting a new revelation of God in the light of the apostolic movement and the divine deeds? What are the controlling threads which weave together the characters and incidents in Acts?

Statement of Purpose

There is no single human character acting throughout the Acts narrative. Yet the main human characters share a common experience (the divine encounter) and a common concern (the divine redemptive plan). The role of divine characters, thus, is crucial to the understanding of the Acts narrative as one coherent work; the controlling line which governs the development of the story and interconnects characters and incidents falls on divine characters—God, Jesus or/and the Spirit—who are present throughout the narrative as is shown through various points of view. Among divine characters God is the one presented most frequently and evenly throughout the narrative (Jesus' name occurs 69 times, the Holy Spirit 55 times and God 160 times).[3] Therefore, the role of God in the

---

[1] Robert Maddox, *The Purpose of Luke-Acts* (Edinburgh: T. & T. Clark, 1982) 19-23; French L. Arrington, *The Acts of the Apostles* (Peabody: Hendrickson, 1988) xxxvi.

[2] For those scholars who consider Acts as a narrative and compare it with other Hellenistic literature see Loveday Alexander, 'Fact, Fiction and the Genre of Acts,' *NTS* 44 (1998) 380-99; James M. Dawsey, 'Characteristics of Folk-Epic in Acts,' *SBLSP* 28 (1989) 317-25; Richard I. Pervo, *Profit with Delight* (Philadelphia: Fortress Press, 1987); Susan Marie Praeder, 'Luke-Acts and the Ancient Novel,' *SBLSP* 20 (1981) 269-92.

[3] Actually, θεός occurs 167 times of which seven refer to other gods; τὸ πνεῦμα occurs 70 times of which fifteen refer to evil or human spirits. Moreover, God is men-

plot is crucial to grasping the author's intention and the characterisation of God will definitely shed light on the soul of the Acts narrative. The purpose of this study is to investigate God's role in the narrative world; through this exercise the questions above will, more or less, be answered. The narrative approach, which carries multiple points of view and allows a close look at a character from various perspectives, will be adopted to grasp a thorough portrait of God. Interestingly, from the standpoint of such literary approach, God inevitably gets the spotlight.[4] God's interrelationship with other divine and human characters will be the central concern of this study whereby God's role in the author's intention is revealed. That is, does God serve to amplify other characters (e.g. Jesus, Peter, Paul)? Or, rather, do other characters function to bring a new perspective on God? In other words, is the Acts narrative character-centred or God-centred? It is by his relationship to other characters that God's role in the narrative will present itself. Who God is, what his interest is and how he acts will come to light through the study.

Clarification of Terminology

The narrative approach differs from historical studies mainly in its full focus on the text. The metaphors of window and mirror are often borrowed to illustrate the difference between the two.[5] Historical studies look at texts as windows

---

tioned in every chapter except Acts 25; Jesus is absent in Acts 12, 14, 23, 27 and the Spirit in Acts 3, 12, 14, 17, 18, 22-27.

[4] Cf. Ben Witherington III, *The Acts of the Apostles: A Socio-Rhetorical Commentary* (Grand Rapids: Eerdmans, 1998) 72-74; Mark Reasoner, 'The Theme of Acts: Institutional History or Divine Necessity in History?' *JBL* 118 (1999) 635-59. In the past decade, the characterisation of God has gradually become an observable topic when scholars adopt the narrative approach to examine a narrative text. See James W. Watts, 'The Legal Characterization of God in the Pentateuch,' *HUCA* 67 (1996) 1-14; Paul Danove, 'The Narrative Function of Mark's Characterization of God,' *NovT* 43 (2001) 12-30; D. Francois Tolmie, 'The Characterization of God in the Fourth Gospel,' *JSNT* 69 (1998) 57-75; Marianne Meye Thompson, '"God's Voice You Have Never Heard, God's Form You Have Never Seen": The Characterization of God in the Gospel of John,' *Semeia* 63 (1993) 177-204; Robert L. Brawley, 'Abrahamic Covenant Traditions and the Characterization of God in Luke-Acts' in J. Verheyden (ed.), *The Unity of Luke-Acts* (BETL 142; Leuven: Leuven University Press, 1999) 109-132.

[5] Norman R. Petersen, *Literary Criticism for New Testament Critics* (Philadelphia: Fortress Press, 1978) 24; Mark Allan Powell, *What Are They Saying about Acts?* (Mahwah: Paulist Press, 1991) 106; Robert J. Karris, 'Windows and Mirrors: Literary Criticism and Luke's Sitz im Leben,' *SBLSP* 16 (1979) 47-58; Stephen A. Geller, 'Through Windows and Mirrors into the Bible: History, Literature and Language in the Study of Text' in *A Sense of Text: The Art of Language in the Study of Biblical Literature* (Winona Lake: Eisenbrauns/Dropsie College, 1983) 3-40.

Introduction 3

through which one learns about the historical world indicated in the text; the narrative approach regards texts as mirrors from which one constructs the narrative world without regard to its historical world. The former views the text as a means of understanding its historical world; the latter centres on the world presented in the narrative.[6] The former attempts to seek insights through the communication between the historical author and reader; the latter allows insight to emerge from the communication between the implied author and reader (or even the narrator and narratee) within the text itself. See the following diagram for the relationship between historical and narrative approaches.[7]

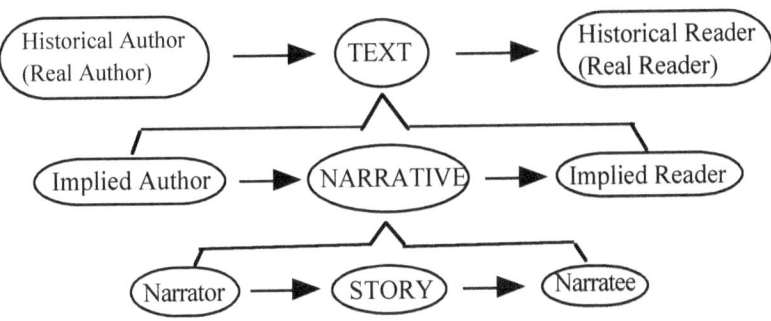

Here the term *story* indicates 'the signified or narrative content,' *narrative* 'the signifier, statement, discourse or narrative text itself,'[8] and *text* 'the message component of a larger communication model.'[9] For example, the text of Acts may be considered as ancient rhetorical history, seeking to teach and persuade;[10] the Acts narrative subsumes events and summary, describing the apostolic movement; there are selective stories in Acts, telling what happened to the apostles. As noted, this study aims to explore God's role in the narrative. The definition of certain terminology relevant to the investigation of character and characterisation will be elucidated in order to pave the way for the introduction of the methodology for this study.

---

[6] Powell, *About Acts*, 106.

[7] Mark Allan Powell, *What is Narrative Criticism?* (Minneapolis: Fortress Press, 1990) 27.

[8] Gérard Genette, *Narrative Discourse: An Essay in Method* (Ithaca: Cornell University Press, 1995) 27.

[9] Powell, *Narrative Criticism*, 19-20. Narrative approach views the text as complete in itself and investigates its significance from the narrative context; historical studies are not satisfied with the text itself and detect its significance from the historical context.

[10] Darrell L. Bock, *Acts* (Grand Rapids: Baker Academic, 2007) 8-12.

The Narrator and the Implied Author

In the above diagram it is necessary to distinguish three types of senders and receivers while communicating a message. The historical author is the real person who writes the text; the implied author is the image of the author as revealed in the deployment of the narrative work; the narrator, a rhetorical device created by the implied author, is the person who tells the story as revealed in the voice inscribed in the text. Correspondingly, the historical reader is the person, individual or collective, to whom the historical author intends his text to be read; the implied reader is the image of the recipient presupposed within the text itself; the narratee is the textual figure to whom the narrator tells the story.[11] For example, most scholars argue that Luke is the historical author; even though one may disagree with Luke as the real author, all concur in that there must be a person (the implied author) who composes the Acts narrative; the phrase such as 'then Peter said...' reveals the existence of the narrator.

A narrative approach emphasises 'the need to separate the act of *writing* from the act of *narrating*, that is, to distinguish between the *author* and the *narrator*. Essentially, the narrator is 'either a character who narrates or the author' of a narrative.[12] 'In fictional narratives, the narrator is a rhetorical device invented by the author in order to tell the story in a certain way.... In non-fictional narratives, therefore, the narrator represents the author.'[13] The biblical narrative belongs to the latter so the terms of implied author and narrator are interchangeable. In this study, however, the *implied author* will be used to highlight the hand behind the literary composition while *narrator* simply represents the voice telling the story.

The narrator is *omniscient* and *omnipresent*, being capable of 'constantly transferring the point of view from one place to another' and discerning one's heart;[14] thus, his voice, representing the perspective of the implied author, is

---

[11] Daniel Marguerat and Yvan Bourquin, *How to Read Bible Stories* (London: SCM Press, 1999) 15; Petri Merenlahti and Raimo Hakola, 'Reconceiving Narrative Criticism' in David Rhoads and Kari Syreeni (eds.), *Characterization in the Gospel: Reconceiving Narrative Criticism* (Sheffield: Sheffield Academic Press, 1999) 22. For further discussion on the implied author and narrator see Shimon Bar-Efrat, *Narrative Art in the Bible* (JSOTSup 70; Sheffield: Sheffield Academic Press, 2000) 13-45; R. Alan Culpepper, *Anatomy of the Fourth Gospel* (Philadelphia: Fortress Press, 1983) 15-20; William S. Kurz, *Reading Luke-Acts: Dynamics of Biblical Narrative* (Louisville: Westminster/John Knox Press, 1993) 9-16; Allen James Walworth, *The Narrator of Acts* (unpublished PhD dissertation, Southern Baptist Theological Seminary, 1984) 19-77.

[12] Richard Walsh, 'Who Is the Narrator?' *PT* 18 (1997) 495-513, citing 505.

[13] Merenlahti and Hakola, 'Reconceiving,' 37.

[14] Bar-Efrat, *Narrative Art*, 17; cf. Robert Scholes and Robert Kellogg, *The Nature of Narrative* (New York: Oxford University Press, 1966) 272-73; George Savran, 'The Character as Narrator in Biblical Narrative,' *Prooftexts* 5 (1985) 1-17, esp. 11.

trustworthy. The presence of the narrator is sensed when he overtly manifests himself, in either the first or third person,[15] in supplying explanation, commentary or summary. The narrator may also be sensed in a covert way when he expresses his attitude through the connotations of the words which describe the characters and events or even through the protagonists' speech.[16] In general, the narrator depicts the story in an objective manner though occasionally giving his own elucidation and interpretation; he frequently hints at his attitudes which can be detected from his subtle use of the literary scheme. The overall function of the narrator is 'to allow the narrative to be read as... something reported as fact'[17] and to make the narrative world 'appear as reality.'[18]

Character

Character is 'an individual or collective figure in the narrative, assuming a role in the plot.'[19] As created by the implied author to fulfil a particular role in the story[20] and represented in a dramatic or narrative work, characters 'are interpreted by the reader as being endowed with particular moral, intellectual, and emotional qualities by inferences from what the persons say... and from what they do.'[21] The way of classifying characters varies. Forster first proposes a rough distinction between *flat characters* with a single trait and *round characters* with several traits.[22] Berlin modifies this into three character types—the *full-fledged character* (i.e. the round character), the *type* (i.e. the flat character) and the *agent* who is a mere function of the plot and is not characterised at all.[23] Harvey divides characters into three groups: *protagonists* 'whose motivation and history are most fully established' and who are the soul of the narrative; *background characters* who are 'cogs in the mechanism of the plot' establishing human contexts for the protagonists to be realised in depth; and *intermediate figures* who act 'as a foil, creating perspective,' and 'as a buttress, sup-

---

[15] For further discussion on the first- and third-person narration (i.e. the involvement and noninvolvement of the narrator in the story) see Franz Karl Stanzel, *A Theory of Narrative* (Cambridge: Cambridge University Press, 1988); also his article 'Teller-Characters and Reflector-Characters in Narrative Theory,' *PT* 2 (1981) 5-15.
[16] Bar-Efrat, *Narrative Art*, 23-45.
[17] Walsh, 'Narrator,' 499.
[18] Stanzel, *Narrative*, 17.
[19] Marguerat and Bourquin, *Bible Stories*, 60.
[20] Powell, *Narrative Criticism*, 51.
[21] M.H. Abrams, *A Glossary of Literary Terms*, 7th edn. (Fort Worth: Harcourt Brace College Publishers, 1999) 32-33.
[22] Edward Morgan Forster, *Aspects of the Novel* (London: Penguin Books, 1990) 73-81.
[23] Adele Berlin, *Poetics and Interpretation of Biblical Narrative* (Winona Lake: Eisenbrauns, 1994) 23.

porting and extending' the story of the protagonists.²⁴ Harvey further divides intermediate figures into two groups: the card (a comic or caricatured figure, creating an atmosphere of pleasurable relaxation) and the ficelle (a means to an end, carrying various functions to reveal the protagonists and the plot progression).²⁵ Hochman proposes eight categories that allow the reader to conceptualise the images of characters from the texts.²⁶ His scheme is a detailed system for defining the qualities of characters from many facets in literature.

Forster's dualistic categories are too simple for the complex human context in Acts. Berlin asserts that there is no real line separating the three character types and leaves the focus of studying the characters on the degree of characterisation rather than the kind of characterisation;²⁷ this is not suitable for defining the relationship between characters. Hochman's eight categories emphasise the kinds of characters within a literary work; this framework accentuates the individuality of characters and is not applicable to analysing the interrelationships either. However, Harvey's classification, which relies on characters' relationship to the protagonists and the plot (i.e. characters' 'different degrees of centrality in the narrative'),²⁸ is most pertinent to this study, especially in Acts where there is no protagonist acting throughout the narrative and characters function as a plot device.²⁹

In this study, the terms used by Harvey will be modified to fit into the setting of Acts. The term *major characters* (protagonists in Harvey's category) indicates the primary characters, Peter and Paul, who alternately stand in the spotlight on the narrative stage. *Minor characters* will be applied to those who are closely associated with major characters and partake in the plot progression.³⁰ They are what Harvey calls the *ficelle* in the category of intermediate figures.³¹ In Acts, minor characters can be categorised into three groups—the believers, the God-fearers and the opponents. *Background characters*, such as John and Silas in Acts, will not enter into the discussion of this study since they contribute little to the plot progression. The term *main charac-*

---

²⁴ W.J. Harvey, *Character and the Novel* (London: Chatto & Windus, 1970) 56, 68.
²⁵ Harvey, *Character*, 58-68.
²⁶ Baruch Hochman, *Character in Literature* (London: Cornell University Press, 1985) 86-140. Each of these categories has its polar opposite: stylization–naturalism, coherence–incoherence, wholeness–fragmentariness, literalness–symbolism, complexity–simplicity, transparency–opacity, dynamism–staticism, closure–openness.
²⁷ Berlin, *Biblical Narrative*, 32.
²⁸ James Garvey, 'Characterization in Narrative,' *Poetics* 7 (1978) 63-78, citing 67.
²⁹ Walworth, *Narrator*, 80; John A. Darr, *On Character Building: The Reader and the Rhetoric of Characterization in Luke-Acts* (Louisville: Westminster/John Knox Press, 1992) 39.
³⁰ The term *minor characters* is also used by Bar-Efrat (*Narrative Art*, 86).
³¹ According to Harvey's definition there is no *card* character in Acts.

ters will be used occasionally to indicate both major and individual minor characters who are crucial to the plot progression (i.e. Peter, Paul, Stephen, Philip, Barnabas and James).

Point of View

The distinction between the characters and the narrator in characterisation is related to *point of view*.[32] The term 'is used rather broadly in literary criticism to designate the position or perspective from which a story is told.'[33] Through a 'variety of perspectives' not only do 'we establish a character's reality'[34] but also characters 'may be characterized in differing degrees or in different dimensions.'[35] On the surface level, a general distinction in points of view is made among 'those of the characters, the narrator, and the audience.'[36] At the structure level, a number of techniques are employed to provide a multiple-faceted perspective on the story for the reader.

Uspensky suggests four levels of point of view in the compositional structure (from the narrator's standpoint). The *ideological* plane refers to the viewpoint which the implied author assumes when he evaluates and perceives the world he describes. The viewpoint may be expressed through the narrator, characters or the use of certain speech characteristics. The *phraseological* plane refers to the perspective which the implied author adopts for narrating. The perspective can be detected from the linguistic features in speech. The *spatial-temporal* plane refers to the position in space and time where the narrator tells the story from the standpoint of a character. The shifting of the standpoint presents the events from various perspectives and in temporal sequence. The *psychological* plane refers to the viewpoint from which the implied author constructs his narration. This can be achieved through the implied author's use of the subjective viewpoint of particular characters or by his objective description of the events.[37] The ideological plane touches the deep compositional structure regarding the system of ideas that shape the work (*what* the implied author wants to communicate). The phraseological, spatial-temporal and psychological planes deal with the surface one regarding the perspective of the narrative voice (*who*, as the eye of a camera), the standpoint of narrating (*where*, as plac-

---

[32] Garvey, 'Characterization,' 64.
[33] Berlin, *Biblical Narrative*, 46.
[34] Harvey, *Character*, 52, citing from K. Burke, *A Grammar of Motives* (New York: Prentice Hall, 1945) 504.
[35] Garvey, 'Characterization,' 67.
[36] Scholes and Kellogg, *Nature*, 240.
[37] Boris Uspensky, *A Poetics of Composition* (Los Angeles: University of California Press, 1983) 8-100.

ing the camera in different positions for taking pictures) and the viewpoint of constructing the story (*how*, as using a camera with zoom lens to take pictures).

Chatman asserts three senses of the viewpoint's relation to the narrative voice (from the character's standpoint): the *perceptual* point of view—the eyes through which the narrative events are perceived; the *conceptual* point of view—presenting someone's world view, attitudes and way of thinking; and the *interest* point of view—concerning someone's interest-vantage (i.e. characterising one's interest, profit, etc.).[38] The perceptual and conceptual viewpoints refer to the character in an active state (i.e. the character as the subject whose perspective is taken for narrating) while the interest point of view is in a passive state (i.e. the character as the object—the concern presented from the perspective in narrating).[39] For the former points of view, the characters are present; for the interest point of view, the characters are absent.

Roughly speaking, Chatman's perceptual viewpoint echoes Uspensky's phraseological, spatial-temporal and psychological planes in the surface compositional structure. His conceptual viewpoint corresponds to Uspensky's ideological planes in the deep compositional structure.[40]

The above survey shows the variety and complexity of the point of view which can refer to the perspectives of the narrator and characters or the aspects of composing and perceiving the narrative. The combination and the interplay of points of view provide the complex human context which is important for characterisation. Although there are many apparently dominant viewpoints arising from the individual scenes, from the perspective of the narrative as a whole, all are subordinate to the overriding viewpoint of evaluating a character.[41] Moreover, 'points of view do not focus in a single central point, but produce a sort of diffused subject, consisting of several centers, with relations between them creating additional layers of meaning.'[42] Through point of view 'a text acquires a specific orientation towards its sentient center.'[43] The multiple-layer of meaning in reading a text is the outcome of the coalescence of points of view in both the surface and deep compositional structure. This can be well observed in the Acts narrative; for example, Peter's speech in Acts 2 presents his *conceptual point of view* about the significance of the Pentecostal phenomena as well as the *interest point of view* of God concerning the divine redemptive will/plan in Jesus.

---

[38] Seymour Chatman, *Story and Discourse* (Ithaca: Cornell University Press, 1980) 151-52.
[39] Cf. Berlin, *Biblical Narrative*, 48.
[40] Adele Berlin, 'Point of View in Biblical Narrative' in *A Sense of Text*, 71-113, citing 85.
[41] Uspensky, *Composition*, 9.
[42] J.M. Lotman, 'Point of View in a Text,' *NLH* 6 (1975) 339-52, citing 340.
[43] Lotman, 'Point of View,' 341.

Introduction

The *interest point of view* is 'helpful in discussing biblical narrative because often the object of the story's interest is not the same character from whose point of view the story is told.'[44] This is particularly true of our main focus, the characterisation of God in Acts, since God is an offstage character yet his redemptive will/plan is the narrative interest. We shall see later in this study that God is brought into attention and becomes the 'sentient center' mainly through the *interest point of view*.

Plot

Plot in the macro-narrative (the narrative as a whole) is 'systematization of the events which make up the story: these events are linked together by a causal link (configuration) and inserted into a chronological process (sequence of events).'[45] Plot in micro-narratives (narrative episodes) is 'the dynamic, sequential element,'[46] which refers to the transforming actions that bring new knowledge about a character or simply indicate a character's doings.[47] Moreover, plot organises events and actions for thematic interest, artistic and emotional effect, and determinate affective response.[48] Plot is the body of the narrative as Scholes and Kellogg explicate.

> Quality of mind (as expressed in the language of characterization, motivation, description, and commentary) not plot, is the soul of narrative. Plot is only the indispensable skeleton which, fleshed out with character and incident, provides the necessary clay into which life may be breathed.[49]

In short, plot regards the deployment of events and actions, which are always associated with characters. Plot is utterly the work of the implied author which serves to communicate his mind through the development of the story in the narrative. In Acts, repetition is one of the literary techniques important to the plot in the macro-narrative (e.g. the conspicuous parallel between Peter and Paul). The repetition of divine encounter and of elucidation of God's salvific will/plan not only interconnects the characters' stories and communicates the narrative theme but also reinforces the image of God emerging from the narrative presentation, which further serves the implied author's aim of persuasion.

---

[44] Berlin, *Biblical Narrative*, 48.
[45] Marguerat and Bourquin, *Bible Stories*, 41; cf. also Bar-Efrat, *Narrative Art*, 93; Forster, *Aspects*, 87.
[46] Scholes and Kellogg, *Nature*, 207.
[47] Marguerat and Bourquin, *Bible Stories*, 56.
[48] Abrams, *Literary Terms*, 224; Bar-Efrat, *Narrative Art*, 93; Kieran Egan, 'What is a Plot?' *NLH* 9 (1978) 455-73, citing 470.
[49] Scholes and Kellogg, *Nature*, 239; cf. Bar-Efrat, *Narrative Art*, 93.

Characterisation

Characterisation is the literary technique of constructing and presenting characters. Bar-Efrat asserts a double-track of characterisation, namely, the direct and indirect shaping of the characters. The *direct shaping* reveals characters' outward appearance and inner personality through the voices of the narrator or other characters; the *indirect shaping* discloses characters' inner state through their speech and actions and through minor characters who take part in the network of interpersonal relations in both the speech and acts of main characters.[50] Alter suggests a scale of characterisation:

> Character can be revealed through the report of actions; through appearance, gestures, posture, costume; through one character's comments on another; through direct speech by the character; through inward speech, either summarized or quoted as interior monologue; or through statements by the narrator about the attitudes and intentions of the personages, which may come either as flat assertions or motivated explanations.[51]

The techniques in this scale are disposed in the order which is based on their capacity to increasingly explicate the character's inner life. Berlin proposes four basic techniques for characterisation: *description*—which tells of characters' status or physical features; *inner life*—which tells of characters' thoughts, emotions and motivations; *speech and actions*—which present characters through what they say and do; *contrast*—which presents characters by contrasting them with other characters, with their earlier actions or with the expected norm.[52]

Among these literary techniques for characterisation, a broad distinction, which is based on the implied author's point of view, is frequently made: telling and showing.[53] In *telling*, the implied author intervenes authoritatively through the narrator's voice 'in order to describe, and often to evaluate, the motives and dispositional qualities of the characters.'[54] In *showing*, the implied author presents the characters talking and acting through statements that convey either their own point of view or other characters' viewpoint concerning them;[55] that is, the implied author may adopt any character's point of view to

---

[50] Bar-Efrat, *Narrative Art*, 47-92.

[51] Robert Alter, *The Art of Biblical Narrative* (London: George Allen & Unwin, 1981) 116-17.

[52] Berlin, *Biblical Narrative*, 34-41.

[53] The agents of these two modes of narrative transmission are identified by Stanzel as tell- and reflector-character which refer to how the narrator communicates his story ('Teller-Characters,' 5). Walsh, on the other hand, argues that a distinct narrative agent is not required ('Narrator,' 497).

[54] Abrams, *Literary Terms*, 34.

[55] Powell, *Narrative Criticism*, 52.

tell and show things about a character. Taking Barnabas as an example, the narrator tells that he is a good man, full of the Holy Spirit and faith (Acts 11:24); the implied author, via the narrator, shows that he sold his land and brought the money to the apostles (Acts 4:37). In brief, characterisation can be done directly by the voice behind the narrative stage (from the narrator's viewpoint) and indirectly by those performing on the stage (from characters' viewpoint, that is, how they describe an onstage character or how the character acts on the narrative stage).[56]

Taking the characterisation of God into account, see the following diagram for the double-track characterisation from various points of view.[57]

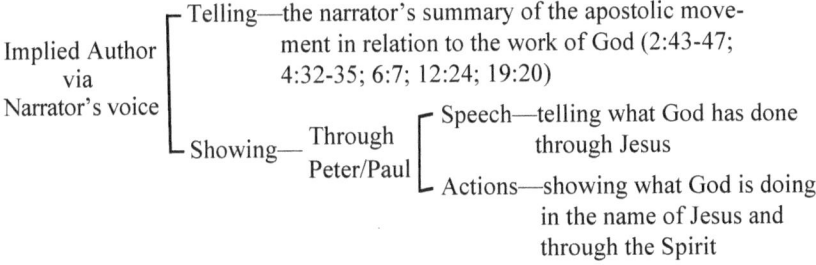

As the diagram reveals, characterisation in Acts is inclined more towards showing than telling.[58] This study will scrutinise the implied author's indirect characterisation of God through the major and minor characters' speeches concerning him and their interactions with him or his will (i.e. *showing* God from the characters' viewpoints). The direct characterisation of God will be examined through investigation of the direct narrative descriptions and evaluations concerning the work of God (i.e. the narrator's *telling* of God through his commentary and narrative plot).

As indicated, the interplay of points of view makes the characterisation of God complicated. In the micro-narratives and the surface compositional struc-

---

[56] For more discussion relevant to characterisation see William H. Shepherd, *The Narrative Function of the Holy Spirit as a Character in Luke-Acts* (SBLDS 147; Atlanta: Scholars Press, 1994) 78-90; Robert W. Funk, *The Poetics of Biblical Narrative* (Sonoma: Polebridge Press, 1988) 134-61; Alter, *Biblical Narrative*, 114-30; Thomas Docherty, *Reading (Absent) Character: Towards A Theory of Characterization in Fiction*, Oxford: Clarendon Press, 1983; Elizabeth Struthers Malbon and Adele Berlin (eds.), *Characterisation in Biblical Literature*, Semeia 63, Atlanta: Scholars Press, 1993; Elie Assis, 'Chiasmus in Biblical Narrative: Rhetoric of Characterization,' *Prooftexts* 22 (2002) 273-304.

[57] Shlomith Rimmon-Kenan defines this double-track characterisation as *direct definition* and *indirect presentation* (*Narrative Fiction: Contemporary Poetics*, 2nd edn. [London: Routledge, 2003] 59-67).

[58] Darr, *Character Building*, 44.

ture, God is characterised indirectly through the narrator's showing of what other characters say about him and how they react to their understanding of him, and directly and explicitly through the narrator's telling of the outcome of God's work. In the macro-narrative and the deep compositional structure, since God's redemptive plan is one of the thematic concerns, the implied author's selection and deployment of the micro-narratives serves as an implicit way of presenting God. A thorough investigation of the characterisation of God, thus, will explore the representation of God from the multiple points of view of characters and the double-layer structure of the narrative.

Methodology

In light of the communication in speech acts, a narrative subsumes three aspects of meaning: *locution*—the linguistic meaning communicated through the grammatical composition; *illocution*—the intention behind the linguistic communication; *perlocution*—the effect of the linguistic communication upon the hearer.[59] For example, Peter says, 'it is necessary to obey God rather than men' (Acts 5:29). The locutionary meaning expresses the necessity of obeying God; the illocutionary meaning may indicate a simple assertion of truth, an exhortation or a warning (i.e. the implication of Peter's notion of God); the perlocutionary meaning conveys expected effects (e.g. the leaders may repent or believe in Jesus) which Peter, the speaker, cannot guarantee they will occur. Both the locutionary and illocutionary aspects of meaning rely highly on the context.[60] These two aspects convey the implied author's world view which he communicates through the main characters; they will also be the concern of this study. The investigation of the locutionary and illocutionary meaning of the story lays a firm foundation for exploring its perlocutionary meaning, in which most critics are interested yet they so often fail to scrutinise the locutionary and illocutionary meaning.[61] It is the purpose of this book to analyse the locutionary and illocutionary aspects of the narrative. Although it is not our focus in the chapters that follow, the perlocutionary meaning of the narrative will be briefly indicated in the concluding remarks to show the implied author's overall expectation on the implied reader who is inferred from the text.

As noted, the implied author is a covert yet influential figure who constructs a narrative world in which characters and events serve as indicators to convey his ideas and align the reader's view with his. Each character, individual or collective, plays a part to animate the narrative world. Each event, the account

---

[59] Chatman, *Story and Discourse*, 161-62; Susan Sniader Lanser, *The Narrative Act: Point of View in Prose Fiction* (Princeton: Princeton University Press, 1981) 70-72.

[60] Lanser, *Narrative Act*, 72.

[61] Such a failure leads to various assumptions of the implied author's expectation on his reader, which may not be the very concern of the narrative.

of particular interactions among characters, is interconnected in line with the plot to communicate the narrative theme; this is the implied author's very interest. With regard to the implied author's characterisation of the offstage God in Acts, which brings a deeper understanding of the thematic points, it requires a distinctive way of characterisation. Although absent from the narrative stage, through the *interest point of view* God's redemptive will/plan keeps him, in the figurative sense, always onstage, either in the foreground or background; that God carries out his salvific will through divine and human agents reveals his nature since the redemptive plan is the invisible God's perfect self-expression and self-manifestation. People's actions reveal their innermost selves—'A person's nature is revealed by deeds; action is the implementation of character, and individuals are disclosed through their deeds no less than through their words.'[62] Since the invisible God acts through his agents, their interactions with God's salvific plan insinuate God's nature, that is, through the actions of God's agents in disclosing God's salvific plan and in interpreting divine deeds the reader builds the character of God. As the readers conceptualise their image of God indirectly from what God is doing through his agents, such an image is modified as they perceive and know more about how God's divine and human agents carry out his redemptive plan.

In Phelan's rhetorical interpretation of narrative there are two fundamental components (mimetic and thematic) of a non-fictional narrative character. The mimetic component creates the impression that characters are real people; the thematic component generates the characters' significance in the narrative.[63] Mimetic characterisation regards a character's complex interactions with other characters:

> The fundamental matrix within which we construct a character is the web of interrelationships that develops among all of the figures in the story world. In other words, characters are delineated largely in terms of each other, just as we are defined by our relationships in real life.[64]

---

[62] Bar-Efrat, *Narrative Art*, 77.

[63] James Phelan, *Reading People, Reading Plots: Character, Progression, and the Interpretation of Narrative* (Chicago: University of Chicago Press, 1989) 2-3. Actually, Phelan asserts that a narrative character has three components (mimetic, thematic and synthetic). The synthetic component, conveying an awareness of knowing that a fictional character is a construct, however, does not apply to our investigation of the portrayal of God in Acts since the narrator composes his narrative as a historiography. The examination of the mimetic component does not aim at revealing how the narrator makes God alive but helps the reader perceive what image of the hidden God the narrator intends to communicate. The thematic component serves as a plot line along which characters and incidents are deployed.

[64] Darr, *Character Building*, 41.

To present the mimetic characterisation of God, the implied author adroitly adopts various characters' viewpoints to present their relationships with God in order to establish God's reality and arouse the reader's interest and involvement to share the narrator's world view.[65] Since God is an invisible, offstage character in Acts, other characters' relationships with him are reflected in their response to his salvific plan—the common concern of major and minor characters, as well as divine and human characters. The literary technique for mimetic characterisation in Acts is mainly the narrator's *showing*. In *showing*, the characterisation of a character is done directly through the character's speech and actions and indirectly through other characters' viewpoints; therefore, the divine and human characters' speeches and actions concerning God and his salvific plan will first be investigated in order to explore the characterisation of God in the mimetic stratum (i.e. the surface compositional structure).

Thematic characterisation pertains to a character's role within the plot. 'Character and plot are interdependent and both are essentials of narrative. Audiences "actualize" plot in terms of character and character in terms of plot.'[66] In other words, a character's role in the plot development portrays the character from the implied author's point of view. To highlight the thematic characterisation, the implied author uses the overt narrator to elucidate and comment on the happenings which adumbrate his thoughts concerning the narrative theme; he also uses the covert narrator adopting characters' points of view to convey the theme. The literary technique for thematic characterisation is through the overt narrator's *telling* the thematic points in the narrative summary and the covert narrator's insinuation of the narrative theme concealed in the plot.[67] Whereas the overt narrator touches upon the surface compositional structure, the covert narrator deals with the deep compositional structure. To explore the characterisation of God in the thematic stratum, God's role in the plot will be investigated, which is shown in the function of God's salvific will/plan (i.e. his self-expression) in the narrative development.

In real life, the invisible God is known through his written Word and through his people's interacting with his will in accordance with the Word. People may reinforce or modify their conceptual image and understanding of God as they experience how God works in their and others' lives through their faith in him and in his Word. Ostensibly, God's people are characterised by their deeds in response to and words concerning God's will in their lives. Intrinsically, they make manifest God's will from which other people construct their image of

---

[65] Bar-Efrat, *Narrative Art*, 16.
[66] Darr, *Character Building*, 39; see also Abrams, *Literary Terms*, 224; Bar-Efrat, *Narrative Art*, 77; Walworth, *Narrator*, 80-84. Seymour Chatman, however, counteracts characters as a derivative product of plot and views them as a paradigm of traits; see his 'On the Formalist-Structuralist Theory of Character,' *JLS* 1 (1972) 57-79, esp. 58; *Story and Discourse*, 119-34.
[67] Bar-Efrat, *Narrative Art*, 14.

God, that is, God is characterised indirectly through his people's deeds and words concerning him. Similarly, as an invisible and offstage character in Acts, God is presented by the implied author indirectly in how characters interact with his redemptive will/plan. In mimetic characterisation, the investigation of how characters represent God may seemingly portray the characterisation of characters; in the deep compositional structure of each micro-narrative, however, the new insights of God allow the implied readers to modify their image of God. This will be made clear in the thematic characterisation of God when the implied author's view from the macro-narrative is taken into account. Since God is made known through his agents, a clear cut of characterisation between God and his agents is sometimes ambiguous. This study may touch characterisation of certain characters when they shed light on the characterisation of God; this study also pays great attention to God's redemptive plan through which the nature of God is revealed. In short, the indirect portrayal of an invisible character—God—is done through his divine and human agents and through the disclosure of his salvific will/plan.

To examine the characterisation of God, the first chapter of this book briefly defines the purpose of this study and the terminology and methodology for the study. Chapters Two to Five will investigate the characterisation of God in mimetic stratum *shown* in characters' speeches and actions (Chapter Two—heavenly characters; Chapters Three and Four—major characters, Peter and Paul; Chapter Five—minor characters). From the points of view of these characters, their speeches concerning God reveal their conceptual presentation of him; their reactions to and their interactions with others regarding God's will/plan express their personal/interpersonal presentation of God. Chapter Six will investigate the characterisation of God in thematic stratum *told* by the overt narrator in the story and confided by the covert narrator through the plot in the macro-narrative. The thematic portrayal of God, which conveys the implied author's conceptual presentation of God, will reinforce the mimetic image of God emerging from the preceding chapters which communicates the implied author's perceptual presentation of God. The final chapter will conclude this study with the characteristics of the characterisation of God; here, a particular portrait of God in Acts will be drawn and the questions which were raised in our statement of purpose will be answered.

PART I

MIMETIC CHARACTERISATION OF GOD—SHOWING

CHAPTER 2

The Characterisation of God by Heavenly Characters

The biblical portrayal of God as a character is unique since 'most dimensions associated with character—physical appearance, social status, personal history, local habitation—do not apply to him at all.'[1] In fact, the absence of tangible aspects to God's portrait serves as a distinct way of characterising God. Such absence paves the way for a new comprehension of God which, as Sternberg indicates,

> impresses on the reader from the very beginning the message that the whole Bible will dramatize with variations: the qualitative distance that separates God from humans *and* pagan gods, both existing in matter and time and space and society. So nothing "material" is told, by way of preliminaries *or* retrospect, because for one there is nothing to tell; and the mind must attune itself to radically new coordinates of divinity.[2]

That the *material* dimension of God is not delineated in the Bible not only makes God's uniqueness and supremacy over other characters stand out but requires a distinctive method of constructing the portrait of God in the biblical narrative. In the Old Testament narrative, God speaks of his will to people, directly or indirectly through the prophets, in the first person.[3] While investigating God's sayings and doings in Acts, surprisingly, there is no direct dialogue, speech or action from him.[4] Nevertheless, God's will and plan are fully recognised through the performance of characters in Acts. Although God is hidden, his plan is initiated and inspired by the divine characters. Moreover,

---

[1] Meir Sternberg, *The Poetics of Biblical Narrative: Ideological Literature and the Drama of Reading* (Bloomington: Indiana University Press, 1987) 323.

[2] Sternberg, *Biblical Narrative*, 323.

[3] For the direct speeches of God to people see Gen 3:9-19; 6:13-7:4; 9:1-17; 12:1-3; Exod 3:4-22; 20:1-17; 1 Sam 8:7-9; etc.; for God's speeches spoken in the first person through the prophets see 1 Sam 10:18; Isa 43-45; Jer 31:31-7; Ezek 36:22-37; Hos 11:1-11; Joel 2:28-31; Zech 10: 6-12; Mal 3:1.

[4] Compared with the Old Testament narrative, the direct speech of God in the New Testament narrative is much less. Still, God's voice from heaven is found three times in the gospel narrative: Jesus' baptism (Mt 3:17; Mk 1:11; Lk 3:22), the Transfiguration (Mt 17:5; Mk 9:7; Lk 9:35) and one of Jesus' final discourses (Jn 12:28); yet there are none in Acts.

through the human characters' decoding of the divine deeds, God's will is manifested. To be specific, God never personally steps unto the arena of Acts, yet his will is unequivocally disclosed through the heavenly revelators (Jesus, the Spirit and angels). By the interactions between heavenly and human characters and by human characters' deciphering of the divine revelations, the reader is able to perceive God's will and plan. Briefly put, God, though invisible and covert, becomes the focus and is made known overtly by means of a twofold portrayal—by the divine interventions in human history and through human characters' interpretation of the divine deeds.

The presentation of God by the heavenly characters, thus, is fundamental to the characterisation of God; this further serves as the foundation for human characters' characterisation of God. The purpose of this chapter is to scrutinise the speeches and actions of the heavenly characters in order to sketch out, from the divine point of view, a picture of God and his inner world as it is presented in the narrative world. The divine utterances will first be examined to expose the conceptual recognition of divine revelations. Then the divine interactions with human characters will be investigated to ascertain the significance of the revelations.

Conceptual Characterisation

It is noteworthy that there is no formal speech by any heavenly character in Acts. All the divine speeches appear in dialogue form. Out of the mouth of a vivid character in the narrative world the content of a dialogue attracts the reader's attention. By this, not only does the trustworthy authority behind the divine utterances stand out but each divine utterance, carrying a prophetic nature and a divine purpose,[5] evokes the reader's curiosity and concern for what will happen next and, thus, serves as a key to the development of the narrative plot. The divine utterances bear either the promises or commands of sending, instructing or heartening the believers to the divine mission to accomplish God's plan. Although infrequent and laconic, the divine utterances demand a thorough investigation since they provide crucial clues to knowing God in the narrative.

Jesus

Four utterances of the risen Jesus are found in the narrative: the words to the believers before the Ascension (1:4-8), the dialogue with Paul and Ananias regarding Paul's calling (9:4-16) and the continual promises to assure Paul of the divine presence and protection (18:9-10; 23:11). Before his return to God,

---

[5] Jean-Noël Aletti, *Quand Luc raconte. Le récit comme théologie* (Lire la Bible 115; Paris: Cerf, 1998) 25.

Jesus' major concern is the kingdom of God (1:3) for which he commissions the believers (1:8). Although ascending to God in heaven (cf. 7:55-6), Jesus' concern for the kingdom of God continues as he commissions and cares for Paul who is the unique vessel for the expansion of the kingdom. Jesus' words reflect a divine plan and purpose behind the sequential events[6] as well as the divine authority over and love for those carrying out the plan.

The first scene of Acts narrates Jesus' final work on earth in which his last words to the believers convey a command to wait for the Holy Spirit (1:4) and a promise of the Spirit's empowerment (1:8). Here Jesus twice refers to God as the Father (1:4, 7). The epithet of God implies 'one who combines aspects of supernatural authority and care for his people.'[7] This fatherhood divinity is 'responsible for the origin and care of all that exists' (cf. 17:25-28).[8] Jesus' acknowledging of himself as the Son of God manifests both God's supreme authority and loving care over all. This reveals Jesus' personal relationship to God as Son to Father,[9] and draws the attention to the Father's sovereign authority (cf. 1:7, ὁ πατήρ... ἐν τῇ ἰδίᾳ ἐξουσίᾳ).[10] Certainly, God the Father in his supreme authority guarantees the fulfilment of his promise and in his loving care assures the very best for his people (cf. Lk 11:13, the bestowal of the Spirit).

Moreover, the phrase *the promise of the Father* implies a divine purpose and plan underlying the promise ever since it was made long before.[11] God progressively makes his will known in human history and his promise of the Spirit is first foretold by the prophet.[12] As the time draws near, both John the forerunner of Jesus and Jesus himself highlight it. Here Jesus reconfirms what he said about the Spirit earlier on (1:5; cf. Lk 24:49), which is also the testimony of John the Baptist (cf. Mt 3:11; Mk 1:8; Lk 3:16), and announces the approach of the realisation of God's promise. Jesus further specifies God's will: a plan of mission, that is, the Spirit-empowered believers are to be Jesus' witnesses to the end of the earth (1:8).[13] From the believers' perspective, Jesus' words ignite

---

[6] Marion L. Soards, *The Speeches in Acts* (Louisville: Westminster/John Knox Press, 1994) 24.
[7] L&N, §12.12.
[8] BDAG, 787.
[9] For the Lukan use of πατήρ see Appendix One.
[10] Cf. Donald Guthrie, *New Testament Theology* (Leicester: Inter-Varsity Press, 1981) 82.
[11] James D.G. Dunn, *The Acts of the Apostles* (Peterborough: Epworth Press, 1996) 8.
[12] Besides the promise of Joel 2:28-29 there are other important references to the Spirit in the new epoch to come (Isa 44:3; Ezek 36:27).
[13] F. Scott Spencer, *Acts* (Sheffield: Sheffield Academic Press, 1997) 26; John B. Polhill, *Acts* (NAC 26; Nashville: Broadman Press, 1992) 85. In contrast to Peter G. Bolt's use of *witnesses* for the first-hand eyewitnesses of Jesus ('Mission and Witness' in I. Howard Marshall and David Peterson [eds.], *Witness to the Gospel* [Grand

conjecture about what God is going to do through the Spirit as they learn about the kingdom of God through Jesus (1:3). To some extent they are convinced that the restoration of Israel is at hand;[14] thus they ask the time of the restoration (1:6). Yet Jesus affirms only God's sovereign authority in determining the timing (1:7) and God's way of consummating his own plan (1:8). The geographical indication of Jesus, whose utterance bears a prophetic force, provides a programmatic hint for the development of God's mission.[15] At this moment, the universal significance of Jesus' commission is still ambiguous to the believers. As the divine characters gradually unveil God's will in the narrative, the believers are led to comprehend fully that the nature of the mission in God's plan is worldwide (i.e. not just geographical but racial).

After the Ascension, Jesus, from heaven (9:3), appears to Paul in person and Ananias in a vision (9:4-6, 10-16). By Jesus' two-stage revelation Paul is divinely called into the mission of God. The sending of Ananias signifies not only a divine witness to Jesus (9:17) but to Paul (9:15-16, 18). Like his commission to the believers (1:8; ἔσεσθαί μου μάρτυρες), Jesus calls Paul to be his witness (9:15). Although God is never in view in Paul's conversion, the whole event (Jesus' revelation and commission) is perceived by Paul as the predeterminate will of God (22:14); moreover, Paul is convinced that his witness to Jesus is faithful service to God (23:1; 24:16; 26:19, 21). From Paul's perspective there is a divine plan/purpose behind the Christophany. Foremost, the universal significance in Jesus' commissioning of Paul parallels that of his early commission of the believers for God's mission; therefore, Jesus' calling of Paul continues and promotes God's plan of mission.

Paul's mission at Corinth is fortified by the Lord appearing to him in a vision (18:9-10). In light of the mention of Lord in 18:8 (ἐπίστευσεν τῷ κυρίῳ) the Lord who appears to Paul is probably Jesus since Jesus is the object of human faith for God's salvation (cf. 3:16; 10:42; 13:39). The present imperative of prohibition, which carries the idea of 'stop an action already in progress,'[16]

Rapids: Eerdmans, 1998] 191-214, citing 192-93), this study will adopt a broad definition for *witnesses*, i.e. those who testify to Jesus.

[14] Polhill, *Acts*, 84.

[15] Acts 1:8 is further argued to provide a programmatic skeleton for the development of the plot. See Soards, *Speeches*, 24; Polhill, *Acts*, 85-86; Mikeal C. Parsons, *The Departure of Jesus in Luke-Acts* (JSNTSup 21; Sheffield: JSOT Press, 1987) 155. Daniel R. Schwartz, however, argues that the verse provides simply a basic structure to the first and second stages of the divine mission ('The End of the ΓΗ [Acts 1:8]: Beginning or End of the Christian Vision?' *JBL* 105 [1986] 669-76, citing 675; cf. Aletti, *Luc raconte*, 38-39).

[16] James A. Brooks and Carlton L. Winbery, *Syntax of New Testament Greek* (Washington: University Press of America, 1979) 116. The following μὴ σιωπήσῃς (aorist prohibitive subjunctive), which bears the idea of 'forbid the intention of an action' (108), implies that Paul has already been preaching (cf. the present imperative of

of φοβοῦ in 18:9 suggests Paul is in 'a considerable degree of trepidation in his early preaching in Corinth (1 Cor 2:3).'[17] Jesus' promise, thus, strengthens and encourages Paul who needs spiritual heartening. The locution in Jesus' saying reminds the reader of the parlance employed by God in the Old Testament. Μὴ φοβοῦ... διότι ἐγώ εἰμι μετὰ σοῦ is often addressed to God's servants who have been given a calling or entrusted with a mission yet are in fear or distress (Gen 28:15; Exod 3:12; Deut 31:23; Josh 1:9; Isa 41:10; Jer 1:8).[18] Moreover, the expression λαός ἐστί μοι recalls the language God uses of his people (cf. 15:14; Exod 5:1; 6:7; 19:5; Jer 7:23; 11:4; 24:7; Ezek 11:20; 36:28). The resemblance of the wording between Jesus and God may signify that Jesus is in 'a function and status equal to those of God the Father himself.'[19] So Jesus' timely assurance of safekeeping and invigoration whispers of divine compassion and hints at the most considerate, divine care.

At Paul's trial in Jerusalem the Lord appears to him again and promises that Paul would witness to him in Rome just as in Jerusalem (23:11). The clause διεμαρτύρω τὰ περὶ ἐμοῦ (you have testified things about me) indicates the person who speaks is Jesus since Jesus is the heart of Paul's witness in Jerusalem (22:3-21; 23:6). Once more, Jesus assures Paul of the divine plan for him to witness in Rome (see the use of δεῖ in relation to the divine utterance signifying the *must* of the divine plan in the narrative: 1:16; 9:6; 17:3; 23:11; 27:24).[20] The word θάρσει (to have courage), which conveys the meaning 'to have confidence and firmness of purpose in the face of danger or testing',[21] denotes Paul again in need of encouragement. As in Corinth, Jesus' promise invigorating Paul in time of trial whispers divine care. Both Jesus' utterances in Corinth and in Jerusalem communicate a twofold message: there is a divine

---

λάλει) and should not begin to be silent (cf. Howard Marshall, *The Acts of the Apostles* [Leicester: Inter-Varsity Press, 1980] 296).

[17] Dunn, *Acts*, 244; Barclay M. Newman and Eugene A. Nida, *A Translator's Handbook on the Acts of the Apostles* (London: United Bible Societies, 1972) 351; cf. Martin M. Culy and Mikeal C. Parsons, *Acts: A Handbook on the Greek Text* (Waco: Baylor University Press, 2003) 347.

[18] Marshall, *Acts*, 296; cf. Rudolf Pesch, *Die Apostelgeschichte*, 2 Teilbd. (Zürich: Benziger Verlag, 1986) 149. The presence of God is also deemed to be the assurance of prosperity and the promise of the victory over, and deliverance from, enemies in the Old Testament (cf. Gen 31:5; Exod 33:16; Josh 14:12; Jdg 16:20; 1 Sam 3:19; see also Acts 7:9).

[19] Marshall, *Acts*, 296.

[20] Luke Timothy Johnson, *The Acts of the Apostles* (Collegeville: The Liturgical Press, 1992) 399. Johnson further indicates that the use of δεῖ 'functions as a programmatic prophecy which shows the direction the plot will continue to take' (399); cf. Pesch, *Apg*, 2:245.

[21] L&N, §25.156.

plan and purpose behind which Jesus' promise is assured; the divine care always turns up faithfully and in time.

In summary, the episodes of the Ascension and Paul's conversion concern Jesus' commission of his witnesses. The former commission is to the collective believer whereas the latter is to a particular individual. Both commissions, assigning people to partake in God's universal mission, reveal Jesus' authority over the believers and God's sovereignty over the events. While Jesus plays a dominant role in the scene, the major concern in both episodes is the plan of God which underlies Jesus' command and promise and leads to 'a God-willed sequence of events.'[22] Overall, Jesus' final words on earth first appear as an inscrutable enigma for the believers. As the work of God continues, such a puzzle turns into a revelatory signal, which inspires the believers' interpretation of God's deeds (cf. 11:16). Foremost, Jesus, calling people to be his witnesses, never leaves them alone but keeps them in his divine care and oversight in accordance with God's purpose and plan.

The Holy Spirit

The utterance of the Holy Spirit is found in three scenes: Philip's evangelism with regard to the Ethiopian eunuch (8:29); Peter's evangelism to Cornelius' household (10:19-20); the sending of Barnabas and Saul for the divine task at the Antioch church (13:2). All the sayings of the Spirit carry a command, either to an individual or a collective character, to further the divine mission in conformity to God's will. Although succinct, each saying of the Spirit precisely directs the believers to a new stage of the mission in God's plan.

The Spirit's first spoken word is significant since it initiates the first Gentile evangelism recorded in the narrative. After the angel's rough command to Philip (8:26), the Spirit precisely directs him to the Ethiopian eunuch (8:29)[23] which gives Philip an opportunity to evangelise a Gentile. This evinces that the very first step of Gentile mission is actuated by divine intervention.[24] The second utterance of the Spirit is also connected to Gentile evangelism (10:19-20). Peter is decisively instructed to go with three Gentile visitors while given no explanation to his vision. The Spirit's precise indication of the number of visitors, the timing of their arrival and even Peter's inner world[25] manifests the

---

[22] Ernst Haenchen, *The Acts of the Apostles* (Oxford: Basil Blackwell, 1971) 144.

[23] It is proposed that Philip needs further confirmation before accosting a person of higher social status. See Marshall, *Acts*, 162; C.K. Barrett, *The Acts of the Apostles*, vol. 1 (Edinburgh: T & T Clark, 1994) 427.

[24] Haenchen, *Acts*, 311.

[25] The phrase μηδὲν διακρινόμενος in the present context can indicate 'doubting nothing' (L&N, §31.37) or imply 'making no distinction' (in light of 15:9; cf. L&N, §30.113; Barrett, *Acts*, 1:511). Either option uncovers the perplexity of Peter's inner life. For a further discussion of the meaning of διακρίνομαι see Peter Spitaler,

Spirit's omniscience and sovereign authority over the whole event. The reason given to Peter for going with the visitors is ἐγὼ ἀπέσταλκα αὐτούς (I have sent them). The first person emphatic pronoun ἐγώ accentuates the divine initiative of the event. As narrated earlier in this episode, the sending of these men is the instruction of God's angel (10:3). Here the Spirit identifies his will with God's. By the Spirit's sending of Peter to the Gentiles (cf. 11:12) Peter perceives God's authority and will over the whole event of the breakthrough of the Gentile mission (cf. 15:7).[26]

The last saying of the Spirit appears in the service at the Antioch church (13:2); this is a Gentile-dominated church (cf. 11:20-21). Again the Holy Spirit speaks in the first person in order to send out Barnabas and Saul for the great Gentile mission, the task for which the Spirit has called them. The incipient commission of Saul to God's universal mission is, however, from Jesus (9:15). As the Spirit identifies his will with God's in sending Peter to a Gentile household (10:3, 20), the Spirit here identifies his calling with Jesus' in sending out Saul to the Gentile mission. The perfect tense of προσκέκλημαι in 13:2 (as well as that of ἀπέσταλκα in 10:20) connotes that the present directive is an ongoing act following a previous event. Such a continuing incident actuated by the Spirit signifies a progressive realisation of the divine plan. Essentially, the three utterances of the Spirit are all related to the breakthrough of God's universal mission. While the first two regard the Gentile mission with racial concern, the last has geographical interest (see also 16:6-7; the Spirit, though communicating without a word, forbids the mission team from going to a certain mission field).

In sum, while Jesus' geographical indication provides a programmatic hint for the development of God's mission (1:8; from Jerusalem, Judea and Samaria to the ends of the earth), the Spirit's directives actuate each new stage of the mission in God's plan (Philip and Peter in Judea; Paul to the ends of the earth, cf. the open ending in 28:31). The Spirit enforces Jesus' commission to his witnesses and causes them to carry on the mission.[27] In other words, Jesus announces the programme of God's plan for the universal mission by commissioning his witnesses; the pioneering Spirit carries it into execution by direct-

---

'Διακρίνεσθαι in Mt. 21:21, Mk. 11:23, Acts 10:20, Rom. 4:20, 14:23, Jas. 1:6, and Jude 22—the "Semantic Shift" That Went Unnoticed by Patristic Authors,' *NovT* 49/1 (2007) 1-39.

[26] Barrett, *Acts*, 1:511; Marshall, *Acts*, 187; Ju Hur, *A Dynamic Reading of the Holy Spirit in Luke-Acts* (JSNTSup 211; Sheffield: Sheffield Academic Press, 2001) 148.

[27] R.F. O'Toole, 'Activity of the Risen Jesus in Luke-Acts,' *Bib* 62 (1981) 471-98, citing 486; cf. Gerhard Schneider, *Die Apostelgeschichte*, vol. 1 (Freiburg: Herder, 1980) 192-93.

ing the chosen ones to particular tasks which will advance the divine mission.[28] By scrutinising the Spirit's sayings one finds no indication of how the Spirit speaks.[29] Although the specific manner of the divine communication remains unknown, the lack of mention of human agency leaves the focus solely on the Spirit and thus draws the attention to the divine authority. Moreover, the Spirit, as the revelator or mouthpiece of God and Jesus,[30] identifies his own will and authority with theirs in the events of reaching out to the Gentiles. This elucidates that the Gentile mission is, utterly and ultimately, inaugurated and approved by the supreme authority of the one Divinity. The divine, infallible guidance and timing in these events reveal the divine sovereignty over all. By divine interventions God's will is done in its due course and in line with his purpose and plan.

Angels

The speech of angels in the narrative appears in various forms.[31] The direct utterance of angels is found in four episodes: the deliverance of the apostles (5:20), Philip's approach to the eunuch (8:26), Cornelius' summons of Peter (10:4-6) and the deliverance of Peter (12:7-8). There is one indirect speech of an angel narrated by Paul (27:23-24). Angels in 10:4-6 and 27:23-24 are explicitly characterised as *the angel of God* whilst in 5:20, 8:26 and 12:7-8 as *the angel of the Lord*. The latter probably refers to the angel of God as well since it is a very common Old Testament expression (cf. 7:30-31).[32] Additionally, the two men with bright clothing at the Ascension may implicitly refer to angels

---

[28] Daniel Marguerat rightly points out that 'the Spirit sets in place a relationship between theology and practice' (*The First Christian Historian* [SNTSMS 121; Cambridge: Cambridge University Press, 2002] 125).

[29] For the manner of the Spirit's communication to an individual, Marshall regards it as an inward assurance or guidance (*Acts*, 162, 187) and Dunn takes it as an inner conviction (*Acts*, 138, 217). For the divine communication to a group, most commentators consider that the Spirit speaks through human agencies i.e. the prophets among the group (Marshall, *Acts*, 216; Dunn, *Acts*, 173; Haenchen, *Acts*, 396; Barrett, *Acts*, 1:605).

[30] Dunn, *Acts*, 173.

[31] Although only one angel appears each time (except 1:10) they *may* or *may not* be the same angel. In this study the plural *angels*, in a collective sense, will be employed.

[32] For the exchangeable use of *the angel of God* and *the angel of the Lord* in the Old Testament see Gen 16:7; 21:17; 22:11; 28:12; Exod 3:2; 14:19; 32:34; Num 22:31; Jdg 2:1; 5:23; 13:6; 2 Sam 24:16; 1 Kgs 19:7; 2 Kgs 1:3; 1 Chr 21:12; Isa 37:36; Zech 1:12; 3:6. Such an understanding may have passed onto Jews in New Testament times; cf. Hur, *Spirit*, 171.

(1:10; cf. 10:30).³³ The utterances of angels, the messengers and representatives of God, are mainly instructing the human target to preach or approach the salvation of Jesus in conformity to God's will.

After delivering the apostles from prison (5:19), the angel commands them to go and speak in the temple τὰ ῥήματα τῆς ζωῆς ταύτης (5:20, the words of this life). Ἡ ζωὴ αὕτη may mean 'the new life offered by Jesus as the ἀρχηγὸς τῆς ζωῆς (3:15, the author of life).'³⁴ The purpose of this deliverance is to proclaim the message of the salvation of life accomplished by Jesus whom God raises from death (3:15).³⁵ The command of preaching *the words of life* profoundly signifies that the risen Jesus is God's very message for salvation.³⁶ Another angelic deliverance happens at Peter's potentially fatal imprisonment (12:4-11). The angel awakens Peter and orders him to clothe himself and follow him (12:7-8). Here the angelic speech provides a dramatic effect to vivify the unexpected deliverance (cf. 12:6, the two soldiers beside Peter do not hear the angel). It ironically reinforces the sovereign power of the divine deliverance (cf. 12:9, 15-16; it is hardly to be believed that Peter would have been saved).³⁷ Both angelic deliverances expose God's sovereign authority and saving power over deadly human force.

The other two direct, angelic sayings appear in the first stage of reaching out to the Gentiles. When Philip evangelises the Ethiopian eunuch, it is an angel takes the lead to direct him to the place for evangelism (8:26)³⁸ whereas the

---

33   A man ἐν ἐσθῆτι λαμπρᾷ in 10:30 definitely refers to the angel (cf. 10:3). In light of 10:30, the wording of ἐν ἐσθήσεσι λευκαῖς in 1:10 suggests that the two men are angels since λαμπρός and λευκός can carry the same meaning, i.e. 'bright, shining, radiant' (cf. L&N, §14.50).

34   Barrett, *Acts*, 1:284. Barrett further asserts that ζωή is used to express the content of the gospel in Acts (cf. 11:18; 13:46, 48) which is much more common in John and Paul. Comparing it with the phrase ὁ λόγος τῆς σωτηρίας ταύτης in 13:26, τὰ ῥήματα τῆς ζωῆς ταύτης in 5:20 is understood as the salvation of Jesus; cf. Marshall, *Acts*, 118; Haenchen, *Acts*, 249; Johnson, *Acts*, 97.

35   Marshall, *Acts*, 118.

36   For a thorough investigation of the risen Jesus as the word of God's salvation see the speeches to the Jews by Peter and Paul in Chapter Three and Four.

37   While the apostles are commanded to witness in the Temple at the first angelic deliverance, Peter goes away secretively (cf. 12:17). This may imply deadly persecution at that time.

38   *The angel of the Lord* in 8:26 probably refers to the angel of God (cf. 10:3; 27:23). It may be supported by the latter use of *the Spirit of the Lord* in 8:39 where the Lord very likely refers to God in the light of 5:9. See H. Douglas Buckwalter, *The Character and Purpose of Luke's Christology* (SNTSMS 89; Cambridge: Cambridge University Press, 1996) 203; John Cochrane O'Neill, 'The Use of *Kyrios* in the Book of Acts,' *SJT* 8 (1955) 155-74, esp. 158-59; James D.G. Dunn, *The Christ and the Spirit: Christology*, vol. 1 (Edinburgh: T & T Clark, 1998) 249; Gerhard Von Schneider, 'Gott und Christus als ΚΥΡΙΟΣ nach der Apostelgeschichte' in Josef

Spirit further directs him to the person. Appearing to Cornelius in a vision (10:4-6), the angel guides him to the way of obtaining salvation. Again, the Spirit opportunely directs Peter to show Cornelius the way of salvation (10:19-20) and implements the work which the angel initiates. The correlated speeches of angels and the Spirit enforce the divine initiative of Gentile evangelism and strongly assure the will of God (cf. 11:17; 15:8).

Besides divine deliverance and guidance, angels also communicate divine promise. The first angelic utterance recorded in the Ascension episode regards a universal promise (1:10-11). As the believers witness how Jesus ascends into heaven in a tangible way, likewise, the way Jesus departs guarantees his second advent on earth. Although not indicated explicitly, the main point of the opening episode, which concerns the kingdom of God and the witness of Jesus (1:3, 8), suggests a divine plan in the interim between Jesus' two advents. During the shipwreck the angelic message (27:24) confirms Jesus' earlier promise to Paul (23:11) and simultaneously reassures Paul of a safe arrival at Rome. The present imperative of μὴ φοβοῦ indicates Paul in fright and in need of invigoration; the perfect tense of κεχάρισται (to have given) reinforces the assurance of God's promise as it is fulfilled. The singling out of *an angel of God* emphasises 'the source and authority behind the angel and his message.'[39] The opportune and infallible strengthening of the angel expresses God's understanding and concern for his messenger. In line with God's plan, Paul, again and again, is heartened by the divine assurance in Corinth (18:9-10), in Jerusalem (23:11) and now at the shipwreck on the way to Rome (27:23-4). Paul, thus, can be sure that 'the purpose of God is still overseeing events' (27:25).[40]

That the angelic message is believed to be God's not only unveils God's will (cf. 1:11; 5:29; 10:13-15, 34; 27:25) but instructs and strengthens believers to do God's will in accordance with his plan (5:20; 8:26; 10:4-6; 27:24). The angelic sayings in the divine deliverances manifest the mighty and invincible power of God (5:20; 12:7-8); those in the Gentile mission convey a divine plan behind the divine interventions and disclose the omniscience and omnipotence of God (8:26; 10:4-6, 13-15); those communicating the divine promises express God's predeterminative will and plan as well as his loving care (1:11; 27:24). In general, the angelic utterances pilot humans to do God's will by leading Jesus' witnesses to testify to the words of life and by pointing people to salvation.[41]

Zmijewski and Ernst Nellessen (eds.), *Begegnung mit dem Wort* (Bonn: Hanstein, 1980) 161-74, citing 163.

[39] Culy and Parsons, *Acts*, 521.
[40] Dunn, *Acts*, 306; cf. Pesch, *Apg*, 2:291; Polhill, *Acts*, 524.
[41] Hur also notes that the angelic speaking and acting are particularly related to revealing God's will in witness-contexts (*Spirit*, 173).

Summary

A divine plan and purpose, which governs the speeches and actions of the heavenly revelators, can be evidently perceived while investigating the divine utterances.[42] That Jesus' last words on earth elucidate God's will and plan specifically serve as a theme to, and a hint for, the development of the narrative. The Spirit and angels progressively promote God's will and make it fully known, especially their close cooperation at the first stage of Gentile mission.[43] Yet the Spirit, along with Jesus, is more concerned with the plan of God being manifested and realised whereas angels are more concerned with the human target to do God's will. This can be observed in that the utterances of Jesus and the Spirit appear at the most crucial moment of God's mission plan (i.e. the commission and the Gentile evangelism).[44] Yet angels, coming alongside Jesus and the Spirit, instruct and strengthen the believers of God and/or Jesus to partake in God's mission plan.[45]

Although distinct in performance, the heavenly characters act on one supreme authority with Jesus and the Spirit performing as God himself (see their use of first person in 18:10 and 10:20) and angels on behalf of God (see the reference of God in third person, 10:4; 27:24). The divine authority of Jesus' words is undoubted since the title *Lord* is referred to both God and Jesus (cf. 2:36, 39; 4:29, 33).[46] The words of the Spirit and angels are equally recognised as the voice of God (compare 10:5-6 with 10:20 and 27:23-24 with 27:25).[47] Both 'represent the same divine power'[48] and 'serve the same purpose of directing events in accordance with the will of God.'[49] All heavenly revelators are regarded as acting for one Divinity and their voice thus possesses the supreme authority of God. No word is of God yet his will and plan is recognised

---

[42] Robert L. Mowery, 'Lord, God, and Father: Theological Language in Luke-Acts,' *SBLSP* (1995) 82-101, citing 92.

[43] Hur rightly indicates that the Spirit and angels 'are closely linked to both Jesus' and his disciples' witness-mission' (*Spirit*, 174).

[44] Aletti, *Luc raconte*, 41-42.

[45] Hur asserts that the role of both the Spirit and angels is parallel to that of the risen Jesus: revealing God's purpose/will by empowering, directing and guiding Jesus' witnesses (*Spirit*, 144, 172). Yet Hur does not distinguish the work of the Spirit from that of angels.

[46] Buckwalter, *Christology*, 185-86; cf. Schneider, 'ΚΥΡΙΟΣ,' 171-73. Turner further argues Jesus' sharing in God's lordship of the Spirit (cf. 16:7); see Max Turner, 'The Spirit of Christ and "Divine" Christology' in Joel B. Green and Max Turner (eds.), *Jesus of Nazareth Lord and Christ* (Grand Rapids: Eerdmans, 1994) 413-36, esp. 435-36. Jesus' share in God's lordship will be thoroughly investigated in the discussion of Peter's speech in Acts 2.

[47] Dunn, *Acts*, 138.

[48] Haenchen, *Acts*, 349.

[49] Barrett, *Acts*, 1:427.

throughout the narrative by means of the utterances of heavenly characters. No presentation is by God himself yet all events are driven in conformity to his purpose by virtue of divine interventions. God's sovereign authority and power are declared in the divine commands. His compassion and loving care are breathed out while those doing his will are strengthened by the heavenly revelators in time of adversity and in need of encouragement. As the divine sovereignty assures that all ongoing events correspond to God's plan, the divine care and oversight guarantee the fulfilment of God's promise to the doers of his supreme will. Overall, the utterances of heavenly characters reveal God as sovereign, caring, faithful and powerful.

Personal/Interpersonal Characterisation

Interestingly enough, no interaction between God and the heavenly characters is found in the Acts narrative. Each heavenly character acts for God and in his authority. Although functioning independently, their performances are closely correlated in order to achieve the plan and purpose of God. Moreover, by God's omnipotent authority the divine utterance, which unveils the will of God, carries a prophetic function that in turn makes the utterance itself a signal to the development of the narrative plot. So far as it is discussed, there is a divine plan behind the divine utterances yet the essence of the plan is still unspecified. No definition of the plan is given by the divine revelators except Jesus' last words on earth (1:4-8) which form the very first divine utterance in the story. This offers, however, only a sketchy image and further elucidation is needed for a thorough picture of God's plan. As indicated, Jesus and the Spirit not only act in the status of God but also mutually open a new page for God's mission plan. The interrelationship between God and them, thus, is crucial for the scrutiny of God's plan. As the feature of God's plan and purpose is divulged, his inner world is uncovered.

Broadly speaking, there are three points of view to look at the interrelationship between God, Jesus and the Spirit in the narrative—those of characters, the narrator and the reader.[50] Through the personal interactions with heavenly revelators and the interpersonal interactions with other fellows the characters perceive God's will. Underneath the plot, the deployment of incidents and characters, lies the narrator's recognition of God. In following the signals laid by the narrator the reader constructs their image of God. The communication between the narrator and the reader can be well illustrated by a dot-to-dot picture. Characters and incidents in the narrative world resemble the dots in the picture which carry the message of the narrator. The narrator deploys the dots to communicate his designed picture which the reader deciphers by filling up the gap between the dots.

---

[50] Cf. Scholes and Kellogg, *Nature*, 240.

As noted, the revelators, acting as one Divinity (though each functions as a distinct character)[51] and without interaction between them, make God's plan known only by their interacting with human characters (who are the pictorial dots of the narrator). It is, thus, impossible to unveil the features of God's plan, which are concealed in the divine interrelationships, through the viewpoint of the heavenly revelators. Such divine interrelationships, however, are fully disclosed in the speeches of the major characters in the narrative. Therefore, to scrutinise the divine interpersonal portrayal of God from the divine perspective, the reader's point of view will be adopted in order to provide an alternative way to perceive the divine interrelationships between God and Jesus/the Spirit. Marguerat clearly indicates that 'following the characters of the story the reader is called to identify, in the opacity of what took place, a divine logic of salvation.'[52] The aim of this section is to probe the personal/interpersonal characterisation of God by the heavenly revelators with the assistance of the reader's eyes. By this investigation the image of God will be particularly focused on the divine interrelationships constructed by the reader in order to provide a latent-yet-essential picture of God and his plan.[53]

Jesus

The opening scene of Acts skims swiftly over what Jesus did and taught from the beginning until the day of the Ascension; this gives a brief summary of the previous narrative work (1:1-2). Then, while the narrator recounts Jesus' final work after his resurrection, the screening slows down and the lens remains on Jesus' teaching of the apostles (1:3). As the narrator silences himself, Jesus speaks. His last words serve as an introduction to the forthcoming story. This comprises the command of waiting for, and the promise of receiving, the Spirit in order to be Jesus' witness (1:4-5, 8). Only by the Spirit's empowerment are the believers able to be Jesus' witnesses. To be witness is a narrative theme and related to the kingdom of God (1:3; 8:12; 19:8; 20:25; 28:23, 31). The Acts narrative, thus, delineates the impact of Jesus in human history and depicts how his witnesses are empowered by the Spirit for the mission of God.

Most may assume that the rest of the story is about the Spirit's empowerment of the believers while Jesus, finishing his work on earth, ascends into

---

[51] The tangible and dramatic performances of Jesus and angels undoubtedly characterise them as characters (see Jesus in 1:4-9; 9:4-16 and the angel in 5:19-20; 12:7-11). Only through his assertive words is the Spirit undisputedly regarded as a character (10:19-20; 13:2). See Marguerat, *Historian*, 110; Hur, *Spirit*, 129-30; Shepherd, *Spirit*, 90-97.

[52] Marguerat, *Historian*, 91.

[53] The divine relationships also shed new light on the image of God from the other points of view (i.e. the characters and the narrator) which will be scrutinised in the following four chapters.

heaven. The heavenly Jesus, however, remains active in human history and vigilant to oversee his witnesses.[54] The preface also suggests an implication of the continual work of Jesus (1:1, ὧν ἤρξατο ὁ Ἰησοῦς ποιεῖν τε καὶ διδάσκειν). The exalted Jesus, receiving the Holy Spirit from the Father, first pours him out upon the believers (2:33; cf. 2:2-4).[55] At Stephen's martyrdom Jesus is at God's right hand to witness for him as Stephen has witnessed for Jesus (7:55-6).[56] Moreover, the heavenly Jesus calls out Paul (9:3-6), commis-

---

[54] Whether Luke presents an *absentee christology* has been debated. For its advocator see C.F.D. Moule, 'The Christology of Acts' in Leander E. Keck and J. Louis Martyn (eds.), *Studies in Luke-Acts* (London: SPCK, 1968) 159-85, esp. 179-80; two works by Geoffrey Lampe, *God as Spirit* (Oxford: Clarendon Press, 1977) 72 and 'The Lucan Portrait of Christ,' *NTS* 2 (1955-56) 160-75, esp. 174-75; J.A. Ziesler, 'The Name of Jesus in the Acts of the Apostles,' *JSNT* 4 (1979) 28-41, esp. 37-38. For those who modify this view to having a certain connection between the heavenly Jesus and the believers see Hans Conzelmann, *The Theology of St Luke* (London: Faber and Faber, 1960) 186; George W. MacRae, '"Whom Heaven Must Receive Until the Time": Reflections on the Christology of Act,' *Int* 27 (1973) 151-65, esp. 160-64; compare the two works of Eric Franklin, 'The Ascension and the Eschatology of Luke-Acts,' *SJT* 23 (1970) 191-200, esp. 197 and *Christ the Lord* (London: SPCK, 1975) 55; Moule later modifies his view in *The Origin of Christology* (Cambridge: Cambridge University Press, 1977) 104-05. For those who attest the heavenly Jesus' active presence in communication with the believers on earth see Parsons, *Departure*, 161-62; Buckwalter, *Christology*, 180-84; Aletti, *Luc raconte*, 40; I. Howard Marshall, *Luke: Historian and Theologian* (London: Paternoster Press, 1997) 179; Max Turner, 'The Spirit of Christ and Christology' in Harold H. Rowdon (ed.), *Christ the Lord* (Leicester: Inter-Varsity Press, 1982) 168-90, esp. 183; Max Turner, 'Jesus and the Spirit in Lucan Perspective,' *TynB* 32 (1981) 3-42, esp. 40; O'Toole, 'Risen Jesus,' 471-98; Powell, *About Acts*, 47; Maddox, *Purpose*, 139; Keith Warrington, 'Acts and the Healing Narratives: Why?' *Journal of Pentecostal Theology* 14/2 (2006) 189-217.

[55] The active role of the heavenly Jesus can also be affirmed in the change of his relation to the Spirit. The earthly Jesus is, by the Spirit, conceived in Mary's womb (Lk 1:35), confirmed at his baptism (Lk 3:22), led into the wilderness (Lk 4:1) and empowered for his ministry (Lk 4:14-15). The heavenly Jesus, however, promises the Spirit (1:4-5), pours out the Spirit upon the believers (2:4, 33) and empowers the believers with the Spirit for his own witness (1:8; 4:8-12). Cf. Earl Richard, 'Pentecost as a Recurrent Theme in Luke-Acts' in Earl Richard (ed.), *New Views on Luke and Acts* (Collegeville: Liturgical Press, 1990) 133-49, citing 134; C.F. Evans, '"Speeches" in Acts' in Albert Descamps and André de Halleux (eds.), *Mélanges Bibliques* (Gembloux: Éditions J. Duculot, 1970) 287-302, citing 298.

[56] Aletti, *Luc raconte*, 31. In Stephen's vision, that Jesus stands at God's right hand indicates only a static relationship between God and Jesus. There is no interaction between them.

sions him (9:15) and opportunely strengthens him (18:9-10; 23:11; cf. 9:16).[57] Even at Paul's westward mission journey Jesus 'continues to take an active role'[58] as seen in the portrayal of the Spirit as *the Spirit of Jesus* (16:7), 'a phrase which emphasises how Jesus himself through the Spirit was guiding the progress of the gospel.'[59] Although in heaven, Jesus' care is present (18:10) through either visions (9:10-16; 18:9; 22:17-21) or the Spirit (16:7).[60]

No explicit indication of Jesus' personal interaction with God is denoted yet Jesus' calling to be his witness is regarded as God's will (4:18-19; 5:28-29) and is with God's help (26:22-23). It is by the speeches of the major characters, Peter and Paul, that the reader learns more about the relationship and interactions between Jesus and God and thus knows more about God through Jesus.[61] By the indicator dots and through the reader's eyes it becomes apparent that the whole of Jesus' life is intended by God to carry out his will and plan.[62] Jesus is proved to be of God by the miraculous deeds God performs through him (2:22; 10:36, 38); his death is in accordance with God's foreknowledge and purpose (2:23; 3:18); God raises him up from death (2:24, 32; 3:15, 26; 4:10; 5:30; 10:40; 13:30, 33, 34, 37; 17:31); God exalts him (2:33; 5:31; cf. 3:13; 7:55); he receives the Spirit from God the Father and gives him to the believers (2:33); finally, God will send him again to the world (3:20-21; cf. 1:11). By doing God's will, Jesus is called God's holy servant (4:27, 30) and the Son of God

---

[57] As Paul is led into a new continental mission, where the influence of Judaism is less and the persecution of the Jews and the challenge of the polytheistic Gentiles increase, the heavenly Jesus interacts more closely with him (18:9-10; 23:11).

[58] Johnson, *Acts*, 285.

[59] Marshall, *Acts*, 263. Also, Buckwalter asserts that 'certainly Acts 2:33 and 16:7 indicate for Luke that the Spirit represents, if not mediates, the exalted Jesus' continued presence and activity' (*Christology*, 180). Cf. Guthrie, *Theology*, 547; William J. Larkin, 'The Spirit and Jesus "on Mission" in the Postresurrection and Postascension Stages of Salvation History: The Impact of the Pneumatology of Acts on Its Christology' in Amy M. Donaldson and Timothy B. Sailors (eds.), *New Testament Greek and Exegesis* (Grand Rapids: Eerdmans, 2003) 121-39, esp. 134-38.

[60] The heavenly Jesus seems notably to be interested in Paul. The pattern of Paul's commission differs from that of the apostles. The apostles are called and taught by the earthly Jesus and are finally commissioned at Jesus' ascension into heaven. In contrast, Paul is first called and commissioned by the heavenly Jesus and then comes Jesus' comfort and teaching (cf. also 2 Cor 12:1-10).

[61] Robert L. Mowery, 'Direct Statements Concerning God's Activity in Acts,' *SBLSP* 29 (1990) 196-211, citing 201. The relationship between Jesus and God is mainly expounded in the speeches except in 9:20 where the narrator indicates the content of Paul's proclamation, i.e. Jesus is the Son of God.

[62] Cf. Robert L. Mowery, 'The Divine Hand and the Divine Plan in the Lukan Passion,' *SBLSP* 30 (1991) 558-75, esp. 568-71.

(9:20). Foremost, God makes him Lord and Christ (2:36), ruler and saviour (5:31; 13:23) and judge (10:42; cf. 17:31).[63]

As outlined above, there are two stages of Jesus' performance in the light of his relation to God in the narrative: the earthly and the heavenly Jesus. The earthly Jesus, though performing his ministry powerfully and actively (10:38b), is fully passive before and compliant to God, that is, he submits himself fully to God's will (2:23). The scrutiny of the relationship between God and Jesus reflects a God-dominated one.[64] In elucidating the purpose of Jesus' mission on earth, both Peter and Paul refer back to God's old promise (2:30-31; 3:18, 25; 13:23) and its fulfilment (2:36; 13:23),[65] behind which lies a purpose and plan of God.[66] This brings God into the spotlight in their witness to Jesus. God is the author who causes Jesus' resurrection, exaltation and second advent (2:24, 32, 36; 3:13, 15, 20, 26; 4:10; 5:30, 31; 10:40; 13:23, 30, 33, 34, 37; 17:31; God in an active role),[67] the ultimate agent who vindicates Jesus' status (2:22a; 10:42; God as a witness of Jesus' standing)[68] and the intermediate agent who acts through Jesus (2:22b; 10:36; God as a fortifier of Jesus' witness).[69] By and large, throughout Jesus' earthly ministry as narrated in Acts, God plays a very active role (cf. in the descriptions of the God-Jesus relation, either God is the subject of an active verb with Jesus its object or Jesus is the subject of a passive verb with God its direct agent).[70] This signifies that God dominantly and actively communicates a message to the world through Jesus. God initiates

---

[63] For God's role in the story of Jesus see also Mowery's two articles: 'God's Activity,' 199-201; 'God,' 95-101.

[64] Leon Morris, *New Testament Theology* (Grand Rapids: Zondervan, 1986) 149.

[65] Christopher M. Tuckett, 'The Christology of Luke-Acts' in Verheyden (ed.), *Unity*, 133-64, citing 158; Marshall, *Luke: Historian*, 105.

[66] Powell, *About Acts*, 40; John T. Squires, *The Plan of God in Luke-Acts* (SNTSMS 76; Cambridge: Cambridge University Press, 1993) 2, 137-39.

[67] It is noteworthy that God is the subject and Jesus the object in these verses. The only passive expression of Jesus being exalted occurs in 2:33a where ὑψωθείς functions as a temporal participle providing an additional circumstance to the main thought *Jesus pours out the Spirit*. The active expression of God attaches the witness of Jesus to the plan of God.

[68] Here the emphasis is on God as the direct agent (cf. the direct passive concept or voice). In 2:22a, Jesus is proved to be of God by the miraculous deeds God performs through him. In Jesus' vindication God is the direct agent and the miracles are the indirect agent. The ὑπό in 10:42 indicate God as the direct agent who appoints Jesus to be a judge.

[69] God is also presented in the role of indirect agent (cf. indirect passive) as he performs miracles through Jesus (2:22b) and sends the word to Israel through Jesus (10:36). Here the cooperative relation is in view yet it slightly emphasises God in order to fortify the witness of Jesus.

[70] See also Jacob Jervell, *The Theology of the Acts of the Apostles* (Cambridge: Cambridge University Press, 1996) 31-32.

salvation in the salvific activity of Jesus; therefore, in the narrative, before 'soteriology is christocentric, it is theocentric.'[71] Specifically speaking, by Jesus' submission, not only does Jesus magnify God's sovereignty and authority, nor merely does he manifest God's will and saving plan (2:36-9; 10:36-43),[72] but also he himself becomes the very message of God,[73] that is, the Word of salvation (13:23, 26). As Jesus' last words on earth communicate God's plan of mission, the interpretation of his life on earth reveals it to be a mission plan of salvation.[74]

The heavenly Jesus, however, acts independently and actively on the authority of God.[75] After being exalted, he receives the Holy Spirit from the Father and then pours the Spirit out upon the believers (2:33; Jesus in an active role). Through his own name Jesus' authority and power prevails.[76] In his name the believers receive the heavenly blessings (i.e. the forgiveness of sin, the Spirit, miraculous healings; cf. 2:38; 3:16; 4:12, 30; 16:18; 22:16; Jesus as an agent). His commission and overseeing of Paul never fail (9:3-16; 18:9-10; 23:11; Jesus in an active role). In Jesus is the divine care of his witnesses assured; by him is the bridge for the heavenly blessings built; through him comes the Spirit to consummate the plan of God.

In sum, the earthly Jesus passively complies with the will of the heavenly Father yet actively fulfils the will of the Father God on earth. The heavenly Jesus shares God's authority on high and sovereignly takes part with the believers, his witnesses. The earthly Jesus is in submissive relation to God; the heavenly Jesus is in equal relation to him.[77] In the light of his relationship with God, the earthly Jesus characterises God as an authoritative and almighty Father; the heavenly Jesus characterises him as a sovereign Lord and a gentle shepherd (looking after his people, as the title *Father* also suggests).

---

[71] Joel B. Green, 'Salvation to the End of the Earth: God as Saviour in the Acts of the Apostles' in Marshall and Peterson (eds.), *Witness*, 83-106, citing 98.
[72] Morris, *Theology*, 151, 173-75, 181; Guthrie, *Theology*, 461.
[73] Larry W. Hurtado, *Lord Jesus Christ* (Grand Rapids: Eerdmans, 2003) 342.
[74] Powell, *About Acts*, 40.
[75] There is no indication of the heavenly Jesus' relation to God except in Stephen's vision (7:56). His active role in the believers' lives is expressed in the verses where Jesus is the subject of an active voice verb (2:33; 9:3-16; 18:9-10; 23:11).
[76] Ziesler, 'Name of Jesus,' 30. See also Buckwalter who asserts that Jesus' name implies 'the personal, active presence of transcendent deity among his people' (*Christology*, 183); Marshall regards it as 'the living power of Jesus at work in the church' (*Luke: Historian*, 179).
[77] Buckwalter, *Christology*, 184-91; Hur, *Spirit*, 142-43; Michael Allen Salmeier, 'Ordainer of Times and Seasons': The Portrayal of God in the Book of the Acts of the Apostles* (unpublished D.Phil. Thesis, Linacre College of Oxford University, 2005) 92-100.

The Holy Spirit

Doubly promised by God the Father and Jesus, on the day of fulfilment the hidden Spirit vigorously steps into the human arena (2:1-4). He is associated with the plan and purpose of God (1:8; 2:33, 39) and is foretold a long time previously (2:16-21).[78] The Spirit prophetically speaks through human agents (1:16; 4:25; 20:23; 21:11; 28:25; cf. 11:28; 21:4),[79] assertively guides the believers into a new stage of God's mission (2:1-4; 8:29, 39; 10:19; 13:2; 16:6-7),[80] mightily empowers the believers to bear witness to Jesus or God (2:4; 4:8, 31; 9:17; 13:9; cf. 1:8),[81] definitively evinces the divine approval and presence to God's people (in a collective sense, i.e. the Spirit falls on a group of people, see 8:15, 17; 10:44, 47; 11:15; 19:2, 6; cf. 2:2-3),[82] and is undisputedly recognised as the master over the church (5:3; 20:28) and as a sign of the presence of the divine power within a spiritual person (6:3, 5; 7:55; 11:24; cf. 6:8, 10; 13:52).[83]

---

[78] Robert L. Mowery, 'God the Father in Luke-Acts' in Richard (ed.), *New Views*, 124-32, citing 131.

[79] The prophetic nature of the Spirit's utterance is a divine form of witness. From the characters' point of view, the Spirit speaks through human agents in the past (1:16; 4:25; 28:25) and present (20:23; 21:11) and God speaks through the Spirit (4:25). From the narrator's point of view, however, humans are empowered by the Spirit and thus speak through the Spirit (11:28; 21:4). The former is aware of the Spirit's participation in human utterance while the latter observes the Spirit as an agent causing the speech.

[80] Guthrie, *Theology*, 549; Aletti, *Luc raconte*, 40; James B. Shelton, *Mighty in Word and Deed* (Peabody: Hendrickson Publishers, 1991) 125-27.

[81] The phrase πλησθῆναι πνεύματος ἁγίου is used to indicate the empowerment of powerfully and boldly bearing oral witness. Πίμπλημι, which means 'to cause something to be completely full' (L&N, §59.38), occurs nine times in Acts. Five occurrences refer to the believers being filled completely with the Spirit (2:4; 4:8, 31; 9:17; 13:9); four to those being fully filled with amazement (3:10), jealousy (5:17; 13:45) and confusion (19:29). See also Hur, *Spirit*, 168; Shelton, *Mighty*, 139-41; Max Turner, *Power from on High* (JPTSup 9; Sheffield: Sheffield Academic Press, 2000) 166. Turner further points out 'the words "filled with Holy Spirit" usually designate short outbursts of spiritual power/inspiration rather than the inception of long-term endowment of the Spirit' (168).

[82] The direct indwelling of the Spirit in the believers appears in the structure as either the Spirit falling upon–ἐπέπεσεν or ἦλθε– the believers (i.e. the Spirit as the subject of a sentence, see 10:44; 11:15; 19:6; cf. 2:2-3) or the believers receiving–λαμβάνειν–the Spirit (i.e. the believers as the subject of a sentence, see 8:15, 17; 10:47; 19:2).

[83] In the phrase of πλήρης πνεύματος ἁγίου, the Spirit signifies a trait of a spiritual person (7:55). It often accompanies other spiritual dispositions, e.g. wisdom (6:3), faith (6:5; 11:24) and joy (13:52, here the verb πληροῦν takes the place of the adjective πλήρης). See Hur, *Spirit*, 168; Shelton, *Mighty*, 137-39; Turner, *Power*, 165.

Stepping onto the human stage as the fulfilment of God's promise, the Spirit closely interacts with the believers and his relation to God turns into a two-tier relationship of which the indicator dots are mainly found in Peter's speeches and the narrator's narration. The Spirit dependently serves as God's intermediary (4:25) or gift (5:32; 15:8; cf. 2:17-18; 10:45) in his relation to God towards humans yet acts independently on the authority of God in his own relation with the believers (8:29; 10:19-20; 13:2). While the Spirit's attached relation to God keeps him in the background of the stage to whisper God's will, the detached relation moves him to the foreground to act out God's plan. Put briefly, the Spirit's attached role makes him a *commentator* of God's will; the detached role makes him a *director* of God's mission of witnessing to Jesus.[84]

Both the attached and detached roles of the Spirit may appear chiastically (8:17, 29; 10:19-20, 44) or simultaneously (2:1-11). In his attached relation to God, the Spirit as God's intermediary, before descending upon the believers, prophesies concerning Jesus through human agents (4:25; cf. 3:18, 24; 28:25) and empowers the earthly Jesus (10:38; cf. 1:2). Being sent by God and Jesus to the believers, the Spirit inaugurates the 'apostolic testimony to the risen Christ and his gospel,'[85] and a new faith community is formed (chs. 2-4). Then, the Spirit as God's gift[86] signifies the divine presence (2:17-18; 19:2-6)[87] and particularly indicates God's approval and acceptance of the (semi)Gentile believers as he did to the Jewish believers at Pentecost (8:15-17; 10:47; 11:15;

Turner further clarifies, '[t]he Lukan use of these expressions [*filled with Holy Spirit* and *full of Holy Spirit*] allows that a person might on many occasions be "filled with Holy Spirit" while nevertheless remaining "full" of the Spirit: the two types of metaphor make different but complementary assertions' (*Power*, 168).

[84] Hur, *Spirit*, 179.

[85] Joseph A. Fitzmyer, 'The Role of the Spirit in Luke-Acts' in Verheyden (ed.), *Unity*, 165-83, citing 174.

[86] Hur indicates that the expression of the Spirit as a gift (or a thing) characterises the Spirit as a 'non-person like' character (*Spirit*, 156). From this perspective Hur argues the Lukan narrator does not intend to elucidate whether or not the Spirit *is* a person; however, the narrator '*shows* that the *personal* activity of the Spirit dynamically participates in believers' affairs as signifying the divine (God's and/or the risen Jesus') intervention or manifestation' (158). This is what Max Turner already argued that the Spirit is a personal character presented metaphorically ('Spirit Endowment in Luke-Acts: Some Linguistic Consideration,' *VoxE* 12 [1981] 45-63, citing 57-60). In the light of the Spirit's relationship with God, his detached role presents him as a personal being whilst his attached role makes him like an impersonal force since he acts simply as God's intermediary.

[87] Turner, *Power*, 406. Turner elucidates that 'God's "Spirit" is virtually always synecdoche for God himself, and is usually a way of speaking of God's *presence* while preserving his transcendence' ('Christology,' 422).

15:8).[88] In his detached relation to God, the Spirit as the divine, personal power[89] enables the believers to bear witness to Jesus in words (4:8, 31; 6:10; 9:17, 22), in deeds (6:8; 13:9-11; cf. 7:55, empowering Stephen for the coming martyrdom)[90] and in life (6:3, 5; 11:24; 13:52).[91] Foremost, as God's revelator, the Spirit himself witnesses for Jesus (5:32; cf. 2:33),[92] guides the crucial breakthrough of God's mission racially (8:29; 10:19-20; 11:12) and geographically (13:2; 16:6-7),[93] oversees and shepherds the church (5:3; 20:28) and reveals the impending events to believers (11:28; 20:23; 21:4, 11). In brief, the Spirit aligns himself with God in unveiling God's will while functioning as God's intermediary and gift and in advancing God's mission plan and enabling the

---

[88] Marguerat, *Historian*, 116-17, 125-26; Jacob Jervell, *The Unknown Paul* (Minneapolis: Augsburg, 1984) 107.

[89] Few regard the Spirit as a mode of God's activity, an impersonal, active power through which God interacts with people. See Jervell, *Theology*, 44; Jervell, *Unknown*, 115; G.W.H. Lampe, 'The Holy Spirit in the Writings of St. Luke' in D.E. Nineham (ed.), *Studies in the Gospels* (Oxford: Basil Blackwell, 1957) 159-200, esp. 160. Nonetherless, the personal status of the Spirit can be clearly discerned in 5:3; 16:7. See G. Stählin, 'Τὸ πνεῦμα Ἰησοῦ (Apostelgeschichte 16:7)' in Barnabas Lindars and Stephen S. Smalley (eds.), *Christ and Spirit in the New Testament* (Cambridge: Cambridge University Press, 1973) 229-52, esp. 252; F.F. Bruce, 'The Holy Spirit in the Acts of the Apostles,' *Int* 27 (1973) 166-83, esp. 173. Max Turner explicitly indicates the Spirit as a powerful numinous character who somehow conveys the numinous sense of God's presence and activity ('The Spirit of Prophecy and the Power of Authoritative Preaching in Luke-Acts: A Question of Origins,' *NTS* 38 [1992] 66-88, citing 70).

[90] In Acts the power of the Spirit is often connected with the word and miracle (Jacob Jervell, *Die Apostelgeschichte* [Göttingen: Vandenhoech & Ruprecht, 1998] 115; Jervell, *Unknown*, 86; Leo O'Reilly, *Word and Sign in the Acts of the Apostles* [Analecta Gregoriana 243; Roma: Editrice Pontificia Università Gregoriana, 1987] 166). Yet no explicit link is made between miracles and the Spirit's work; instead, the work of the Spirit, a Spirit of prophecy, aims at the proclamation of the Word (Marguerat, *Historian*, 118-21; cf. Jervell, *Unknown*, 109-12). Robert P. Menzies even strongly argues that the reception of the Spirit signifies receiving prophetic empowerment for mission (*The Development of Early Christian Pneumatology* [JSNTSup 54; Sheffield: JSOT Press, 1991] 245-77).

[91] Turner, *Power*, 408. Turner further indicates that the Spirit nurtures, shapes and purifies the faith community ('The "Spirit of Prophecy" as the Power of Israel's Restoration and Witness' in Marshall and Peterson [eds.], *Witness to the Gospel*, 327-48, citing 347).

[92] Marguerat indicates the Spirit himself *is* the witness; he is the enabling power to witness to Jesus (*Historian*, 115; cf. Hur, *Spirit*, 155). Hur further asserts that the Spirit-inspired or empowered human characters as witnesses to both God and Jesus (*Spirit*, 170).

[93] Hur, *Spirit*, 148; Guthrie, *Theology*, 543, 546-47.

believers to do God's will while performing as God's power and revelator (i.e. acting as he is God).[94]

Acting independently with the power and authority of God, the Spirit is recognised as God himself. Lying to the Spirit is considered by Peter as lying to God (5:3-4); resisting God is nothing less than resisting the Spirit (7:51, see the rebellion of Israel throughout her history in Stephen's speech); the Spirit identifies his will with God's (10:3, 19-20); and finally, in the Jerusalem council, the decision of the faith community, which is driven by God (15:7-11, 14-18), is regarded as the will of the Spirit (15:28). By these indicators the reader learns that God is still at work in human history and interacts with his people dynamically. It is in the power of the same Spirit that both Jesus and the believers carry out the saving plan in conformity with the purpose of God.[95] While the earthly Jesus is the content of God's word to the world, the Spirit is God's design to empower the believers for the witness of Jesus (1:8). Therefore, Jesus makes God's saving plan manifest; the Spirit enables God's loving purpose to be achieved. In their relationships to God, whereas the earthly Jesus' passive role makes manifest God's saving will, the Spirit's attached role affirms it; whereas the heavenly Jesus' active role announces and assures God's plan, the Spirit's detached role promotes and fortifies it.

To be specific about the characterisation of God, the Spirit, in his attached relation to God, characterises God as a plan-designing and purpose-driven deity embracing sovereign authority. In the light of his will of salvation (5:31; 13:23), God's authoritative plan and purpose whisper his powerful love. In his detached relation to God, the Spirit characterises God as a supreme Lord with omnipotent authority. Such sovereignty and omnipotence direct all things in keeping with God's will and thus assure the consummation of God's plan. The divine invincible power and authority are fully presented as the Spirit 'pulls the believing community ahead in order that the plan of God can be accomplished.'[96] Besides the relational portrayal of God by the Spirit, the prophetic nature of the Spirit,[97] whether in the past or present, either in prophecy

---

[94] Although indicating the significance of the Spirit's presence and activities, Salmeier does not clarify the Spirit's relationship with God in the narrative (*Ordainer*, 109-20).

[95] John H. Sieber, 'The Spirit as the "Promise of My Father" in Luke 24:49' in Daniel Durken (ed.), *Sin, Salvation, and the Spirit* (Collegeville: Liturgical Press, 1979) 271-8, citing 274; cf. Dunn, *Acts*, 8. Hur indicates that the Spirit signals 'God's intrusive presence or power working within Jesus and his disciples as God's human agents' (*Spirit*, 161).

[96] Marguerat, *Historian*, 117.

[97] The Spirit as a spirit of prophecy is discussed by many scholars. See Jervell, *Unknown*, 96-121; Jervell, *Theology*, 51; Marguerat, *Historian*, 119; Turner, *Power*, 404-18; Turner, 'Restoration,' 334.

or guidance, magnifies God's omniscience and omnipresence since through the Spirit God reveals his will trans-temporally and trans-spatially.

Angels

Unlike Jesus and the Spirit, who are parts of God's saving plan and who are also the divine agents to actuate God's mission plan, angels only play the role of God's agents to carry out God's will. Although not with the same status as Jesus and the Spirit in relation to God, angels still serve as the representatives of God who act with God's authority and power. Their major tasks in the narrative are to announce God's will (1:11; 27:23; cf. 7:30, 35, 53), instruct believers to do God's will (8:26; 10:3-6) and implement God's will (5:19; 12:7-11; 12:23).

Acting on behalf of God, angels reveal Jesus' second advent to the believers (1:11), deliver the apostles (5:19; 12:7-11) and execute the divine judgement on Herod (12:23). Cooperating with the Spirit, angels initiate the vital breakthrough of Gentile evangelisation and accelerate God's mission plan by directing Jesus' witness (8:26, 29) and the believer of God (10:3-6, 19-20) to do God's will. Such a double confirmation of God's purpose by the two heavenly revelators—through the tangible guidance of angels (outwardly, either in vision or in person) and the impalpable lead of the Spirit (inwardly)[98]—makes God's will incontestable and indisputable (11:12-18). In parallel with the heavenly Jesus, an angel announces God's will and continues Jesus' care for Paul by renewing Jesus' earlier promise to Paul at the fatal shipwreck (27:23; cf. 23:11). Again, out of the omnipotent authority, on which the angel acts, streams God's loving care and protection which ensure God's mission plan.

Unlike the angelic work in the Gospels, which is essentially christocentric,[99] the angelic activities are believer-centred in Acts. Angels not only reinforce God's will, revealed to the believers by Jesus and the Spirit, but also pilot and escort them to carry out God's will. The divine deliverance and judgement implemented by angels appear at the religious and political persecutions by which God's sovereign authority and almighty power are magnified. The angelic instruction and promise, coming alongside that of the Spirit and Jesus, happen at both stages of Gentile mission; through this God's will of worldwide mission is fortified and the believers are encouraged to carry on the mission in keeping with God's plan. The overall angelic work manifests God as a sovereign, authoritative and powerful figure.

---

[98] The angel probably appears to people in a tangible way since he can be recognised as an angel. The Spirit, however, is a spirit communicating in an intangible way.

[99] M.J. Davidson, 'Angels' in Joel B. Green, Scot McKnight and I. Howard Marshall (eds.), *Dictionary of Jesus and the Gospels* (Leicester: InterVarsity Press, 1992) 8-11, citing 11.

Summary

To summarise, all the heavenly characters act on one divine authority with one determinate purpose. In the narrative arena they closely interact with human characters to carry out God's predeterminative plan. Although performing independently, they act as one Divinity.[100] The authority of their utterances is enhanced by divine interventions and acknowledged by human compliance. The divine deliverance, instruction, guidance and safekeeping primarily fall upon the major characters, Peter and Paul, whom God has uniquely chosen for the particular tasks (15:7; 26:19-22). In line with God's saving plan and purpose, the divine utterances signal God's will; the divine interventions pilot believers to do it; consequently, the believers are convinced and commit themselves vigorously to it.

Taken into account individually, each revelator plays a distinctive role in disclosing God's inner world. Jesus himself becomes the Word of God to reveal God's saving plan and universal mission. His interactions with the believers occur at the most crucial moments either to initiate a new stage of God's plan (commissioning the believers, 1:4-8; pouring out the Spirit, 2:33; commissioning the Gentile missionary, 9:14-16; involvement in the westward mission, 16:7), or to invigorate the particularly chosen witnesses, Stephen (the first martyr, 7:55) and Paul (the first assigned missionary, 18:9-10; 23:11). The Holy Spirit actuates the mission in accordance with God's universal saving plan. Similar to Jesus' role, the Spirit co-initiates the crucial stages in God's mission plan (descending into the human arena, 2:1-4; directing the Gentile evangelism, 8:29; 10:19-20; sending out the Gentile missionaries, 13:2; guiding the westward mission, 16:6). Besides this, the Spirit empowers Jesus' witnesses (4:8, 31; 6:10; 7:55), authenticates the Gentile mission (8:17, 39; 10:44-45) and partakes in the community life (in a general way, 9:31; 13:52; or in particular, 11:28; 19:6; 20:23; 21:4, 11).[101] Angels drive the believers to carry out God's will of the universal mission for salvation. Alongside Jesus and the Spirit, angels, providing specific help and instruction, guard and direct the believers (of God and/or Jesus) to do God's will (5:19-20; 8:26; 10:3-6; 12:7-11, 23; 27:23-24).[102] The most unique angelic work is revealing Jesus' second advent (1:11). Above all else, Jesus is the manifestation of God in the physical realm when he becomes the content of God's saving Word and commissions the believers for God's mission. The Spirit presents God in the metaphysical realm as

---

[100] Cf. Mowery attributes the activities of supernatural agents to God ('God's Activity,' 209-10).

[101] Marguerat also points out the Spirit, acting in and for the faith community, reaches only believers (*Historian*, 112).

[102] Hur, *Spirit*, 172.

he is connected with the manner of the believers' witnessing to Jesus and carrying on God's plan.[103] In making God's will and care palpable to the believers, angels steer them to carry out God's mission. In short, Jesus is the manifestation of God's will of salvation; the Spirit is the realisation of God's power in consummating God's will; angels are the representatives of God in helping people to do God's will.

Conclusion

The divine representation of God can be well illustrated by a telescopic lens. While zooming in, one gets a close-up of elements of a landscape. While zooming out, a vista of the larger landscape can be viewed. The divine utterances and the narrator's narration resemble the zoom-in lens by which a close-up of present events, actuated by the heavenly revelators, is perceived. Through what the heavenly revelators say (the divine utterances) and what they do (depicted in the narration) the work of the veiled God receives attention and is magnified; by this the readers construct their image of God. Similarly, the speeches of Peter and Paul resemble a zoom-out lens by which the whole picture of God's plan is perceived. It is through this perspective that God's purpose and will behind the divine work are unfolded entirely. From the microscopic (zoom-in) view, a God with sovereign authority and saving power emerges from the performance of Jesus; a God with omnipotent authority and dynamic power emanates from the presentation of the Spirit; a God with supreme authority and protective power flows from the representation of angels. Along with the unchallenged authority and invincible power come God's omniscience and omnipresence. From the macroscopic (zoom-out) view, the portrait of God displays, in the light of his saving plan and purpose, a loving Father and caring Lord who holds in his hand the omnipotent sovereignty and authority and who embraces his people in his mighty kingdom.

The ostensible disappearance of God does not signify his withdrawal or absence from human history but indicates his distinct manner of involvement. As the preceding discussion has shown, God's saving purpose and plan leave him always in the interest of the reader and constantly bring him into focus. With reference to the divine characterisation, Sternberg points out:

---

[103] See Jervell who argues that the Spirit is concerned with the ways of preaching the gospel. He asserts the boldness of Jesus' witnesses is a gift of the Spirit (*Theology*, 50); even the miracles, which authenticate the preaching, are also Spirit-empowered works (*Unknown*, 88, 110-12). Marguerat explicates '[t]he Spirit is at the service of the expansion of the Word' (*Historian*, 121). See also Allison A. Trites, *The New Testament Concept of Witness* (SNTSMS 31; Cambridge: Cambridge University Press, 1977) 150-51.

> In the absence of overt exposition, the reader must piece it together for himself by extrapolating features from dramatic givens. We infer divine motive (as cause) from act or response (as effect); check that inferred motive against later acts supposed to issue from it; generalize recurrent instances or lines of action into attributes and the various attributes into a theocentric world picture, subject at any moment to further retrospective adjustment as well as deepening or specification.[104]

This chapter marks the beginning of our marching into the theocentric world of Acts. It starts from the vital perspective of the self-characterisation of God. Performing independently to carry out God's plan, the heavenly revelators share the authority and power of God (10:20, 38; 18:9-10; 27:24) and act as one Divinity, in one authority, of one power and for one purpose. Their actions, being associated with each other, reflect a tightly cooperative presentation to introduce God and unveil his will (cf. 10:34; 18:11; 27:24).

To conclude, there is a word which God gives to the world and communicates through divine and human agents. Being sent by God (10:36; 13:26; cf. 3:26), Jesus becomes the content of the word and throughout his earthly life he characterises God as an authoritative Father. The heavenly Jesus, the Spirit and angels perform actions on behalf of the one God,[105] which enable the believers to be Jesus' witnesses in conformity to God's will. They portray God as a supreme, sovereign, authoritative and omnipotent Lord. The divine utterances, carrying a prophetic nature, not only ensure the realisation of the divine mission plan but also serve as the indicatory dots to sketch the framework of God's saving plan. The examination of the portrayal of God in the rest of this study will consider the heavenly revelators as a collective character acting on behalf of God. Moreover, God is also characterised by other heavenly signals (e.g. miracles, visions) which are deployed by the narrator to enhance the narrative theme and achieve the plot (which will be taken into account in Chapter Six). Turning to God's human agents, commissioned by Jesus, the believers are to proclaim God's very Word (that which is a part of God's plan) and throughout their lives they also characterise God in ways which will be explored in the next three chapters.

---

[104] Sternberg, *Biblical Narrative*, 322.
[105] Beverly Roberts Gaventa, 'Initiatives Divine and Human in the Lukan Story World' in Graham N. Stanton et al. (eds.), *The Holy Spirit and Christian Origins* (Grand Rapids: Eerdmans, 2004) 79-89, citing 81; Larkin, 'Pneumatology,' 134.

CHAPTER 3

The Characterisation of God by Major Characters (I)—Peter

Characters are the crucial component in the narrative world which thus receive greater attention than other components of the narrative.[1] 'All readers of literature carry around with them notions about character and incident, in the form of unconsciously consulted touchstones which shape their evaluations of literary works.'[2] The Acts narrative attracts the reader by the dramatic and tense scenario of incidents and by the characters' fidelity to the mission of God. Although no single character runs through the narrative, each episode coheres as a whole with the development of an undergirding theme. Therefore, characters in Acts belong to what Scholes and Kellogg call developmental characterisation, 'in which the character's personal traits are attenuated so as to clarify his progress along a plot line which has an ethical basis.'[3] Such developmental formation itself is 'primarily a plot formulation rather than a character formulation. It involves seeing the character at long range, with limited detail, so that his change against a particular background may be readily apparent.'[4] Reading Acts, one observes how the major characters, Peter and Paul, are transformed by divine power in keeping with God's purpose which undergirds the development of the story in the narrative world.

As discussed in the previous chapter, the undergirding theme is related to the mission plan of God's salvation. In order to thoroughly and profoundly comprehend the divine plan, an investigation of the performance of major characters, the mouthpiece of the implied author,[5] is needed. God, the veiled yet vigorous character who never steps on the narrative stage, gets the attention through major characters' personal relationship with heavenly revelators and their interpersonal relationships with other human characters. This chapter will focus on Peter's presentation of God; it will scrutinise his interpretation of divine deeds and his interactions with heavenly and human characters.

The leadership of Peter, one of Jesus' inner circle of apostles (Lk 8:51; 9:28; Mk 14:33), is well recognised throughout Jesus' earthly ministry (Lk 9:20, 33;

---

[1] Bar-Efrat, *Narrative Art*, 47.
[2] Scholes and Kellogg, *Nature*, 160.
[3] Scholes and Kellogg, *Nature*, 169.
[4] Scholes and Kellogg, *Nature*, 168.
[5] Bar-Efrat, *Narrative Art*, 47. Eventually, it is the implied author who arranges the characters' words to convey the story and its meaning to the implied reader.

12:41; 19:28; 22:8, 31; 24:34). After the Ascension, Peter dominantly takes the lead of the Jewish mission in the Acts narrative. The first part of the story is mainly about his saga, especially his interpretation of the divine deeds and his witness to the divine revelation. Peter's speeches will be scrutinised first to uncover his notion of God in light of God's redemptive plan. Then his interactions with heavenly revelators and other human characters will be investigated for his full characterisation of God.

Conceptual Characterisation

Several speeches and interlocutions of Peter are recorded: speeches at the choosing of Matthias (1:16-32), at Pentecost (2:14-40), at the healing of a lame man (3:12-26), before the Jewish leaders (4:8-12, 19-20; 5:29-32) and concerning the Cornelius incident (10:34-43; 11:5-17; 15:7-11); and various succinct interlocutions (5:3-4, 8-9; 6:2-4; 8:20-23; 9:34, 40; 10:14, 26-29, 47; 12:11). These speeches are significant to Christology; nevertheless, discussion over matters contained in the speeches will be entered into only insofar as it touches upon the relevant notion of God. The speech at the choosing of Matthias chiefly relates to Peter's making up the Twelve,[6] and thus will not be brought into discussion. The succinct interlocutions will be taken into account in the next section since they concern Peter's interactions with other characters. In light of Marguerat's distinction between 'narrative (which describes history) and speech (which deciphers the action of God within history),'[7] Peter's elucidation of divine deeds plays an important part in contributing to the characterisation of God in the story. The divine interventions are not themselves an end but a means of knowing God and of unfolding his will (especially his saving plan for humankind). Such a disclosure of the divine intentions is mainly put in Peter's mouth.

The Speech at Pentecost (2:14-40)

After the Ascension, the first divine intervention is the descent of the Spirit on the day of Pentecost (2:4). In responding to the bewilderment and misunderstanding of the Jews (2:14-15) Peter gives a crucial speech to elaborate the cause of the phenomena at Pentecost (2:16-36). Although Jesus is the main concern in the content of the speech, the literary structure implicitly brings God

---

[6] The Twelve are closely linked with the preaching to Israel, especially the judging of the twelve tribes of Israel (Lk 22:30). With regard to the Twelve in the kingdom, it is necessary to replace the role of the disqualified Judas yet no need is required for the martyr James (12:2). See Richard F. Zehnle, *Peter's Pentecost Discourse* (Nashville: Abingdon Press, 1971) 107.

[7] Marguerat, *Historian*, 103.

into focus in a way which convinces the Jews that what happened is the fulfilment of God's promise through Jesus. The reality that God is continually at work in history with regard to his promise to his people stirs up and invigorates Peter's audience. Thus, many are deeply pricked in their hearts (2:37) and respond to Peter's evangelism (2:41).

According to the literary structure, the speech can be divided into three segments. Two direct addresses to the audience, with Peter calling attention to his words, set forth the why (2:14) and the how (2:22) of what is happening. The two inferential conjunctions of οὖν, which lead to the climax of Peter's main speech at Pentecost (2:33, 36), echo the cause introduced in 2:17-21 and announce the significance of the happening. The logic of Peter's argument can be clearly observed from the structural outline of Acts 2:14-36.

2:14 ἄνδρες Ἰουδαῖοι καὶ οἱ κατοικοῦντες Ἰερουσαλὴμ πάντες,
 ... ἐνωτίσασθε τὰ ῥήματά μου — the why of the happening

    Elucidation (vv. 15-16) [the Jews' understanding]
        οὐ ... (v. 15)
        ἀλλά ... (v. 16)

    Confirmation: scriptural support (vv. 17-21) [God's design]
        The promise of the Spirit (vv. 17-18)
        The promise of salvation in the name of the Lord (v. 21)[8]

2:22 Ἄνδρες Ἰσραηλῖται,
 ἀκούσατε τοὺς λόγους τούτους — the how of the happening

    Elucidation (vv. 22-24) [the Jews vs. God]
        Ἰησοῦν τὸν Ναζωραῖον ... ἀπὸ τοῦ θεοῦ
        (v. 22; Jesus' earthly ministry is ultimately of God)[9]
        τοῦτον τῇ ὡρισμένῃ βουλῇ καὶ προγνώσει τοῦ θεοῦ
        (v. 23; Jesus' death is in conformity with God's will)[10]
        ὃν ὁ θεὸς ἀνέστησεν
        (v. 24; God is the author of Jesus' resurrection)[11]

---

[8] Since this study concerns the relational characterisation of God, 2:19-20 (which indicates God's awesome deeds in the natural world) is not discussed here. Commentators' interpretation of these two verses differs as their relevance to the circumstances of Pentecost is considered. Barrett doubts their necessity (*Acts*, 1:137-38); F.F. Bruce associates them with the darkness on Good Friday (*The Acts of the Apostles*, 3rd edn. [Grand Rapids: Eerdmans, 1990] 121); Marshall views them as the signs of the end of the world (*Acts*, 74).

[9] Ἀπό reinforces the *genitive of source* use of τοῦ θεοῦ which indicates Jesus' origin.

[10] Note the use of dative of rule; 'the dative substantive specifies the rule or code a person follows or the standard of conduct to which he or she conforms.' See Daniel B. Wallace, *Greek Grammar Beyond the Basics* (Grand Rapids: Zondervan, 1996) 157.

[11] The subject use of θεός indicates God initially taking the action to raise up Jesus.

Confirmation (vv. 25-32; focusing on Jesus' resurrection)
[God's design]
  Scriptural evidence (vv. 25-28)
  Explanation (vv. 29-31; cf. Ἄνδρες ἀδελφοί)[12]
  Present witness (v. 32; comp. τοῦτον τὸν Ἰησοῦν ἀνέστησεν ὁ θεός with v. 24)

2:33, 36 οὖν . . . a mark for conclusion (vv. 33-36)
— the significance of the happening

The fulfilment of the promise of the Spirit (vv. 33-35)
[God's design]
  Explanation (v. 33)
  Scriptural evidence (vv. 34-35)

The realisation of the Lord of salvation (v. 36)
[The Jews vs. God]
  κύριον αὐτὸν καὶ χριστὸν ἐποίησεν ὁ θεός,
  τοῦτον τὸν Ἰησοῦν ὃν ὑμεῖς ἐσταυρώσατε

Peter, after first refuting the Jews' mockery (2:14-15), expounds that the cause of the phenomenon (i.e. tongue-speaking) at Pentecost is the fulfilment of God's promises pre-announced through the prophet Joel (2:16-21; cf. Joel 2:28-32). Two universal promises are specified, that is, the promise of the Spirit (2:17-18) and the promise of salvation in the name of the Lord (2:21).

---

[12] The three vocatives of ἄνδρες (2:14, 22, 29) are employed by some as a mark for the major division of the speech (Soards, *Speeches*, 32; Zehnle, *Pentecost Discourse*, 27). However, the use of the last vocative (ἄνδρες ἀδελφοί) slightly differs from that of the first two (ἄνδρες Ἰουδαῖοι, ἄνδρες Ἰσραηλῖται). Most commentators retain no mention of the implication of these terms (such as, Bruce, Dunn, Johnson, Marshall). Barrett presumes the function of these vocatives as 'to show the end of the quotation and the beginning of Peter's own words' (*Acts*, 1:139). Haenchen expresses the growing of a sense of intimate address in these appellations (*Acts*, 179; also Witherington, *Acts*, 139).

Ἰουδαῖοι and Ἰσραηλῖται are the ethnic name of a person who belongs to a nation (L&N, §93.172; §93.183) whereas ἀδελφοί refers to a person who is a member of the same nation (L&N, §11.57). The former identifies the audience ethnically; the latter identifies the speaker with the audience. The former as a formal address calls to listen (cf. 2:14, ἐνωτίσασθε τὰ ῥήματά μου; 2:22, ἀκούσατε τοὺς λόγους τούτους); the latter as an intimate address may serve to draw near to and win over the audience (Eduard Schweizer, 'Concerning the Speeches in Acts' in Keck and Martyn [eds.], *Studies in Luke-Acts*, 208-16, citing 211). The response of the audience in the same intimate address in 2:37 shows that Peter has achieved rapport, cf. Zehnle, *Pentecost Discourse*, 27.

The former relates to a new relationship between God and his people;[13] in other words, the Spirit of God will dwell in human beings, and no distinction of such a relationship is made in race, sex, age or status; this highlights the universality of the promise of the Spirit. The latter declares God's awesome deeds in the cosmos on the great day of the divine judgement (from the perspective of the relationship between God and the universe). Yet God prepares a salvation for whomever calls upon the name of the Lord. The use of πᾶς (an adjective expression of the totality)[14] and ὃς ἄν (a construction indicating 'a generic subject')[15] doubly accentuates the universality of the promise of salvation. Undoubtedly, the two promises of God convey the divine concern and plan for humankind regarding the universality of salvation.[16]

Peter's second call for attention brings Jesus into the centre of his presentation (2:22-32). Ostensibly, a new topic is entered into yet the relation between God's promises and Jesus' life will gradually be proven. The undergirding thought in this segment is how God's promises are achieved. Here, whenever Jesus is indicated, he appears in the first position of the sentences and in the accusative case: he is of God (v. 22); his death is in conformity with God's purpose (v. 23); God is the author of his resurrection (v. 24); and the apostles are the witnesses of the resurrection (v. 32). Not only does the content of the speech concentrate on Jesus' life but also the expression of the first position lets him get the spotlight.[17] In his earthly ministry, Jesus is the agent of God to carry out the very mission of God. God communicates a message to the world by the miraculous deeds through Jesus (v. 22) and, foremost, by his resurrection from death, the very miracle of God (vv. 23-24). The word ὡρισμένῃ con-

---

[13] The phrase ἐπὶ πᾶσαν σάρκα (2:17) need not be considered that the Spirit of God will come upon all but all his people. The ὑμῶν in verse 17 implies that the receivers of the Spirit are God's people (cf. Joel 2:23, Israelites); the μου (God) in verse 18 unquestionably makes the receivers of the Spirit God's people.

[14] L&N, §59.23 and §59.24; BDAG, 782.

[15] Wallace, *Beyond*, 478.

[16] Barrett, *Acts*, 1:134.

[17] Robert C. Tannehill, *The Narrative Unity of Luke-Acts*, vol. 2 (Minneapolis: Fortress Press, 1990) 36. Gustavo Martin-Asensio, *Transitivity-Based Foregrounding in the Acts of the Apostles* (Sheffield: Sheffield Academic Press, 2000) 160-64, 171. Tannehill asserts that the pronoun (esp. 2:36; cf. also 2:23, 24, 32; 3:25, 26), referring to Jesus, is placed in the first position in the sentence and thus emphasised. Martin-Asensio protests that it is a matter of stylistic effect (the complement-initial clauses, cf. 2:36; 7:35) that Jesus is the character 'who is central to the episode's plot, yet who at the same time appears sidelined and incapacitated in light of his own inactivity and the events initiated almost wholly by others' (164). Either from the perspective of the clause-initial position or the framework of the author's larger literary strategy, Jesus gets the focus in the speech.

veys a definite decision of God,[18] that implies the life of Jesus carries the very purpose of God. With regard to Jesus' life, Peter lays a great emphasis on his resurrection. A quotation of David in Psalms 16:8-11 is cited to attest why death cannot imprison Jesus (vv. 25-28). As assured by the prophet David,[19] the resurrection is necessary for God's promise of the everlasting throne to David himself with regard to Christ, the Anointed One (vv. 30-31).[20] The clause τοῦτον τὸν Ἰησοῦν ἀνέστησεν ὁ θεός in verse 32 echoes back to that in verse 24 (ὃν ὁ θεὸς ἀνέστησεν) and presents a literary unit asserting the theme of resurrection. Two resurrections are indicated in this literary unit: the prophesied resurrection of the Messiah by David (2:29-31)[21] and the witnessed resurrection of Jesus by the apostles (2:32).[22] The demonstrative pronoun τοῦτον, singling out Jesus with an emphatic flavour, specifies Jesus' resurrection and identifies it with that of the Messiah, Christ.[23] Such an identification is not without proof but will soon be made clear in its following context, namely, the descent of the Spirit.

---

[18] L&N, §30.83.

[19] Cf. Joseph A Fitzmyer, 'David, "Being Therefore a Prophet...",' *CBQ* 34 (1972) 332-39. Fitzmyer argues that 'David, the reputed author of the psalms according to both Luke and a Qumran author, was considered to have been gifted also with prophecy from the Most High God in contemporary Palestinian Jewish tradition' (338).

[20] Robert F. O'Toole, 'Acts 2:30 and the Davidic Covenant of Pentecost,' *JBL* 102 (1983) 245-58, esp. 251-53, 55. O'Toole understands 2:30 in light of God's promise to David in 2 Sam 7:12-16. The reestablishment of the ancient glories of the Davidic kingdom is one of the essential notions of Jewish expectation of Messiah, cf. Lawrence H. Schiffman, 'The Concept of the Messiah in Second Temple and Rabbinic Literature,' *RE* 84 (1987) 235-46, esp. 236.

[21] The immortalisation of τὸν ὅσιον is later expounded as the Messiah rather than David himself (2:29-31). Commentators (e.g. Marshall, Johnson, Witherington) translate τὸν ὅσιον as *the Holy One* which carries 'the sense of superior moral qualities and possessing certain essentially divine qualities in contrast with what is human' (L&N, §88.24). Although the term is later understood as a reference to the Messiah (2:31), the use of the first person (David) in 2:27 suggests, to the audience, a more appropriate interpretation, i.e. 'the devout, godly, dedicated one' (L&N, §53.46; Barrett, *Acts*, 1:145-46). However, according to Peter's later elucidation, he may carry in mind the meaning of the Holy One (cf. 3:14).

[22] The witness of Jesus' resurrection is the personal mission of the apostles (2:32; cf. 1:22).

[23] Although messianism develops variegatedly among different Jewish groups, Peter endows the term Χριστός, which later prevails in the faith community, with his own interpretation of God's Christ which is indissoluble from Jesus' death and resurrection. For further discussion on the first century messianism see Schiffman, 'Messiah,' 237-41; J.H. Charlesworth, 'From Jewish Messianology to Christian Christology Some Caveats and Perspectives' in Jacob Neusner, William S. Green and Ernest

The third segment, containing a repeated οὖν (2:33, 36), interlocks the resurrected Jesus and God's two promises introduced in the first segment. Besides being crucial in Jesus' own life, the resurrection serves as a key to the fulfilment of God's promises (cf. 2:33-36). The significance of Jesus' resurrection is first related to the happening at Pentecost (2:33-35). It is the exalted and triumphant Jesus who receives the promise of the Spirit from the Father and pours him out (v. 33). God is the initiator and Jesus the mediator of the pouring out of the Spirit. Another quotation of David in Psalms 110:1 is further cited to confirm the pre-announcement of Christ's exalted status in heaven (vv. 34-35). Furthermore, Jesus' exaltation, being proved by his pouring out of the Spirit, serves as a verification to affirm his glorious status, Lord and Christ (v. 36).[24] In other words, the outcome of Jesus' resurrection doubly fulfils God's two promises—the Spirit and the salvation in the Lord.

Later, in his instruction to the heart-pricked Jews, Peter specifically indicates that salvation embraces the forgiveness of sins and the gift of the Spirit.[25] His two commands (μετανοήσατε and βαπτισθήτω... ἐπὶ τῷ ὀνόματι Ἰησοῦ Χριστοῦ) denote the means to salvation.[26] As the resurrection of Jesus is crucial to the fulfilment of God's promise of salvation, the name of Jesus is vital to the receiving of God's salvation. This *saving* name of Jesus echoes back to the *saving* name of the Lord (2:21) which God foretells long before and is further exploited in Peter's later speeches.

There is a significant development of God's lordship while examining the use of κύριος in Peter's speech at Pentecost. Among the seven occurrences of

---

Frerichs (eds.), *Judaisms and Their Messiahs at the Turn of the Christian Era* (Cambridge: Cambridge University Press, 1987) 225-64, esp. 251-54; William Horbury, *Jewish Messianism and the Cult of Christ* (London: SCM Press, 1998) 64-108; N.T. Wright, *Jesus and the Victory of God* (London: SPCK, 1996) 481-89.

[24] Jervell indicates that the title Christ 'is attached to the scheme of promise-fulfilment: Jesus fulfils the promises to the people of God' (*Theology*, 27).

[25] After Peter's instructions to 'repent and be baptised in Jesus' name' and indications of 'the forgiveness of sins and the reception of the Spirit' (the former precedes the latter, cf. the future tense of λήμψεσθε in verse 38), the use of σώθητε in his concluding words (v. 40) implies that his previous instructions and indications of the divine promise are closely related to the salvation of God.

[26] Μετανοέω signifies 'to change one's way of life as the result of a complete change of thought and attitude with regard to sin and righteousness' (L&N, §41.52). This change involves both attitude and behaviour and is, theologically, connected with faith (cf. Marshall, *Acts*, 81). The baptism in the name of Jesus is an external sign of internal repentance and remission of sins (cf. Bruce, *Acts*, 3rd edn., 129; Marshall, *Acts*, 81; Barrett, *Acts*, 1:154). For the various meanings and significance of the name of Jesus see Lars Hartman, '"Into the Name of Jesus:" A Suggestion concerning the Earliest Meaning of the Phrase,' *NTS* 20 (1974) 432-40; J.A. Ziesler, 'The Name of Jesus in the Acts of the Apostles,' *JSNT* 4 (1979) 28-41; Buckwalter, *Christology*, 182-84.

κύριος, five appear in the OT quotations. After Peter's first call to listen, three scriptural quotations (2:17-21, cf. Joel 2:28-32; 2:25-28, cf. Ps 16:8-11; 2:34, cf. Ps 110:1), followed by his interpretation, are given to support that the Pentecostal happening is the fulfilment of God's promises and Jesus is the key of the realisation. Κύριος first appears twice in the quotation of Joel (2:20-21). As the Jewish audience first hear this scriptural quotation, 'the reference would be clearly to Yahweh.'[27] Yet there is an ambiguity of such a recognition since Yahweh speaks in the first person in the prophecy. It is likely that God refers κύριος to a person other than himself. Another occurrence of κύριος happens in the second scriptural quotation which clearly refers to God (2:25).[28] The other figure in this quotation is recognised as the Messiah (2:27, τὸν ὅσιόν σου; cf. 2:29-31). Κύριος occurs twice in the third quotation (2:34). The first refers to God; the second to the Messiah. Two lordships are specifically presented in the quotation and their relationship is depicted later by Peter.

The last two uses of κύριος are found in Peter's elucidation of God's promises. One appears in his climactic conclusion, κύριον αὐτὸν καὶ χριστὸν ἐποίησεν ὁ θεός (2:36). Here Jesus is fully identified with the Messiah (2:31) and the Lord (compare the indication of ὄνομα in 2:21 and 2:38).[29] It is God who makes Jesus both Lord and Christ. Jesus, thus, shares the divine name of Lord.[30] In light of this sharing of the divine name, Peter may understand the title κύριος in 2:21 as referring to Jesus instead of to Yahweh.[31] The other usage occurs in Peter's authoritative instruction toward the heart-pricked Jews (2:39, κύριος ὁ θεὸς ἡμῶν). The combination of κύριος and θεός insists on the lordship of God as being also admitted by the audience (cf. the use of ἡμῶν). Throughout Peter's speech the sovereign lordship of God is incontestable yet the lordship of Christ is gradually proven and affirmed. Both lordships are equally valued as Dunn points out:

---

[27] Marshall, *Acts*, 74. Cf. Buckwalter, *Christology*, 183; Huub van de Sandt, 'The Fate of the Gentiles in Joel and Acts 2: An Intertextual Study,' *ETL* 66/1 (1990) 56-77, esp. 76.

[28] Marshall, *Acts*, 76; Barrett, *Acts*, 1:145; Haenchen, *Acts*, 181; Dunn, *Acts*, 30.

[29] Zehnle, *Pentecost Discourse*, 62.

[30] Darrell L. Bock, *Proclamation from Prophecy and Pattern: Lucan Old Testament Christology* (Sheffield: Sheffield Academic Press, 1987) 264. Bock rests his contention on the following assertion: 'as a result of his exaltation to the right hand of God (Ps 110:1), Jesus now mediates God's salvation as a "co-regent"' (264). The concept of 'co-regent' is also seen in Bock's other article on 'Jesus as Lord in Acts and in the Gospel Message,' *BSac* 143 (1986) 146-54, citing 148. The term is later introduced and employed by: Tuckett, 'Christology,' 149; Buckwalter, *Christology*, 188.

[31] Buckwalter, *Christology*, 185. For detailed discussion on the reference of κύριος in 2:21 see Bock, *Proclamation*, 165-69.

The same text made clear the relationship of the two lordships: Jesus had been given lordship by the Lord God (2:36). That also meant that when both were spoken of as κύριος within the same context there need be no confusion, for the lordship of Jesus was a derivative lordship, but as derived from the Lord God it was in effect an expression of God's lordship.[32]

It is evident that by Jesus' death and resurrection not only does Jesus' name possess the saving power of the promised name of God (2:21) but also God's promise of salvation is accomplished. Such 'a messianic death is a part of God's plan.'[33] Yet in the light of God's power Jesus' death signifies a new stage of God's plan being on the way and by God's power Jesus' exaltation inaugurates the new stage of God's saving plan (2:33).[34] This way of death-resurrection-exaltation toward salvation signifies God's supreme power over death. The suffering and rejection of Jesus, therefore, serves as a distinct way of magnifying God's extraordinary might and power which guarantee the realisation of God's promise and the consummation of his plan.

While the content of the speech evinces Jesus causing God's promises to be realised, the skeleton of the speech discloses that God is at work and authoritatively carrying out his own promises. Throughout Peter's speech, God is either the subject or agent of an ergative verb. This indicates that God takes the initiative in human history (2:17-21) and is the author and designer of Jesus' life (2:22-36). The passive role of Jesus, presented in the accusative case (except in verse 33, where the linchpin of God's promise to the present incident is highlighted), leaves the stage to God and the Jews acting toward Jesus. A contrast of what they do to Jesus is constantly pointed out in the speech (cf. *you* and

---

[32] Dunn, *Christology*, 252-53; also Turner, '"Divine" Christology,' 435; Buckwalter, *Christology*, 184-91 (asserting Jesus as Yahweh's co-equal); Salmeier, *Ordainer*, 108.

[33] Hurtado, *Christ*, 170.

[34] The dative τῇ δεξιᾷ may function as means (by the right hand of God) or place (to the right hand of God). The former highlights the power and authority of God (L&N, §76.4) whereas the latter stresses the high status and honour beside God (L&N, §87.36). Both are applicable to the present verse (cf. 5:31). At first thought, if reading the text in a descriptive level, it may favour the locative sense since the fact of what has been happening is in view. While understanding it in a significant level, the text may prefer the instrumental sense for the dynamic power of God undergirds Peter's whole argument. That the context presents God's great deeds among his people may suggest that a slight gravity lies in God's power (2:11, 41, 43, 47). Furthermore, when the place of right side is clearly implied in a context, the phrase ἐκ δεξιῶν (note the plural form of δεξιά) is always employed in Lukan writings (2:25, 34; 7:55, 56; also Lk 1:11; 20:42; 22:69; 23:33). Therefore, the ambiguous use of the singular δεξιᾷ may be understood in a figurative or symbolic sense, that is, by the power of God (L&N, §76.4; BDAG, 218; Barrett, *Acts*, 1:149; Bruce, *Acts*, 3rd edn., 126).

God in 2:22, 23, 33, 36). Additionally, the whole speech as a literary unit conceives also a contrast between God's design and the Jews' doings (cf. the divine promises, purpose and prophecy in 2:17-18, 21, 23, 27, 34 vs. the Jews' malicious act in 2:23, 36).[35] From such a literary strategy of contrast emanates God's overruling power which rules over the deadly force and amplifies God's omnipotent authority in keeping with his own plan.[36]

By the literary strategy, that is, a God-centred structure with Jesus-centred content, in which the Scripture is quoted to reveal the divine world view,[37] Peter successfully and convincingly introduces Jesus to the Jews. According to the rabbinic teaching, the Jews may have believed that 'the return and outpouring of the Spirit on all Israel would accompany the Messianic Age.'[38] Grounded on the Jewish messianic hope, Peter shows 'God's design in history and the centrality of Jesus to the plan,'[39] and powerfully attests to the Pentecost event as the pouring out of the Spirit which signals that the age to come is at present. Such an old era of expectation leading to a new era of realisation is part of God's design which 'involves a promise-fulfilment perspective.'[40] What is new to the Jews is 'Jesus as the mediator in the dispensing of the Spirit.'[41] As discussed above, the Pentecost event is ultimately and utterly of God, and Jesus is the linchpin to effectuate God's promise and consummate God's redemptive plan toward humans. Peter's speech provides a picture of God's saving plan through Jesus toward humankind, from which emerges an image of a silently compliant Jesus with an authoritatively almighty Father behind him. The portrait of this Father-Son image further reveals the divine care for the well-being of humankind in providing salvation (i.e. through the name of Jesus comes the forgiveness of sin and the bestowal of the Spirit). In the speech at Pentecost

---

[35] The most prominent contrast is shown in the literary style in 2:32 (τοῦτον τὸν Ἰησοῦν ἀνέστησεν ὁ θεός) and 2:36 (τοῦτον τὸν Ἰησοῦν ὃν ὑμεῖς ἐσταυρώσατε).

[36] Martin-Asensio, *Foregrounding*, 163.

[37] Bill T. Arnold, 'Luke's Characterizing Use of the Old Testament in the Book of Acts' in Ben Witherington III (ed.), *History, Literature and Society in the Book of Acts* (Cambridge, Cambridge University Press, 1996) 300-23, citing 309.

[38] O'Neill, 'Kyrios,' 160. O'Neill supports his assertion by indirectly quoting the Midrash remarks from Abrahams: 'The Holy One, blessed be He, said: In this world individuals were given prophetic power, but in the world to come all Israel will be made prophets, as it is said (Joel ii. 28).' See Numbers Rabba cited by I. Abrahams, *Studies in Pharisaism and the Gospels*, 2nd Series (New York: Ktav Publishing House, 1967) 127; cf. Bock, *Proclamation*, 169.

[39] Darrell Bock, 'Scripture and the Realisation of God's Promises' in Marshall and Peterson (eds.), *Witness of the Gospel*, 41-62, citing 41.

[40] Bock, 'Realisation,' 41; also 45. Cf. Stanley E. Porter, 'Scripture Justifies Mission: The Use of the Old Testament in Luke-Acts' in idem (ed.), *Hearing the Old Testament in the New Testament* (Grand Rapids: Eerdmans, 2006) 104-126, esp. 126.

[41] Bock, *Proclamation*, 347, n. 50.

The Speech at the Healing of the Lame Man (3:12-26)

Peter's second speech about God-Jesus after the Ascension is recorded in the episode of healing the lame man in the temple. Not only does this great miraculous healing lead Peter to explore further the power of the name of Jesus and God's plan in Jesus but it offers Peter another great opportunity to witness (cf. 4:4). Similar to the Pentecost speech, Peter connects the incident with Jesus by referring its cause to God's risen Christ (3:15-16; cf. 2:31-33). Zehnle states that Peter's speeches in Acts 2 and 3 are strikingly similar.[42] However, after a thorough investigation of their themes and structures, the similarities are found solely in the elements of Peter's argument.[43] While comparing the similar elements, different emphases appear on the themes which show a significant development of Peter's comprehension of the divine plan in relation to humankind.

The main structure of Acts 3:12-26 is based on two antitheses, a contrast and a correspondence, which divide the speech into two segments. The first segment is composed of a sharp contrast between God and the Jews in which the cause of the healing is elucidated (3:12-18, led by Ἄνδρες Ἰσραηλῖται). The second segment finds a corresponding relation between God and the Jews in which the exhortation of repentance is expressed (3:19-26, signalled by οὖν). Jesus, appearing in the accusative case throughout the speech,[44] plays a passive role and stands in between God and the Jews. Again, Jesus conveying of a message of God is the focal interest of the speech. The structure of the speech insinuates God is at work in history whereas the content concerns God's revelation in Jesus through the prophets (in the past) and the expectation of the audience's repentance (at present). See the following structural outline for the flow of Peter's argument.

3:12 ἄνδρες Ἰσραηλῖται — the cause of the healing
    [God's work on Jesus versus the Jews' deeds towards Jesus]
    God's power over human forces (3:13-14)
    Witnesses of God's power against human villainy (3:15-16)

---

[42] Zehnle, *Pentecost Discourse*, 19-23.
[43] Zehnle claims the similarities in elements—a reference to the situation, the Jesus-kerygma, an announcement of salvation and a call to repentance (*Pentecost Discourse*, 24-26).
[44] Only in 3:16 does Jesus occur in the genitive of either possessive use or instrumental use.

By the apostles (v. 15)
By the healing (v. 16)

God's plan higher than human plot (3:17-18)

3:19 οὖν — the exhortation of repentance
[God's plan in Jesus versus the Jews' corresponding response]

God's plan in Jesus for the Jews (3:19-24)
[from God's perspective]
    The way of salvation (vv. 19-21)
    The crux of judgement (vv. 22-24)

The Jews' status before God (3:25)
[from the Jews' perspective]
    Sons of prophets (v. 25a)
    Sons of covenant (v. 25b)

Conclusion: God's design for the Jews (3:26)

GOD'S WORKS ON JESUS VS. THE JEWS' DEEDS TOWARD JESUS

In the first segment, the Jews in Jerusalem are convicted of guilt for what they have done to Jesus (3:13c-15a). However, God sovereignly overrules their wickedness and raises Jesus from death (3:13, 15b); this is verified by the apostles (3:15c) and demonstrated by the healing power in the name of Jesus (3:16). Nevertheless, a chance for forgiveness remains for the Jews since they acted in ignorance (3:17), and their evil deeds are within God's all-knowingness (3:18). Three salient contrasts are found in this segment to enforce God's plan which is higher than human conspiracy (3:13-18).

Following a rhetorical question (3:12), which reflects the internal false assumption of the audience, lies the first contrast of God and the Jews (ὑμεῖς in 3:13-14). Both are presented in an emphatic form. The two epithets of God (v. 13a, ὁ θεὸς Ἀβραὰμ καὶ [ὁ θεὸς] Ἰσαὰκ καὶ [ὁ θεὸς] Ἰακώβ and ὁ θεὸς τῶν πατέρων ἡμῶν) convey the identity of God and thus vindicate Peter as affirming the same God as the Jewish audience. The two emphatic personal pronouns ὑμεῖς[45] in the first position of a clause highlight the doings of the Jews (vv. 13c, 14). The figure Jesus standing in between actuates the opposition:[46]

| God | → | Jesus | ← | 'You' |
| (ὁ θεός, v. 13a) | | (Ἰησοῦν, v. 13b) | | (ὑμεῖς, vv. 13c-14) |

---

[45] Barrett, *Acts*, 1:195.

[46] As the literary strategy of contrast in Acts 2, Jesus appears in the accusative case which implies his passive role which leaves the spotlight remaining on God and the Jews.

The malice of the Jews' conspiracy is amplified by two ancillary antitheses: the decision about Jesus by the Jews versus that by Pilate (cf. παρεδώκατε καὶ ἠρνήσασθε vs. κρίναντος... ἀπολύειν in v. 13c); and the status of Jesus versus that of a man the Jews ask for (τὸν ἅγιον καὶ δίκαιον vs. φονέα in v. 14). No matter how spiteful and threatening the human intrigue is, God powerfully and authoritatively glorifies his servant Jesus.[47] The greater the hostility, the more powerful the authority of God.

In the second contrast, the apostles (ἡμεῖς in v. 15c) and the healing (v. 16) are added as witnesses to verify God's resurrecting power in Jesus and disprove the Jews' actions towards Jesus.

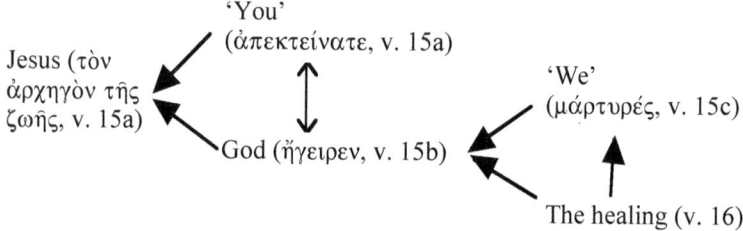

A series of actions against Jesus by the Jews is introduced (cf. vv. 13c-14, παρεδώκατε, ἠρνήσασθε twice, ᾐτήσασθε ἄνδρα φονέα) and then their opposition reaches its peak, i.e. they kill Jesus (v. 15). In responding to these serially opposed actions, God takes only one action (v. 15b, ὃν ἤγειρεν ἐκ νεκρῶν). From this series of antitheses of rhetorical strategy emanates a God of history who is serenely sitting on the throne, calmly watching over people who intrigue against him, and patiently waiting to consummate his plan in his own timing. Neither do the cunning human plots foil God's plan nor do the greatest human forces confine God's power. On the contrary, the invincible power and authority of God overrules all human opposition.

Not only does the witness of the apostles verify God's vindication of Jesus through the resurrection but also the present healing of a man born lame confirms Peter's witness and thus fortifies God's mighty deed in Jesus (vv. 15c-16). On the grounds of faith in the name of this resurrected Jesus, the man is healed (v. 16). Both Jesus' name (v. 16b, ἐστερέωσεν τὸ ὄνομα αὐτοῦ) and the accompanying faith (v. 16c, ἡ πίστις ἡ δι᾽ αὐτοῦ ἔδωκεν... τὴν ὁλοκληρίαν

---

[47] Although παῖς conveys the meanings of *child* and *servant*, in the light of Isaiah 52:13 the suffering servant of God may be in view (Marshall, *Acts*, 91; Johnson, *Acts*, 67; Haenchen, *Acts*, 205). The context, however, indicates the glorified status of Jesus as Barrett denotes, 'it is God's act of vindication after suffering that gives significance to the servant' (*Acts*, 1:194). For further discussion on the messianic servanthood of Jesus see Jacques Ménard, '*Pais Theou* as Messianic Title in the Book of Acts,' *CBQ* 19 (1957) 83-92, esp. 88-89; Bock, *Proclamation*, 188-90; Buckwalter, *Christology*, 256-57; Hurtado, *Christ*, 190-92; Franklin, *Christ*, 61-64.

ταύτην)⁴⁸ are significant to the healing since 'the name is ineffective unless faith in it is present.'⁴⁹ The healing power from Jesus' *name* which signifies his divine authority, power and presence⁵⁰ is a manifestation of Jesus' sharing of God's lordship. The healing, therefore, serves as God's vindication of his suffering Christ (cf. 3:18). Because the man's healing in the name of Jesus is so powerful and dramatic (cf. 3:6), Peter's witness implicitly points out the deviation of the Jews from God. The witness of the apostles and the healing incident, thus, convict the disbelieving Jews in Jerusalem of guilt.

This leads to the third contrast of God and the Jews (3:17-18) where the sharp opposition declines in order to pave the way for a later calling of the Jewish audience to repent. Regardless of what has been done, νῦν ἀδελφοί, Peter gently ascribes the Jews' opposition to their ignorance, which implies the possibility of being forgiven,⁵¹ as well as their leaders (3:17). Ultimately, God foreknows all things and his plan is higher than theirs (3:18). The suffering of God's Christ is part of God's plan and thus a fulfilment of what he foretold through the prophets. Even though God's plan is higher than human intrigue, the Jews cannot be excused from their ignorance and are in need of repentance.

---

48 The meaning of the phrase ἡ πίστις ἡ δι' αὐτοῦ is uncertain since αὐτοῦ may refer to Jesus himself (Marshall, *Acts*, 92) or his name (Haenchen, *Acts*, 207). As Ziesler asserts that the name of Jesus may indicate Jesus himself ('Name of Jesus,' 35-36), whichever meaning it is makes not much difference. Another debate is that ἡ δι' αὐτοῦ means *faith caused by him* (αὐτοῦ as an agent) or *faith in him* (αὐτοῦ as a means), cf. Barrett, *Acts*, 1:200. It is difficult to discern the meaning. However, comparing another phrase ἐπὶ τῇ πίστει τοῦ ὀνόματος αὐτοῦ, where *faith in his name* clearly functions as a means, the different expression of ἡ δι' αὐτοῦ may imply the use of agent and thus emphasise the divine initiative (cf. 16:14). The other debate is whose faith is in view. There is no mention of the faith of the lame man. The man may not have faith in Jesus but he does expect to receive something from the apostles (3:5). We do see, however, Peter's faith in Jesus' name (3:6; cf. Marshall, *Acts*, 92; Witherington, *Acts*, 182). Just as Christ's name and human faith actuate the healing, the human desire precedes human faith and actuates the divine initiating of faith (cf. 3:8-9, the lame man later shows his faith in God).

49 Haenchen, *Acts*, 207.

50 David Peterson, 'The Worship of the New Community' in Marshall and Peterson (eds.), *Witness*, 373-95, citing 381. Arguing its semitic original, Irene W. Foulkes asserts that the phrase τὸ ὄνομα Ἰησοῦ turns a Jewish formula of *the name of Yahweh* to Christian use. In its OT context the expression connotes 'with God's commission' or 'on God's authority' and is equated with God himself ('Two Semantic Problems in the Translation of Acts 4.5-20,' *BT* 29 [1978] 121-25, citing 122; also Hans Bietenhard, '"Ονομα' in *TDNT*, 5:242-81, esp. 255-56, 277).

51 Buckwalter, *Christology*, 112; Marshall, *Acts*, 92.

GOD'S PLAN IN JESUS VS. THE JEWS' CORRESPONDING RESPONSE

The second segment of the speech aims at calling the audience to repent (3:19-26). God's plan in Jesus, spoken through the prophets (3:21, 24), is first introduced in order to evoke a corresponding response by the Jews. From God's perspective, human repentance is needed because Jesus is his design for salvation and judgement (3:19-24).[52] Then the Jews' status before God is accentuated (cf. the emphatic personal pronoun ὑμεῖς in 3:25). That the Jews are a means of God's promise of the universal blessing is indicated in order to invigorate their turning towards God's will. From the Jews' perspective, their repentance is needed because they bear a noble, yet ignored, mission of God. Lastly, God's blessing designed first for the Jews is concluded in to confirm their privilege before God and thus instigate their repentance (3:26).

God's Plan in Jesus for the Jews (from God's Perspective)

The inferential conjunction οὖν with two imperatives marks Peter's intention in the previous argument (3:19a, μετανοήσατε καὶ ἐπιστρέψατε).[53] Repentance can be understood in individual and/or collective sense as Barrett comments:

> Repentance has personal and corporate aspects and is called for in the present; the blotting out of sins similarly is both personal and corporate, and in its personal aspect belongs to the present; the coming of the Messiah means corporate redemption in the future.[54]

The emphasis, however, may be laid on the individual in the light of the distributive pronoun ἕκαστον employed by Peter in his later exhortation of repentance (3:26). In order to evoke the Jews' conversion to God, God's plan in Jesus is succinctly presented, conveying both the rewarding aspect (3:19-21) and the warning aspect (3:22-24).

---

[52] The notion of the Day of the Lord is indicated earlier by Peter in 2:20. This concept is found in prophetic literature: at a certain time God will bring salvation to the righteous and punish the wicked (Ezek 30:3; Joel 1:15; 2:31-32; Amos 8:10; 9:11-15; Mic 4:1, 6; Zeph 1:14-18; Mal 4:1-3). See Schiffman, 'Messiah,' 236. Peter probably adopts the twofold notion of the Day of the Lord as positive and negative reasons to evoke the repentance.

[53] The word μετανοέω bears the idea of 'chang[ing] one's way of life as the result of a complete change of thought and attitude' (L&N, §41.52); ἐπιτρέφω conveys the notion of 'chang[ing] one's manner of life in a particular direction, with the implication of turning back to God' (L&N, §41.51). The former connotes a turning away from evil; the latter a turning toward God. Two verbs, as two sides of one coin, signify a full conversion (Barrett, *Acts*, 1:202-03; Haenchen, *Acts*, 208; Marshall, *Acts*, 93; Witherington, *Acts*, 184).

[54] Barrett, *Acts*, 1:203.

The Characterisation of God

The rewarding aspect of God's plan in Jesus is depicted as the purpose of repentance. Three purposes are indicated by εἰς τό with an infinitive and ὅπως ἄν with two subjunctives (3:19b-21): the removal of sins (v. 19b; cf. 2:38), the coming of the times of refreshing (v. 20a) and the coming again of Jesus (vv. 20b-21). The primary consequence of repentance is the wiping away of personal sins which leads to a universal expectation of God's blessing and Jesus' second coming. Grounded on the forgiveness of sin, times of refreshing come from God (v. 20a).[55] The word ἀνάψυξις may imply a relief or a refreshing state from a previous stage;[56] this is alluded to in the preceding infinitival clause ἐξαλειφθῆναι ὑμῶν τὰς ἁμαρτίας. As compared with the two promises of repentance in Peter's previous speech (2:38, the forgiveness of sins and the reception of the Spirit), a parallel thought may be implied in the first two purposes of repentance here (if so, probably the times of refreshing is in view of the reception of the Spirit).[57] Furthermore, in the light of 3:26 the times of refreshing may refer to a present and individual realisation of God's blessing through Jesus while the Jews turn away from their wickedness (cf. the adverbial use of the telic participle εὐλογοῦντα in present tense).

Subsequently, Peter takes his account of the exploits of God in Jesus further; besides the removal of sins and the times of refreshing, there is the second advent of Jesus (3:20b-21). The word προκεχειρισμένον, which conveys the notion of 'express[ing] preference of someone for a task'[58] and 'choos[ing] for a particular purpose in advance,'[59] implies God designating a certain mission to Jesus and indicates the mission being proposed before Jesus' first coming to the Jews (cf. the perfect tense and ὑμῖν in v. 20b). God's sending again of Jesus is made clear in verse 21 which expresses the necessity of Jesus' remaining in heaven until the time of restoration of all things. Ἀποκατάστασις, signifying a 'change to a previous good state,'[60] suggests 'a restoration of the original order of creation,'[61] including all things and all people,[62] which is 'the realisation of all prophetic promises.'[63] The design of Christ's two comings is utterly of God

---

[55] Commentators usually consider the times of refreshing as the final stage of salvation, i.e. the times of restoration (Hans Conzelmann, *Acts of the Apostles* [Philadelphia: Fortress Press, 1987] 29; cf. Marshall, *Acts*, 93), or indicate the ambiguity of the relationship between the two 'times' (Dunn, *Acts*, 46; Johnson, *Acts*, 69).

[56] The word ἀνάψυξις can mean either 'relief from distressful, burdensome circumstances' (L&N, §22.35; cf. BDAG, 75) or 'a state of cheer and encouragement after a period of having been troubled or upset' (L&N, §25.148).

[57] Cf. Barrett, *Acts*, 1:205.

[58] BDAG, 891.

[59] L&N, §30.89.

[60] L&N, §13.65.

[61] Haenchen, *Acts*, 208.

[62] Barrett, *Acts*, 1:207.

[63] Haenchen, *Acts*, 208.

who speaks through prophets (3:18, 21). Regardless of the Jews' opposition to Jesus, God turns it into the way of blessing in the present (the removal of sins and the times of refreshing) and in the future (the times of restoration). In brief, in Jesus salvation is found (cf. 2:21, 36; 4:12) and the salvific blessing received (3:26); this is the set plan of God. The purposes of repentance, thus, unveil the divine saving programme and provide the incentive to evoking the audience's repentance.

The warning aspect of God's plan in Jesus is delineated in Mosaic prophecy supported by other prophets as well (3:22-24). The Mosaic prophecy is cited to warn against those who disobey the word of the Moses-like prophet,[64] in whom Peter, perhaps, carries the notion of the Prophet-Messiah.[65] Those who resist this God-appointed prophet will be destroyed and removed from the people of God (v. 23). As the Jews are pointed out as being opposed to God's Christ in the previous segment, their repentance is definitely demanded. The need of repentance is also foretold by all the prophets after Moses (from Samuel onwards, v. 24). The phrase πάντες οἱ προφῆται echoes this in verse 21. What God speaks through the prophets further discloses the nature of τὰς ἡμέρας ταύτας, i.e. the messianic days (v. 24), which are both the days of salvation (including the times of refreshing and restoration, vv. 19-21) and adjudication (vv. 22-23). The repetition of the prophets as God's spokesmen progressively and double-facetedly uncovers God's plan in Jesus and highlights God's initiative in designing and revealing his plan (3:18, 21, 24). Moreover, the indication of the totality of the prophets may signify Peter's comprehension of the christocentric fulfilment of all the prophetic promises (cf. πάντες in verses 18, 24 and ἀπ' αἰῶνος in verse 21).[66] Either the rewarding or warning aspect of such a christocentric revelation of God's plan reflects the necessity of repentance for the Jews.

The Jews' Status before God (from the Jews' Perspective)

After a microscopic view of the christocentric revelation in history is presented, a macroscopic view of the Jews' status in God's plan is specified (3:25). The Jews are the sons of the prophets who inherit the prophecies of the prophets, and who 'could expect to see the fulfilment of the promises… [and] benefit

---

[64] The scriptural reference is probably a combination of Deuteronomy 18:15, 18-19 and Leviticus 23:29. The original context of Deut 18, warning Israelites against adopting the magical practices of pagans in order to ascertain God's will, and Lev 23:29 are not applicable to the present context. Yet the combination forms a severe warning which powerfully achieves Peter's goal.

[65] Bock, *Proclamation*, 190. For the first-century Palestinian Jews the Messiah may be either a king, a high priest or a prophet (Bruce, *Acts*, 3rd edn., 145; Schiffman, 'Messiah,' 237-39; cf. Charlesworth, 'Messianology,' 228).

[66] No specific prophet and his scriptural reference is indicated (3:18, 21, 24). Barrett considers the use of the totality of the prophets as hyperbole (*Acts*, 1:202).

from them.'⁶⁷ Additionally, they are the sons of the covenant who inherit the promises God made with Abraham in the covenant.⁶⁸ The promises embrace the universal blessing through Abraham's descendants with christological realisation.⁶⁹ The tracing back to Abraham (cf. 3:13) offers a panoramic look at God's plan of universal blessing conceived in the covenant. The God who covenants with Abraham also designs the way, which is further communicated by all prophets, of consummating his own promises. Being the sons of the prophets and the covenant, the Jews not only inherit the promises of God in the covenant but also receive the assurance of their realisation heralded by the prophets (cf. 3:18, 21, 24). In short, the God of covenant is at work completing his own plan and promises and the work is achieved through God's Christ.⁷⁰ Accordingly, the Jews are God's means of blessing all the nations yet their denial and refusal of God's very promise, God's Christ, obstruct them from being a blessing to others. They are, thus, in need of reminding of their honourable yet ignored mission from God and should repent and turn towards God.

God's Design for the Jews

The fact that God's blessing in Jesus is first designed for the Jews indicates the privilege of the Jews in God's plan (3:26). This is proven by God first sending Jesus to them⁷¹ in order to bless them by turning each of them from their evil ways.⁷² As Peter explicitly states, such a prerogative as receiving God's blessing requires their repentance, especially for killing Jesus (3:15, 17). In the sec-

---

67   Marshall, *Acts*, 96.
68   Sabine van den Eynde, 'Children of the Promise: On the ΔΙΑΘΗΚΗ-Promise to Abraham in Lk 1,72 and Acts 3,25' in Verheyden (ed.), *Unity*, 469-82.
69   The OT references of the Abrahamic covenant are Genesis 12:3; 22:18, where the *seed* is often taken in an individual sense, referring to Christ (Haenchen, *Acts*, 209; Eynde, 'Children,' 472; Max Wilcox, 'The Promise of the "Seed" in the New Testament and the Targumim,' *JSNT* 5 [1979] 2-20, esp. 12-13). In the light of ὑμεῖς ἐστε οἱ υἱοὶ τῶν προφητῶν καὶ τῆς διαθήκης (3:25), the indication of the covenant highlights the role of Abraham's descendants as a blessing to all nations.
70   Soards, *Speeches*, 42.
71   Although it could refer to Jesus' resurrection, ἀναστήσας is better understood in the sense of verse 22 as the first sending of Jesus as God's servant (cf. Barrett, *Acts*, 1:213; Bruce, *Acts*, 3rd edn., 146; Dunn, *Acts*, 48; Haenchen, *Acts*, 210; Marshall, *Acts*, 96; Alexis Léonas, 'A Note on Acts 3,25-26,' *ETL* 76/1 [2000] 149-61, citing 160).
72   The meaning of the infinitive phrase ἐν τῷ ἀποστρέφειν is ambiguous in its instrumental or temporal use. The former speaks of the divine action (i.e. by turning each of you from your evils); the latter the human action (i.e. while each of you turns from your evils). Since God's plan and initiative are implied throughout the speech, the former may gain more weight (cf. 5:31; Bruce, *Acts*, 3rd edn., 146; Dunn, *Acts*, 48; Barrett, *Acts*, 1:214).

ond segment of the speech, the divine plan in Jesus and the Jews is put forth to induce the audience's corresponding reaction, namely, repentance. The striking contrasts presented in the first segment reveal God's supreme and invincible authority in carrying out his plan. The expectation of the corresponding response, thus, is urgent since God's plan never fails and the only way to regain their status before God and inherit the salvific blessing is to return to God.

GOD REVEALED IN THE PRESENTATION OF JESUS

Alongside the antitheses, which show up God's omnipotent authority and judgement, the presentation of Jesus unveils the divine design in the theocentric world. Jesus is characterised by three epithets. The first epithet παῖς signifies Jesus as a suffering servant of God as he suffers under the Jews (3:13).[73] The second epithet, *the holy and righteous one* in contrast with a *murderer* (3:14), stresses the moral innocence of the suffering servant.[74] The third epithet turns Jesus' humiliated status to a glorious one in which God plays a pivotal role in raising him from death and making him *the founder of life* (3:15).[75] The combination of the suffering and the exaltation of God's holy servant (cf. 4:27) introduces a distinctive image of Christ Jesus to the Jews. Such an image is significant to the Jews who may bear various notions about the Messiah,[76] for it is God himself, in whom the Jews believe, who now vindicates Jesus and communicates a message to the world through him. Through Jesus come the removal of sin, the times of refreshing and restoration. Here Peter brings out what God foretells through the prophets in different ages and makes the pieces

---

[73] Cf. Franklin, *Christ*, 61; Buckwalter, *Christology*, 256.

[74] Barrett, *Acts*, 1:196; Franklin, *Christ*, 62; Buckwalter, *Christology*, 256-57.

[75] Ἀρχηγός conveys two fundamental connotations: 'a person who as originator or founder of a movement continues as the leader' (L&N, §36.6; cf. BDAG, 138) and 'one who causes something to begin' (L&N, §68.2). Since Jesus is the cause of salvation, the latter connotation, which signifies 'initiator, founder, originator,' provides a better rendering (for a common translation of 'the author of life' see Bruce, *Acts*, 3rd edn., 141; Marshall, *Acts*, 91; cf. Barrett, *Acts*, 1:198).

[76] In early Judaism most of the Jews yearn for the coming of one or two messiahs with various beliefs about the Messiah. Charlesworth indicates that the early Christians 'obviously inherited the many tributaries of Early Judaism, not only those concerning the Messiah and other messianic figures, but also the independent one concerning the belief in the resurrection of the dead' ('Messianology,' 254). Thus, Peter's emphasis on God's initiative in vindicating Jesus as the very Messiah is crucial to the Jewish audience. For detailed discussion on the Jewish concepts of the Messiah see Schiffman, 'Messiah,' 235-41; James H. Charlesworth (ed.), *The Messiah: Developments in Earliest Judaism and Christianity* (Minneapolis: Fortress Press, 1992) 79-115, 276-95; John J. Collins, 'Jesus and the Messiahs of Israel' in Hermann Lichtenberger (ed.), *Geschichte—Tradition—Reflexion*, vol. 3 (Tübingen: J.C.B. Mohr, 1996) 287-302.

of the divine revelation into a whole picture; this concerns God's plan and Jesus Christ is its focal point. The God of Abraham is bringing up a new perception of his own Christ other than the Jews' conventional notion of the Messiah or messiahs. Grounded in the theocentric programme, Peter convincingly communicates the message of Jesus to the Jews and powerfully provokes the Jews' conversion.

Peter's speeches on the day of Pentecost and at the Temple healing are extraordinarily influential (2:41; 4:4). Both present Jesus as God's Christ. Yet in Acts 2 Jesus' exalted and glorified status is highlighted; in Acts 3 the servant status of Jesus' innocent suffering is accentuated. Both introduce God's power in the name of Jesus. Yet in Acts 2 Jesus' name bears saving power as he shares God's saviour-lordship; in Acts 3 it carries healing power since the divine lordship bears the authority of exercising divine power.[77] The latter further puts 'in evidence the role of the confession of faith by the witness.'[78] Both recognise Jesus as the mediator of God's salvation. Yet Acts 2 reveals God's design of Jesus as the mediator of the descent of the Spirit and Acts 3 Jesus' name, accompanying faith, as the mediator of divine blessings. While Acts 2 acclaims God mightily carrying out his promise in the messianic age, Acts 3 claims the need for repentance since God's Christ, whom the Jews killed, is the only way for God's salvation. Both speeches are so powerful because of the representation of the Messiah in the context of the theocentric programme. In Jesus God's universal saving plan and salvific blessings are perceived and consummated. Peter is concerned with the christocentric fulfilment of God's promises foretold by the prophets and presents it in a theocentric framework.[79] Through the God-centred skeleton of the speeches the message of Jesus is effectively made acceptable to the Jews. Such a theocentric christology is fundamental to Peter's witness of Jesus and crucial to Peter's new insight of God. God is actively and powerfully at work, faithfully and authoritatively keeping his promises, and compassionately and tolerantly waiting to bless his people.

The Speeches before the Jewish Leaders
(4:8-12, 19-20; 5:29-32)

As Jesus, standing in between God and the Jews, provokes the hostility of the unbelieving Jews and their leaders towards himself, Peter's witness of Jesus

---

[77] Bock, *Proclamation*, 264.
[78] Marguerat, *Historian*, 103.
[79] Marguerat, *Historian*, 102. Here 'Scripture is used in a polemical way, against Jewish opponents of the gospel, as well as in a positive way, to expound the significance of Jesus and his saving work' (David Peterson, 'The Motif of Fulfilment and the Purpose of Luke-Acts' in Bruce W. Winter and Andrew D. Clarke [eds.], *The Book of Acts in Its Ancient Literary Setting* [Grand Rapids: Eerdmans, 1993] 83-104, citing 99).

agitates especially the enmity of the Jewish leaders and results in the official arrest (4:1-3). While the Temple healing gives Peter an opportunity to bear witness to Jesus before the Jews, the arrest offers him another opportunity of witnessing Jesus before the Jewish leaders (4:8-12, 19-20). The crux of the trial is the cause of the healing rather than what the apostles preached (4:7; cf. 4:2). This allows Peter straightforwardly to point out God's healing power and saving purpose in the name of Jesus (4:10, 12). Being questioned about the source of healing power,[80] Peter refers the very cause to the divine authority via Jesus' name (4:10; cf. 3:16). Peter's use of the word σωθῆναι in a double sense (to heal in v. 9 and to save in v. 12) enables him to use the healing as a proof of the saving power of the resurrected Jesus.[81]

Similar to the literary structure used constantly, the contrast between God and the Jewish leaders in 4:10 provides a context to enforce the divine vindication of Jesus (God's witness), followed by explicit testimony of the healed lame man (human witness).

Such a contrast is reinforced in the metaphorical expression of Psalm 118:22 (4:11).[82] The builders are identified with the Jewish authorities (note the additive word of ὑμῶν in the scriptural quotation, cf. 4:5-6). In contrast, the divine reversal of human action 'brings honour to an originally rejected object'[83] and turns the evil human machinations to God's own purpose.[84] What they have despised is now becoming the very foundation of salvation (4:11-12).[85] The use of a double negative, which strongly emphasises an assertion (οὐκ... οὐδενί... οὐδέ...), specifies that Jesus is 'the only source and ground of salvation avail-

---

[80] The question (4:7, ἐν ποίᾳ δυνάμει ἢ ἐν ποίῳ ὀνόματι ἐποιήσατε τοῦτο ὑμεῖς) indicates that the Jewish leaders 'suspect idolatry behind the act of the apostles. They think that a sinister power is at work and that the name of a false god was named at the healing' (Bietenhard, '"Ονομα,' 277).

[81] Haenchen, *Acts*, 217; Soards, *Speeches*, 47; Foulkes, 'Semantic,' 124.

[82] Marshall, *Acts*, 100.

[83] Soards, *Speeches*, 46.

[84] Barrett, *Acts*, 1:228.

[85] Κεφαλή means 'the cornerstone or capstone of a building, essential to its construction' (L&N, §7.44). It is figuratively referred to Jesus as the fundamental stone of the salvation of God.

The Characterisation of God 65

able for mankind.'[86] Moreover, the phrase δεῖ σωθῆναι accentuates a must of salvation in Jesus which introduces the divine necessity of God's plan.[87] In short, God's authoritative saving plan is only found in Jesus.

Additionally, God's salvation is designed for all humankind. Jesus is 'the central vehicle for God's saving purpose on a universal scale.'[88] God's vindication of Jesus in the resurrection and through the healing confirms the significance of Jesus' name for salvation which Peter interprets with universal application.[89] The apostles' witness of the saving power and the healing power in Jesus' name is ascribed to the will of God (4:19-20). What they experienced and witnessed is, thus, doing God's will. The double negative (v. 20, οὐ δυνάμεθα... μὴ λαλεῖν) reflects a strong affirmation of the apostles' submission to God.[90] By and large, Peter's speech before the leaders is a succinct compendium of his previous two speeches which concern both God's saving power (Acts 2) and healing power (Acts 3) in Jesus' name. Again, the christocentric belief is conveyed in a theocentric framework.[91] By such a literary strategy, salvation in Jesus is justified. It is God himself who is at work in Jesus' life and communicates through him a message of salvation to the world.

Another confrontation between the apostles and the Jewish leaders arises from the numerous healings at the Temple (5:12) and the continuous proclamation of Jesus (5:28). Similarly, the animosity of the leaders leads to the arrest and imprisonment of the apostles (5:17-18). After being miraculously delivered and arrested again, the apostles (with Peter their delegate) get another opportunity to bear witness to Jesus before the leaders (5:29-32).[92] Peter's speech here is a compact summary of his previous preachings.[93] He first emphasises the necessity of their submission to God (5:29; cf. 4:19) where a contrast of θεός and ἄνθρωποι is laid for the immediate context to assert God's supreme authority (cf. 3:30-31). Again, the divine authority is amplified by means of an antithesis between God's act to Jesus and the Jews' (v. 30).

---

[86] Barrett, *Acts*, 1:233.
[87] Barrett, *Acts*, 1:233; Soards, *Speeches*, 46.
[88] Dunn, *Acts*, 54.
[89] Green, 'Salvation,' 97; also Soards, *Speeches*, 46; Tannehill, *Narrative Unity*, 2:39-40.
[90] Barrett, *Acts*, 1:238. Note the use of the emphatic personal pronoun ἡμεῖς.
[91] Jervell, *Theology*, 30.
[92] Haenchen regards all the apostles speaking 'with divinely inspired unanimity' (*Acts*, 251). Often speaking for the apostles (2:14; 3:11-12; 4:7-8), Peter may again take the lead to reply to the accusation (cf. Barrett, *Acts*, 1:288; Marshall, *Acts*, 119).
[93] Bruce, *Acts*, 3rd edn., 172; Witherington, *Acts*, 232, n.154. Soards denotes that 'the speech is brief but multifaceted' (*Speeches*, 51).

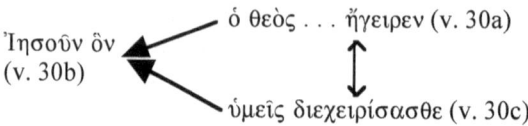

In his authority and power God raises Jesus from death and exalts him to be a leader and a saviour (vv. 30a, 31a). The epithets of Jesus unveil God's saving purpose. Ἀρχηγός, corresponding to ἀρχηγὸν τῆς ζωῆς in 3:15,[94] conveys the meaning of *founding leader* in relation to life (5:31)[95] which is specifically defined by the second epithet σωτήρ. God makes Jesus a saviour to bring repentance to Israel (cf. 3:26) which results in the forgiveness of sins (v. 31b, cf. 2:38). In addition to the giving of the Spirit (2:33), the exalted Jesus gives repentance and forgiveness which are also God's work.[96] God, appearing as the subject of the ergative verbs in 5:30-32, highlights that all the determinative actions in relation to Jesus are God's:[97] resurrection (v. 30a), exaltation (v. 31a) and the bestowal of the Spirit (v. 32b). Behind these actions lie God's supreme authority and invincible power as Soards indicates: 'implicit in this declaration about the work of God through the exalted Jesus are the themes of divine necessity and divine authority, for the idea of determinative divine action dominates this construction.'[98]

Lastly, the message of God's salvation in Jesus is testified by both the apostles and the Spirit within them (5:32). God's vindication of Jesus is always accompanied by human witness (cf. 2:32; 3:16; 4:20). Here a divine witness is added, namely, the Spirit whom God gives to those who obey him to notarise the apostles' witness and fortify God's mighty deeds (5:32b).[99]

---

[94] Haenchen, *Acts*, 251; Soards, *Speeches*, 52; Barrett, *Acts*, 1:290.

[95] Without the descriptive genitive τῆς ζωῆς the word ἀρχηγός probably simply means *pioneer leader* or *founding leader* (Barrett, *Acts*, 1:290; cf. L&N, § 36.6; O'Toole, 'Risen Jesus,' 492).

[96] In the light of the theocentric contexts of 2:37-39, 3:19 and 5:31, the repentance and the forgiveness of sins are of God (see God's promise in 2:39, God as the agent of the passive verbs of κατενύγησαν in 2:37 and ἐξαλειφθῆναι in 3:19, and God the subject of making Jesus a saviour to give forgiveness in 5:31).

[97] Dunn, *Acts*, 69.

[98] Soards, *Speeches*, 52.

[99] Larkin points out that 'the Spirit bears witness by empowerment in witness' ('Pneumatology,' 130). Soards indicates a twofold testimony by the Spirit: the Spirit authenticates the kerygma and vouches for the early Christian community (*Speeches*, 53).

The Characterisation of God 67

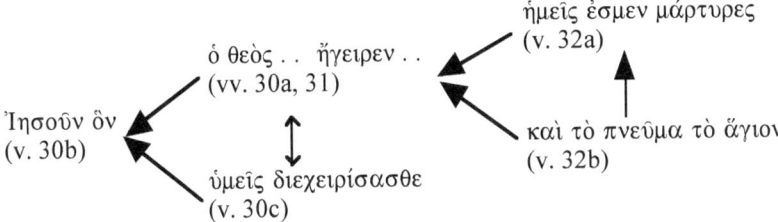

It is precisely the same God, whom the Jewish leaders confess (see ὁ θεὸς τῶν πατέρων ἡμῶν in v. 30), about whom Peter now witnesses to his saving plan in Jesus. Accordingly, what Peter proclaims is the realisation, not the contradiction, of Jewish belief.[100] The killing of Jesus by the Jewish leaders is, thus, an act against their own God. Contrarily, the apostles are on God's side with the confirmation of the Spirit and the miraculous healings (5:12-16).

The essential elements of Peter's notion of God's revelation in Jesus are presented in this pithy speech from four points of view: a literary scheme of contrast to amplify God's omnipotent authority (God's perspective); Jesus' death, resurrection and exaltation (Jesus' angle); the necessity of repentance which leads to the forgiveness of sins and the reception of the Spirit (human aspect); the witness of the apostles with the Spirit within them (the apostles' view). From these facets appears a thorough picture of God's authoritative saving plan and purpose in Jesus (to be a saviour), to the world (to repent and receive forgiveness and the Spirit) and for the believers (to be witnesses).

Overall, both speeches before the Jewish leaders emphasise God's saving plan and work in Jesus which manifests God's sovereign authority and invincible power over the apostles' witness and over human opposition and in achieving the divine purpose.

The Speeches concerning the Cornelius Incident

Being inspired by the heavenly vision (10:11-16), Peter realises that no one should be called defiled or unclean (10:28). Such a transformation of mind makes Peter's speech to Cornelius' household full of the universal implication of God's salvation in Jesus (10:34-43) which was already evident in his previous speeches (2:17, 21, 39; 3:25; 4:12). The two defence speeches concerning the Cornelius incident (or the Gentile evangelism) further highlight God's work and will in the realisation of this universal salvation (11:4-17; 15:7-11).

THE SPEECH TO CORNELIUS' HOUSEHOLD (10:34-43)

Having heard Cornelius' depiction of the divine visitation (10:31-33), Peter proclaims God's will of a universal saving programme to this Gentile house-

---

[100] Barrett, *Acts*, 1:289.

hold (10:34-43). The speech can be divided into two segments: God's impartial nature (10:34-35) and God's work for universal salvation (10:36-43). Each of Peter's statements about God or Jesus is followed by proof to fortify his presentation. First, the nature of God (10:34) is confirmed by the divine acceptance of the God-fearer (10:35). Similarly, the second segment of the speech is grounded on a corresponding structure in which every divine activity is followed by human witness. As conceived in the previous speeches, the theocentric framework with christocentric content allows Peter to introduce Jesus well to these God-fearing Gentiles. The speech begins with the universal application of God's justice (10:34) and ends with the universal realisation of Jesus as Judge, explicitly, and Saviour, implicitly (10:42-43). The focus of the speech gradually shifts from God to Jesus in order to amplify God's saving plan in Jesus. See the following outline for the five statements of God and/or Jesus followed by human witnesses.

v. 34 προσωπολήμπτης ὁ θεός [God as the subject; the nature of God]	v. 35 (Cornelius as an evidence)
v. 36 τὸν λόγον (a message through Jesus) [God as subject; the sending of Jesus]	v. 37 ὑμεῖς οἴδατε
v. 38 Ἰησοῦν [God/Jesus interacting; the earthly Jesus]	v. 39 ἡμεῖς μάρτυρες
v. 40 τοῦτον [God as subject; the raising of Jesus]	v. 41 μάρτυσιν... ἡμῖν
v. 42 παρήγγειλεν (Jesus) [Jesus as subject; the resurrected Jesus]	v. 43 οἱ προφῆται μαρτυροῦσιν

The impartiality of God is the basis which leads to the worldwide realisation of God's salvation in Jesus. The divine interventions in the lives of Peter and Cornelius pilot Peter to perceive God showing no favouritism (cf. 10:28, 30-31). Peter's declaration of God's impartiality is further defined as 'God accepts everyone who fears him and performs righteousness' (10:35; cf. 10:2). The phrase ἐν παντὶ ἔθνει in the first position of the clause highlights the worldwide range of God's acceptance of the God-fearer.[101] Obviously, the two criteria in 10:35 imply that the divine visitation of Cornelius is evidence for God's impartiality since he meets the criteria and gets the divine approval (10:30-33).

Following the introduction of God's just nature, the speech turns to three crucial activities of God in relation to Jesus: the sending of Jesus (v. 36), the empowering of Jesus (v. 38) and the raising of Jesus (v. 40). Regardless of the

---

[101] Barrett, *Acts*, 1:519.

The Characterisation of God 69

difficulty of the sentence construction resulting from ὅν,[102] the notion of God sending Jesus to proclaim a message of peace to the sons of Israel is explicit in verse 36. The circumstantial participle of means (εὐαγγελιζόμενος) defines how the action of the main verb ἀπέστειλεν is carried out, that is, God sends the word by *announcing the gospel* of peace.[103] By the explanation τὸν λόγον is portrayed as the good news of peace.[104] Moreover, while the main clause indicates the indirect object of God's action, the participial clause denotes the agent of it. In other words, God sends the good news of peace to the sons of Israel through Jesus. Peter's notion of God sending Jesus as a messenger first to Israel is seen earlier in 3:26; in the light of this ὁ λόγος is the message of God's salvation in Jesus. This Jesus is the Lord of all (cf. 2:21, 36; 3:21),[105] which indicates Jesus as the saving Lord of both the Jews and the Gentiles. Tuckett further asserts, 'Jesus is Lord *of all* and this justifies salvation being made available to Gentiles... But the dominant actor in the inauguration of the Gentile mission is primarily God, rather than the Lord Jesus' (cf. Acts 15).[106] After all, God is a God of impartiality. Conjointly his saving plan is for all as Jesus shares his universal lordship.[107] Jesus' events throughout the whole of Judea are well known so that the Gentile audience can also witness them (ὑμεῖς οἴδατε, Cornelius' household, 10:37).

In addition to divine preaching through Jesus (10:36), God performs mighty works through Jesus as well (10:38).[108] The cause of Jesus' powerful ministry is God's anointing of him with the Spirit and power. The word χρίειν conveys the idea of assigning 'a person to a task, with the implication of supernatural

---

[102] Whether the original text carries ὅν is doubted. Without it the construction of verse 36 is quite straightforward (τὸν λόγον is the object of the main verb ἀπέστειλεν). With it (ὅν becomes the object of the ἀπέστειλεν) the whole sentence is left unfinished (cf. the suspension of τὸν λόγον). According to the rule of textual criticism (the more difficult reading is more likely to be original one), ὅν may be taken as the original. Yet one should also admit that for some unknown reasons or not yet discovered knowledge the implied author leaves a grammatical problem. See Barrett, *Acts*, 1:521-22; Bruce M. Metzger, *A Textual Commentary on the Greek New Testament*, 2nd edn. (Stuttgart: Deutsche Bibelgesellschaft, 1994) 333-34.

[103] Wallace, *Beyond*, 628-29; L&N, §33.215. Commentators often indicate the scriptural allusions in the wording of verse 36 (cf. Ps 107:20; Isa 52:7). See Bruce, *Acts*, 3rd edn., 261; Dunn, *Acts*, 142; Marshall, *Acts*, 191; Soards, *Speeches*, 73.

[104] Λόγος conveys the meaning of a *message* rather than the personified λόγος in John. Cf. Barrett, *Acts*, 1:521; Haenchen, *Acts*, 352; Soards, *Speeches*, 74.

[105] Both the contexts of 3:26 and 10:36 convey the universal implication of God's salvation. To the Jewish audience, 3:25 points to Israel as a channel for the universal blessing; to the Gentile audience, 10:36 specifies that Jesus is the universal Lord.

[106] Tuckett, 'Christology,' 152; cf. Barrett, *Acts*, 1:522.

[107] Dunn, *Acts*, 142.

[108] Marshall, *Acts*, 192.

sanctions, blessing, and endowment.'[109] Such a divine assignment signifies God's presence with Jesus. The believers themselves (ἡμεῖς, cf. 10:23, Peter and those with him) are the witnesses of God's wonders through Jesus, i.e. Jesus' earthly ministry (10:39). The believers also witness Jesus' death. Unlike Peter's previous speeches to the Jews, the tension reflected in the contrast between God and the Jews is diminished in order to lay the emphasis on the fact of Jesus being put to death by the Jews which leads to God's third crucial activity through Jesus. God vindicates Jesus by raising him from death (10:40). God performs various wonders through Jesus yet Jesus himself is God's very wonder. Again, the believers are the witnesses of God's great deed in Jesus (10:41). Προχειροτόνειν, which means 'to choose for a particular purpose in advance,'[110] signifies that the believers are designated by God to be the witness of Jesus. Their witness of Jesus is accentuated by the depiction of their personal relationship with him after his resurrection.[111] The believers' witness of Jesus' earthly ministry (including his death and resurrection) expresses the ultimate authority and plan of God which direct human history.

While the earthly Jesus is empowered by God and closely interacts with God, the resurrected Jesus acts on his own authority in commanding the believers to be his witnesses (10:42; cf. 1:8). The content of the witness is defined as that Jesus, being given a task by God,[112] is a judge of both ζώντων καὶ νεκρῶν (which includes all people and echoes Jesus' status *Lord of all*).[113] Jesus' mission of sharing the role of universal judge with God is a new feature in Peter's speeches.[114] God makes Jesus both the Lord of all (2:36; 10:36)[115] and the Judge of all (10:42). Not only do the believers bear witness to Jesus but also the prophets witness about him (10:43). No indication of the specific prophets again suggests Peter's understanding of the christocentric fulfilment of the prophecies.[116] The gist of the prophetic witness is that those who believe in him shall receive the forgiveness of sins through his name. The forgiveness of sins may signify salvation in Acts.[117] Comparing 10:43 with Peter's notion of forgiveness in his earlier speeches, one finds that faith is another side of

---

[109] L&N, §37.107.
[110] L&N, §30.89.
[111] Marshall, *Acts*, 193.
[112] L&N, §37.96.
[113] Johnson, *Acts*, 193.
[114] Marshall, *Acts*, 193; Dunn, *Acts*, 144.
[115] Cf. C. Kavin Rowe, 'Luke-Acts and the Imperial Cult: A Way Through the Conundrum?' *JSNT* 27 (2005) 279-300, esp. 297-300.
[116] H. Douglas Buckwalter, 'The Divine Saviour' in Marshall and Peterson (eds.), *Witness to the Gospel*, 107-23, citing 119.
[117] Green contends that '"forgiveness" can appear in balanced apposition with "salvation" in Acts, or as a synecdoche for "salvation"' ('Salvation,' 95), see also the connection of the forgiveness of sins with the reception of the Spirit in 2:38.

repentance (cf. 2:38; 3:19; 5:31; which stress repentance leading to forgiveness of sins). For the Jews, who killed Jesus, repentance is emphasised so that they may receive God's salvation; for the God-fearing Gentiles, who have believed in God, faith in Jesus is demanded since God's saving plan is in Jesus. To both the Jews and the Gentiles salvation in Jesus' name is solemnly asserted because salvation comes in Jesus alone (cf. 2:38; 4:12; 10:43). God's sharing of the lordship with Jesus, thus, makes Jesus the universal Judge (10:42; cf. 3:22-23) and Saviour (10:43; cf. 2:38; 4:12; 5:31).

Besides the crucial depiction to God's work in Jesus, the speech to the Gentile household amplifies and unfolds two themes conceived in Peter's earlier speeches to the Jews: the universality of God's salvation in Jesus and the witness of God's plan in Jesus. While the universal implication of God's salvation is subtly indicated in Peter's speeches (cf. 2:21; 3:25-26; 4:12), God's universal saving plan is enhanced and highlighted in this speech[118] as Jesus is recognised as the Lord of all who plays the roles of both Judge and Saviour. To consummate his saving plan, God sends Jesus to the Jews to bring forth the Word of salvation; Jesus sends the apostles (believers) to the world to bear witness to the Word (i.e. Jesus' earthly ministry-death-resurrection-exaltation through which Jesus is made the universal Saviour-Judge).

THE SPEECH TO THE JEWISH BELIEVERS (11:5-17)

Peter's speech to Cornelius' household provides a thorough picture of the divine saving plan and gets the divine approval (10:44). However, a dispute about Peter being ritually defiled by entering into the Gentile house is raised by some Jewish believers (11:2-3). This, nevertheless, offers Peter an opportunity to testify to God's universal saving will by interpreting God's work throughout the Cornelius' incident (11:5-17).[119] The speech is presented from Peter's points of view, through three angles, to justify his associating with the Gentiles. Peter's personal divine encounter is first elucidated (11:5-12) and followed by that of Cornelius (11:13-14). Succeeding the instructions in the human-divine encounters, the divine approval, pre-announcement and initiative are indicated to vindicate the Gentile mission (11:15-17). The speech ends with a rhetorical question which fully justifies Peter's evangelism to the Gentiles (11:18).

Peter's two divine encounters express the divine initiative in edifying and directing him for the further realisation of God's saving plan (11:5-12).[120] His heavenly vision is delineated in order to introduce a new teaching of God

---

[118] Hans F. Bayer, 'The Preaching of Peter in Acts' in Marshall and Peterson (eds.), *Witness to the Gospel*, 257-74, citing 268; also Soards, *Speeches*, 73.

[119] Linda M. Maloney, *'All that God Had Done with Them'* (New York: Peter Lang, 1991) 68.

[120] Brian Rapske, 'Opposition to the Plan of God and Persecution' in Marshall and Peterson (eds.), *Witness to the Gospel*, 235-56, citing 240-41.

(11:5-10), that is, ἃ ὁ θεὸς ἐκαθάρισεν, σὺ μὴ κοίνου (v. 9). The vision is faithfully repeated to the audience from the narrator's depiction with few significant variations (10:10-16). The narrator expresses the heavenly vision as a whole in terms of τὸν οὐρανὸν ἀνεῳγμένον; Peter adds ἐκ τοῦ οὐρανοῦ to stress the heavenly origin of each individual element in the vision (i.e. a vessel and a voice in 11:5, 9; cf. 10:11, 15); this intensifies the divine initiative of the message conveyed in the vision. In Acts 10 Peter replies to the heavenly voice with emphasis on *never* for self-defence (from the narrator's point of view, 10:14, οὐδέποτε ἔφαγον πᾶν κοινὸν καὶ ἀκάθαρτον) while in Acts 11 he shifts the emphasis to *defiled and unclean* for the present debate (from his own point of view, 11:8, κοινὸν ἢ ἀκάθαρτον οὐδέποτε εἰσῆλθεν εἰς τὸ στόμα μου).[121] The Jewish audience is able to identify and sympathise with Peter fully. Nonetheless, they should also give ear to the divine teaching communicated through the heavenly vessel and voice which dramatically contradicts their conventions and consciousness. This revelation is absolutely from above yet its significance is confused.

Immediately the second divine encounter sets Peter on the journey of exploring the new realisation of God's will (11:11-12). As the heavenly vision leaves a puzzle for Peter and his present Jewish audience, the divine command from Peter's perspective solves the dilemma. The subtle change of the word διακρίνω from middle voice (*doubt*, 10:20)[122] to active voice (*make a distinction*, 11:12)[123] sheds light on Peter's new comprehension of God's will. In Acts 10 the narrator states Peter's perplexity (see διηπόρει *to be very perplexed* in 10:17)[124] and the Spirit's confirmation of him going with the Gentile visitors and doubting nothing (see ὅτι ἐγὼ ἀπέσταλκα αὐτούς in 10:20, which is omitted in Acts 11). As indicated, Peter's concern in Acts 11 is the issue of the *defiled and unclean*. The change of the verb to active voice expounds the divine will of making no distinction between human beings.[125] Such a subtle change reflects Peter's perception of the divine revelation on the one hand and allows him to express the divine will in an explicit way on the other (see also the active voice of διακρίνω in 15:9). That Peter retrospectively elucidates the Cornelius incident with his new insight of God's will is further supported by the subtly shifted order of the event. The narrator indicates that Peter is commanded by the Spirit without knowing who the visitors are (10:19-20); Peter specifies the Caesarean visitors and then the Spirit's command (11:11-12). This makes Peter's point clear that the Spirit commands him to make no distinction

---

[121] Note the word in the first position of a clause.
[122] L&N, §31.37.
[123] L&N, §30.113.
[124] L&N, §32.10.
[125] Barrett, *Acts*, 1:540; Marshall, *Acts*, 196; Witherington, *Acts*, 363; Dunn, *Acts*, 150.

between Jews and Gentiles. Overall, the divine initiative in the divine instructions is featured greatly in Peter's divine encounter.

Complying with the divine command, Peter learns about the other side of the divine work in relation to himself (11:13-14). While the heavenly vision and the Spirit enlighten Peter for the next stage of God's saving plan, an angel pilots Cornelius to partake in it. The divine visitation and direction of Cornelius, depicted from Cornelius' angle by Peter, point Cornelius to the way of salvation. In comparison with Cornelius' own narration of the divine encounter, one omission and one addition appear in Peter's citation of it. The omission of God's acceptance of Cornelius leaves the focus on the divine directive (11:13; cf. 10:31-32) in order to heighten the divine initiative. Moreover, Peter specifies that the angel informs Cornelius of his bearing of a message of salvation for them (11:14) whereas the narrator indicates that Cornelius himself expects only a message from God through Peter (10:33). The additional note on the content of the message reveals Peter's discerning and enhancing of God's will that salvation now also applies to the Gentiles. The indication of the angelic informer again accentuates the divine initiative. Thus far, Peter amplifies the divine initiative in these two divine-human encounters which guide the events in accordance with the will of God.

Lastly, Peter turns to the divine justification of God's will for the Gentile evangelism (11:15-17). He first recalls the descent of the Spirit as the indication of divine approval and acceptance of these God-fearing Gentiles (11:15). In regard to the descent of the Spirit, the prepositional clause, ἐν τῷ ἄρξασθαί με λαλεῖν, intensively dramatises the divine initiative while the fact is narrated as ἔτι λαλοῦντος τοῦ Πέτρου τὰ ῥήματα ταῦτα (10:44). Additionally, a comparative clause, ὥσπερ καὶ ἐφ' ἡμᾶς ἐν ἀρχῇ, is added to 'make the parallel with the event of Pentecost more emphatic.'[126] The Spirit falling upon the Gentiles, thus, not only reinforces the divine initiative but places the Gentile household in the same standing as the earliest faith community (cf. 2:1-11).[127] Accordingly, what Jesus foretells about the baptism of the Spirit before his ascension is endowed with universal implication (1:5; 11:16).[128] For the earliest Jewish believers water baptism precedes the baptism of the Spirit. These God-fearing Gentiles, however, experience it the other way round (10:44-48). As Jesus is the harbinger of the mission of the Spirit (1:5, 8), the Spirit pioneers and affirms the mission to the Gentiles (10:19, 44; 11:12, 15; cf. also 8:29; 13:2; 16:6, 7). Therefore, Peter fully justifies himself as conforming to the step of the Spirit. Ultimately God is attributed as the author of the gift of the Spirit

---

[126] Barrett, *Acts*, 1:541.
[127] Barrett, *Acts*, 1:541.
[128] The reminder of Jesus' words probably serves to justify Peter's baptising of Cornelius' household (cf. 10:47-48).

to whoever believes in the Lord Jesus (11:17; cf. 2:39).[129] Faith in Jesus, which applies to both Jews and Gentiles, is the key to receiving God's gift. The supreme and unsurpassed authority of God emerges as he makes his intention lucid through Jesus and the Spirit. Finally Peter challenges the Jewish audience with a rhetorical question which expresses 'a clear recognition of the authority of God and the involvement of God directing the course of events.'[130]

The Cornelius incident, the God-initiated event, decidedly discloses and instructs God's will for Gentile evangelism.[131] Joining in Peter's journey of investigating God's will, the Jewish believers are convinced and thus submit their wills to God's (11:18). What is recognised is that God also grants repentance unto life even to the Gentiles (see 5:31, repentance is first given to Israel, cf. also 3:26). The generic use of the article in τοῖς ἔθνεσιν signifies that the reference is not to Cornelius' household alone but to all the Gentiles as a class.[132] The response of the audience adequately echoes Peter's argument of God's impartiality (10:34). As God leads Peter to realise his plan of universal salvation, what God has done also prompts the Jewish believers to acknowledge his will. Now God's universal saving purpose is authoritatively made known to the faith community.

THE SPEECH AT THE JERUSALEM COUNCIL (15:7-11)

The Jewish believers who hear Peter's justification of the Gentile mission glorify God over his salvation also given to Gentiles (11:18). Nonetheless, the great debate within the community evinces that not all the believers realise the full implications of God's approval and acceptance of the Gentiles (15:1-2, 5). Much forceful dispute arises even among the leaders of the community (15:6).[133] The gist of the debate is whether circumcision and Mosaic Law are the requisites of salvation for the Gentiles rather than whether the Gentiles can partake in salvation. The latter issue is resolved as God's initiative is shown in his authoritative leading of the Gentile evangelism (11:4-17). The former focuses on the requirements for Gentiles to enter into salvation, by which they consequently become members of the faith community whose primary members are Jews. Obviously, Peter's speech in Acts 11 does not 'settle the question of Gentile membership in the church.'[134] The essence of the Acts 15 debate is

---

[129] This implies that Cornelius' household have faith in Jesus (cf. 10:43).

[130] Soards, *Speeches*, 79.

[131] Schneider, *Apg*, 2:82; Gerhard Schneider, 'Καθεξῆς' in *EDNT* 2:221; Florian Wilk, 'Apg 10,1-11,18 im Licht der lukanischen Erzählung vom Wirken Jesu' in Verheyden (ed.), *Unity*, 605-17, citing 611.

[132] Barrett, *Acts*, 1:543.

[133] The word ζήτησις expresses 'forceful differences of opinion' (L&N, § 33.440).

[134] Shepherd, *Spirit*, 205.

how the believing Gentiles are accepted into the community rather than whether or not they can be accepted.[135] The dilemma concerns the fact that certain Jewish believers still keep the God-given law (15:5, especially those from Pharisee sect) which demands the Jews separating from the Gentiles. The pragmatic difficulty is how the community makes the two separated groups into one. Apparently, two different issues are merged and cause bewilderment, that is, the requisite for universal salvation and the art of living community life in unity. For the earliest Jewish believers, both the Mosaic Law and the Gentile mission find their roots in God. Which crucial element then should be considered as the key to the gate of salvation? While those from the Pharisee sect assert that the key is keeping circumcision and Mosaic Law (15:5), Peter contends that faith is the key. Only if the confusion of the two issues is clarified can the dilemma be solved.

By and large, Peter's speech at the Jerusalem council clears up the first issue (15:7-11) while James' provides a way for the second. Peter's speech presents three aspects: God's work towards the Gentiles (15:7-9), your act towards the believing Gentiles (15:10, those who urge law-keeping) and our belief towards believing Gentiles (15:11, those who propose law-freeing). Peter first draws the attention of the audience back to the will and deeds of God, the subject of the main verbs in 15:7-9, who holds the absolute authority. God chooses and sends Peter to the Gentiles, alluding to the Cornelius incident, so that they may hear the Word and believe (15:7). The unique use of τὸν λόγον τοῦ εὐαγγελίου echoes God's announcing the gospel to Israel (10:36, τὸν λόγον... εὐαγγελιζόμενος). God first preaches the gospel to Israel through Jesus and then, through Peter's witness, the gospel is heard by the Gentiles. The Gentiles' faith in Jesus as God's purpose for Peter's evangelism is specified in order to support Peter's later argument on the necessity of faith for salvation. Not only does God aim to let the Gentiles hear and believe the gospel but he himself bears witness to them by giving them the Spirit (15:8). Here God is particularly characterised as the one who knows the hearts of people.[136] This epithet of God implies that God looks at people's innermost beings and thus wills to purify their hearts by faith (15:9; cf. 10:15; 11:9). Peter's point is clear that the gift of the Spirit and the purification of hearts (probably Peter's other expression of *forgiveness of sins*) are by faith,[137] which is gradually highlighted as the key for salvation to all in Peter's speeches concerning the Gentile believers (10:43; 11:17; 15:7-9). It is the inward faith rather than the outward legal observance which leads to

---

[135] Mark A. Plunkett, 'Ethnocentricity and Salvation History in the Cornelius Episode (Acts 10:1-11:18),' *SBLSP* 24 (1985) 465-79, citing 476-77.

[136] L&N, §28.12; BDAG, 509. Haenchen indicates that God knowing all hearts is 'a favourite expression of post-apostolic Christendom' (*Acts*, 162).

[137] The reception of the Spirit often accompanies the forgiveness of sins in Peter's speeches (2:38; 5:31-32) and personal experience (10:43-44). See Barrett, *Acts*, 2:717; Marshall, *Acts*, 249.

the divine witness and purification.[138] The universal application of human faith in Jesus as the means to God's salvation is considerably accentuated as seen in the phrase καθὼς καὶ ἡμῖν (15:8, the bestowal of the Spirit) and μεταξὺ ἡμῶν τε καὶ αὐτῶν (15:9, the purification of hearts).

After reminding the audience of God's authoritative work and will regarding salvation, Peter points out that their present stance towards the Gentiles is tempting God (15:9). Since God, through his activities, makes clear his intention of incorporating the Gentiles into his people apart from circumcision and Mosaic Law, those who attempt to impose the legal observance on the Gentiles are thus tempting God (15:10). Even though the legal observance is burdensome to themselves, and even their fathers, the strong keeping of the convention and custom in Jewish Palestinian environment obstructs the Jewish believers from the full conviction of God's salvation through faith to all. The ironic question raised to the audience suggests Peter's connotation of opposing law-keeping. Contrarily Peter concludes with a succinct statement of his belief about the very base of salvation (15:11). The crucial point is that the grace of Jesus is the necessity for salvation for both the Jews and the Gentiles.[139] What is implied is that salvation to all is entirely by the grace of the Lord Jesus so that faith in him is the only requisite for salvation. The issue of legal observance, therefore, becomes 'a secondary matter.'[140]

As noted, the believing Jews' adherence to the legal observance causes confusion about the basis and requisite for salvation. Peter clarifies that the base of God's universal salvation is the divine grace of Jesus (15:11) and the requisite of salvation is human faith (15:9).[141] Succeeding Peter's elucidation of the foundation of salvation, James affirms Peter's argument and then wisely gives his own suggestion to make possible the unity of the faith community (15:14-21). As a result, 'the Council removed the wall of separation and hostility between Jewish and Gentile Christians. The apostolic decision bore witness to the universality of the Gospel. The Council did not create a new faith but expressed the one which already existed.'[142] Peter's powerful speech can be attributed to his God-centred contention.[143] While in Acts 11 God's activities makes his will realised, in Acts 15 the significance of God's will causes the disputation to vanish. The gate of salvation is opened to all by God through Jesus' grace (15:11, the principle of grace) whereas the unity of the one people

---

[138] Dunn, *Acts*, 201; Marshall, *Acts*, 249-50.

[139] Dunn, *Acts*, 201; Barrett, *Acts*, 2:720-21.

[140] Marshall, *Acts*, 250.

[141] John Nolland, 'A Fresh Look at Acts 15.10,' *NTS* 27 (1981) 105-15, esp. 108-11.

[142] Veselin Kesich, 'The Apostolic Council at Jerusalem,' *VSQ* 6/3 (1962) 108-17, citing 113.

[143] Mowery points to God as the ultimate agent of the Cornelius event ('God's Activity,' 205).

of God is preserved by the believers' compliance to God's will and through their mutual consideration (15:10, 19-21, the principle of love).

In summary, the theocentric argument dominates Peter's three speeches concerning the Cornelius incident. Acts 10 is expounded to the Gentile household that God's impartiality leads to the universal application of his salvation. In Acts 11 and 15, it is elucidated to the Jews that God takes the lead in Gentile evangelism. Four prominent motifs are woven together to manifest God's universal saving purpose: God's activities through Jesus to make the way possible for universal salvation; God's initiative in giving instructions to achieve the Gentile evangelism; God's approval of the Gentile salvation by bestowing the Spirit on them; the necessity of human faith in Jesus as a response to God's salvation. The recognition of God's work in the Gentile household represents the acknowledged ideal of God's will for the Gentiles.[144] Peter's God-focused presentations not only reflect God's mighty work in convincing Peter of his will of universal salvation but magnify God's sovereign authority in carrying out his salvific plan.

Summary

To conclude the speeches of Peter, we note that each speech carries a basic theocentric tone. Those to the Jews provide a close-up on God's saving purpose through Jesus whereas those to the Gentiles offer a wider angle of God's saving plan in the theocentric world.[145] The salient themes found in the speeches to Jews are: the divine or prophetic promises are fulfilled christocentrically (2:30-36; 3:18, 21-24); God's saving and healing power are made effective in the name of Jesus (2:38; 3:16; 4:10, 12); God's authority is amplified in the contrast between how God/the apostles and the Jews act towards Jesus (2:23-24; 3:14-15; 4:10; 5:30-32). The striking themes found in the speeches concerning Gentiles are: God's salvation is offered without distinction between Jews and Gentiles (10:34-35, 43; 11:15, 17; 15:8-9); Gentile evangelism is utterly by divine initiative and intervention (10:47; 11:5-15; 15:11). The common themes which are progressively developed throughout Peter's speeches are: God is at work in human history to consummate his universal salvation (2:17, 21, 38; 3:25; 4:12; 10:42; 11:15-17; 15:8-9);[146] God designates Jesus as the

---

[144] Jouette M. Bassler, 'Luke and Paul on Impartiality,' *Bib* 66 (1985) 546-52, citing 551.

[145] Robert C. Tannehill, 'The Functions of Peter's Mission Speeches in the Narrative of Acts,' *NTS* 37 (1991) 400-14, citing 401.

[146] The universal application of salvation is implied in Peter's early speeches and becomes the main issue discussed in his later speeches.

universal Saviour (2:21, 36; 5:31) and Judge (3:22-24; 10:42);[147] faith in Jesus is the only way to God's salvation (2:38; 4:12; 10:43; 11:17; 15:9); the believers' witness to Jesus is the divine will of carrying out God's mission for salvation (2:32; 3:15; 5:32; 10:39, 41-42; 11:5-17; 15:7-11). Overall, it is God, through heavenly revelators, who initiates and accomplishes the universal salvation and who further makes manifest his own will and plan. What God demands is people's faith in Jesus and witness to his salvation. Peter's speeches sketch a thorough picture of God's saving will with christocentric realisation in the theocentric programme conducted by God's sovereign authority and power. From Peter's overall speeches appears a God of the universe who graciously offers a promise of salvation, steadily keeps that promise, powerfully fulfils it, and makes it known. The divine activities, carried out by heavenly and human characters, in keeping with this divine redemptive plan further reveal God as sovereign, omnipotent, faithful, and loving.

Personal/Interpersonal Characterisation

Besides the characterisation of God in his speeches, Peter's interactions with other characters also shed light on this characterisation. Peter first experiences the divine deeds and the account of his experiences serves not only as a disclosure of God's will but an offer of God's salvation for others.[148] McBride elucidates that 'in the gradual process of revelation the experience and the interpretation of the experience are mutually dependant.'[149] Investigation of Peter's experience of the divine and human encounters, therefore, will enhance the exposition of his conviction of God. In this section, Peter's divine encounters will first be explored to bring out his personal characterisation of God. Then his interactions with other human characters, with the implication of his interpretation of the divine encounters, will be investigated to bring forth the impact of such divine experiences in the narrative world.

Personal Characterisation—Divine Encounters

The divine encounters, though succinct in narration, dramatically and significantly characterise Peter's performance on the stage: these comprise his experience of the ascension of Jesus (1:9-11), the descent of the Spirit (2:4), various

---

[147] Jesus as a Saviour is explicitly or implicitly expressed throughout Peter's speeches. Jesus as a Judge, however, is only explicitly indicated in 10:42 and implicitly connoted throughout the speeches while Peter warns the audience of God's will in Jesus (3:22-24; 11:17; 15:10).

[148] Denis McBride, *Emmaus: The Gracious Visit of God According to Luke* (Dublin: Dominican Publications, 1991) 101.

[149] McBride, *Emmaus*, 101.

miraculous healings (3:7; 5:15-16; 9:34, 40), the divine punishment (5:5, 10), divine deliverances (5:19; 12:7-10) and divine instructions (10:11-16, 19-20). Each divine intervention plays a crucial role in the plot progression as it not only inspires and assures Peter of God's saving plan but opens up a door for Peter's witness to God.

On Jesus' last day on earth the apostles may have understood Jesus' promise of the Spirit coming in a few days as also the time of restoring the kingdom of Israel (1:5-6).[150] Probably bearing this notion, Peter takes the lead in choosing Matthias in place of Judas for the purpose of the judging role of the Twelve in the kingdom of Israel (Lk 22:30).[151] On the day of Pentecost, however, the descent of the Spirit turns Peter to God's two promises in Joel. Peter then announces the inauguration of the messianic time as he elaborates on the double fulfilment of God's promises in the resurrected Jesus (2:14-36). The apostles' interest in the kingdom of God, the core of Jesus' preaching (1:4), played out in Israel is now shifted to the messianic concern. Following the numerous miracles by the apostles (2:43), Peter's powerful healing of a man born lame further convinces Peter of the reality of the messianic time,[152] which is believed to be marked by miraculous healings (cf. Lk 7:20-22; Mt 11:2-5; Jn 7:31; 20:30-31).[153] Peter thus determinedly affirms the presence of the messianic time by pointing out that in Jesus Christ alone come the salvation and judgement of God (3:12-26; 4:12).[154]

The Old Testament concept of God is not significantly challenged and changed in the Second Temple period; the Jews still believe in 'a God who exercised power directly in the human sphere.'[155] By miracles God takes the initiative to reveal himself and his will and to manifest his authority and power in accomplishing his plan.[156] Peter's experiences of the divine deeds, thus, bring him to a fresh understanding of God at work in human history for his very purpose (2:16-21; 10:34-43). His interpretation of the divine deeds reflects his conviction of Jesus as God's promised Messiah through whom alone

---

[150] Those with Jesus on Ascension Day probably includes other believers, see 1:21-22.

[151] See footnote 6 in this chapter. McBride distinguishes the function of the Twelve as a stationary one and the apostles a missionary one (*Emmaus*, 182).

[152] In the allusion to Isaiah 35, a messianic passage in the first century, O'Reilly asserts that the healing of a lame man is 'a concrete realization of the messianic salvation promised for the last times' (*Word*, 129).

[153] Bruce indicates that 'the ideas of healing and salvation which it conveys (cf. 4:9f., 12) are frequent in Jewish thought and language about God' (*Acts*, 3rd edn., 173).

[154] The Messiah also tends to be regarded as 'the Executor of divine judgement' (Psalms of Solomon 17:21-25); see Herntrich Büchsel, Κρίνω, *TDNT* 3:935.

[155] Alan J. Avery-Peck, 'Miracles in Judaism, the Classical Statement' in Jacob Neusner, Alan J. Avery-Peck and William Scott Green (eds.), *The Encyclopaedia of Judaism* (Leiden: Brill, 2000) 888-97, citing 890.

[156] Avery-Peck, 'Miracles,' 889.

comes the salvation of God (4:12). His theocentric presentation of God's salvation in Jesus further signals and stimulates the Jews to speculate on God's will at the present time (2:22-37; 11:5-18).

Moreover, the divine punishment within the faith community (5:1-11), the amazingly powerful healings among the people (5:12-16) and the angelic deliverance of the apostles (5:19) profoundly aggrandise and invigorate Peter's conviction of God at work in human history to accomplish his saving plan in Jesus. So at his second confrontation with the Jewish leaders Peter, with other apostles, resolutely asserts that they are witnesses of God's designated *saviour* Jesus (5:29-31). Peter's increasing conviction of God's revelation can be lucidly observed in his using the epithets of Jesus and in his two confrontations with the Jewish leaders. The development of Peter's recognition of Jesus from the Lord sharing the lordship with God (2:21, 36) to the Saviour sharing the saviourship with God (3:15; 4:12; 5:31; cf. Ps 42:11; 43:5) signifies his progressive and determined conviction of God's saving will in Jesus.[157] Moreover, in comparison with the similar terms in 4:19, the significance of the two emphatic words Peter uses in 5:29 exposes his increasingly steadfast confession in complying with God's will. To submit oneself to God is not simply a proper or right matter (4:19, δίκαιος) but a must (5:29, δεῖ), nor is it solely paying attention to and obeying (4:19, ἀκούω)[158] but, rather, submitting to authority by obedience (5:29, πειθαρχέω).[159] As Peter is progressively inspired and convinced by the divine interventions, *God's will of salvation in Jesus* is gradually unfolded and affirmed while Peter witnesses it to the Jews.

As the witness of Jesus grows,[160] the divine interventions powerfully authenticate the outreaching of God's saving programme. By laying their hands on the Jews' half-brothers, Peter and John testify to the divine approval of Samaritan salvation (8:14-17). Travelling around, Peter again testifies that the messianic blessing diffuses throughout Judea (9:32-42). Moreover, the divine instructions lead Peter to perceive and witness God's will of Gentile salvation (10:9-43). The descent of the Spirit upon the Gentile household assures the Gentile mission not only for Peter's own sake but for the law-keeping Jews (10:44-48; 11:1-18; 15:1-11). As the mission of God is carried out step by step, the deadly threat of the king Herod enters the arena to destroy God's particularly chosen witness (12:1-6). Yet the angelic deliverance of Peter manifests that God's authority and power triumph over those of human beings and ensure the con-

---

[157] Note Peter's expression of Jesus' saviourship is increasingly specified in his use of vocabulary (see the use of σωτηρία or σῴζω for indicating Jesus' saviourship in 2:21; 4:12 and σωτήρ to pinpoint Jesus' status as saviour in 5:31).

[158] L&N, §36.14.

[159] L&N, §36.12.

[160] The growth of the witness of Jesus is seen in the witness expansion from the apostles to the disciples (Acts 6-8) geographically from Jerusalem to Antioch and racially from Jews to Gentiles (Acts 8-11).

summation of the divine mission (12:7-23; see Peter's crucial defence for God's will of Gentile salvation later in Acts 15).[161] Similar to Peter's mission in Jerusalem, the more Peter is empowered and instructed by the divine interventions the more *God's plan of universal salvation* is spread and validated as Peter strengthens the Samaria and Judea believers, evangelises the God-fearing Gentiles and contends with the Jewish believers.

Fundamentally speaking, it is God himself who powerfully and vigourously initiates, reveals and authenticates his salvation in Jesus by means of divine intervention. Peter is especially chosen by God's gracious favour for the mission of unfolding God's saving will and plan to the Jews. Peter's speeches in Acts function as cogs in the mechanism to invigorate the realisation of God's salvation in Jesus and to promote the recognition of God's universal salvation. By Peter's witness God's saving programme is unveiled and fortified; by his compliance with God's will God's universal mission is prompted and strengthened. Behind Peter's witness and evangelism lies God's sovereign authority and power shown in the divine interventions which pilot the divine mission, shape Peter's speeches and pave the way for Peter's witness of God's will.

Interpersonal Characterisation—Interactions with Other Human Characters

Because of the prophetic and authentic nature of divine intervention, Peter's personal experiences of the divine encounters play a pivotal role in disclosing God's will in the narrative plot. His interactions with other human characters, who perform a minor role in providing a human context for Peter to be realised in depth, enhance the manifestation of God's will.[162] In other words, Peter's divine encounters function as a controlling thread undergirding the development of the narrative. His interactions with human characters add supporting threads to colour and vivify the story and, at the same time, to highlight the momentous facets of the divine plan. Through the human context, constructed by various collective characters, a brilliant portrayal of God is presented and the divine will is gradually manifested and confirmed as Peter interacts with these groups. Peter's human interactions, alongside his God-vindicated speeches, thus merit a thorough investigation for the image of God and will be looked into from four angles: his interactions with the Jewish crowd, the Jewish leaders, the believers as a whole in Jerusalem and, finally, the believers in Samaria and Judea and the Gentiles. Each angle presents a different perspective of Peter's witness to God and undoes a coil of the unfolding narrative plot.

---

[161] In the context that the church was praying to God and Herod did not give the glory to God (12:5, 23), the κύριος in 12:7, 11, 23 probably refers to God (Haenchen, *Acts*, 384; Schneider, *Apg*, 2:105; Dunn, *Acts*, 163; Maloney, *God Had Done*, 104; Beverly Roberts Gaventa, *The Acts of the Apostles* [Nashville: Abingdon Press, 2003] 184).

[162] Bar-Efrat, *Narrative Art*, 86.

INTERACTIONS WITH THE JEWISH CROWD

Peter's interactions with the Jewish crowd are characterised by miracles (2:5-13, 43; 3:1-10; 5:12-16) and two significant speeches which follow-up the divine deeds (Acts 2-3). At each single miracle, the crowd's perplexed questionings (2:12-13) and amazed expressions (3:10-11) establish a moment of intensity in the narrative world in which Peter is allowed to move to a certain depth of realisation.[163] By seeing the sequential and various miracles, the crowd's chorus of high regard for the apostles (2:43; 5:13) creates a social background into which another human relationship merges to further the plot (4:5-7; 5:17-28).[164] The Jewish crowd, as a collective character, functions as a background character who paves the way for the major character Peter to be realised in depth and thus enables Peter to fully expose his witness of God while the divine deeds impressively shepherd him. Moreover, the Jewish crowd provides a social setting to introduce Peter's interactions with the Jewish leaders into the scene which will be discussed in next section.

Although believing that God may interfere in human history, the Jews still need a further indication of the implications suggested by these miraculous deeds, particularly the healings (cf. 3:12), since there are miracle workers of all kinds in the Roman Empire.[165] Peter's speech then controls the interpretation of the miracle and steers the astonished Jews to speculate about God's will. To Jews, the divine miracles 'function to confirm that divine favour, authority, or approval rest on the miracle-worker delivering his message.'[166] As the Jewish crowd recognises the miracles as divine deeds the miracles, in turn, authenticate the divine origin of Peter's authority to deliver God's will as well as Peter's proclamation of God's saving plan in Jesus.

At the descent of the Spirit, the perplexity and bewilderment of the Jewish crowd over the Pentecostal phenomena open a door for Peter's witness. Although in early Judaism there is the inconsistent use of the term 'messiah,'[167] Peter's *promise-fulfilment* motif gives the figure of God's promised Messiah a

---

[163] Cf. Harvey, *Character*, 56.
[164] Cf. Harvey, *Character*, 56.
[165] Daniel Marguerat, 'Magic and Miracle in the Acts of the Apostles' in Todd E. Klutz (ed.), *Magic in the Biblical World* (London: T & T Clark, 2003) 100-24, citing 100.
[166] Andy M. Reimer, *Miracle and Magic* (Sheffield: Sheffield Academic Press, 2002) 89-90. This notion can be clearly perceived in the believers' prayer. While facing the threat of the Jewish leaders, they ask God to strengthen their proclamation of the word by performing miracles through Jesus' name (4:29-30).
[167] William Scott Green and Jed Silverstain, 'The Doctrine of the Messiah' in Jacob Neusner and Alan J. Avery-Peck (eds.), *The Blackwell Companion to Judaism* (Malden: Blackwell Publishers, 2000) 247-67, citing 252-53; William Scott Green, 'Messiah in Judaism: Rethinking the Question' in Neusner, Green and Frerichs (eds.), *Judaisms and Their Messiahs*, 1-13, esp. 2-4.

diachronic dimension;[168] this catches the Jews' attention since it highlights that the God of the old time is working here and now. His theocentric presentation of Jesus Christ, which focuses on the fulfilment of God's promises (2:14-36), converts the Jews to Jesus, God's promised Messiah (2:37-39). At the healing of a man born lame, Peter first accentuates the healing power coming from faith in Jesus' name (3:16) and thus establishes 'between healing and faith, a dialectical relation where the word of the witness plays a decisive role.'[169] He then expounds the divine salvation and judgement and calls for repentance. The former speech discloses how God achieves his saving plan in Jesus; the latter unveils the necessity of human response in faith and repentance for God's salvation. As a result, Peter's two significant and powerful speeches win a large number of Jews for God's Christ (2:41; 4:4).

Peter's last interaction with the Jewish crowd is full of various miraculous healings in such a marvellous way (5:15-16) that it divides the crowd into two. As in 2:43, the apostolic miracles cause a certain fear in the Jewish crowd (5:12-13) yet many come to faith in Jesus because of the dynamic life within the faith community (2:47; 5:14). That the miraculous awesome deeds come alongside Peter's evangelism to the Jews, without indicating the content of his speech, dramatically signifies that it is ultimately by such divine interventions that God's salvation in Jesus is made manifest to the Jews and it is the Lord God who draws the Jews to himself.[170]

In summary, miracles authenticate Peter's authority as being from above and vindicate his witness (i.e. the interpretation of divine deeds)[171] and thus convince the Jews that Jesus is God's promised Messiah. The single divine miracle preceding Peter's speeches (Acts 2-3) steers Peter's witness to God's Christ through whom alone comes the saving and healing power of God. The necessity of participating in God's salvation is expounded as repentance and faith in Jesus. The various and numerous miracles alongside Peter's evangelism portray God at work and evoke the Jews' faith in Jesus (5:14). Seeing the divine deeds and perceiving God's will through Peter's witness, the Jews turn from perplexity and astonishment to the full conviction of God's saving Word (2:41-42; 4:4;

---

[168] Green and Silverstain, 'Messiah,' 254.

[169] Marguerat, 'Magic,' 101.

[170] The reference of the Lord, God or Jesus, in 2:47 and 5:14 is ambiguous. Even if the phrase προσετίθεντο πιστεύοντες τῷ κυρίῳ in 5:14 suggests the Lord is Jesus, the passive voice of προστίθημι still indicates that there is another agent who adds a number of believers to the faith community (cf. Dunn, *Christology*, 250). In 2:47, the narrator's use of τοὺς σῳζομένους as a reference to the believers, which is the only occurrence in Acts, probably implies that God is the Lord who adds the saved souls to the community (note the active voice of προσετίθει in 2:47). Its context also indicates that they praise God. This further corresponds to the Jewish concept of God alone providing salvation (cf. Schneider, 'ΚΥΡΙΟΣ,' 168).

[171] O'Reilly, *Word*, 172.

5:14) and glorify God (2:47; 4:21). By Peter's crucial witness of God's very Word, Jesus becomes recognised as God's Christ by many of the Jews. God is perceived as actively and powerfully stepping into human history to bring hope and salvation to his people.

INTERACTIONS WITH THE JEWISH LEADERS

Besides providing a setting for Peter's witness to God's Christ, the Jewish crowd paves the way for Peter's further witness to their leaders as well. The Jewish leaders as a collective antagonist function as a background against which the main interest of Peter stands out.[172] They act as a foil to Peter, creating a perspective of depth for Peter to reinforce his witness.[173] Their opposition thus plays a structural role in the narrative, highlighting Peter by contrast and providing emphasis and colour to Peter's witness.[174]

Both the two encounters between Peter and the Jewish leaders, resulting from the great impact of Peter's powerful witness and miracles among the Jews, lead to Peter's trials before the Sanhedrin. The first encounter happens at the healing of the lame man. The significant influence of Peter's proclamation among the Jews brings on the leaders' hostility and provokes them to arrest Peter and John (4:1-3). Yet Peter boldly witnesses to God's salvation in the name of Jesus Christ alone (4:9-14).[175] Because of the healed man's presence and the crowd's high regard for the healing, the leaders are unable to punish the apostles but simply forbid them to preach Jesus' name (4:16-17). The quandary of the leaders reflects their justification of Peter's witness of God in a negative parallel (4:19-20).

The second encounter between the apostles as a whole, with Peter as their spokesman,[176] and the Jewish leaders occurs after numerous apostolic miracles which provoke the leaders' jealousy and the arrest of the apostles (5:12-18). The angelic deliverance of the apostles, however, turns the leaders' control upside down. Here a more detailed narration regarding the Jewish authorities is given; the emphasis is laid on the leaders' losing control of the event.[177] This

---

[172] Bar-Efrat, *Narrative Art*, 86.

[173] Harvey, *Character*, 63.

[174] Bar-Efrat, *Narrative Art*, 86.

[175] Peter's use of the verb (σέσωται) for healing in 4:9 reinforces his assertion of God's salvation (Barrett, *Acts*, 1:228; Marshall, *Acts*, 100). Robert C. Tannehill further suggests that 'the healed lame man is the continuing symbol of the salvation for all offered in Jesus' name' ('The Composition of Acts 3-5: Narrative Development and Echo Effect,' *SBLSP* 23 [1984] 217-240, citing 225).

[176] Andrew C. Clark, 'The Role of the Apostles' in Marshall and Peterson (eds.), *Witness to the Gospel*, 169-90, citing 172-73.

[177] Tannehill, 'Composition,' 227.

trial increases in tension as the apostles' witness of the Word grows.[178] The core of the conflict is preaching the name of Jesus which appears as a condemnation to the leaders themselves (5:27-28) and which the apostles regard as obeying the will of the same God whom the leaders believe (cf. ὁ θεὸς τῶν πατέρων ἡμῶν, 5:29-32). Unable to block them from preaching Jesus, the leaders attempt to gain control by killing the apostles (5:33). Ironically, by Gamaliel's exhortation, which turns the leaders to respecting God's authority,[179] the apostles are released (5:34-40). Throughout the incident the leaders' incapability of suppressing the apostolic mission in Jerusalem speaks of God's sovereign authority overruling their deadly force.

While Peter's speeches to the Jewish crowd stress God's Christ through whose name salvation comes (2:21, 36, 38; 3:16), his speeches to the Jewish leaders underline God's salvation alone in the name of the risen Jesus (4:10, 12; 5:30-31). Jesus' name is the crux of Peter's preaching (2:38; 3:16; 4:10, 12) yet an annoyance to the Jewish leaders (4:18; 5:28). Peter regards his witness as being of God whilst the leaders consider it human.[180] Not only does Peter's witness tie in Jesus and God but it also challenges the decision, the abnegation and crucifixion of Jesus, made by these Jewish authorities. In Peter's speech, Jesus stands in the centre of the conflict between God and the Jews; similarly, Jesus' name stands in between Peter and the Jewish leaders while Peter comes alongside God. Yet, the more the persecution, the stronger the witness (5:41-42). A dynamic life flows from within the apostles because behind such confrontations with the leaders is divine empowerment and invigoration (4:8; 5:19-20).

Specifically speaking, Peter, devoting himself fully to God's sovereign will, acts as a reflector which shares God's power and authority. His witness accompanied by the divine approval reveals God's saving will in Jesus and reflects God's authority and power upon him. The leaders, on the contrary, focusing on their own power and authority, are unable to discern the divine origin of the apostolic witness buttressed by the angelic deliverance and are shown to be powerless in their human authority. Ostensibly, it is an encounter of human power between Peter (the apostles) and the leaders; in reality, it is a combat between divine and human authority concerning the origin of Peter's witness. By negative parallel, the increase of the leaders' fury, and them being out-of-

---

[178] Tannehill, *Narrative Unity*, 64; Scott Cunningham, *'Through Many Tribulations' The Theology of Persecution in Luke-Acts* (JSNTSup 142; Sheffield: Sheffield Academic Press, 1997) 193; Polhill, *Acts*, 164.

[179] A comparison between 4:19 and 5:29 reveals the apostles' firmness. While in 4:19 the leaders are left to make their own judgement, in 5:29 the apostles' firm assertion implicitly condemns them.

[180] See the theme of Gamaliel's speech which focuses on what is human and what from God (5:38-39); this will be investigated in Chapter Five.

control of the events, magnifies God's invincible authority and fortifies Peter's witness.

INTERACTIONS WITH THE BELIEVERS AS A WHOLE IN JERUSALEM

As a part of the human context, the believers as a whole walk closely with Peter. Their performance serves as a positive parallel to fortify Peter's witness. The dynamic and communal life within the faith community is like a living witness which enhances Peter's oral witness. In Acts, the very first group of believers is emphatically characterised by their eyewitness of the ascension of the risen Jesus (1:9-11).[181] After the Ascension the believers stay together with one mind in prayer (1:14) and follow Peter's leading (1:15-26). Together they experience the descent of the Spirit (2:1-4). The great impact of Peter's two speeches among the Jews considerably increases the number of believers (2:41; 4:4) who devote themselves to the apostolic teaching (2:42). This growing faith community then becomes a parallel support for the apostles' mission in Jerusalem. While within the faith community the ministry of the apostles as a whole is highlighted (2:42, 43; 4:33, 35, 37; 6:2), within the ministry of the apostles Peter's witness is accentuated (2:14-41; 3:1-26; 4:8-12; 5:1-11, 12-16, 29-32). The faith community and the apostles as a whole, thus, perform as a human backing to invigorate and embolden Peter (2:14; 4:23-31; 5:29; 12:3-17) and as a corporate witness to Peter's proclamation of Jesus' resurrection (1:21; cf. 10:39).[182] Peter, in turn, acts as a leading figure of the apostles and of the community, that which is made clear at the first stage of outreach (8:14); that is, to carry out God's mission in Jerusalem.

Although dynamic in life, there exists an internal crisis in the community. This, similar to the function of the Jewish crowd in the narrative world, provides a background which allows Peter's witness of God to be realised in depth and provides a social setting to further the plot. Peter, with the other apostles, has to confront the menacingly spiritual and collective divisions within the community. The Ananias and Sapphira incident presents a division of mind which leads to spiritual corruption; it is a disregarding of God (5:1-11). Peter authoritatively brings out the tension between Satan and God and adjudges Ananias' lying to the Spirit and to people as lying to God (5:3-4). The divine judgement of death instantly following Peter's verdict about Ananias and Sapphira manifests God's awesome power over this deception which threatens the spiritual purity of the church (5:5, 10). Their death also evinces that the divine power is active through Peter and in the community; anti-divine power has no

---

[181] Andy Johnson, 'Resurrection, Ascension and the Developing Portrait of the God of Israel in Acts,' *SJT* 57 (2004) 146-62, citing 150. Note the one noun (ὀφθαλμῶν) and four verbs in relation to sight. The four verbs are used in pairs by the narrator (βλέπω, ἀτενίζω) and angels (ἐμβλέπω, θεάομαι) for a structural highlight.

[182] McBride, *Emmaus*, 183.

part in the community's integrity.[183] As the fear of God grows in the church (5:5, 11), the spiritual unity remains and God is dignified. This further leads to the divine power mightily falling on the apostles and the increasing growth of the church (5:12-14). Here God's power appears as awe-inspiring and almighty.

The other crisis in the church is the Hellenistic Jews' complaint to the Hebrews about the neglect of caring for their widows (6:1).[184] This exposes a possible split within the consolidated community. As the apostles elucidate their priority in prayer and the ministry of God's Word, the Seven among the disciples are chosen for the caring ministry (6:2-6). It is the first time in Acts that the term *disciple* is introduced; this clearly indicates two statuses among the believers—the apostles and the disciples. The choosing of the Seven, on the one hand, clarifies the apostles' primary task as preaching God's Word and, on the other, unfolds the stage of the disciples for God's mission. The former manifests that the Word of God is crucial to the growth of the church (6:7); the latter introduces the relevant characters and incidents which lead to the first stage of the outreach of God's mission (see next section). Overall, these two crises in the church, having been solved by God's awesome power and the apostles' faithful devotion to God's Word, result in the increase of the believers and the growth of the Word.

Besides the internal crises, the most dreadful crisis to the faith community is Herod's persecution, which was intended to kill their leaders, the apostles, in order to please the Jews (12:1-6). As a powerful leading figure in the community, Peter becomes one of Herod's targets. Although the killer Herod seems to be victorious in the beginning, as he kills James, God ultimately triumphs over him as Herod is killed by an angel. God's sovereign authority and invincible power is seen fully in his admission of letting James be killed and in his willfulness of delivering Peter.[185] By comparison with the persecution by the Jewish leaders, King Herod's persecution indicates that the opposition has extended from a religious force to a political one. However, no force is able to defeat God's plan for his witness (see Peter's crucial defence for God's will

---

[183] Robert F. O'Toole, 'You Did Not Lie to Us (Human Beings) but to God (Acts 5,4c),' *Bib* 76 (1995) 182-209, citing 188, 197, 208.

[184] The contrast between the Hellenists and Hebrews is probably based on the linguistic connotation, that is, 'a Greek-speaking Jew in contrast to one speaking a Semitic language' (L&N, §11.93). For further discussion on the issue see C.F.D. Moule, 'Once More, Who Were the Hellenists?' *ExpT* 70 (1958-59) 100-102; Martin Hengel, *Between Jesus and Paul* (London: SCM Press, 1983) 8-11; David A. Fiensy, 'The Composition of the Jerusalem Church' in Richard Bauckham (ed.), *The Book of Acts in Its Palestinian Setting* (Grand Rapids: Eerdmans, 1995) 213-36, esp. 234-35; Craig C. Hill, *Hellenists and Hebrews* (Minneapolis: Fortress, 1992) 22-24; Barrett, *Acts*, 1:307-9; Marshall, *Acts*, 125-26; Bruce, *Acts*, 3rd edn., 180-81; Haenchen, *Acts*, 260; Schneider, *Apg*, 1:406; Pesch, *Apg*, 1:227.

[185] Barrett, *Acts*, 1:573.

later in Acts 15) nor can any power override God's saving will (Herod's forceful threat is amplified by the irony that the believers pray for Peter yet disbelieve his deliverance, 12:5, 15). This episode greatly manifests God's sovereignty as being much greater than that of an earthly king; there is, therefore, no impediment of the witness of God's Word (12:24).[186]

In Jerusalem, Peter spearheads the mission of God and makes manifest God's will. It is by way of a variety of perspectives that the reality of Peter's witness to God is established. The Jewish crowd provides a background for Peter to elaborate on God's saving plan in Jesus; the Jewish leaders reinforce, through a negative parallel, his witness to God's salvation; the believers as a whole fortify his witness to God's Word through a positive parallel. The divine miracles pioneering Peter's speeches vindicate his witness to God's Christ; the apostles' joy over sufferings magnifies God's salvation and deliverance over human threats and persecutions; the dynamic life of the church upholds Peter's witness to God's Word while the crises in it present opportunities for its growth and for the expansion of God's mission. The believers in Jerusalem, thus, as a collective character, strengthen and confirm the reality of Peter's witness to God's Word. God's authority and power, which ensure the divine mission, are fully recognised in the life and the crises of the church as the believers remain faithful to the apostolic teaching and Peter (the apostles) to God's Word.

INTERACTIONS WITH THE BELIEVERS IN SAMARIA AND JUDEA AND WITH GENTILES

Outside Jerusalem, Peter's performance in relation to the local faith community shifts from an authoritative leader to an authoritative backer. As noted, the disciples, particularly Philip (Acts 8), are introduced onto the narrative stage and pioneer the first stage of God's outreaching mission; this is kindled by Stephen's witness of God and martyrdom (Acts 7) and intensified by the persecution of the church in Jerusalem (8:1).[187] Such breaking through expands the witnesses of the Word from the apostles to the disciples, the location of witness from Jerusalem to Samaria and Judea and the recipients of witness from Jews to Samaritans and Gentiles. Philip initiates the Samaritan mission (8:5-8) and Gentile evangelism in Judea (8:26-39),[188] while Peter and John are delegated, by the apostles in Jerusalem, to reinforce the Samaritan mission (8:14-17).[189] There Peter confronts Simon the sorcerer with his utilitarian faith (8:18-23).

---

[186] For the significant function of this unique episode in the plot see Chapter Six.

[187] See Chapter Five for the significance of Stephen and Philip in God's outreaching mission. Here the emphasis falls on Peter's interactions with the believers as a whole outside Jerusalem.

[188] Tannehill, *Narrative Unity*, 2:110.

[189] God's withholding of the Spirit could be to show the unity and cooperation of the apostles and the Seven (Barrett, *Acts*, 1:412), to evince the full incorporation of the Samaritan believers into the faith community in Jerusalem (Marshall, *Acts*, 157) or

Peter's utterance reveals that the Spirit is utterly God's gift which one can obtain only by having the right manner of heart before God. Like his relation to the church in Jerusalem Peter, with divine authority, also strengthens the believers and challenges the avaricious one in the Samaritan church. Yet, unlike in his leading role in the Jerusalem church, Peter as a backer briefly supports the ministry of Philip in Samaria and then goes back to Jerusalem (8:25).

Similarly, travelling in Judea, Peter strengthens the believers in the local church (9:32-43). The miracles he performs invigorate the believers and draw many who hear to faith in the Lord (9:35, 42). In the semi-Gentile regions of Judea,[190] miracles are connected with the miracle worker's faith. The connection of miracles with faith in Jesus is crucial in a society in which various beliefs exist behind miraculous signs.[191] Moreover, Peter's ministry in Lydda and Joppa, 'almost purely Jewish places on the coastal plain,'[192] is expressly specified; this signifies Peter particularly as the apostle of the Jews in *Jewish* Palestine—Jerusalem, Judea, Galilee, Samaria (9:31).[193] Again, Peter's role as a backer and promoter is conspicuous. As the witness of God's Christ is firmly rooted in the Jerusalem church and expanded geographically, Peter's role in the church subtly veers from a pioneer disclosing God's saving will to a fortifier strengthening God's outreaching mission. Wherever Peter goes, the divine authority and power are with him to encourage the believers and to promote God's mission.

While Peter still stays in Joppa, divine vision and instruction steer him to Gentile evangelism (10:9-48). That such divine deeds take the initiative in the Cornelius incident (an angel speaks to Cornelius, 10:3; a heavenly voice and the Spirit speak to Peter, 10:13, 15, 19-20) manifests that the mission is absolutely of God's determination and authority.[194] Receiving the command in the vision, Peter hesitates to implement it (10:13-14). This reveals his allegiance to Jewish convention which then becomes an obstacle to God's universal mission. By complying with the Spirit's instruction, Peter learns the other side of the story and perceives God's universal saving will (10:30-48). He thus breaks through Jewish convention and makes God's will manifest to the Jewish be-

---

to denote the divine authority and power upon the apostles for the narrative plot (cf. 19:1-7; the parallel between Peter and Paul).

[190] Marshall, *Acts*, 179.

[191] F. Gerald Downing, 'Magic and Scepticism in and around the First Christian Century' in Klutz (ed.), *Magic in the Biblical World*, 86-99. In his argument, Downing concludes that there is 'no widespread evidence for any widespread *firm* belief in "magic" or in "miracle" whichever term is chosen, in the world where the Christian movement began' (99). See also Chapter Four, p. 131 n. 204.

[192] Martin Hengel, 'The Geography of Palestine in Acts' in Bauckham (ed.), *Acts in Its Palestinian Setting*, 27-78, citing 59.

[193] Hengel, 'Palestine,' 60-61.

[194] Barrett, *Acts*, 1:511.

lievers. He first defends God's will before the law-keeping believers in Jerusalem (11:1-18) and later attests it in front of the leaders of the Jerusalem church to legitimate God's will (15:6-11). Throughout Peter's refutation, God's initiative is amplified and it is highlighted that exactly the same experience of the Spirit's descent was shared by the Jewish and Gentile believers. To the Jewish believers, 'the descent of the "holy Spirit" upon the gentiles was "the finger of God,"'[195] a sure sign of the divine presence and approval. Peter therefore effectively defends God's universal saving will and enables Gentile believers to be fully accepted into the faith community as one people of God.

With regard to the Gentile mission, it is utterly the work of God. Peter, whilst in need of having his mindset transformed, is entrusted with the mission in particular. As the divine manifestations lead him to the realisation of God's will, Peter becomes a powerful witness of God's will in the Jerusalem church. In the process of insisting on God's will for Gentile salvation, Peter acts as an explorer of God's Gentile mission and as a promoter of God's will. Ostensibly, Peter is one of the pioneers of the Gentile mission; substantially, the divine guidance to the Gentile evangelism is primarily God enlightening Peter of the divine will and through him the Jerusalem church is convinced to accept the Gentile believers and made ready for the next stage of God's universal mission.[196] Therefore, the divinely edifying significance behind the Cornelius event predominates over the Gentile evangelism itself.

Generally speaking, it is the disciples who spearhead the first stage of God's outreaching mission. Peter as a backer, bearing the divine authority and power, witnesses the mission which is invigorated by the divine deeds in Samaria and Judea. In the Cornelius event Peter perceives and witnesses God's will of Gentile salvation and then becomes a witness of it in the Jerusalem church. Through Peter the Jewish believers' notion of ethnic identity is converted in accordance with God's will and thus the Jerusalem church is transformed and ready for God's universal mission. Ultimately, it is God who transforms his people to his will and who upholds them with power and authority for his mission. Peter's interactions with the believers outside Jerusalem reflect God's omniscience (in knowing the ethnic favouritism of Peter and the Jewish believers), wisdom (in convincing them of the divine will of universal salvation), and omnipotence (in steering and empowering Peter to participate in God's universal mission plan).

---

[195] Yehezkel Kaufmann, *Christianity and Judaism: Two Covenants* (Jerusalem: Magnes Press, 1988) 156.
[196] McBride, *Emmaus*, 199.

Summary

In submitting himself to the divine revelation, Peter not only apprehends God's progressive saving plan but faithfully carries out God's mission. His role shifts from the leader of the Jewish ministry in Jerusalem to being a backer of the disciples' ministry in Samaria and Judea and, then, from a backer of the predominately Jewish mission to being an advocate of God's Gentile mission. Throughout Peter's life the authority and power of God are explicitly seen in convincing Peter of God's salvation in Jesus and for the Gentiles. Peter's bold and sturdy witness of God's will in turn testifies to God's authority and power over him and over human affairs.

While the divine interventions pilot Peter's witness and mission, the human interactions provide emphasis and colour to his witness. The Jewish crowd provides a background for Peter to introduce God's Christ; the Jewish leaders to highlight God's salvation in Jesus' name; the believers in Jerusalem to specify the importance of God's Word; and the believers outside Jerusalem to unveil God's universal mission. Peter's overall mission is mainly to the Jews and Jewish believers (even the Gentile evangelism is for edifying the believing Jews and Herod's persecution is for pleasing Jews). From these various perspectives of Peter's witness to God, a tapestry of the divine plan is thoroughly portrayed; the God of Israel is progressively and profoundly recognised as the God of all[197] and God's sovereign authority and power are manifested in his overruling of human lives for his will of universal salvation.

Conclusion

In the Jewish monotheistic context, miracles precede and shape Peter's speeches concerning God's salvation in Jesus whose resurrection fulfils God's promise of salvation (2:21).[198] From Peter's speeches *a God of Israel* emerges who gives a new revelation in Jesus which is a continuance of God's salvation for his people (see the highlight on salvation in Jesus throughout Peter's speeches, 2:36, 38; 3:26; 4:12; 5:31; 10:43; 11:17; 15:11).[199] As miracles are regarded, in Jewish context, as the signals of divine communication and approval,[200] the miraculous deeds, miracles (speaking in tongues, 2:6-12; healing the lame man, 3:6-7) or divine vision/instructions (10:9-20), which precede Peter's main speeches, not only give him inspiration regarding God's will of

---

[197] Marguerat, *Historian*, 37.

[198] Richard Bauckham, 'Kerygmatic Summaries in the Speeches of Acts' in Witherington (ed.), *History, Literature and Society*, 185-217, esp. 213-14.

[199] See the promise-fulfilment motif underlying Peter's speeches which signifies the 'continuity in the economy of God's dealings with his people' (O'Reilly, *Word*, 120).

[200] René Latourelle, *The Miracles of Jesus and the Theology of Miracles* (New York: Paulist Press, 1988) 286.

salvation through Jesus and to Gentiles but powerfully certify his witness of God's will. This makes Peter's speeches fundamentally miracle-shaped (i.e. speeches and miracles are mutually informed and attested), that is, the interpretation of the divine initiative events (evangelic speeches, 2:14-39; 3:12-26; 10:34-43) or the defense for God's will revealed in these events (defensive speeches, 4:8-12, 19-20; 5:29-32; 11:5-17; 15:7-11). The former focuses on God's saving or healing power in the name of Jesus (to Jews and God-fearers, 2:38; 3:16; 10:43); the latter centres on God's supreme authority over salvation in Jesus (to Jewish leaders, 4:19; 5:29) and over Gentile mission (to Jewish believers, 11:17; 15:10). Noteworthily, the universal nature of God's salvation is increasingly acknowledged in Peter's speeches from universal implication (2:21, 39; 3:25; 4:12) to universal application (10:34-35, 43; 11:17; 15:8-11). Such miracle-shaped speeches, with their single focus, convincingly make known *God's Word—the divine will of the universal salvation in Jesus*. Furthermore, they manifest the absolute initiative of God in promising salvation in the past and consummating it at the present time.

Whereas miracles are closely associated with Peter's oral witness to God's will, the heavenly revelators steer Peter towards God's mission to the Jews. The earthly Jesus commissions Peter to be his witness; the Spirit conducts him to the first stage of Gentile mission (a preparatory step with ethnic concern); angels rescue him for further witness. In observing Peter at long range, his shift away from the Jewish expectation (from the national concern to the messianic concern of the kingdom of God) and convention (from the identity of ethnic purity to the new perspective of God's people) reinforces the reality exposed in his speeches that God actively steps into human history to bring about the divine redemptive plan. Peter, being gradually transformed into conformity with God's will, effectively turns the Jews to God's Christ and the Jewish believers to God's will of universal salvation. Either as a leading witness in Jerusalem or as a backer for other witnesses outside Jerusalem, Peter is divinely empowered to be the witness of God's very Word even at the persecution of Jewish leaders. Throughout Peter's life (speeches and actions) God is characterised as a sovereign God, authoritatively and powerfully taking the initiative to unfold his will of universal salvation in Jesus and to empower Jesus' witnesses to carry out the divine mission plan. Behind God's provision of salvation lies his mighty and gracious love.

CHAPTER 4

The Characterisation of God by Major Characters (II)—Paul

While the first part of the Acts narrative mainly delineates Peter's saga, the second deals with Paul's. As Peter carries out the mission to the Jews in Jerusalem and the first stage of God's outreaching mission in Samaria and Judea, the Jerusalem church is adequately equipped for the second stage of outreach: the Gentile mission, to which Paul, the divinely chosen one, is particularly assigned. As the story moves towards the Gentile mission the major character on the stage is changed whilst God remains the same. The God to whose will Peter devotes himself is also the God to whose mission Paul commits himself. Through Peter, God's will of universal salvation in Jesus is realised in the Jewish context; through Paul, God's salvific plan of universal mission is recognised and consummated in the Gentile context. The aim of this chapter is to explore the presentation of God in Paul's speeches and actions in order to unveil the narrative Paul's portrayal of God.

Conceptual Characterisation

There are seven main speeches and several interlocutions in Paul's performance. Those interlocutions with reference to Paul's notion of God will be discussed in the next section as they are part of Paul's interactions with others (14:22; 16:18, 31; 18:6-7; 19:2-4; 26:29; 27:21-26; 28:25-29). Paul's speeches at Pisidian Antioch, Lystra and Athens are often categorised as *the missionary speeches* (13:16-41; 14:15-17; 17:22-31)[1] whose aim is evangelism.[2] His farewell speech to the Ephesian elders at Miletus exposes his personal philosophy of ministry (20:18-35). His three trial speeches are well known as *the apologetic speeches* (22:1-21; 24:10-21; 26:2-23)[3] in which Paul defends himself. As

---

[1] Stanley E. Porter, *The Paul of Acts: Essays in Literary Criticism, Rhetoric and Theology* (Tübingen: Mohr Siebeck, 1999) 131; also Schneider, *Apg*, 1:96; Schweizer, 'Speeches,' 210-13; G. Walter Hansen, 'The Preaching and Defence of Paul' in Marshall and Peterson (eds.), *Witness to the Gospel*, 295-324, esp. 297-317; Jack T. Sanders, *The Jews in Luke-Acts* (London: SCM Press, 1987) 54.

[2] Martin-Asensio, *Foregrounding*, 117.

[3] Porter, *Paul*, 151; also Schneider, *Apg*, 1:96; Hansen, 'Defence,' 317-24; Fred Veltman, 'The Defense Speeches of Paul in Acts' in Charles H. Talbert (ed.), *Perspectives on Luke-Acts* (Edinburgh: T & T Clark, 1978) 243-56, esp. 253; Jervell, *Theology*, 85.

far as this study is concerned, the missionary speeches will be thoroughly investigated since they convey Paul's presentation of God to Jews and Gentiles. The farewell and apologetic speeches, mainly regarding Paul's ministry and personal witness to Jesus, will enter into discussion only if they touch upon the portrayal of God.

The Speech at Pisidian Antioch (13:16-41)

Paul's first recorded speech in Acts is given at the synagogue in Pisidian Antioch (13:16-41). After the scriptural reading on the Sabbath, Paul is invited to share any message of encouragement with the audience (13:15).[4] This allows Paul to freely deliver whatever he considers as the most important message to the audience; this is 'a Jewish-oriented audience'[5] with God-fearers among them (13:16).[6] Like Peter's speeches to the Jewish crowd in Jerusalem, the focal point of Paul's speech to the Jews in diaspora is the resurrected Jesus who,[7] also, is presented theocentrically.[8] Paul presents Jesus as God's promised Saviour by recounting God's great saving deeds towards the Israelites; among these the resurrection of Jesus is the greatest.[9]

Reflecting God's work in Israel's history, Paul's speech can be divided into three segments. The two direct addresses call the audience's attention to God's saving deeds in the past and at present (vv. 16b, 26). The two inferential conjunctions of οὖν call for the audience's response to God's saving promise (vv. 38, 40). Fundamentally, God's salvation undergirds Paul's whole argument (cf. 13:46).[10] This can be clearly perceived in the flow of thought which is grounded in God's great saving deeds toward Israel in the past (13:17-25) and God's greatest saving deed, the fulfilment of the Davidic promise, at present (13:26-37). Finally, the reality of God's salvation is elucidated in a positive exhortation of faith in Jesus and in a negative admonition of unbelief (13:38-41). As the interactions between God, along with his saving promise, and the collective characters are specified, the theme of God's salvation un-

---

[4] For argument concerning a genuine synagogue sermon see J.W. Bowker, 'Speeches in Acts: A Study in Proem and Yelammedenu Form,' *NTS* 14 (1967-68) 96-111.
[5] Porter, *Paul*, 132.
[6] For further discussion on the God-fearers see Chapter Five and Appendix Two.
[7] Hansen, 'Defence,' 300.
[8] Marguerat, *Historian*, 102.
[9] Hansen, 'Defence,' 301; C.A. Joachim Pillai, *Apostolic Interpretation of History: A Commentary on Acts 13:16-41* (Hicksville: Exposition Press, 1980) 30, 103; Mark L. Strauss, *The Davidic Messiah in Luke-Acts* (JSNTSup 110; Sheffield: Sheffield Academic Press, 1995) 178.
[10] Hansen, 'Defence,' 297; Evald Lövestam, *Son and Saviour: A Study of Acts 13,32-37* (Lund: CWK Gleerup, 1961) 6-7.

folds and stands out. See the structural outline of Acts 13:16-41 for Paul's presentation of God's promise of salvation in Jesus.[11]

13:16-25 God's great saving deeds in Israel's history
[God vs. Historical Israelites]
Ἄνδρες Ἰσραηλῖται καὶ οἱ φοβούμενοι τὸν θεόν (v. 16b)

God initiates the deliverance of Israel (vv. 17-20a)
— *According to God's mighty power, leading them out of Egypt and into the promised land*

God raises human deliverers for Israel (vv. 20b-22)
— *According to God's authority, giving them judges and kings*

God brings a Saviour Jesus to Israel (vv. 23-25)
— *According to God's promise, having John the Baptist as a witness*

13:26-37 God's greatest saving deed at the present time
[God's promise vs. Us]
Ἄνδρες ἀδελφοί, υἱοὶ γένους Ἀβραὰμ καὶ οἱ ἐν ὑμῖν φοβούμενοι τὸν θεόν (v. 26)
— *The word of salvation is to all of us*

The Jews in Jerusalem versus Jesus (vv. 27-29)
— *They fulfil the prophecy of Jesus' death by their ignorance*

God and the earliest believers in Jerusalem versus Jesus (vv. 30-31)
— *They witness God's greatest deed of raising Jesus*

We (Paul and Barnabas) versus Jesus (vv. 32-37)
— *We proclaim the good news about Jesus' resurrection*

13:38-41 The reality of God's salvation in relation to human response [You vs. Jesus]
Οὖν, ἄνδρες ἀδελφοί, a positive perspective (vv. 38-39)
— *Faith in Jesus leads to the forgiveness of sins and justification*

Οὖν, βλέπετε, a negative perspective (vv. 40-41)
— *Disbelieving Jesus results in destruction*

---

[11] The scholars who argue from a rhetorical perspective tend to outline the speech in the framework that singles out the direct address: proem (13:16b), historical narration (vv. 17-25), proposition (v. 26), scriptural proof (vv. 27-37) and epilogue (vv. 38-41). See George A. Kennedy, *New Testament Interpretation through Rhetorical Criticism* (Chapel Hill: The University of North Carolina Press, 1984) 125; cf. also Porter, *Paul*, 132; Witherington, *Acts*, 407. Those who emphasise the themes mainly sketch out the speech in three segments: vv. 17-25, vv. 26-37 and vv. 38-41, although there may be further division within each segment according to the theme. See Soards, *Speeches*, 80; Pillai, *History*, 1.

GOD'S GREAT SAVING DEEDS IN ISRAEL'S HISTORY (13:16-25)

Paul's use of the appellation of the audience (ἄνδρες Ἰσραηλῖται καὶ οἱ φοβούμενοι τὸν θεόν) and the epithet of God (ὁ θεὸς τοῦ λαοῦ τούτου Ἰσραήλ) subtly ties in the God of Israel's history and the present audience (13:16-17). It makes the historical events considerably relevant to the audience while the historical distance is shortened by identifying the individual Israelites with the nation Israel, an ethnic entity.[12] Paul's speech begins by sketching the salvation history of Israel;[13] this centres on 'the constancy of God's care for Israel.'[14] God, being the focal figure of the delineation of Israel's ancient history (13:17-22), is highlighted by his initiative towards the people Israel as exposed by the syntactical structure. Throughout the historical account God is the subject of nine of the ten indicative verbs and the three participles which all bear an active sense.[15] This signifies that God is the author of the history of Israel through which he communicates his plan. Such a plan is unfolded as God's greatest saving agent is introduced (13:23-25), as the things concerning this Saviour are fulfilled in accordance with the Scripture (13:26-37) and as the need of human faith for salvation is spelt out (13:38-41).[16]

God's relation to Israel is inaugurated at the divine election (v. 17a). Thenceforward God's actions regarding Israel converge upon the course of salvation. The emphasis is first laid on God taking the initiative to exalt Israel in Egypt

---

[12] L&N, §11.58; 93.183. Whether the God-fearers are devout proselytes or Gentile sympathisers, to some extent, they identify themselves with the ethnic Jews and have congregated at the synagogue.

[13] Scholars, especially commentators, often indicate the similarities and differences between Paul's speech in Acts 13 and Stephen's in Acts 7. See Haenchen, *Acts*, 408; Johnson, *Acts*, 230-31; Dunn, *Acts*, 179; Bruce, *Acts*, 3rd edn., 303; Soards, *Speeches*, 81; Martin-Asensio, *Foregrounding*, 113-16; Squires, *Plan*, 70 n. 170. The significance of each speech depends on its context while that of rehearsing Israel's history in these two speeches is determined by the narrator's deployment of the speeches in the narrative as a whole.

[14] Squires, *Plan*, 70.

[15] The nine indicative verbs are: ἐξελέξατο (v. 17a), ὕψωσεν (v. 17b), ἐξήγαγεν (v. 17c), ἐτροποφόρησεν (v. 18), κατεκληρονόμησεν (v. 19b), ἔδωκεν (vv. 20; 21b), ἤγειρεν (v. 22b) and εἶπεν (v. 22c). The three participles are: καθελών (v. 19a), μεταστήσας (v. 22a) and μαρτυρήσας (v. 22c). All are in the active voice except the deponent verb ἐξελέξατο which also conveys an active meaning. The only verb referring to something other than God regards the Israelites' request for a king (v. 21a, ᾐτήσαντο). Here the two verbs in the quotation (one referring to God, one to David) are not taken into account since they are not the direct actions in the narration (cf. Squires, *Plan*, 70; Porter, *Paul*, 134).

[16] Squires, *Plan*, 71.

and deliver them by his great power (v. 17).[17] Furthermore, God takes care of them in the wilderness (v. 18)[18] and makes them inherit the land of Canaan (v. 19). For about 450 years God powerfully cares for the people he has elected (v. 20a).[19] The silence of Moses and Joshua as God's agents for delivering the Is-

---

[17] The phrase βραχίονος ὑψηλοῦ literally means 'exalted arm,' an idiom for great power (L&N, §76.5), which is in perfect accord with the OT usage with reference to the plague traditions in the account of the Exodus (Karen Martens, '"With a Strong Hand and an Outstretched Arm" The Meaning of the Expression חזקה ובזרוע נטויה ביד,' *SJOT* 15 [2001] 123-41).

[18] There is a textual variation between ἐτροποφόρησεν (put up with) and ἐτροφοφόρησεν (took care of). Both are singularly equally well attested (Metzger, *Textual Commentary*, 357; Johnson, *Acts*, 231). Early scholars argue that the two terms are similar in meaning since ἐτροποφόρησεν is perhaps derived from τροφοφορέω, for φ is replaced by π on the ground of euphony (*Beg*, 4:149; Haenchen, *Acts*, 408 n. 5). Moulton, however, disclaims this phonetic change (J.H. Moulton and W.F. Howard, *A Grammar of New Testament Greek, vol. 2: Accidence and Word-Formation* [Edinburgh: T & T Clark, 1929] 109). Further, the probable allusion of verse 18 is found in Deut 1:31 where the LXX also carries such a variation. Recent scholars consider the reading of the LXX text, which is less prevalent, to be the original (ἐτροποφόρησεν) since the scribes would tend to conform the text to that of the majority (ἐτροφοφόρησεν); see Metzger, *Textual Commentary*, 357; Newman and Nida, *Translator's Handbook*, 253. Such an evaluation is based on presuming the tendency of the scribes was to adapt Luke's word to that of the majority text. It is, however, possible that Luke adopts ἐτροφοφόρησεν in the majority text yet the scribes who favour ἐτροποφόρησεν or Hebrew text (נשא means 'bear, carry') substitute the word for ἐτροφοφόρησεν. This explains why ἐτροφοφόρησεν 'is supported by a slightly stronger diversity of manuscript evidence and seems more suited to the context' (Newman and Nida, *Translator's Handbook*, 253). Eventually, the context is the vital factor for determining the text while the external evidence is undecided. As the context concerning God's care is taken into consideration, ἐτροφοφόρησεν is usually preferred. See *Beg*, 3:120; Barrett, *Acts*, 1:632; Johnson, *Acts*, 231; Diane G. Chen, *God as Father in Luke-Acts* (SBL 92; New York: Peter Lang Publishing, 2006) 149, 215 n. 2. Robert P. Gordon also indicates the Targumic influence in this speech by presenting the Targumic expression of סופיק צורכא which describes God's care for Israelites in the wilderness as well as presenting a parallel to ἐτροφοφόρησεν ('Targumic Parallels to Acts XIII 18 and Didache XIV 3,' *NovT* 16 [1974] 285-89, citing 285-86).

[19] The phrase ὡς ἔτεσιν τετρακοσίοις καὶ πεντήκοντα is better interpreted with the preceding verse since the following phrase καὶ μετὰ ταῦτα signals a temporal transition (Newman & Nida, *Translator's Handbook*, 255). In light of 7:6, this well presents a conformity and consistency within the narrative. The period of 450 years thus includes 400 years in Egypt (v. 17; 7:6), 40 years in the wilderness (v. 18) and the remaining 10 years for the acquisition of the land (v. 19). See Marshall, *Acts*, 223; Bruce, *Acts*, 3rd edn., 304; Haenchen, *Acts*, 408; Newman and Nida, *Translator's Handbook*, 254.

raelites from Egypt into the promised land leaves the spotlight on God alone. By this, God himself is characterised as a powerful deliverer in Israel's primeval history (13:17-20a).

While inhabiting the promised land, the human agents as deliverers are indicated and brought onto the stage (13:20b-22). God's authority is conspicuously portrayed in the transitions of human deliverers (see God's *giving* of judges to Israel and *removing* and *raising up* a king for them).[20] The judges function as the deliverers of Israel under the oppression of nations (from the perspective of the divine design)[21] and Israel's asking for a king intends a similar function (1 Sam 8:20; from the perspective of human desires). The saving nature of these leaders paves the way for introducing the ultimate Saviour of Israel who is closely related to God's promise to David.[22] The king David, thus, is particularly indicated as having God's high regard for being a man after God's heart who will do all God's will (v. 22).[23] The scriptural quotation as God's testimony for David connotes that David is the ideal king of Israel to whom God promises that his seed will be an eternal throne (v. 23; cf. 2 Sam 7:12-16).[24] The phrase κατ' ἐπαγγελίαν implies that 'God works in relation to a plan' with regard to his salvation.[25] This promised seed of David, with its messianic expectation,[26] is now identified with Jesus as a saviour (v. 23) and, as will be ex-

---

It is further noticed that the use of the dative for duration of time is unusual. Bruce indicates the dative as implying point of time and expressing 'he gave them their land as a possession in the 450th year' (*Acts*, 304). Yet, from the narrative perspective, Bar-Efrat provides a pellucid elucidation: 'Expressions denoting points of time make a considerable contribution to the sense of narrated time. They cannot indicate duration, however, unless they are connected with one another, establishing internal relations between themselves or with events in the narrative' (*Narrative Art*, 145).

[20] Soards, *Speeches*, 82-83.
[21] See Judges 3:9, 15 in LXX where God raising judges for Israel is described as ἤγειρεν κύριος σωτῆρα τῷ Ισραηλ. The notion of judges as deliverers is obvious (Pillai, *History*, 17).
[22] Lövestam, *Saviour*, 6.
[23] For further discussion on the quotation composed from Psalm 89:21; 1 Samuel 13:14 and Isaiah 44:28 see Barrett, *Acts*, 1:636; Bruce, *Acts*, 3rd edn., 305-6; Marshall, *Acts*, 224; Johnson, *Acts*, 232.
[24] Marshall, *Acts*, 224.
[25] Soards, *Speeches*, 83.
[26] Wilcox points out: 'The "messianic" interpretation of 2 Sam. vii. 12-16 in Jewish circles before the Christian era is supported by evidence from 4QFlor i 10-13' ('Promise,' 11). Christopher G. Whitsett further indicates the combination of 2 Samuel 7 and Psalm 2 by Jewish messianic exegetes ('Son of God, Seed of David: Paul's Messianic Exegesis in Romans 1:3-4,' *JBL* 119 [2000] 661-681, citing 677); cf. Otto Betz, *What Do We Know about Jesus?* (London: SCM Press, 1968) 88-89; Lövestam, *Saviour*, 7, 12.

posed later, that Jesus is the very Saviour of God (13:26-40). Even John the Baptist, the one who is believed to be a prophet (Mt 21:25-26; Mk 11:30-32; Lk 20:4-6),[27] serves as a witness to Jesus (vv. 24-25).[28]

GOD'S GREATEST SAVING DEED AT THE PRESENT TIME (13:26-37)

As Jesus is introduced unto the arena, the narration reaches 'the midpoint in the line of redemptive history with reference to which both past and present and future are to be evaluated.'[29] Paul's addressing of the audience as υἱοὶ γένους Ἀβραάμ subtly reminds them that they are the descendants of the one whom God promises to bless and that now God's blessing has come.[30] Paul then gives a summary of his main concern in the speech: ἡμῖν ὁ λόγος τῆς σωτηρίας ταύτης ἐξαπεστάλη (13:26). *The word of this salvation* denotes 'God's significant intervention in the redemptive act accomplished by and in Jesus;'[31] this is especially through the events of Jesus' death and resurrection (13:27-31) which are in conformity to the pre-announcement of the Scripture (13:32-37). Here ἡμῖν includes all the present Israelites (including the God-fearing audience) as the following presentation unfolds. Four collective characters in relation to ἡμῖν can be observed: the Jews in Jerusalem (vv. 27-28), the earliest believers in Jerusalem (v. 31), we (Paul and Barnabas, v. 32, 43) and you (the audience, v. 32, 16). Although playing a passive role, Jesus is the main interest by consecutively being the object on whom all these collective characters act.[32] No

---

[27] Ulrich Wilckens emphasises that 'Johannes hat hier [Ac 13:24-25] ganz die Funktion eines Propheten' (*Die Missionsreden der Apostelgeschichte: Form- und Traditionsgeschichtliche Untersuchungen* [Neukirchen-Vluyn: Neukirchener Verlag des Erziehungsvereins, 1963] 51). Pillai further considers John as 'an eschatological prophet' (*History*, 27).

[28] Marshall, *Acts*, 224; Soards, *Speeches*, 84. Lövestam asserts that Jesus as the Saviour 'is introduced in the normal apostolic manner with the baptismal ministry of John' (*Saviour*, 7).

[29] Pillai, *History*, 30.

[30] Brawley, 'Abrahamic Covenant,' 121. For the fulfilment of God's promise to Abraham see also Nils A. Dahl, 'The Story of Abraham in Luke-Acts' in Keck and Martyn (eds.), *Studies in Luke-Acts*, 139-58, esp. 148-49.

[31] Pillai, *History*, 30-31.

[32] While God is the subject throughout the historical account (13:17-23), Jesus is the object throughout the christocentric presentation (13:27-37) except in the last clause in verse 37. Although in both the infinitive clause in verse 28 (ἀναιρεθῆναι αὐτόν) and the relative clause in verse 31 (ὃς ὤφθη) the referents for Jesus (αὐτόν and ὅς) serve as a subject functionally and syntactically; the passive verbs still make Jesus the receiver of the actions of the verbs. In reference to his interactions with human characters, thus, Jesus is the object throughout. In his relation to God, God resurrects Jesus (v. 37a, Jesus as an object); therefore, it is emphasised that Jesus no longer decays (v. 37b, Jesus as a subject).

matter how the human characters act for or against Jesus, the emphasis on the scriptural fulfilment of Jesus' death and resurrection (vv. 27, 29, 32, 33) manifests that 'God is still the overarching, controlling figure whose own divine purposes were accomplished through Jesus.'[33]

Because of their ignorance of God's promised Saviour, and the prophetic words about him, the Jews in Jerusalem who cause the death of Jesus ironically fulfil the scriptural prophecy (vv. 27-28). Paul's concern here is not the conviction of these Jews but God's overruling of the event of Jesus' death.[34] Both the words ἐπλήρωσαν (v. 27b; with the implication of fulfilling a purpose)[35] and ἐτέλεσαν (v. 29a; for an end result)[36] connote a divinely designed end in the context of the fulfilment of prophecies. In spite of the human intent, what is done to Jesus fulfils what has been foretold in the Scripture and thus is a part of God's plan.[37] While Jesus' death is certain (v. 29b) God raises him from death (v. 30). As noted, the resurrection of Jesus is the greatest and most unique intervention of God in accomplishing his salvation. This divine mighty deed is first testified by human witnesses who are the earliest believers of Jesus and who witness of Jesus' death and resurrection to the Jews in Palestine (v. 31; cf. 1:3-11).[38]

Now to the Jews in the diaspora and the Gentile God-fearers (ὑμᾶς) Paul and Barnabas (ἡμεῖς) announce the good news, *God's promise made to the fathers* (v. 32; cf. v. 23),[39] which regards God's resurrecting Jesus in accordance with the prophetic witness of the Scripture (vv. 33-35). The two explanatory conjunctives of ὅτι are employed to further elucidate the fulfilment of the promise made to the fathers (vv. 33-34)[40] and are followed by an inferential conjunctive διότι to affirm Jesus' resurrection (v. 35).[41] The first ὅτι explicates that *God has fulfilled the promise to their children* by raising up Jesus for *us*

---

[33] Soards, *Speeches*, 84.
[34] Bruce, *Acts*, 3rd edn., 303; Witherington, *Acts*, 411.
[35] L&N, §13.106. BDAG (829) specifies that the active πληρόω conveys the fulfilment of divine predictions which are 'partly of God, who brings divine prophecies to fulfilment (Ac 3:18)... partly of humans who, by what they do, help to bring divine prophecies to realization... (Ac 13:27).'
[36] L&N, §13.126.
[37] Witherington, *Acts*, 411; Soards, *Speeches*, 85.
[38] Marshall, *Acts*, 225; Witherington, *Acts*, 411; Barrett, *Acts*, 1:644; Johnson, *Acts*, 234.
[39] Lövestam, *Saviour*, 7; Marshall, *Acts*, 226; Bruce, *Acts*, 3rd edn., 309; Johnson, *Acts*, 234. As the fulfilment of God's promise to the fathers is in view, *we* and *you* are considered as one. See Martin-Asensio, *Foregrounding*, 122.
[40] L&N, §91.15; BDAG, 732.
[41] BDAG, 251.

(ἡμῖν, see also v. 26)[42] to be the Messianic Son of God as it is testified in Psalm 2:7 (v. 33); this is interpreted messianically in the pre-Christian Jewish exegesis, especially associated with the opposition and rebellion against God and the anointed king.[43] An early connection of Psalm 2:7 (the king's status as the son of God) with 2 Samuel 7:12-16 (the promised Davidic king as the son of God) in Psalms of Solomon 17:23-24 (the expectation of the Davidic king, the Messiah) justly elucidates the Messianic Son of God as the fulfilment of God's promise to the Davidic king (13:23, 32-33).[44] Although first-century perspectives of the Messiah vary in detail, the expectation of a Davidic king as a deliverer is a widespread tradition; this is now applied to Jesus.[45] Here, the divine sonship is connected with the risen Jesus who is recognised as the Messianic Son of God at his resurrection.[46] This is further specified by the second ὅτι

---

[42] The textual problem of 13:33 probably results from ἡμῶν (the best attested variation) being a primitive corruption of ἡμῖν. See B.F. Westcott and F.J.A. Hort, *The New Testament in the Original Greek* (London: Macmillan, 1909) 585; Metzger, *Textual Commentary*, 362; *Beg*, 3:124; Marshall, *Acts*, 226 n.1; Barrett, *Acts*, 1:645; Bruce, *Acts*, 3rd edn., 309.

In the light of the emphasis on the present audience's relation to God's salvation in 13:26 (see the first position of ἡμῖν in the sentence), here, ἡμῖν is probably the indirect object of ἀναστήσας rather than ἐκπεπλήρωκεν which highlights the significance of Jesus' being the Son of God to the audience. See Metzger, *Textual Commentary*, 362; Barrett, *Acts*, 1:645.

[43] Lövestam, *Saviour*, 22-23; Huub van de Sandt, 'The Quotations in Acts 13,32-52 as a Reflection of Luke's LXX Interpretation,' *Bib* 75 (1994) 26-58, citing 31-32.

[44] Lövestam, *Saviour*, 15-23; Whitsett, 'Son of God,' 677-78; Strauss, *Messiah*, 35-43; Marshall, *Acts*, 226; Barrett, *Acts*, 1:646; Moule, 'Christology,' 174; Eduard Schweizer, 'The Concept of the Davidic "Son of God" in Acts and Its Old Testament Background' in Keck and Martyn (eds.), *Studies in Luke-Acts*, 186-93, citing 190; Chen, *Father*, 131-35, 163.

[45] Strauss, *Messiah*, 55.

[46] Ἀναστήσας can refer to God's bringing of Jesus onto the stage of history (without ἐκ νεκρῶν; cf. 3:22, 26; 7:37) or God's raising up of Jesus from death (13:34). The former, a minority view, refers to Jesus' earthly life (Bruce, *Acts*, 3rd edn., 309-10; Richard N. Longenecker, 'The Acts of the Apostles' in Frank E. Gaebelein [ed.], *The Expositor's Bible Commentary*, vol. IX [Grand Rapids: Zondervan, 1981] 207-573, citing 428; Martin Rese, *Alttestamentliche Motive in der Christologie des Lukas* [Gerd Mohn: Gütersloher Verlagshaus, 1969] 83-86). The latter speaks of Jesus' resurrection as proof of his identity as the Messianic Son of God (cf. Rom 1:4; Marshall, *Acts*, 226; Lövestam, *Saviour*, 9-11, 39, 42; Soards, *Speeches*, 86 n. 226; Pesch, *Apg*, 2:38; Schweizer, 'Davidic "Son of God",' 187, 190; A.E. Harvey, *Jesus and the Constraints of History* [London: Duckworth, 1982] 166-67). While surveying the use of ἀνίστημι in Acts, the phrase ἐκ νεκρῶν is not decisive in its indication of Jesus' resurrection but the immediate context is (cf. 2:24, 32). Here the immediate context regarding Jesus' resurrection gives weight to the latter view (vv. 30-31, 34).

clause which expounds God's raising up Jesus from death as the fulfilment of the Davidic blessings announced in the LXX Isaiah 55:3 (v. 34).⁴⁷

The Old Testament context of Isaiah 55:3 speaks of God's renewal of the everlasting Davidic covenant with the people Israel according to God's steadfast love promised to David (חַסְדֵי דָוִד הַנֶּאֱמָנִים, the sure lovingkindness of David) which is often related to 2 Samuel 7 and Psalm 89.⁴⁸ The LXX, however, translates חסדי into τὰ ὅσια which signifies the covenanted blessings,⁴⁹ namely the Davidic promise of the everlasting kingdom and throne, more than simply being a reference to divine favour.⁵⁰ In the light of the LXX understanding, the quotation in Acts highlights the fulfilment of God's promised blessings to David with its implications at the present time. That δώσω ὑμῖν replaces διαθήσομαι ὑμῖν διαθήκην αἰώνιον makes this even clearer. What God will give his people in order to bring the promised blessings is the resurrection of Jesus so that Jesus' ceasing to undergo decay ensures the everlasting dominion of the Messiah.⁵¹ The word διαφθοράν, appearing in each verse of 13:34-37, holds these verses together as a unit in order to attest to the significance of Jesus' resurrection. As in 2:27, Psalm 16:10 is further cited to affirm Jesus' resurrection (v. 35) in which the repeated word-stems of δώσεις τὸν ὅσιον specify the essence of the promised blessings and attest the resurrection of Jesus (vv. 36-37).⁵² The contrast between David (who, having served *God's purpose in*

Moreover, as a speech of Paul, the latter view better presents his notion if the implied author is faithful to his composite message (cf. Rom 1:4; for discussion on Paul's concept of Jesus' Davidic messiahship see Whitsett, 'Son of God,' 661-81; Leslie C. Allen, 'The Old Testament Background of (ΠΡΟ)'ΟΡΙΖΕΙΝ in the New Testament,' *NTS* 17 [1970-71] 104-8). Nonetheless, since the emphasis of the quotation of Psalm 2 is on the standing of Jesus' divine sonship, ἀναστήσας may simply be understood in the sense of coming into a position (7:18, 37; cf. L&N, §13.81) yet with Jesus' resurrection in mind.

47 Schneider, *Apg*, 137; Bock, *Proclamation*, 248; Strauss, *Messiah*, 165.
48 Claus Westermann, *Isaiah 40-66* (London: SCM Press, 1969) 283; Klaus Baltzer, *A Commentary on Isaiah 40-55* (Minneapolis: Fortress Press, 2001) 471. For detailed discussion on the different interpretations of the quotation see Strauss, *Messiah*, 168-74; Bock, *Proclamation*, 249-54.
49 L&N, §33.290; BDAG, 728; Lövestam, *Saviour*, 75, 78; Sandt, 'Quotations,' 34; John J. Kilgallen, 'Acts 13,38-39: Culmination of Paul's Speech in Pisidia,' *Bib* 69 (1988) 480-506, citing 500.
50 Brevard S. Childs, *Isaiah* (Louisville: Westminster John Knox Press, 2001) 434-35; J. Alec Motyer, *The Prophecy of Isaiah* (Leicester: Inter-Varsity Press, 1993) 454; John N. Oswalt, *The Book of Isaiah Chapters 40-66* (Grand Rapids: Eerdmans, 1998) 438; Strauss, *Messiah*, 171.
51 Lövestam, *Saviour*, 71-72, 79-80; Marshall, *Acts*, 227-28; Strauss, *Messiah*, 173; Bock, *Proclamation*, 254, 256.
52 Kilgallen even indicates that Jesus (τὸν ὅσιον) is the mediator of τὰ ὅσια ('Speech in Pisidia,' 494).

his own generation, saw corruption) and Jesus (who, having been raised by God, does not see corruption) connotes that Jesus' resurrection is a part of God's plan to the present generation.[53]

Not only is God's pivotal saving act (resurrecting Jesus, v. 30) testified by eyewitnesses (v. 31) but it is also certified by the scriptural proof which concerns the promise-fulfilment (vv. 32-37).[54] The indication of the promise regarding a saviour (vv. 23, 32) and its fulfilment (v. 33; see the perfect tense of ἐκπεπλήρωκεν) elucidates the realisation of God's saving plan. The dative objectives τῷ Ἰσραήλ in 13:23 and ἡμῖν in 13:26, 33 refer the time of realisation to the present.[55] The confirmation of Jesus' resurrection is framed with the scriptural testimonies. While ἀναστήσας Ἰησοῦν indicates God's bringing of the risen Jesus to be the Messianic Son of God (v. 33; Ps 2:7), ἀνέστησεν αὐτὸν ἐκ νεκρῶν points out Jesus' resurrection as God's fulfilment of the blessings of the Davidic promise (vv. 34-35; Isa 55:3; Ps 16:10). Jesus' resurrection, thus, signifies that he holds the eternal status of the Messianic Son of God and the everlasting dominion of the Davidic Messiah.[56] What undergirds the whole event of Jesus' death and resurrection is God's faithfulness in fulfilling his promise and his lovingkindness in providing salvation. Jesus' death is essential for God's saving purpose; Jesus' resurrection is essential for the realisation of God's saving promise.

THE REALITY OF GOD'S SALVATION IN RELATION TO HUMAN RESPONSE (13:38-41)

Strauss points out that the quotation of Isaiah 55:3 in 13:34 carries a double (descriptive and prophetic) function: 'to demonstrate the eternal nature of the Davidic promises and to show the application to the hearers brought about by the fulfillment of the promise in Jesus.'[57] As the Davidic promise in respect of God's salvation is realised in Jesus, the reality of its application is exposed in people's response to God's greatest saving deed at present. It is elucidated from both positive and negative perspectives introduced by two conjunctions (οὖν). The first οὖν indicates the blessings through Jesus, namely forgiveness of sins

---

[53] Sandt, 'Quotations,' 36. David's serving of God's plan (vv. 22, 36; both of the words θέλημα and βουλή belong to the same word-group, conveying the notion of 'intent, purpose and plan' [L&N, §30.59; 30.57]) can be perceived at his preparing the way for God's promised Saviour as well as his prophetic witness of Jesus' resurrection (vv. 33, 35; see Squires, *Plan*, 71).

[54] Haenchen, *Acts*, 411; Lövestam, *Saviour*, 72; Strauss, *Messiah*, 157.

[55] Sandt, 'Quotations,' 33.

[56] Lövestam indicates the divine sonship and eternal dominion (the quotations from Ps 2:7 and Isa 55:3) as the characteristics of God's promise to David (*Saviour*, 81).

[57] Strauss, *Messiah*, 172; cf. Bock, *Proclamation*, 254.

and justification to the one who believes (vv. 38-39).⁵⁸ Διὰ τούτου in verse 38 parallels ἐν τούτῳ in verse 39. Both accentuate Jesus as the means by which God brings forth the Davidic blessings.⁵⁹ Forgiveness is an essential blessing offered through the Saviour Jesus as Peter also emphasises (2:38; 5:31; 10:43). The typical Pauline term δικαιόω highlights the fundamental blessing through Jesus, that is, the right relationship with God.⁶⁰ Those who believe what God has done in Jesus receive the promised blessings whereas those who disbelieve remain in destruction as another οὖν indicates.

The second οὖν points out the prophetic warning of disbelief (vv. 40-41). By contrast the stern warning gives weight to faith in God's present work in Jesus.⁶¹ The original prophecy of Habakkuk 1:5 expounds the consequence of disbelieving God's work through the Chaldeans (Hab 1:5-11, LXX). Here the quotation is applied to warn of the seriousness of disbelieving God at work through Jesus. Paul's additional remark in 13:46 unveils, by a negative inference, that ἡ αἰώνιος ζωή is substantially what God offers through Jesus. The eternal life inclusively states that forgiveness of sins and justification enable the believers to share God's life through Jesus the founder of life (cf. 3:15; 5:20).

To summarise Paul's speech in Pisidian Antioch, then, God's consistent care for Israel (13:17-22) is continually shown in the provision of a Saviour in accordance with God's promise to David (13:23-25) which is realised and culminates in God's raising up of Jesus from death (13:26-37). By this risen Jesus, God brings the Davidic blessings by offering forgiveness of sins and justification to all who believe, including Jews and Gentiles (13:38-41, 46-47). In other words, only those who believe God's work in Jesus, which is the Word of God (13:46a), are able to partake in God's salvation, eternal life (13:46b). While taking a long perspective of God's saving deeds towards Israel, the panorama lucidly shows up the divine plan⁶² of salvation under the framework of the Davidic promise-fulfilment in which God's faithfulness and lovingkindness stand out. God's saving power overruling human forces and the power of death further speaks of his sovereign and invincible authority over humankind and all things.

---

[58] Sandt points out that 'the content of the ὅσια Δαυίδ for "you" (ὑμῖν) is specified in a concrete offer of salvation in vv. 38-39' ('Quotations,' 38). See also Kilgallen, 'Speech in Pisidia,' 499-501.

[59] Ἐν τούτῳ may refer to πιστεύων or δικαιοῦται. As it stands in contrast to ἐν νόμῳ, it is probably understood as the means by which one is justified rather than the object of one's faith.

[60] L&N, §34.46; Marshall, *Acts*, 228; Barrett, *Acts*, 1:651.

[61] Commenting on the additional word ἔργον in the quotation, Sandt indicates that '[t]his repetition, giving extra weight to the "work" occurring in Habakkuk's text, has been inserted purposely' ('Quotations,' 45).

[62] Squires, *Plan*, 71.

The Speech at Lystra (14:15-17)

After seeing Paul healing a man born lame the crowd at Lystra superstitiously regard Paul and Barnabas as gods and attempt to offer them sacrifices (14:8-13). Paul and Barnabas, being called *the apostles* by the narrator (14:4, 14),[63] respond as a collective character giving a concise speech on the notion of the true God (14:15-17). As the apostles intend to restrain the crowd from sacrificing to themselves, their speech reveals the true nature of God (14:15a-b) and his status in relation to the world (14:15c-17). See the following outline for the flow of the apostles' thought:

14:15a-b The nature of God unveiled in the apostles' self-clarification
    A supreme being other than human beings (v. 15a)
    A living God other than futile gods (v. 15b)

14:15c-17 The identity of God disclosed in God's work towards the world
    The Creator of the universe (v. 15c)
    The Sustainer of humankind (vv. 16-17)

THE NATURE OF GOD UNVEILED IN THE APOSTLES' SELF-CLARIFICATION (14:15a-b)

A rhetorical question is first asked to keep the crowd from offering up sacrifices to the apostles, and then followed by the reason for such restraint (14:15a). That the apostles are of the same human nature as the crowd not only points out the falseness of worshipping human beings but implies a supreme being of the true God who alone is worthy of human worship. Moreover, God's

---

[63] Throughout Acts the word ἀπόστολοι is applied to the Twelve (with Matthias replacing Judas). Referring οἱ ἀπόστολοι to Paul and Barnabas has been suggested as reflective of Luke's use of various sources or his unthoughtful use of an earlier source. Yet Clark argues that the use of ἀπόστολοι hints at Luke's recognition of 'Paul and Barnabas as playing a role similar to that of the twelve apostles' ('Apostles,' 185). Since Luke is quite consistent in applying οἱ ἀπόστολοι to the Twelve, the term οἱ ἀπόστολοι in Acts 14 is probably 'in the sense of commissioners from the church of Antioch' (Bruce, *Acts*, 3rd edn., 319; see also Barrett, *Acts*, 1:671-72; Witherington, *Acts*, 419-20). Perhaps those commissioned by a local church to perform certain Christian work are addressed as ἀπόστολοι in Luke's time (cf. Rom 1:19; 16:7, where Paul considers James, Andronicus and Junias as apostles and this implies that some, other than the Twelve, are deemed to be the apostles). Moreover, Stephen G. Wilson argues concerning the qualification and function of an apostle (*The Gentiles and the Gentile Mission in Luke-Acts* [Cambridge: Cambridge University, 1973] 112-20). The qualification aspect (to have been with Jesus throughout his ministry, 1:21-22) may refer to the Twelve whereas the function aspect (to be a witness of the Resurrection) rightly includes Paul and Barnabas. The latter better explains Barnabas' status of an apostle since Paul, as the Twelve, is commissioned by Jesus (chs. 9, 22, 26) yet Barnabas only by the church in Jerusalem (11:22) and in Antioch (13:3).

nature is further specified in the purpose of the apostles' visit which is for evangelism so that the crowd may ἀπὸ τούτων τῶν ματαίων ἐπιστρέφειν ἐπὶ θεὸν ζῶντα (14:15b). On the one hand, the anarthrous epithet of God intensifies the *living* nature of God.[64] Ζῶν signifies 'physical life in contrast to death'[65] as well as beings in reality that are not subject to death. In the latter sense it is most comprehensively applied to God who is never subject to death.[66] On the other hand, the contrast between τῶν ματαίων and θεὸν ζῶντα reinforces the explicit characterisation of God as a *living* God in the sense of his significance.[67] Τῶν ματαίων may be an expression for idols or Gentile idolatry (cf. Jer 2:5; Rom 1:21).[68] The preceding demonstrative τούτων makes it clear that the futile things are regarding the apostles as gods (14:11-13), the blind worship of human beings without regard to the true nature of God. Moreover, in the light of the meaning of ματαίων, the living God is the meaning and significance of all existence while the futile gods return to emptiness and worthlessness.[69] In brief, while τῶν ματαίων features the vanity and futility of idols, θεὸν ζῶντα accentuates the perpetuation and reality of the true God. God is evinced as the *living* One in reality whereas gods are futile in vanity. The good news to the crowd at present, thus, is that there is only one living true God in contrast to their futile gods.

THE IDENTITY OF GOD DISCLOSED IN GOD'S WORK TOWARDS THE WORLD (14:15c-17)

Successively, the following two relative pronouns (ὅς) reveal God's identity in the light of his work towards the world. It is the absolutely active works of God

---

[64] A.T. Robertson, *A Grammar of the Greek New Testament in the Light of Historical Research* (Nashville: Broadman Press, 1934) 794. The anarthrous θεὸν ζῶντα conveys the qualitative force. Investigating the object (either the Lord or God) of the phrase ἐπιστρέφειν ἐπί in Acts, all other occurrences are with article (9:35; 11:21; 15:19; 26:18, 20). The anarthrous use, thus, is exceptional and obviously signifies the very *living* nature of God.

[65] BDAG, 424.

[66] BDAG, 425.

[67] Berlin points out that contrast is one of the ways of characterisation (*Biblical Narrative*, 40).

[68] Most commentators indicate ματαίων as a description of idols found in the OT (Haenchen, *Acts*, 428; Marshall, *Acts*, 238; Bruce, *Acts*, 3rd edn., 323; Johnson, *Acts*, 249; Dunn, *Acts*, 191.

[69] The word μάταιος conveys the idea of 'being useless on the basis of being futile and lacking in content' (L&N, §65.37). By contrast God is understood to be the significance and meaning of all.

that make him manifest to the world.⁷⁰ The first relative clause elucidates God's authoritative power of creating the whole universe which makes him unshared and unparalleled. This presents God as the Creator of the universe and spells out the very identity of the one true God (14:15c). The universe, in turn, is evidence which leads people to 'recognise the existence, power and goodness of the Creator.'⁷¹ The second relative clause expounds God's relation to humankind, especially the Gentiles in the past (14:16-17). Ostensibly, 'God did not intervene in the affairs of the Gentiles, as he did intervene in the affairs of Israel.'⁷² Substantially, God evermore makes himself known to the Gentiles through his providential care which testifies to God's continual goodness for humankind and thus signifies God as the Sustainer of humankind. Through the revelation of the natural world God's existence, authority, power, goodness and care are no longer veiled.

In short, the speech to the Gentile audience enfolds the fundamental notion of God regarding his nature and identity. Contrary to the crowd's deeds of considering the apostles as gods, God's nature is distinctly recognised as the supreme being and the one living, true God. In conformity to God's deeds towards the world, God is identified as the Creator of the universe and the Sustainer of humankind. Underneath the notion of God lie the oneness, power, authority, self-revelation and goodness of God.

The Speech at Athens (17:22-31)

Being upset at the excessive idolatry (the city was *full of* idols, 17:16), Paul disputes with those he encounters at Athens (17:17-18). As a controversy arises between him and the Epicurean and Stoic philosophers, Paul is brought to the Areopagus to elucidate his 'new teaching' (17:19-20). Although Jesus and the resurrection are the kernel of the dispute (v. 18), God is the core of Paul's speech (17:22-31). For Paul, in order to perceive the salvation in Jesus, one has to first acknowledge the one true God in the world. By subtly adopting the inscription at their altar Paul skilfully introduces the true God to the audience. See the following outline for Paul's presentation of God in this compact speech which first clarifies the essential nature of God and ends with God's plan in Jesus who is the key point of contention.

---

[70] Six out of the eight verbs are in active voice with God as their subject (ἐποίησεν, εἴασεν, ἀφῆκεν, ἀγαθουργῶν, διδούς and ἐμπιπλῶν). The other two deponent verbs (παρῳχημέναις and πορεύεσθαι) serve as modifiers to two nouns (γενεαῖς and ἔθνη). Dean P. Béchard indicates the theme of the speech as God's self-disclosure ('Paul Among the Rustics: The Lystran Episode [Acts 14:8-20] and Lucan Apologetic,' *CBQ* 63 [2001] 84-101, citing 100).

[71] Marshall, *Acts*, 239; cf. Porter, *Paul*, 140-41.

[72] Barrett, *Acts*, 1:681.

17:22-24a Identification of an Athenian unknown god with the one true God[73]
    Point out an Athenian unknown deity (vv. 22-23)
    Bring out the God of creation (v. 24a)

17:24b-29 Elucidation of the nature of God the Creator
    Supreme over the creation (v. 24b)
    — *Lord of heaven and earth*
    Self-sufficient from the creation (v. 25)
    — *Giver of life and all things*
    Sovereign over humankind (vv. 26-27)
    — *Ruler of humankind*
    Self-existent from humankind (vv. 28-29)
    — *Begetter of humankind*

17:30-31 Explication of the plan of God in Jesus
    Past: God disregarded human ignorance (v. 30a)
    Present: God commands all to repent (vv. 30b-31)
    — *Reason for humankind's repentance (v. 31a)*
    — *Proof for God's judgement (v. 31b)*

IDENTIFICATION OF AN ATHENIAN UNKNOWN GOD WITH THE ONE TRUE GOD (17:22-24a)

The inscription *to an unknown god*, whom the Athenians ignorantly worship, serves as a way for Paul to introduce the true God;[74] this is the dominant theme

---

[73] It is noticed that ancient authors and travellers speak of altars to unknown gods. Paul's use of an unknown god is considered as a literary device to achieve his purpose. See Hans Conzelmann, 'The Address of Paul on the Areopagus' in Keck and Martyn (eds.), *Studies in Luke-Acts*, 217-30, citing 220; Johnson, *Acts*, 315; Porter, *Paul*, 144. Nonetheless, the ambiguity of the meaning of 'altars to unknown gods' (two or more altars with an inscription 'to an unknown god' or every altar with an inscription 'to unknown gods') and some possible suggestions (ἀγνώστῳ θεῷ might be a suitable inscription for the rededication of a derelict altar with the name of its god missing [by Bruce] or the inscription on an altar erected by Godfearers for the God of the Jews [by Horst]) do not completely rule out what Paul may have seen and said. See Witherington, *Acts*, 521-23; Marshall, *Acts*, 286; Bruce, *Acts*, 3rd edn., 381; C.K. Barrett, *The Acts of the Apostles*, vol. II (ICC; Edinburgh: T & T Clark, 1998) 837-38; Pieter W. van der Horst, 'A New Altar of a Godfearer?' (*Journal of Jewish Studies* 43 [1992] 32-37) in P.W. van der Horst (ed.), *Hellenism – Judaism – Christianity: Essays on Their Interaction*, 2nd edn. (Leuven: Peeters Press, 1998) 65-71, esp. 68-70. For further discussion on the background of unknown gods see *Beg*, 5:240-46; Pieter W. van der Horst, 'The Altar of the "Unknown God" in Athens (Acts 17:23) and the Cult of "Unknown Gods" in the Graeco-Roman World' (*ANRW* II 18, 2, Berlin-New York 1989, 1426-1456) in Horst (ed.), *Hellenism – Judaism – Christianity*, 187-220; Porter, *Paul*, 144 n. 72; Haenchen, *Acts*, 521 n. 2.

[74] Arguing from Hellenistic rhetoric, Zweck asserts that in Acts 17:22-23 the *exordium* functions as an introduction to a deliberation on the topic of religion. See Dean

in the speech.⁷⁵ The use of this inscription enables Paul to point out the Athenians' ignorance about god and draw their attention to his argument about the true God (v. 18).⁷⁶ For the Athenians, Paul's message of God's resurrection of Jesus indicates more than one deity in a sense of lesser gods (note the use of δαιμονίων instead of θεῶν in v. 18).⁷⁷ They might consider God and Jesus as lesser gods. Paul's specification of the singular unknown god clarifies that there is only one God in his proclamation. Moreover, a distinction between this unknown god and Paul's God is expounded in the subtle change of the pronoun/article gender from neuter (ὅ, τοῦτο in v. 23b; an impersonal deity) to masculine (ὁ, οὗτος in v. 24; a personal deity).⁷⁸ By such a nuance Paul evinces the very essence of the true God, a personal Being,⁷⁹ to the audience.

Straightforwardly, Paul associates *an unknown god* with the true God whose very identity is specified as the Creator of the universe, ὁ θεὸς ὁ ποιήσας τὸν κόσμον καὶ πάντα τὰ ἐν αὐτῷ (v. 24a).⁸⁰ At first glance, the word κόσμον, in philosophical usage,⁸¹ replacing the phrase τὸν οὐρανὸν καὶ τὴν γῆν καὶ τὴν θάλασσαν, the essential Jewish expression for God of *the creation* (cf. 4:24;

Zweck, 'The *Exordium* of the Areopagus Speech,' *NTS* 35 (1989) 94-103, esp. 96-100; cf. Dean Flemming, 'Contextualizing the Gospel in Athens: Paul's Areopagus Address as a Paradigm for Missionary Communication,' *Missiology* 30 (2002) 199-214, esp. 202-3.

75 Paul Schubert, 'The Place of the Areopagus Speech in the Composition of Acts' in J. Coert Rylaarsdam (ed.), *Transitions in Biblical Scholarship* (Chicago: University of Chicago Press, 1968) 235-61, citing 249.

76 Witherington, *Acts*, 519; Kennedy, *Rhetorical Criticism*, 130; Zweck, '*Exordium*,' 100; Bruce W. Winter, 'On Introducing Gods to Athens: An Alternative Reading of Acts 17:18-20,' *TynB* 47 (1996) 71-90, citing 84.

77 L&N, §12.26; BDAG, 210.

78 Bruce, *Acts*, 3rd edn., 381; Polhill, *Acts*, 372; Witherington, *Acts*, 524.

79 Barrett, *Acts*, 2:838.

80 This phrase, taken as a pendent nominative which carries an emphatic force (Wallace, *Beyond*, 51-52; cf. Johnson, *Acts*, 315), has always been understood with the following οὗτος (v. 24b). Another possible interpretation of the phrase is by taking it as a nominative of appellation to τοῦτο in verse 23b (Wallace, *Beyond*, 61). By this the whole phrase functions as though it were a proper name which associates *an unknown god* with the true God and, at the same time, spells out God's very identity as the Creator. Logically, this angle strikingly singles out the topic of Paul's following clarification of God (vv. 24b-29). Although indicating that the nominative phrase introduces the topic, Culy and Parsons still connect it syntactically with οὗτος as the traditional view does (*Acts*, 337). Structurally, it closely links together ὅ, τοῦτο and ὁ θεός... and thus adequately steers the audience's view of God from ambiguity to unequivocalness. Moreover, it allows verses 24b and 25, standing in a parallel structure, to emphatically elucidate God's relation to the creation.

81 BDAG, 561.

14:15),[82] seemingly communicates a god in Greek philosophy.[83] The phraseology, however, reflects the fundamental notion of God in the Old Testament.[84] Moreover, the ancillary phrase καὶ πάντα τὰ ἐν αὐτῷ, which would be unnecessary for Greek philosophical thought[85] yet familiar to Jewish thinking (Exod 20:11; Ps 146:6), makes clear that Paul roots his presentation of God in the Old Testament understanding.[86] The nominative phrase, thus, spells out a sovereign, authoritative and omnipotent God who alone creates the whole universe and himself is apart from and transcendent over all the creation. In other words, identifying the unknown god as God the Creator with creating power in his own superlative authority, Paul tells the audience that there is only one God who excludes all the other gods they worship.[87]

---

[82] God as the Creator is indicated in his making (ποιέω) of the world expressed often in the phrase τὸν οὐρανὸν καὶ τὴν γῆν (Gen 1:1; 2:4; Exod 31:17; 2 Kgs 19:15; 2 Chr 2:12; Ps 115:15; 121:2; 124:8; 134:3; Isa 37:16; 42:5; 45:18; 51:13; Jer 39:17) and sometimes in the phrase τὸν οὐρανὸν καὶ τὴν γῆν καὶ τὴν θάλασσαν (Exod 20:11; Ps 146:6; Neh 9:6; Ac 4:24; 14:15; Rev 14:7). See also Gen 14:19, 22; Dan 4:37 and Rev 10:6 where the verb κτίζω replaces ποιέω. The word κόσμος is never employed for God's creating the world in the LXX and NT except the use here and in Greek-speaking Judaism (Wisdom 9:9; 11:17; for another equivalent expression, ὁ κτίστης τοῦ κόσμου, see 2 Macc 7:23; 13:14; 4 Macc 5:25; cf. Marshall, *Acts*, 286).

[83] Martin Dibelius, *Studies in the Acts of the Apostles* (London: SCM Press, 1956) 41.

[84] Bertil Gärtner, *The Areopagus Speech and Natural Revelation* (Lund: Gleerup, 1955) 85-89, 171-73; Wilson, *Gentiles*, 198-99; Kenneth D. Litwak, 'Israel's Prophets Meet Athens' Philosophers: Scriptural Echoes in Acts 17,22-31,' *Bib* 85 (2004) 199-216.

[85] Gärtner, *Areopagus Speech*, 173. Gärtner clearly elucidates that, in the Stoic system, their alleged deity 'is not outside the world, is not transcendent but immanent in the world, and is the one that gives quality and existence to every thing... which can be denoted as speculative and based on the Stoic system of physics' (170). The term κόσμος, thus, is comprehensive enough, from the Hellenic background, for Paul to indicate a God who creates the world.

[86] It has been long debated whether the underlying thought of this speech is from the OT or Greek philosophy. While investigating the whole speech, the fundamental belief is thoroughly biblical. Still, since Paul is trying to reach the Athenian philosophers, his language may echo that of Greek philosophy (Polhill, *Acts*, 370). For those who argue for Greek philosophy see Conzelmann, 'Areopagus,' 217-30; Dibelius, *Acts*, 26-77; David L. Balch, 'The Areopagus Speech: An Appeal to the Stoic Historian Posidonius against Later Stoics and the Epicureans' in David L. Balch, Everett Ferguson and Wayne A. Meeks, *Greeks, Romans, and Christians* (Minneapolis: Fortress Press, 1990) 52-79; Haenchen, *Acts*, 522 n. 5. For those who basically argue for the OT see Gärtner, *Areopagus Speech*, 170-241; Barrett, *Acts*, 2:840; Polhill, *Acts*, 370-71; Bruce, *Acts*, 3rd edn., 382; Marshall, *Acts*, 286; Wilson, *Gentiles*, 199, 210.

[87] Barrett, *Acts*, 2:839.

As the very essence (only one personal divine Being) and identity (the Creator) of the true God are affirmed, Paul establishes a cardinal foundation for the true knowledge of God upon which he lays his argument to convince the audience of the true nature of God and the befitting confession of him (17:24b-31). Paul's concern for the audience is the ignorance expressed in their attitude of allegiance to and regard for deities (cf. ἀγνοοῦντες εὐσεβεῖτε in v. 23b).[88] What Paul declares, thus, signifies an expectation of the appropriate attitude and response to the true God. The more God's nature is attested, the more the audience's superstition and idolatry are implied. 'Along with affirmation of the true nature of God there is refutation of idolatry'[89] which is insinuated throughout the main body of the speech (17:24b-29) and culminates at the calling for repentance in Paul's final word (17:30-31).

ELUCIDATION OF THE NATURE OF GOD THE CREATOR (17:24b-29)

Building on the notion of God the Creator, Paul expounds the true nature of God in the light of his relation to the creation in general (17:24b-25) and to humankind in particular (17:26-29). Such relations are revealed in God's roles and actions towards the creation and humankind which are presented in chiastic order.

> God's role to the creation (v. 24b)
> > God's actions towards the creation (v. 25)
> > God's actions towards humankind (vv. 26-27)
> God's role to humankind (vv. 28-29)

From God's relation to the whole universe emerge, on the one hand, the true knowledge of God's nature and the appropriate worship of him and, on the other hand, the implication of the refutation of idolatry. In verses 24b-27 God is predominantly the subject of the main verbs and participial clauses.[90] The magnificent authority of the Creator is prominent throughout. In verses 28-29 the first person plural, *we*, is the subject since Paul is gently pointing out, from the angle of human relationship to God, the transgression of the audience's

---

[88] The underlying thought of εὐσεβέω is 'to express in attitude and ritual one's allegiance to and regard for deity' (L&N, §53.53). Ἀγνοοῦντες is the adverbial participle of manner which adds '*extra color* to the action of the main verb' (Wallace, *Beyond*, 627), indicating the attitude that accompanies εὐσεβεῖτε.

[89] Zweck, '*Exordium*,' 100. Wilson also indicates that '[t]here is both a positive assessment of their religiosity and worship and a positive condemnation of their idolatry' (*Gentiles*, 210).

[90] Schubert, 'Areopagus Speech,' 250. The main verbs are: κατοικεῖ, θεραπεύεται, ἐποίησεν. The participles in the main participial clauses are: ὑπάρχων, προσδεόμενος, διδούς, ὁρίσας. The other participles, infinitives and εἰ-clause carry a supplementary or explanatory function to enhance Paul's argument on God's nature.

idolatry by indicating it in a collective sense; this paves the way for his calling for repentance (vv. 30-31).

God's Relation to the Creation

God's relation to the creation is articulated in a structural parallel (vv. 24b-25). The two participles, providing the cause for the main verbs, depict the reality of God's standing and doing. The two indicative verbs, with negative markers, characterise God's nature 'in a negative way'[91] and firmly define inappropriate knowledge and worship towards God.

οὗτος   οὐρανοῦ καὶ γῆς ὑπάρχων κύριος
         οὐκ ἐν χειροποιήτοις ναοῖς **κατοικεῖ**

         οὐδὲ ὑπὸ χειρῶν ἀνθρωπίνων **θεραπεύεται** προσδεόμενός τινος
αὐτὸς   διδοὺς πᾶσι ζωὴν καὶ πνοὴν καὶ τὰ πάντα

As the Creator of the universe God is the *Lord* of heaven and earth. The phrase οὐρανοῦ καὶ γῆς indicates the totality of the creation, surely, including humankind.[92] God the Lord of the universe, thus, is not a part of the creation nor is he confined to the world spatial nor does he dwell in hand-made shrines at all (v. 24b). That God is absolutely apart from his creation demonstrates his *supreme* nature which makes him transcendent over the creation. Furthermore, as the Creator of the universe God is also the *Giver* of life, breath and all things as seen in his continual providential care for the creation (v. 25). The present tense of διδούς, in contrast to the aorist tense of ποιήσας in verse 24 and ἐποίησεν in verse 26 (cf. 14:15, 17), clearly elucidates God's continual care for the world he created.[93] Moreover, the adverbial participle προσδεόμενος (as if he needs or lacks something further or in addition)[94] indicates that God has no need of human service and assistance. Rather he always omnipotently provides for all the needs of his creation. God, thus, is an almighty sustainer of the creation and is utterly independent from it. The absolute independence of God from the creation characterises his *self-sufficient* nature.[95]

God's Relation to Humankind

The verb ἐποίησεν resumes the topic of God the Creator with a particular concern for the relationship between God and humankind (vv. 26-29).[96] God's relation to humankind is expounded in a parallel presentation of the relationships

---

[91] Gärtner, *ArVeopagus Speech*, 216, 218.
[92] Barrett, *Acts*, 2:840.
[93] Gärtner, *Areopagus Speech*, 175.
[94] L&N, §57.45; cf. BDAG, 876.
[95] Witherington, *Acts*, 519; Wilson, *Gentiles*, 199-200.
[96] Dibelius, *Acts*, 35; Marshall, *Acts*, 287; Haenchen, *Acts*, 523.

between God and humankind and Paul's claim for humankind's response to God.

> God's actions towards humankind (v. 26)
>   Paul's expectation of humankind's response (v. 27)
> Humankind's relation to God (v. 28)
>   Paul's assertion of humankind's response (v. 29)

Not only does God authoritatively create humankind but he sovereignly rules over human activities (v. 26). God's *sovereign* nature is first disclosed in his creation of humankind to dwell on earth (v. 26a). He creates every human nation (πᾶν ἔθνος) out of ἑνός,[97] which often refers to Adam (cf. Gen 1:27).[98] The following epexegetical infinitive κατοικεῖν clarifies πᾶν ἔθνος and specifies that humankind should dwell on all the earth as God's design (cf. Gen 1:28).[99] Furthermore, God's sovereignty is unveiled by his setting of fixed limits of time and space for humankind (v. 26b). He determines both fixed times and fixed boundaries for humankind's inhabitation.[100] The circumstantial use of

---

[97] The meaning of the phrase πᾶν ἔθνος is in debate: *every nation* (Bruce, *Acts*, 3rd edn., 383) or *the whole race* (Dibelius, *Acts*, 36; Haenchen, *Acts*, 523). Either is possible and communicates the same gist since 'from the one human being came all other human beings whatever their race or national group' (Witherington, *Acts*, 528). Examination of the singular use of ἔθνος in Acts reveals it often refers to *nation* especially occurring with πᾶν (2:5; 10:35). In the light of this usage, the rendering of *every nation* may be a better view.

[98] H.P. Owen, 'The Scope of Natural Revelation in Rom. I and Acts XVII,' *NTS* 5 (1958-59) 133-43, citing 135 n. 3; Barrett, *Acts*, 2:842; Marshall, *Acts*, 287; Witherington, *Acts*, 526; Pesch, *Apg*, 2:137; Balch, 'Areopagus Speech,' 57; Gärtner, *Areopagus Speech*, 229; Wilson, *Gentiles*, 200-1. Gärtner further argues that Jesus is the counterpart to Adam (v. 31) since he is the starting-point of the new humanity (*Areopagus Speech*, 231-32); see also Bruce, *Acts*, 3rd edn., 382-83.

[99] Haenchen, *Acts*, 523. For the epexegetical use of the infinitive see Barrett, *Acts*, 2:842.

[100] The participle προστεταγμένους modifies καιρούς and conveys the meaning of *fixed times* (BDAG, 885). Ὁροθεσίας bears the idea of *fixed boundaries* (BDAG, 724; L&N, §80.5), cf. Johnson, *Acts*, 315. To be more specific, καιρούς may be understood as the seasons of the year or the set epochs of human history; so is ὁροθεσίας referred to either the inhabitable zones of the earth or national boundaries. Marshall prefers the former view since they imply God's providential care for humankind (*Acts*, 288; cf. Haenchen, *Acts*, 523; Dibelius, *Acts*, 33-34; Balch, 'Areopagus Speech,' 54-58). Nonetheless, considering Paul's concern here is God's direct and specific relation to humankind other than the indirect relation through the creation, the latter view may be preferred (cf. Witherington, *Acts*, 527; Porter, *Paul*, 122; Wilson, *Gentiles*, 204-5).

the participle ὁρίσας,[101] which implies God's authority and probably reflects a divine plan behind God's actions,[102] elucidates that 'the determination of man's home *preceded* his creation.'[103] The second epexegetical infinitive (ζητεῖν) spells out God's further design for humankind in the light of his sovereign determination;[104] this is that they may seek God (v. 27a). The divine confinement is designed to make humankind sense their finiteness and drive them to *try to grope for the infinite God.*[105]

As God's sovereign design for humankind is introduced 'the crucial point remains the relation of man to God and his religious potentialities.'[106] Such a possibility of searching for God is made clear in Paul's expectation of humankind's response to God (v. 27b-c). The fourth conditional clause with two optatives, which communicate a subjective possibility,[107] expressing actions in a remote possibility,[108] exposes Paul's personal expectation. The particle ἄρα,

---

[101] Brooks and Winbery give the circumstantial participle a broad definition which indicates an action accompanying the action of the main verb (*Syntax*, 137) whereas Wallace defines it in a strict way. Even though ὁρίσας does not meet one of the five features Wallace suggests for the use of attendant circumstance (i.e. the participle precedes the main verb), the ingressive force of ὁρίσας (introducing a new action) may serve as a key for identifying this usage (*Beyond*, 642).

[102] Soards, *Speeches*, 97. While ὁρίζω is used with reference to God in Acts (2:23; 10:42; 17:31; cf. Lk 22:22) it always signifies an underlying divine plan, especially in the particular assigned task for Jesus. Here the divine determination, though not related to Jesus, may indicate a divine purpose as well.

[103] James Hope Moulton, *A Grammar of New Testament Greek, vol. 1: Prolegomena* (Edinburgh: T & T Clark, 1930) 133; cf. Bruce, *Acts*, 3rd edn., 383; Barrett, *Acts*, 2:842; Newman and Nida, *Translator's Handbook*, 341.

[104] Schubert takes ζητεῖν as a telic infinitive dependent on ὁρίσας ('Areopagus Speech,' 249; Balch, 'Areopagus Speech,' 57). Some scholars take the two infinitives (κατοικεῖν, ζητεῖν) in the sense of purpose and as subordinate to the main verb ἐποίησεν (Newman and Nida, *Translator's Handbook*, 341; Polhill, *Acts*, 374; cf. Barrett, *Acts*, 2:841-42). These two infinitives, however, specify God's intention for humankind (πᾶν ἔθνος ἀνθρώπων) rather than the action ἐποίησεν itself. The epexegetical use (clarifying, explaining or qualifying a noun), thus, provides a better syntactical understanding for ζητεῖν (Wallace, *Beyond*, 607; Bruce, *Acts*, 3rd edn., 383; Dibelius, *Acts*, 35; cf. Haenchen, *Acts*, 523-24).

[105] The verb ζητέω carries the idea of trying to find something, cf. BDAG, 428. It is noticed that the searching for God is a thought existing in Stoic philosophy. Yet it is in an impersonal and intellectual sense since the Stoic philosophers believe in the divine principle (God) pervading all nature. Humankind are kin to it and can grasp it through cultivating reason. See Marshall, *Acts*, 288; Polhill, *Acts*, 375; Witherington, *Acts*, 529; Gärtner, *Areopagus Speech*, 177-78.

[106] Conzelmann, 'Areopagus,' 225.

[107] Brooks and Winbery, *Syntax*, 113.

[108] Wallace, *Beyond*, 484.

conveying a degree of uncertainty,[109] clearly indicates the remoteness of any possibility that humankind might feel around for God and find him.[110] Paul's expectation is based on his belief that God is not far from each one of us. What Paul asserts is that a knowledge of the true God is possible, though not highly probable, and this one God is close to humankind although they do not know him.[111] In short, the creating of humankind to dwell on earth declares God's authority over his creature; the divine determination of historical epochs and national boundaries of humankind highlights God's sovereign rule over human history; the possibility of finding God signifies a divine plan behind the confined human lives.[112]

God's relation to humankind is further unveiled in humankind's dependence on him (v. 28). That human existence utterly depends on God is implied earlier in verses 25-26. The phrase ἐν αὐτῷ points out that God is the very cause that humankind live (compare ζῶμεν with διδοὺς ζωήν in v. 25b), move (cf. v. 26b) and exist (cf. v. 26a). The dominant meaning in the triad is that 'man depends absolutely on God for life and existence.'[113] From the human point of view (note the first person plural of the verbs) Paul argues particularly for God the Creator in relation to humankind and finds his support from the Greek poets who depict humankind as the offspring of God.[114] The poets' depiction also testifies Paul's preceding assertion of the possibility of finding God and the nearness of God. Although γένος is originally understood pantheistically in the poets' use,[115] Paul applies it to the one true God he introduces.[116] Being the procreator of human existence, God should be perceived as a personal God[117] *self-existent* and *self-dependent* from his creature. As the begetter-offspring relationship between God and humankind is affirmed, Paul decisively de-

---

[109] BDAG, 127; L&N, §71.19.
[110] Conrad Gempf, 'Athens, Paul at' in Gerald F. Hawthorne and Ralph P. Martin (eds.), *Dictionary of Paul and His Letters* (Leicester: InterVarsity Press, 1993) 51-54, citing 52.
[111] Conzelmann, 'Areopagus,' 221, 228.
[112] Porter, *Paul*, 122.
[113] Gärtner, *Areopagus Speech*, 193. Gärtner further points out that the dependence of the creation on God is also expressed by one triad in verse 25 (198).
[114] The Greek poets are identified as the Stoic poet Aratus (*Phainomena* 5) as well as Cleanthes (*Hymn to Zeus* 4); see Colin J. Hemer, 'The Speeches of Acts II. The Areopagus Address,' *TynB* 40 (1989) 239-59, citing 243; Owen, 'Natural Revelation,' 136; Haenchen, *Acts*, 525; Barrett, *Acts*, 2:848; Marshall, *Acts*, 289; Bruce, *Acts*, 3rd edn., 385; Polhill, *Acts*, 376; Winter, 'Gods,' 85 n. 52; Porter, *Paul*, 121.
[115] Owen, 'Natural Revelation,' 136-37; Barrett, *Acts*, 2:848; Polhill, *Acts*, 376.
[116] Wilson, *Gentiles*, 208.
[117] Barrett, *Acts*, 2:850.

nounces idolatry (v. 29).[118] If divinity is the cause of humanity, the nature of divine being (τὸ θεῖον) should not be materialised (i.e. less than humans) by being made in any worldly shape or substance. Polhill rightly points out that '[o]nly the creature can express the true worship of the Creator, not the creation of the creature, not something made by human design and skill.'[119] God the Creator, thus, is alone worthy of human worship without any image as the unknown god.[120]

While God's relation to the creation tells of his supreme and self-sufficient nature, God's relation to humankind speaks of his sovereign and self-existent nature. Along with Paul's affirmation of the true nature of God lies a tincture of the refutation of idolatry. The negative expressions of God's nature (vv. 24b, 25a, 29), which carry an implication of what should not have been done, convey 'a correction consonant with the true knowledge of God.'[121] Paul's denunciation of idolatry may allude to a refutation of the audience's idolatry (cf. v. 16). By an inclusive tone, the use of the first person plural (cf. ἡμῶν in v. 27b and the person of the main verbs in vv. 28-29), Paul condemns the audience's idolatry. This implicit condemnation makes way for the zenith of Paul's proclamation, that is, God's plan in Jesus and the necessity of humankind's repentance.

EXPLICATION OF THE PLAN OF GOD IN JESUS (17:30-31)

Paul's final word converges on God's relation to humankind at the present stage (vv. 30-31). That God is the subject of the main verbs and participial clauses again signifies Paul's high regard for God's authoritative plan towards humankind. With respect to idolatry, the one true God, being first introduced as the Creator, is now the Judge. Although patiently enduring idolatry in the past epochs of humankind's ignorance, nowadays God commands that all, everywhere, should repent (v. 30).[122] The paronomasia of πάντας and πανταχοῦ emphasises the totality of humankind which highlights the universal character of God's design of judgement.[123] As noted, the call to repentance is an implicit recognition of the audience's guilt and an unknown god among their other gods is the evidence of their ignorance (v. 23).[124]

---

[118] Note ὀφείλομεν in the obligatory sense with the negative marker οὐκ carries a heavy tone of expressing a prohibition (i.e. *must not, ought not*).

[119] Polhill, *Acts*, 376.

[120] Kennedy, *Rhetorical Criticism*, 130.

[121] Zweck, 'Exordium,' 100; cf. Wilson, *Gentiles*, 208.

[122] Note the substantival use of μετανοεῖν as indirect discourse with πάντας functioning as its subject. Note the imperative sense of μετανοεῖν as well (cf. Wallace, *Beyond*, 603-4).

[123] Soards, *Speeches*, 99.

[124] Soards, *Speeches*, 97, 99; cf. Horst, 'Unknown God,' 218-19.

The reason for the necessity of repentance is in view of the fact (note καθότι indicating the reason based on an evident fact)[125] that God sets a day on which he is going to judge all humankind in righteousness (v. 31). The preposition ἐν indicates the means by which God judges, that is, by an appointed man. The verb ὁρίζω, which is closely associated with the plan of God,[126] accentuates God's authority.[127] The divine appointment is shown in the proof that God raises up this man from death. The resurrection serves as an assurance of the coming judgement of God. Although Jesus is not specified, the audience must not be unfamiliar with his name and resurrection since these are the core dispute between them and Paul (v. 18). Rather, the absence of Jesus' name may signify that 'the speaker is more interested in the theme of judgement than in the details of the process.'[128] Paul's main point is that God, the ultimate Judge, determines both the day and the agent of judgement (cf. 10:42).[129] In view of God's inevitable judgement, with the resurrection 'as proof of the divine appointment of Jesus as judge,'[130] repentance (the turning from idolatry to the true God) is urged and pressed for.[131]

To conclude, Paul, with great emotional concern,[132] is so provoked by idolatry in Athens that within him grows a strong desire to convert the Athenians (v. 16).[133] Idolatry, the worship of gods or images, is an issue regarding what constitutes a god.[134] In refuting idolatry, Paul highlights the superlative authority of the one true God and his true nature. The former excludes other gods; the latter rejects any image of God. As the true knowledge of God is affirmed, the twofold characterisation of idolatry is proved to be ignorant. Facing a purely Gentile audience, Paul attests the absolute authority of the true God by building his argument on the creation which can be easily understood by them (cf. Acts

---

[125] L&N, §89.33.
[126] Schubert, 'Areopagus Speech,' 260; Squires, *Plan*, 2 n. 9.
[127] Soards, *Speeches*, 99.
[128] Barrett, *Acts*, 2:853.
[129] Barrett, *Acts*, 2:852.
[130] Marshall, *Acts*, 290.
[131] Wilson, *Gentiles*, 210. Yet in the light of the fact that only a few respond to Paul, Sandnes argues that Paul's aim is to promote curiosity and create an interest in further information rather than call for repentance. See Karl Olav Sandnes, 'Paul and Socrates: The Aim of Paul's Areopagus Speech,' *JSNT* 50 (1993) 13-26. Sandnes, however, considering the rhetorical strategy and Socrates traditions, fails to take Paul's personal concern into consideration (v.16).
[132] Note the word παροξύνομαι implies severe emotional concern (L&N, §88.189).
[133] BDAG, 780.
[134] B.S. Rosner, 'Idolatry' in T. Desmond Alexander and Brian S. Rosner (eds.), *New Dictionary of Biblical Theology* (Leicester: Inter-Varsity Press, 2003) 569-75, citing 571, 575.

14).[135] Foremost, God's identity as the Creator of the universe contends his superlative authority above all. This transcendent God's relation to the creation and humankind reveal his true nature. In relation to the creation in general, God as the Lord of the world and the giver of all manifests that he is a personal being supreme and self-sufficient. As for humankind, God as their ruler and begetter exposes his sovereignty and self-existence. These divine features not only affirm God's superlative authority but point out the inappropriateness of regarding God as, or even less than, a human being as if he needs a hand-made home and human service and exists in a material form (vv. 24, 25, 29). Committing idolatry, thus, is devaluing the nature and authority of God by bringing God under human control. Consequently, for the idolaters, repentance is required which is Paul's final word drawn from the affirmation of God's true nature and the refutation of idolatry. Repentance is inescapable since God's unparalleled authority will be ultimately and climactically revealed in his coming judgement through the resurrected Jesus. What perplexes the audience is the resurrection (vv. 18, 32) which is foreign to them.[136] Yet Jesus' resurrection powerfully attests to God's superlative authority both in giving life to all, even to the dead (v. 25), and in judging the whole world (v. 31). To be brief, in the Areopagus speech God is characterised as the supreme Creator, being transcendent over the creation and humankind, with superlative authority over the universe and for its existence particularly in human history from the beginning to the end. In light of God as the creator of the universe, throughout the speech the connotation of the refutation of idolatry carries a universal implication, and repentance is required of all accordingly.[137] This further indicates that, in addition to his creating and ruling power, God is a God of justice who holds judging power.

The Speech to the Ephesian Elders (20:18-35)

Leaving his tough yet powerful ministry in Ephesus, after the uproar, Paul travels in Macedonia and Greece (20:1-2). On his way back to Jerusalem Paul summons the Ephesian elders at Miletus (20:17). There he delivers a farewell testimony and admonition (20:18-35). The whole speech centres on Paul's personal witness to the divine ministry done by him from which appears a profound picture of God. Instead of analysing the speech seriatim, which would leave the spotlight on Paul, this study will investigate the portrayal of God in

---

[135] Martin-Asensio, *Foregrounding*, 117.

[136] Bruce, *Acts*, 3rd edn., 387; Polhill, *Acts*, 378; N. Clayton Croy, 'Hellenistic Philosophies and the Preaching of the Resurrection (Acts 17:18, 32),' *NovT* 39 (1997) 21-39, esp. 29-37; Joel Marcus, 'Paul at the Areopagus: Window on the Hellenistic World,' *BTB* 18 (1988) 143-48, esp. 148.

[137] Gärtner, *Areopagus Speech*, 229-33; cf. Schubert, 'Areopagus Speech,' 261.

Paul's testimony thematically, particularly concentrating on Paul's notion of the interrelationship within the divine characters and Paul's reactions to the divine characters. Before a thorough investigation of the picture of God, an outline of the speech will first be given to show the flow of thought and Paul's main concern.[138]

20:18-21 Paul states his past ministry

> Paul's perseverance in ministry (vv. 18-19)
> Paul's faithfulness in preaching (vv. 20-21)

20:22-24 Paul testifies to the divine will for his future

> Paul's impending bondage testified by himself and the Holy Spirit (vv. 22-23)
> Paul's response to the divine will (v. 24)

20:25-31 Paul expresses his present concern for the Ephesian church[139]

> Paul has done his incumbency in the church (vv. 25-27)
> The elders should watch over God's church now (vv. 28-31)
> — *for the Holy Spirit appointed them to shepherd the church (v. 28)*
> — *for apostates will arise in the church (vv. 29-30)*
> — *for Paul has set for them an example of watching over the church (v. 31)*

---

[138] The phrase καὶ (τὰ) νῦν in verses 22, 25, 32 introduces new themes which regard Paul's coming bondage and his concern for the church and elders. See Murray J. Harris, *Jesus as God: The New Testament Use of Theos in Reference to Jesus* (Grand Rapids: Baker Book House, 1992) 133; Haenchen, *Acts*, 595; Duane F. Watson, 'Paul's Speech to the Ephesian Elders (Acts 20.17-38): Epideictic Rhetoric of Farewell' in Duane F. Watson (ed.), *Persuasive Artistry* (JSNTSup 50; Sheffield: JSOT Press, 1991) 184-208, citing 208.

[139] The second person plural may refer to either the Ephesian church (including the elders) or simply the elders. That ὑμεῖς in verse 25 is specified by πάντες, a word for totality, and the relative clause ἐν οἷς διῆλθον κηρύσσων τὴν βασιλείαν, the object of Paul's proclamation, makes clear that ὑμεῖς refers to the church in verses 25-27. Yet in verses 28-31, there is a distinction drawn between the two groups: ὑμᾶς and ποιμνίῳ (a figurative use for the church, v. 28). The word ἐπισκόπους, serving as the apposition of ὑμᾶς, identifies *you* as the elders. It is reinforced by the use of the reflexive and intensive pronouns (v. 28, ἑαυτοῖς; v. 30, αὐτῶν) which carry the demonstrative force (cf. Wallace, *Beyond*, 349-50). Paul's main concern is the coming apostasy within the church which he exhorts the elders to safeguard against. Although the two imperatives (προσέχετε, γρηγορεῖτε in vv. 28, 31) introduce the elders' duty towards the church, Paul's concern is still for the welfare of the church.

20:32-35 Paul gives his final word to the elders[140]
>Paul entrusts the elders to God and his Word (v. 32)
>Paul himself is a living example for the elders (vv. 33-35)

The outline reveals that, perceiving his impending bondage, Paul is very concerned for the Ephesian church while foreseeing its coming peril. He thus urges the elders to faithfully keep up the divine ministry in the church as he did. The first two paragraphs relate to Paul's personal affairs (20:18-24) behind which one can glimpse a close-up of Jesus' relationship with the individual believer. The third paragraph delineates Paul's concern for the church (20:25-31) from which a panoramic view of God's relationship with his people emerges. The last paragraph regards Paul's exhortation of the elders (20:32-35) in which both relationships are enforced. Although different concerns lead to different emphases in Paul's witness, each embraces a portrayal of the interrelationship within the divine characters. Moreover, throughout the speech Paul's faithfulness to the divine commission acknowledges the divine authority over himself and the church.

THE INTERRELATIONSHIP WITHIN THE DIVINE CHARACTERS

As Paul testifies to his ministry in the Ephesian church he points out that the Lord Jesus is the one whom he serves (v. 19) and from whom he receives the ministry (v. 24). The ministry is further defined by the appositional infinitive phrase, διαμαρτύρασθαι τὸ εὐαγγέλιον τῆς χάριτος τοῦ θεοῦ (v. 24b). This reveals that the core of Paul's ministry is to solemnly declare the gospel of God's grace, as Paul indicates earlier in verse 21, in which the content of the gospel is specified, τὴν εἰς θεὸν μετάνοιαν καὶ πίστιν εἰς τὸν κύριον ἡμῶν Ἰησοῦν. 'The two elements in conversion, repentance and faith, are introduced by one article, which has the effect of binding them closely together.'[141] The gist of the gospel is that by faith in Jesus people are able to return to God. This reveals God as gracious to all. The attributive genitive of χάριτος[142] and the

---

[140] The *you* continues its identity in the preceding verse that is supported by an indication of two groups (ὑμᾶς and τοῖς ἡγιασμένοις πᾶσιν, the church) in verse 32 and the intensive pronoun αὐτοί in verse 34. Here Paul's concern turns to the elders themselves.

[141] Barrett, *Acts*, 2:969.

[142] Barrett takes τῆς χάριτος as a genitive of content (*Acts*, 2:972) which signifies the gospel containing God's grace. It may also be taken as an attributive genitive which specifies the innate quality of the gospel, namely, God's gracious gospel. Either use is possible and gives weight to χάριτος (cf. Wallace, *Beyond*, 87, 93). Nonetheless, the former highlights grace itself while the latter underlines the gracious attribute of the gospel. For the former grace is in view; for the latter the gospel. With the use of the similar phrase τῆς χάριτος αὐοῦ, in verse 32, the latter view may be preferred since there τῷ λόγῳ rather than χάριτος is accentuated.

meaning of τῆς χάριτος τοῦ θεοῦ (the unmerited favour of God)[143] also suggest this (v. 24b). Although Jesus is the author and object of Paul's evangelism, getting people back to God is the ultimate aim of Paul's ministry.

With regard to his relation to the church Paul, from a panoramic angle, redefines the kernel of his proclamation, κηρύσσων τὴν βασιλείαν (v. 25)[144] and ἀναγγεῖλαι πᾶσαν τὴν βουλὴν τοῦ θεοῦ (v. 27). The gospel of God's grace relates to the kingdom and the plan of God,[145] behind which lie the divine reign and purpose.[146] The divine kingdom and plan bear upon the church of God (v. 28).[147] Paul further explains that God saves his church,[148] a collective term for those who believe in Jesus (cf. v. 21),[149] by the blood of his Own,[150] that is,

---

[143] Barrett, *Acts*, 2:972; cf. Marshall, *Acts*, 335.

[144] Barrett indicates that it is useless to try to distinguish the proclamations in verses 21, 24, 25 since they are the recognised formulae. See Charles K. Barrett, 'Paul's Address to the Ephesian Elders' in Jacob Jervell and Wayne A. Meeks (eds.), *God's Christ and His People* (Oslo-Bergen-Tromsö: Universitetsforlaget, 1977) 107-21, citing 113. Watson even points out *preaching the kingdom* as a synonymous expression for *testifying to the gospel* ('Farewell,' 200).

[145] The four verbs in the same semantic domain (vv. 21, 24, 25, 27), conveying the idea 'to inform and announce' (ἀναγγέλλω, διαμαρτύρομαι, κηρύσσω; see L&N, §33. 197, 223, 256), introduce the content of Paul's message from different perspectives which are related to each other.

[146] Steve Walton, *Leadership and Lifestyle* (Cambridge: Cambridge University Press, 2000) 80.

[147] The textual variation of τὴν ἐκκλησίαν τοῦ κυρίου, a phrase which appears nowhere else in the NT, is probably intended to remove the difficulty of the following phrase τοῦ αἵματος τοῦ ἰδίου. See Johnson, *Acts*, 363; Bruce, *Acts*, 3rd edn., 434; Marshall, *Acts*, 334 n. 1; Barrett, *Acts*, 2:976; Witherington, *Acts*, 623; Newman and Nida, *Translator's Handbook*, 394; Metzger, *Textual Commentary*, 481; Harris, *Jesus as God*, 135-36; Walton, *Leadership*, 94-98.

[148] The word περιεποιήσατο occurs only three times in the NT (Lk 17:33; Acts 20:28; 1 Tim 3:13). Its fundamental meaning is *acquire* while comparing its use in Luke 17:33, whoever seeks to save his life shall lose it, the idea of *saving* may be in view (Barrett, *Acts*, 2:976; Newman and Nida, *Translator's Handbook*, 395).

[149] Here the church of God carries a catholic sense (Barrett, 'Address,' 114). K.N. Giles not only understands ἐκκλησία as a communal church but further argues it to be Pauline thought rather than Lukan theology ('Luke's Use of the term Ἐκκλησία with special reference to Acts 20.28 and 9.31,' *NTS* 31 [1985] 135-42, esp. 136-37).

[150] Marshall, *Acts*, 334; Witherington, *Acts*, 623. It is further suggested that ὁ ἴδιος is an equivalent of ἀγαπητός and μονογενής (Bruce, *Acts*, 3rd edn., 434; Barrett, *Acts*, 2:977; Schneider, *Apg*, 2:297 n. 47; Johnson, *Acts*, 363; Metzger, *Textual Commentary*, 481-82; Newman and Nida, *Translator's Handbook*, 394-95; Harris, *Jesus as God*, 137-41). See also Walton, *Leadership*, 96-98; Beverly Roberts Gaventa, 'Theology and Ecclesiology in the Miletus Speech: Reflections on Content and Context,' *NTS* 50 (2004) 36-52, citing 48; Jervell, *Apg*, 512.

Jesus (v. 28b). This explanation makes visible the divinely gracious attribute of the gospel (cf. v. 24). In brief, God's grace initiates the gospel of Jesus by whom the way back to God is made possible and in whom those who believe become the people of God, the church, which is a part of God's plan and kingdom.

From the microscopic view of the church, Jesus is the Lord of the individual believer because he is the way back to God; from the macroscopic view of the church, God is the ultimate owner[151] of the collective believer since he saves the church in accordance with his own plan. God's ownership and Jesus' lordship is enforced as Paul entrusts the elders to the care of God and his gracious Word (v. 32). In the light of the phrasing (τῆς χάριτος τοῦ θεοῦ) in verse 24, the Word signifies the gospel (cf. 14:3)[152] with Jesus its subject.[153] The gospel of Jesus is the foundation for those who have been sanctified (v. 32b), another expression for the believers,[154] to receive the divine inheritance (κληρονομία), the transcendent salvation.[155] Again, the Word as the intermediate agent of the divine blessing for the believer projects Jesus' close relationship with the individual believer. God as the ultimate agent of τοῖς ἡγιασμένοις reflects his essential relation to the collective believer. Both God and Jesus work side by side to accomplish God's saving plan in the church. Alongside what God and Jesus have done for the church, the Holy Spirit reveals the divine will to the individual believer (v. 23) as well as appoints the leaders to shepherd the church (v. 28a). The Spirit, thus, continues the divine work of God and Jesus and leads the church on to the completion of God's plan.

PAUL'S REACTIONS TO THE DIVINE CHARACTERS

While Paul's proclamation of the divine message reveals a profound picture of the interrelationship within the divine characters, his reactions to the divine commission, through the profession and actions, confess the absolute divine authority over himself and the church. The profession of the divine authority is first articulated with Paul's use of the title κύριος for Jesus (vv. 19, 21, 24). The recognition of the divine authority also inheres in 'the qualification of the gospel in terms of τῆς χάριτος τοῦ θεοῦ' (vv. 24, 32)[156] and in reference to τὴν βουλὴν τοῦ θεοῦ (v. 27) and, more strikingly, in God's ownership over the church indicated in the phrase τὴν ἐκκλησίαν τοῦ θεοῦ (v. 28). Again, the Spirit's appointing of the elders signifies 'divine initiative and authority in se-

---

[151] Note the function of the possessive genitive of θεοῦ.
[152] Barrett, *Acts*, 2:980; Marshall, *Acts*, 335.
[153] Bruce, *Acts*, 3rd edn., 432.
[154] Polhill, *Acts*, 429; Witherington, *Acts*, 625.
[155] BDAG, 548.
[156] Soards, *Speeches*, 107.

lection of church leadership' (v. 28a).[157] Furthermore, the divine authority is attested to in Paul's whole life as he faithfully proclaims the gospel (vv. 18-27) and perseveringly shepherds the church (vv. 28-35). Paul's handing over of the elders to God and the Word asserts the divine caring power for the elders and the church as well as the divine authority over them (v. 32). Prominently, Paul's testifying of the divine authority is seen in his utterly submitting himself to the Spirit's testifying of his bondage (v. 24).

To sum up, in his personal testimony Paul functions as a narrator delineating his faithfulness to the divine commission which relates to God's saving plan to the church through Jesus under the Spirit's guidance. In Paul's speech, the divine interrelationship can be portrayed in three pictures. First, Jesus is the author of the commission of Paul, the messenger (v. 24), as well as the subject of Paul's message (v. 21). Second, God is the author of salvation (i.e. by grace God initiates the gospel through Jesus and builds up his church, v. 28b) and the hope of the church (i.e. again by grace God cares for his people and provides them with the inheritance, v. 32). Third, the Spirit walks alongside Jesus' messenger and God's church to guide them in line with the divine will and plan (vv. 23, 28a). In responding to the divine commission and plan, Paul testifies to the absolute divine authority over himself and the church which is shown in his faithful proclamation of the gospel, caring for the church and obeying the divine guidance. Fundamentally speaking, it is God who makes known his redemptive plan in Jesus and who will consummate the plan through the partnership of the Spirit. A messenger, who is commissioned by Jesus to proclaim the gospel and to build up the church, is under the guidance of the Spirit and the care of God and Jesus. From Paul's personal testimony the implied readers perceive God as an authoritative figure, who makes his will known through Jesus and the Spirit and sets forth a gracious plan of redemption for his people.

The Trial Speeches

Arrested in Jerusalem (21:27-30), Paul faces several trials in which he gives three major defence speeches (cf. ἀπολογία in 22:1; ἀπολογέομαι in 24:10; 26:2): the speeches to the Jerusalem Jews (22:3-21), before Felix (24:10-21) and before Agrippa (26:2-23).[158] Since the risen Jesus is the core of the dispute between the Jews and Paul, in defending himself, Paul insists that his witness

---

[157] Soards, *Speeches*, 107.
[158] Some scholars categorise Paul's speech to the Roman Jewish leaders as a defence speech (28:17-20). See Porter, *Paul*, 151; Schneider, *Apg*, 1:96, 102. For the above defence speeches, Paul is on trial and in need of permission to defend for himself (21:40; 24:10a; 26:1). For the speech in Rome, though still in prison, Paul takes the initiative of the defence which serves as an opportunity for reaching out to people. The official defence speeches convey Paul's notion of God as the justification for his christocentric ministry; the personal vindication mainly regards the reason of Paul's

to Jesus signifies himself faithfully serving the God of the Jewish forefathers. God as a God of the continuity between the old revelation to the Jews and the new revelation in Jesus, thus, is the common theme in these speeches. Moreover, as the settings of trials vary, the God of the continuity is presented with different emphases in the speeches from which emerge distinct portraits of God. To expose the distinct portrayal of God, especially in Acts 22 and 26, Paul's 'autobiographical' discourses will be compared with the narrator's account (Acts 9). The narrator's chronological narrative represents a third-person, omniscient and objective point of view; Paul's retrospective accounts present a first-person, personal and subjective point of view.[159] The variations in-between and the unique accounts of Paul disclose and highlight Paul's personal understanding of Christophany which leads to his new perspective of God's will and new way of serving God.

THE SPEECH TO THE JERUSALEM JEWS (22:3-21)

The accusation of Paul by the Jews in Jerusalem is twofold: Paul teaches people everywhere against God's people, the law and the holy place (21:28a); Paul brings the Gentiles into the Temple to defile the place (21:28b). Instead of thoroughly exculpating himself from the accusation, Paul elucidates the very cause which draws him away from the stance of the Jews who accuse him. The comparative clause, ζηλωτὴς ὑπάρχων τοῦ θεοῦ καθὼς πάντες ὑμεῖς ἐστε σήμερον (v. 3), unique in the three accounts of Paul's conversion, pinpoints Paul's former zeal for God and former stance as being that of the present Jews (v. 4, see Paul's persecution of τὴν ὁδόν, connoting *Christianity*).[160] Yet the pivot of Paul's conversion is Jesus' appearance to him (22:6-11), the significance of which is specified by Ananias' announcement of God's will (22:14-16). Furthermore, God's will is enforced and furthered by Jesus' commission of Paul in a vision (22:17-21). Paul's encounter with Jesus turns him to a new perception of Jesus as God's new revelation and leads him to a new milestone of serving God, that is, the turning from the persecutor of Jesus' followers to the persecuted witness of Jesus.

---

bondage. Thus the speech in Acts 28 will not be discussed here but in the next section since it is part of Paul's interactions with the Jews.

[159] For the different points of view in the repeated accounts see Sternberg, *Biblical Narrative*, 380-82; Kurz, *Luke-Acts*, 26-27; Daniel Marguerat, 'Saul's Conversion (Acts 9, 22, 26) and the Multiplication of Narrative in Acts' in C.M. Tuckett (ed.), *Luke's Literary Achievement* (JSNTSup 116; Sheffield: Sheffield Academic Press, 1995) 127-55, esp. 136-37; Ronald D. Witherup, 'Functional Redundancy in the Acts of the Apostles: A Case Study,' *JSNT* 48 (1992) 67-86, esp. 73; Marie-Eloise Rosenblatt, 'Recurrent Narration as a Lukan Literary Convention in Acts: Paul's Jerusalem Speech in Acts 22:1-21' in Richard (ed.), *New Views on Luke and Acts*, 94-105, esp. 101-2.

[160] Barrett, *Acts*, 2:1104; Marshall, *Acts*, 168.

To convince his Jewish audience of Jesus as God's new revelation Paul, on the one hand, indicates his faithfulness to the Jewish belief and tradition and,[161] on the other hand, underlines the divine origin of Jesus' revelation and identifies the God of that revelation in Jesus with the God of the Jews. Paul's personal faithfulness to the Jewish religion is highlighted by two distinct indications. First, the foundation of Paul's training is based on *the strictness of the ancestral Law* (v. 3). Compared with *the strict sect of our religion*, in 26:5, the ancestral Law is particularly brought out to stress Paul's adherence to the Jewish belief. Second, while returning to Jerusalem, Paul prays in the Temple which emphasises his devotion to the Jewish tradition (v. 17).[162] Paul's devotion to the Jewish belief and tradition explicitly shows his dedication to the Jewish religion and may implicitly defend the Jews' accusation against him (21:28).

Throughout the speech the divine origin of Jesus' revelation is implied in various ways. At Paul's first encounter with Jesus, the phrase ἐκ τοῦ οὐρανοῦ... φῶς ἱκανόν indicates the heavenly cause of this pivotal experience (v. 6). While comparing it with 9:3, ἱκανόν (a term indicating 'a relatively high point on a scale of extent')[163] is added to amplify Paul's divine encounter. It is reinforced by the indications of Paul's companions as *eyewitnesses* of the heavenly light (v. 9) and the cause of his physical blindness (v. 11, τῆς δόξης τοῦ φωτὸς ἐκείνου) which are absent in Acts 9 and 26. Although δόξα signifies the brightness of the light in physical phenomenon,[164] the divine glory may also be connoted since the source of the light is from above.[165] Paul's second encounter with Jesus in a vision is also a unique account (vv. 17-21). Not only does the vision in the Temple (ἔκστασις, frequently associated with divine action, v. 17)[166] signify the divine origin but makes Paul resemble a prophet who receives a divine commission.[167] Foremost, the divine origin of Jesus' revelation is explicated by Ananias who spells out that Paul's encounter with Jesus is God's will (vv. 14-15). God is first characterised as ὁ θεὸς τῶν πατέρων ἡμῶν (v. 14a). The phrase reveals a God of continuity, that is, the God who appoints Paul's divine encounter with Jesus is exactly the same God

---

[161] Marguerat, 'Conversion,' 147; William R. Long, 'The Paulusbild in the Trial of Paul in Acts,' *SBLSP* 22 (1983) 87-105, citing 104.

[162] Johnson, *Acts*, 390; Wilson, *Gentiles*, 165; Beverly Roberts Gaventa, *From Darkness to Light* (Philadelphia: Fortress Press, 1986) 75.

[163] L&N, §78.14.

[164] BDAG, 257.

[165] Johnson, considering the thematic associations between light and the *glory of God* throughout the Lukan writings, regards δόξα as *glory* which indicates 'God's effective presence in the world' (*Acts*, 389).

[166] BDAG, 309.

[167] Johnson indicates Paul as a prophet like Isaiah in the light of Isaiah 6:1-10 (*Acts*, 390).

of the Jewish forefathers. The new revelation regarding Jesus, thus, is certainly from the God whom Paul faithfully served in the past.

The gist of God's new revelation to Paul is unfolded first through Ananias then by Jesus. The emphasis on Ananias' Jewishness, a devout man according to the *Law* and testified to by other *Jews* (v. 12; cf. 9:10 simply indicating him as a disciple), enhances the credibility of his delivering of God's will.[168] Moreover, the fact that Paul regains his sight evinces a divine confirmation of Ananias' message (v. 12)[169] which relates to the purpose of Jesus' appearance to Paul (v. 10). As Ananias reveals, the Christophany signifies God's threefold appointment of Paul: to know God's will, to see the Righteous One (a messianic title for Jesus [cf. 3:14; 7:52])[170] and to hear his voice (v. 14b). The purpose of this divine appointment, namely God's will, is calling Paul to be Jesus' witness to all, both Jews and Gentiles, with regard to what Paul has seen and heard (v. 15); particularly, Paul is entrusted with the Gentile mission. In the visional interlocution between Jesus and Paul, Jesus reveals the reason for sending Paul to the Gentiles, that is, the Jews' rejection of Jesus (v. 18). Paul's opposition to Jesus discloses his zeal for being a witness to his own people (vv. 19-20);[171] nevertheless, Jesus commissions Paul to go to the Gentiles (v. 21). It is because of this divine, unequivocal command towards the Gentiles that Paul, 'a devout and law-abiding Jew,'[172] regards his Gentile mission as faithfully carrying out God's will.

At the subsequent trial before the Sanhedrin summoned by the commanding officer (22:30), Paul asserts that he lives his life with a clear conscience before God (23:1). What Paul insists is that his zeal for God has never changed; what has changed is his understanding of God's will as a new revelation in the risen Jesus. Paul's personal faithfulness to the Jewish religion enforces his loyalty to the Jewish God. The heavenly origin of Paul's encounters with Jesus reveals that God is delivering a new revelation to Paul through Jesus. Paul's loyalty to God remains the same so the carrying out God's will is, for him, thus to be Jesus' witness to the Gentiles. This unfolds the very cause of Paul's conversion, God's calling of the faithful Jew to Gentiles,[173] as well as the cause of the Jews' persecution of him (v. 22).

---

[168] Wilson, *Gentiles*, 163, 165; Gaventa, *Light*, 73.

[169] Marshall, *Acts*, 356. Dennis Hamm further asserts that Paul's blindness and regaining of sight, while serving as a metaphor for the spiritual counterparts, signify 'Paul's call/conversion as an acting out and fulfilment of Israel's covenant vocation to be a light to the nations' ('Paul's Blindness and Its Healing: Clues to Symbolic Intent [Acts 9, 22 and 26],' *Bib* 71 [1990] 63-72, citing 71).

[170] Barrett, *Acts*, 2:1041; Marshall, *Acts*, 356; Bruce, *Acts*, 3rd edn., 457; Haenchen, *Acts*, 626; Witherington, *Acts*, 672.

[171] Barrett, *Acts*, 2:1044.

[172] Haenchen, *Acts*, 631.

[173] Gaventa, *Light*, 76.

The narrative of Paul's conversion in Acts 9 is essentially christocentric yet it turns out to be theocentric in Acts 22.[174] In Acts 9 (from the authoritative viewpoint of the narrator) Jesus plays a completely active role whilst Paul is utterly passive.[175] In Acts 22 (told as if from Paul's subjective viewpoint), although Jesus is still in an active role, Paul stresses the divine origin of Jesus' appearance and perceives God's authority behind him (vv. 14-15). The twofold revelation of Jesus enhances the divine intervention and will.[176] Arguing from the divine viewpoint, Paul highlights the old God of the new revelation, that is, the new revelation in Jesus originates from the same God in whom the Jews believe.

THE SPEECH BEFORE FELIX (24:10-21)

The Jewish leaders' accusation against Paul before Felix is also twofold: Paul is a troublemaker, stirring up riots among the Jews, and a ringleader of the Nazarene sect (24:5); and Paul attempts to desecrate the Temple (24:6). Besides effectively refuting the twofold accusation, Paul confesses that he worships his ancestral God according to the Way called a sect by the Jews (v. 14a). Even so, Paul insists on his firm adherence to the Jewish belief (vv. 14b-15). The phrase τῷ πατρῴῳ θεῷ again signifies the God of such continuity. The God whom Paul worships is the old God whilst Paul serves him in the new Way (v. 14a, κατὰ τὴν ὁδόν).[177] Nonetheless, this new Way of worship is in conformity with Jewish belief since Paul believes what the Law and the Prophets have written (v. 14b) and has a hope in God for the resurrection of the dead (v. 15). Thus, although being excluded by the zealous Jews from the Jewish religion (note here the word αἵρεσις implying an unjustified group),[178] Paul still judges that his faith in Jesus takes root in Jewish ancestral belief.

Paul focuses his disputation with the Jews on the belief in resurrection (v. 15; cf. 23:6-8) which the Jews (Pharisees, not Sadducees) share. The belief in resurrection is fundamental to the core of Paul's faith in God. No reference to

---

[174] Marguerat, 'Conversion,' 148.

[175] The common theme of the incidents in Acts 8-11 is the divine initiative for the worldwide mission which further reveals the narrator's intention.

[176] Cf. Norman A. Beck, 'The Lukan Writer's Stories about the Call of Paul,' *SBLSP* 22 (1983) 213-18, esp. 216.

[177] Barrett, *Acts*, 2:1104.

[178] L&N, §11.50. It is stated that αἵρεσις conveys the meaning of 'a division or group based upon different doctrinal opinions and/or loyalties and hence by implication in certain contexts an unjustified party or group.' Thus the Christian proclamation is regarded as a heterodox movement within Judaism or even a new faith outside it. See Harry W. Tajra, *The Trial of St. Paul* (Tübingen: J.C.B. Mohr, 1989) 122; Arland J. Hultgren, 'Paul's Pre-Christian Persecutions of the Church: Their Purpose, Locale and Nature,' *JBL* 95 (1976) 97-111, citing 100.

Jesus' resurrection[179] leaves the focus simply on Paul's firm faith in the Jewish hope of resurrection. In clarifying his proclamation about a sect within the Jewish religion, Paul accentuates his tight connection with the Jewish hope of resurrection and thus claims his conscience to be blameless (v. 16) and justifies his faith in the risen Jesus (cf. v. 21). It is by this faith in Jesus that Paul serves his ancestral God in the new Way, which is a way or manner of worship conforming to the shared belief of the Jews.

To defend the otherness of his proclamation Paul, arguing from the Jewish point of view, attests his loyalty to God and the Jewish belief from which emerges a God of the old hope of resurrection.

THE SPEECH BEFORE AGRIPPA (26:2-23)

As Festus introduces Paul to Agrippa he admits that Paul, whom the Jews desperately want to kill (25:24), has done nothing deserving of death (25:25). Having no need to refute a specific accusation, Paul elucidates why the Jews intend to kill him. The speech first affirms that the Jews can bear witness to Paul's former way of life when he lived as a Pharisee according to the strictest sect in the Jewish religion (vv. 4-5). The rest of the speech gives the reason for Paul's change of stance which resulted in the Jews' persecution (vv. 6-23). See the following outline for Paul's main argument.

The cause of the Jews' accusation of Paul (26:6-8)
A hope of God's promise to the Jewish forefathers (v. 6)
A hope regarding the resurrection of the dead (vv. 7-8)

> Paul's persecution of Jesus' followers (26:9-12)
> *In Jerusalem (vv. 9-11a)*
> *In Gentile cities (vv. 11b-12)*

>> Paul's encounter with Jesus (26:13-18)
>> *Jesus' appearance (vv. 13-15)*
>> *Jesus' commission (vv. 16-18)*

> Paul as a witness of Jesus (26:19-22a)
> *Paul's mission in Jewish and Gentile cities (vv. 19-20)*
> *The Jews' persecution and God's help (vv. 21-22a)*

The essence of Paul's proclamation (26:22b-23)
In conformity to the Prophets and Moses (v. 22b)
In reference to Jesus' suffering, resurrection and mission (v. 23)

Structurally speaking, the chiasm-like reversal pattern has Paul's encounter with Jesus as the climax and pivot (vv. 13-18). The fifth segment echoes the first; the fourth echoes the second. By comparison the first counterpart lays out

---

[179] Barrett, *Acts*, 2:1105; Marshall, *Acts*, 378.

the divine authority for Jesus' commission of Paul to the Jews and the Gentiles (vv. 6-8, 22b-23). By contrast the second counterpart attests Paul's faithfulness to the divine appointment (vv. 9-12, 19-22a). The heavenly encounter effectively defends the divine universal mission and justifies Paul's Gentile mission (vv. 16-18).

As indicated in the first counterpart, the cause of the Jews' accusation against Paul bears on the hope of God's promise to their forefathers (vv. 6-7) which relates to the resurrection of the dead (v. 8). Again, the God of continuity undergirds the speech. This is made clear in the use of first person plural (ἡμῶν) which indicates that the God Paul worships is no other than the God of the Jews (vv. 6-7). The genitive use of ἡμῶν in the phrases τοὺς πατέρας ἡμῶν and τὸ δωδεκάφυλον ἡμῶν specifies Paul's full identification with God's promise to their forefathers (v. 6) and the hope of the people Israel (v. 7).[180] The hope of God's promise, fundamental to Paul's defence, regards God's raising up of Jesus as proven by Paul's encounter with him (vv. 13-18). Summarising the essence of his witness, Paul accentuates that what he proclaims has been foretold by the Prophets and Moses (v. 22b-23). In the light of God's promise in verse 6 and *what is about to come*, in verse 22b, the first counterpart conveys a promise-fulfilment motif,[181] which legitimises Paul's witness to the risen Jesus (vv. 13-18, 23). The assertion of the promise-fulfilment, implying a divine plan behind it,[182] affirms the continuity of God's activity in Jesus. This paves the way for Jesus' commission of Paul and attests to Paul's faithfulness to the Jewish God and belief.

The second counterpart continually defends Paul's loyalty to God yet there is a dramatic turning point in his life. Instead of being summarised in one sentence (9:1; 22:4), Paul's persecution of the believers is narrated in detail to project its severity (vv. 10-11). By this Paul's great change from being a terrible persecutor to a person desperately persecuted (v. 21) enhances the actuality and credibility of the divine encounter (vv. 13-18). His proclamation to Jews and Gentiles to repent and turn to God (v. 20) manifests his confession of the divine authority of Jesus' commission (vv. 16-18).[183] Paul then boldly professes his obedience to the heavenly vision (v. 19). The wording τῇ οὐρανίῳ ὀπτασίᾳ clearly indicates Paul's conviction of Jesus' divine revelation (note ὀπτασίᾳ implying the divine power or agency behind it).[184] Paul associates with the Gentiles in compliance with the divine commission and this makes the Jews want to kill him (v. 21). Nonetheless, the help of God shows the divine ap-

---

[180] Δωδεκάφυλον, a collective term, indicates the entire ethnic unit. See L&N, §10.3; Johnson, *Acts*, 433; Barrett, *Acts*, 2:1152.
[181] Marguerat, 'Conversion,' 153; cf. Bruce, *Acts*, 3rd edn., 504.
[182] Soards, *Speeches*, 124; Squires, *Plan*, 145.
[183] Soards, *Speeches*, 125.
[184] L&N, §33.488; BDAG, 717.

proval of Paul's actions and enables him to promote the Gentile mission (v. 22a). While Paul's witness to Jesus fulfils Jesus' calling of him (vv. 16, 18), God's help fulfils Jesus' promise of delivering Paul (v. 17).[185] Paul understands God and Jesus to act on the same divine authority and therefore Jesus' commission serves as a part of God's plan in the light of the promise-fulfilment perception. The second counterpart thus reflects Paul's conviction of God at work in and through Jesus and attests to Paul's faithfulness towards the divine commission to the Gentiles.

Founded on the promise-fulfilment of God and affirmed by Paul's conversion, the exact cause of Paul's shift, namely Jesus' appearance to him (vv. 13-18), stands at the climax and pivot of the speech. The heavenly light and voice make Paul realise that Jesus is alive (vv. 13-15). This greatly challenges his belief (v. 9). The unique addition of the non-Semitic proverb,[186] σκληρόν σοι πρὸς κέντρα λακτίζειν (v. 14b), brings out the futility of Paul's fighting against the divinely ordained plan in Jesus.[187] The absence of Ananias as the divine intermediary closely ties in Paul and the risen Jesus. No mention of Paul's blindness and recovery (a description of his plight) intensifies the actions of Paul and Jesus. Once the heavenly light and voice are identified as Jesus' (vv. 13-15) the divine appointment is given (vv. 16-18). That no further interlocution is indicated (cf. 9:6; 22:10) leaves the focus fully on Jesus' commission which concerns the sending of Paul to be a servant and a witness of Jesus to Jews and Gentiles (vv. 16-17).[188] Its purpose is to open the eyes of all so that they may turn from darkness to light, signifying from the authority of Satan to God, in order that by faith in Jesus they may receive the forgiveness of sins and a share among those who have been sanctified (v. 18; cf. 20:32).

As Paul reveals later, the prophesied task of the risen Christ is to proclaim light (a metaphor for salvation) to the Jews and the Gentiles (v. 23).[189] Here

---

[185] Haenchen, *Acts*, 687; Tajra, *Trial*, 168.

[186] Although the source of the proverb is in debate, most scholars regard it as a Greek proverb; see Barrett, *Acts*, 2:1158; Marshall, *Acts*, 395; Haenchen, *Acts*, 685; Johnson, *Acts*, 435; Witherington, *Acts*, 743.

[187] Gaventa links the proverb to 'the futility of resisting a greater power' in a general sense (*Light*, 83). Some specify it as the futility of resisting God's plan. Yet, interpreting the proverb from Paul's point of view, they consider that the divine plan is related to Paul's future mission (Marguerat, 'Conversion,' 152; Witherington, *Acts*, 743). As far as the narrative itself is concerned, taking it from the heavenly point of view, the divine plan is associated with Jesus since Paul is opposing Jesus' name (v. 9). This divine perspective may imply that Paul increasingly realises he is fighting on the wrong side (cf. Marshall, *Acts*, 395) and thus complies with Jesus' commission (vv. 19-23).

[188] Here *servant* and *witness* are epexegetical, that is, Paul's servanthood is understood in terms of witness (Gaventa, *Light*, 84; cf. Culy and Parsons, *Acts*, 496).

[189] Barrett, *Acts*, 2:1166; Witherington, *Acts*, 745.

Paul is entrusted to be Jesus' witness in continuing the divine universal mission (vv. 16-18). By witnessing the light of Jesus (v. 13) Paul becomes a channel to lead all people to the light of God (v. 18) as Jesus himself pioneers the divine mission of proclaiming light (v. 23). While 22:15, 21 briefly indicate the divine commission of Paul, 26:18 specifies that the commission is for a salvific mission.[190] This divine mission of salvation, embedded in the Prophets and Moses (v. 22b), exposes 'the divine necessity (δεῖ) of Christ suffering as part of God's salvation plan.'[191] God's saving plan, founded on Jesus' death and resurrection,[192] lies behind the divine mission and thus ensures its consummation. Moreover, the universal character of the mission is prominent in both Acts 22 and 26. Yet here the unique and detailed account of Jesus' commission of Paul signifies that 'the encounter with the Risen One plays the essential role of justifying a call to evangelize the Gentiles.'[193] What undergirds Paul's notion is that God is at work in Jesus for a saving plan foreshadowed in the Scripture and he is appointed to be Jesus' witness to carry out the mission of God's universal salvation. The ultimate goal of Paul's mission is, therefore, to turn all people, even the Gentiles, back to God through their faith in Jesus (cf. 20:21). Thus far Paul defends his loyalty to God and legitimates his Gentile mission well.

In comparing Paul's autobiographical account in Acts 22 with that in Acts 26, both argue Paul's faithfulness to the Jewish God and belief yet from different viewpoints: To refute the Jews' ignorant accusation, Paul, arguing from the divine viewpoint (Acts 22), elucidates the divine origin of Jesus' revelation and God's universal mission. To defend his innocence while being persecuted by Jews, Paul, arguing from his personal viewpoint (Acts 26), expounds his fidelity to God's saving plan revealed in and through Jesus. Acts 26 thus gives more weight to Paul's role in the persecution and witness of Jesus and to his personal interpretation of the significance of Christophany. The diminishing of the roles of minor and background characters (Ananias and Paul's companions) also leaves the spotlight on Paul's reaction to Jesus.[194] Even the detailed account of Jesus' commission gives weight to justify Paul's Gentile mission which is a part of God's universal saving plan. From Paul's perspective in the narrative,

---

[190] Witherington, *Acts*, 745.

[191] Witherington, *Acts*, 748; cf. Soards, *Speeches*, 126; Robert F. O'Toole, *The Christological Climax of Paul's Defense: Acts 26* (AB 26; Rome: Biblical Institute Press, 1978) 121.

[192] Investigating the centre of Pauline theology, Joseph Plevnik concludes that Christ's death and resurrection are fundamental to Pauline thought though this is together with acknowledgement of Christ's lordship and God's saving purpose ('The Center of Pauline Theology,' *CBQ* 51 [1989] 461-78). In his following work, he argues that the Spirit belongs to the centre of Paul's theology as well ('The Understanding of God at the Basis of Pauline Theology,' *CBQ* 65 [2003] 554-67, esp. 562-63).

[193] Marguerat, 'Conversion,' 154.

[194] Marguerat, 'Conversion,' 151; Witherup, 'Redundancy,' 77, 79.

one sees Jesus standing at the foreground to reveal God's mission to Paul and God standing in the background to ensure the realisation of the mission through Paul. From the scenery there appears a portrait of God who reveals his universal saving plan in and through Jesus and who enables Jesus' witness to accomplish the divine mission.

In sum, the defensive speeches, in which multiple angles and points can be ascertained, are complicated.[195] With respect to characterisation, although the portrayal of Jesus or Paul is much more explicit in these speeches, the implicit characterisation of God can be grasped in the focal point of these defensive speeches, that is, the resurrection of Jesus by God.[196] As discussed, the justification of the risen Jesus' commissioning of Paul for the universal mission is based on God's will and plan foreseen in Scripture. It is from this perspective that Paul insists on his loyalty to the Jewish God and belief while bearing witness to Jesus and evangelising Gentiles. The distinct portrait of God can be detected from Paul's defence of the divine authority behind Jesus' revelation and of the legitimacy of his Gentile mission. Ostensibly, the defensive speeches are repeated more or less. Witherup points out the significance of such repetition: 'what appeared to be merely repetitious details of slight variation were actually part of a narrative strategy of functional redundancy which intimately connected characterization and plot.'[197] This is particularly true of the characterisation of God in Paul's defensive speeches. By adopting the divine point of view to justify his new way of serving God Paul, in Acts 22, attributes the Christophany to God's authoritative appointing of him to the divine mission through Jesus and, thus, represents a God of new revelation in Jesus. Taking on the Jewish viewpoint in order to refute the otherness of his proclamation Paul, in Acts 24, asserts his believing in Scripture and the Jewish hope and so portrays a God of the old hope of resurrection. As Paul turns to his own angle to defend his innocence before, and fidelity to, God in Acts 26, his argument bases on God's promise-fulfilment and is reinforced by his own conversion. From his defence emerges a God carrying out his universal redemptive plan in the risen Jesus and through Jesus' commission of the witness. Paul's overall defensive speech, again, confides his notion of a sovereign and authoritative God who reveals his salvific will in/through Jesus and who calls his people into his mission plan. God's sovereignty and authority are further made manifest in Jesus' and Paul's submission to his will.

---

[195] With regard to the multifaceted representation of Paul's defence, Neagoe suggests that it establishes the variety of emphases, which present the plurality of angles, 'from which the author seeks to establish the validity of the gospel' (*Trial*, 215).

[196] Hansen, 'Defence,' 321; Tajra, *Trial*, 128.

[197] Ronald D. Witherup, 'Cornelius Over and Over and Over Again: "Functional Redundancy" in the Acts of the Apostles,' *JSNT* 49 (1993) 45-66, citing 47. See also William S. Kurz, 'Effects of Variant Narrators in Acts 10-11,' *NTS* 43 (1997) 570-86, esp. 571; Sternberg, *Biblical Narrative*, 390-93; Alter, *Biblical Narrative*, 91.

Summary

Fundamentally speaking, all these seven speeches of Paul are theocentric. Yet, as the setting of each speech differs, the theocentric assertion is presented basically in two ways. For the evangelic interest, God is the centre of the missionary speeches (13:16-41; 14:15-17; 17:22-31). God, standing in the foreground, though in thematic concern rather than in person, gets the spotlight throughout each scene. God, the ultimate goal to whom Paul turns people back, and his plan are the primary concern of Paul's proclamation. For the interest of Paul's personal affairs, God is moved to the background as Jesus is moved to the foreground. In the background God's plan and will serve as the backing and advocacy for Paul's ministry in the church and mission to the Gentiles which are commissioned by Jesus (20:18-35; 22:1-21; 24:10-21; 26:2-23). God's plan and will are still the fundamental concern even when Paul's interrelation with Jesus becomes the primary interest in the speeches regarding personal testimony.

In the theocentric foreground, the nature of God stands out. The speech to Jews unfolds God's initiative and authority in bringing salvation to his chosen people, his power and faithfulness in carrying out the Davidic promise-fulfilment and his lovingkindness in giving Davidic blessings to all who believe in Jesus (13:16-41). The speeches to Gentiles unveil God as the supreme Creator, self-existent, self-sufficient and self-revealing, who holds the superlative authority, sovereignty and power to show his care to the creation (14:15-17; 17:22-31). In the theocentric background stand the plan and will of God. By obedience to God's will Paul testifies God's sovereignty over the redemptive plan and authority over himself. The speech to the church elders shows Paul's faithfulness to Jesus' ministry and his care for God's church (20:18-35). What is embedded in Paul's assertion is God as the ultimate goal and reason of Paul's proclamation (v. 21) and trust (v. 32), and God's will is all that Paul concerns and desires (vv. 24, 27). The three defensive speeches concern Paul's loyalty to God and the legitimacy of his Gentile mission. Although Paul's interaction with Jesus is stressed, God's will of universal salvation is increasingly reinforced in the speeches. In his defence Paul presents a lucid and pithy picture of God's universal saving plan revealed in Jesus and consummated through Jesus' commission of his witness to Jews and Gentiles. Paul's absolute compliance with God's will also fortifies his oral witness of God's sovereign authority in carrying out the divine plan.

The focal point or concern in the theocentric arena is the resurrection of Jesus which is founded on the promise-fulfilment of God. Setting God in the foreground, Paul intends to make known that the risen Jesus is the way of God's salvation and judgement (13:23; 17:31), from which emerge God's saving and judging power. Correspondingly, human repentance and faith in Jesus are required for receiving God's salvation (13:39; 17:30) since Jesus is the only way back to God (cf. 20:21; 26:18). Setting God in the background, Paul aims to vindicate his commission from the risen Jesus for God's universal mission of salvation (20:24; 22:15, 21; 24:14; 26:19-21) by emphasising the God of continuity and his own loyalty to God (20:27; 22:14-15; 24:14-16; 26:19-22). Nonetheless, the resurrection of the dead becomes a stumbling block for people's faith in Jesus. Such disbelief keeps people away from God's salvation and makes the Jews deny Paul's Gentile mission. The vital issue of such disbelief is failing to believe God's resurrecting power (17:32; 23:6-7; 24:21; 26:8). God's promise of salvation fulfilled in an incredible way not only tests one's faith in God but also amplifies God's saving power. Overall, Paul's speeches expose God's creating, saving, resurrecting and judging power alongside his sovereign authority and unfold God's mission plan for the universal salvation. By participating in this divine ministry Jesus' witnesses share in, and testify to, God's authority and power. In the theocentric foreground God is characterised as the Creator, the Saviour and the Judge, whereas in the theocentric background God is characterised as a saving plan-designer and -master.

Personal/Interpersonal Characterisation

The aim of this section is to examine Paul's interactions with the heavenly and human characters. Similar to those of Peter, Paul's heavenly encounters, signalling the development of the narrative, sketch the framework of his service of God; Paul's interactions with human characters provide a human context which manifests how God's worldwide mission is advanced and achieved. Paul's heavenly encounters, which govern and affect his understanding and service to God, will first be examined to provide a foundation for his interactions with other human characters.

Personal Characterisation—Divine Encounters

As noted in Chapter Two the heavenly revelators take the initiative in carrying out God's mission plan. Now Paul, the second major character in the narrative, divinely appointed by Jesus, is steered to further God's universal mission. The divine interventions, either by the personal revelators or through impersonal vision or miracles, guide Paul's ministry and authenticate his proclamation. While investigating Paul's divine experience, two modes of preternatural connections can be seen: Paul as the object of heavenly instructions delivered by the revelators and/or in visions; Paul as the intermediary of miraculous deeds. The former conveys a divine directive or promise which ensures that the *messenger* Paul does God's will; the latter signifies the divine affirmation which fortifies Paul's *message* of God's will. Both assure God's plan and advance God's mission, from which the implied readers continue to renew or modify their image of God.

PAUL AS THE OBJECT OF HEAVENLY INSTRUCTIONS

There are seven occasions where divine interventions play the active role in steering Paul to do God's will: the Christophany (9:3-18); the Spirit's commission (13:2); the Spirit's guidance of the westward mission (16:6-10); Jesus' promise in Corinth (18:9-10); the Spirit's foretelling (21:4, 11); Jesus' promise in Jerusalem (23:11); an angel's promise in the shipwreck (27:23-24). On the first three occasions Paul is convinced of God's will; on the last four he is strengthened to do God's will.

As revealed in his defensive speeches (22:3-21; 26:2-23), Paul's encounter with Jesus is the critical point in his new perspective of understanding and serving God (9:3-18). The Christophany transforms Paul's belief from Law-centred tenet to Christ-centred faith (13:39).[198] As Jesus conforms the core of Paul's belief to God's will, the Spirit leads him on the journey of God's mission. The Spirit first sends out Paul, together with Barnabas, to the Gentile mission (13:2). Then the Spirit guides Paul to the westward mission, via prohibition, followed by an explicit vision (16:6-10).[199] The divine encounter or directive, which brings about the sequential incident, opens a new page for God's mission and shapes Paul's ministry.

The more God's mission is extended, the more Paul faces the opposing force. Yet the divine care never withdraws from him. During the frightening ministry at Corinth Jesus, appearing in a vision, assures Paul of his presence (18:9-10). As the menacing trial approaches, the Spirit prepares Paul for his coming bondage by revealing it to the disciples (20:23; 21:4, 11). When dire imprisonment comes, Jesus' promise of Paul's witnessing to Jesus at Rome heartens him (23:11) and an angel's reaffirmation of God's will concerning Paul's safe arrival at Rome encourages him (27:23-24). The divine promises and prophecy buttress Paul for the ministry assigned to him and thus enable him to accomplish God's mission.

On the above occasions divine initiative is specified in order to highlight divine authority in inaugurating each new stage of God's mission and to project divine care in providing timely invigoration to God's messenger. Being called into God's mission Paul, the recipient of heavenly instructions, is directed and strengthened by God's revelators in order that he may continually partake in and carry out God's mission in accordance with God's plan. From Paul's divine encounters the implied readers construct an image of God who, through his

---

[198] Jacques Dupont, 'The Conversion of Paul and Its Influence on His Understanding of Salvation by Faith' in W. Ward Gasque and Ralph P. Martin (eds.), *Apostolic History and the Gospel* (Exeter: Paternoster Press, 1970) 176-94, citing 194.

[199] Instead of viewing Paul's vision as the divine guidance, John B.F. Miller emphasises the characters' perception of God's will through their interpretation of Paul's experiences (*Convinced that God had Called Us: Dreams, Visions, and the Perception of God's Will in Luke-Acts* [Leiden: Brill, 2007] 106, 234).

divine agents or visions, sovereignly calls his chosen human agents into his mission of salvation and mightily protects them from evil and empowers them to carry on the mission.

PAUL AS THE INTERMEDIARY OF MIRACULOUS DEEDS

In Paul's divine encounters an image of God emerges from the divine authority carried out by heavenly characters, whereas in the miracles performed by Paul a picture of God appears from Paul's proclamation of God's Word. There are eight occasions when Paul acts as a mediator of God's mighty works: Elymas' temporary blindness (13:11); the multi-miracles (14:3; 19:11-12); the healing of the man born lame (14:8-10); the casting out of the soothsaying spirit (16:16-18); the opening of prison doors (16:25-26); the raising of Eutychus from death (20:9-12); the healings at Malta (28:5-9). Fundamentally, Paul's miracles are associated with his proclamation of God's word in two ways.[200] Intrinsically, miracles are the evidence by which God testifies and fortifies the Word and the salvific essence of the Word prevents miracles from being syncretised into other beliefs or religions in the pagan world.[201] Ostensibly, miracles gradually characterise the miracle-worker Paul as a powerful (i.e. divinely authorised) Word-bearer and his proclamation of the Word is therefore irresistible.

While marching out to the Gentile world of polytheism, the miracles of God's messengers fortify the Word and strengthen human faith (13:12; 14:3; 16:25-34; 19:10-12; 20:9-12). However, miracles also endanger Paul's proclamation by being linked with magic (13:6-11; 16:16-24; 19:13-17; cf. 8:9-24) or by being syncretised into polytheism (14:8-13; 28:3-6; see also the proclamation of Jesus' resurrection in 17:18-19).[202] Magic pervades the first century Roman Empire[203] and functions as a negative backdrop to aggrandise Paul's Gentile mission in the narrative. Therefore, before scrutinising Paul's miracles,

---

[200] Jervell asserts, 'proclamation and miracles in essence belong together' (*Unknown*, 82).

[201] Marguerat, 'Magic,' 114.

[202] Marguerat, 'Magic,' 107; cf. Susan R. Garrett, *The Demise of the Devil: Magic and the Demonic in Luke's Writings* (Minneapolis: Fortress Press, 1989) 86.

[203] Although Downing argues that there is no widespread firm belief in magic in the first century Christian movement, various kinds of magical practice are presented in his argument ('Magic,' 86-99). Alan F. Segal, however, basing his argument on the fact that harmful magic is viewed as criminal in Roman law over several centuries, asserts that magic 'must have been widely practiced — or at least believed to be so' ('Hellenistic Magic: Some Questions of Definition' in R. van den Broek and M.J. Vermaseren [eds.], *Studies in Gnosticism and Hellenistic Religions* [Leiden: E.J. Brill, 1981] 349-75, citing 358). See also David E. Aune, 'Magic in Early Christianity' in *ANRW* II.23.2 (1980) 1507-57, esp. 1519; Howard Clark Kee, *To Every Nation under Heaven* (Harrisburg: Trinity Press International, 1997) 160.

a narrative distinction between miracle and magic is vital for understanding the significance of miracles in Paul's Gentile ministry. Although the definition of magic is disputed by scholars,[204] Reimer, comparing the narrative of *Acts* with that of Philostratus' *Life of Apollonius*,[205] classifies a magician as someone seeking personal gain and ambition through the management of a higher power. This may lead to social and political subversion and is thus regarded as religious deviancy. In contrast, a miracle-worker is featured as having a lack of interest in personal gain and in social and political ambition; rather he is perceived as favouring truth authenticated by use of extraordinary, divine power for salvific ends within an established religion.[206] Intrinsically, whether the mediation of a higher power is for personal ends or for salvific ends determines whether a wonder is magic or miracle. Such a distinction is laid out in Paul's confrontation with magic forces in the syncretistic Gentile world,[207] against which Paul's salvific message and extremely powerful wonders stand out as coming from God.

During Paul's First Missionary Journey

Paul's very first recorded miracle, following his proclamation of God's word (13:5), happens at his confrontation with a magician (13:6-12) in which Paul's divine authority and power over the magic force is highlighted. Two contrasts lie in the episode. The first contrast is between the proconsul Sergius Paulus'

---

[204] Simply categorised, there are mainly two ways of defining magic and miracle among scholars. From the perspective of anthropologists and religionists, a sharp distinction between magic and miracle is made by their respective approaches to a higher power: manipulative or supplicative. See Lucy Mair, *An Introduction to Social Anthropology*, 2nd edn. (Oxford: Clarendon Press, 1992) 229; Howard Clark Kee, *Medicine, Miracle and Magic in New Testament Times* (SNTSMS 55; Cambridge: Cambridge University Press, 1986) 3, 99; H.C. Kee, *Miracle in the Early Christian World: A Study in Sociohistorical Method* (New Haven: Yale University Press, 1983) 62-63. From the sociological perspective, magic and miracle are regarded as religious deviance or opposed factions. Magic is a negative label applied to one's religious opponents while the term miracle, carrying a positive sense, is applied to one's own religion. See Aune, 'Magic,' 1510-16; Segal, 'Hellenistic Magic,' 347-75; Arthur Darby Nock, 'Paul and the Magus' in *Beg*, 5:164-88, esp. 169-71.

[205] Reimer, *Miracle and Magic*, 19-23. Although *Life of Apollonius* is dated in the early third century, Reimer argues convincingly, from both narrative and historical perspectives, for the legitimacy of drawing from the two narrative worlds the criteria separating miracle from magic which may have existed in the first century Graeco-Roman world.

[206] Reimer, *Miracle and Magic*, 249.

[207] Hans-Josef Klauck, *Magic and Paganism in Early Christianity: The World of the Acts of the Apostles* (Edinburgh: T & T Clark, 2000) 52.

seeking to hear God's word and Bar-Jesus' diverting him from the faith (vv. 7-8). Bar-Jesus in the prestigious court of the proconsul may protest his position for economic interests;[208] this provides a clue for judging him as magician or miracle-worker. The second contrast is between the authority of Bar-Jesus a Jewish magician and that of Paul the miracle-worker full of the Spirit (vv. 6, 9).[209] Although the narrator reveals Bar-Jesus' threefold identity (Jew, false prophet, sorcerer), Paul discloses his very nature as demonic stand-in (υἱὲ διαβόλου, v. 10). Accordingly, the punitive miracle of temporary blindness falling upon Bar-Jesus signifies the divine power manifest through Paul (cf. Paul is πλησθεὶς πνεύματος ἁγίου and the miracle is by χεὶρ κυρίου) overmastering magical-demonic power (v. 11).[210] The confrontation between Bar-Jesus and Paul, thus, implies a confrontation between the Spirit and the devil.[211] What is in Paul is greater than what is in Bar-Jesus. This steadily confirms Paul's authority in proclaiming the Word and removes the obstacle for faith in the Word (v. 12). Eventually, God's word, which is fortified by God's own power and which invites human faith (see πίστεως in v. 8 and ἐπίστευσεν in v. 12), is the core of the confrontation and the cause that decisively brings about the miracle.[212]

In the other two accounts of miracles in Paul's first missionary journey, miracles again closely follow Paul's proclamation of the Word and human faith (14:1-3, 8-10). A multi-miracle happens at Iconium where Paul preaches in the synagogue and many come to faith (v. 1). The Word fortified by God himself is expressed in an emphatic way — *God himself testifies to the Word* by performing miracles through his messengers (v. 3).[213] Later, at Lystra, Paul heals a man

---

[208] Marguerat, 'Magic,' 121; Klauck, *Paganism*, 51; Polhill, *Acts*, 293.

[209] Craig S. de Vos indicates that 'the Jews were perceived to be magicians by many Romans, and exorcism was probably the main type of magic associated with Jews in this period' ('Finding a Charge that Fits: The Accusation against Paul and Silas at Philippi [Acts 16.19-21],' *JSNT* 74 [1999] 51-63, citing 60); cf. Garrett, *Demise*, 91. Aune expresses magic as 'a strong undercurrent in Judaism' during the first century ('Magic,' 1520).

[210] Garrett, *Demise*, 86; cf. Haenchen, *Acts*, 398.

[211] Garrett, *Demise*, 80; Gaventa, *Acts*, 195.

[212] Klauck, *Paganism*, 53.

[213] Κύριος in 14:3 refers to God since the Word, which conveys God's salvation in Jesus (13:46-48), is depicted as τῷ λόγῳ τῆς χάριτος αὐτοῦ; cf. Pesch, *Apg*, 2:51; Johnson, *Acts*, 246; Marshall, *Acts*, 233. From Paul's viewpoint the miracle is of God's hand (13:11; cf. 4:29-30), i.e. the miracle-worker acknowledges God's authority. From the narrator's perspective God performs miracles through the hands of his messengers (14:3), i.e. the narrator recognises the messengers' authority delegated by God.

born lame who shows faith in his proclamation (14:9-10).[214] Although the powerful healing gives way to further evangelism, the rooted notion of polytheism makes the Lystrians syncretise Paul's miracle into their belief and prevents them from knowing the one true God (14:11-18; note the speech on monotheism).[215] Specifically speaking, Paul's miracles accompany the salvific message of God (cf. the summary of Paul's proclamation in 13:46-48; the narrator's use of the word σωθῆναι for healing in 14:9) and have no interest in personal gain (cf. the persecution after Paul's proclamation and miracles; 14:5, 19). This distinguishes Paul from magicians and his miracles from magic and thus draws people's attention to, or even faith in, the Word-miracle. This is:

> an interaction where word and miracle work together to cause faith to emerge: sometimes the word needs the miracle to provoke faith, sometimes the miracles require the word to legitimate the act of faith. In the first case, the miracle legitimizes the message and, assuring its credibility, participates in missionary effectiveness.[216]

During Paul's Second Missionary Journey

Paul's first miracle appears at his direct encounter with a magic force (16:16-18), in which lie two confrontations. The first confrontation is between the proclamation of Paul and the 'witness' to his salvific message by a Philippian slave-girl with a soothsaying spirit. Like the confrontation with a magician in Paul's first missionary journey (13:10) this confrontation is, by nature, a confrontation between divine power (ἐν ὀνόματι Ἰησοῦ Χριστοῦ) and demonic power (πνεῦμα πύθωνα).[217] The casting out of the spirit passively

---

[214] Lystra is the first place, in Paul's ministry as well as in Acts, where there is no indication of Jewish influence, i.e. a pure polytheism (note that the proconsul in Paphos has a Jewish magician in his entourage; cf. Klauck, *Paganism*, 56).

[215] A local saga of two gods' visit is often taken as the background of the Lystrians' worshipping of Barnabas and Paul. It is said that two gods (perhaps called Tarchunt and Runt or Pappas and Men, replaced in the Greek version by Zeus and Hermes) visit a village near Lystra and are only treated hospitably by an elderly couple. Later, the couple are richly rewarded while the village is destroyed. See Klauck, *Paganism*, 58-59; Gaventa, *Acts*, 207; Johnson, *Acts*, 248; cf. Conrad Gempf, 'Mission and Misunderstanding: Barnabas and Paul in Lystra (Acts 14:8-20)' in Antony Billington, et al. (eds.), *Mission and Meaning* (Carlisle: Paternoster Press, 1995) 56-69, esp. 60-66; Amy L. Wordelman, 'Cultural Divides and Dual Realities: A Greco-Roman Context for Acts 14' in Todd Penner and Caroline Vander Stichele (eds.), *Contextualizing Acts: Lukan Narrative and Greco-Roman Discourse* (SBLSS 20; Atlanta: Society of Biblical Literature, 2003) 205-32, esp. 220-23.

[216] Marguerat, 'Magic,' 123-24; cf. Werner Kahl, *New Testament Miracle Stories in Their Religious-Historical Setting* (Göttingen: Vandenhoeck & Ruprecht, 1994) 227.

[217] Rick Strelan, *Strange Acts: Studies in the Cultural World of the Acts of the Apostles* (BZNW 126; Berlin: Walter de Gruyter, 2004) 117.

averts the connection of Paul with bewitchment, and prevents the syncretisation of his message, and actively attests that the power on which Paul acts is greater than any magic force and corroborates the purity and clarity of Paul's message. The second contrast is between the missionaries being persecuted for setting the slave-girl free and the slave-girl's masters persecuting the missionaries by imprisonment because of their loss of personal gains (16:19-24). Both confrontations highlight the salvific interest and end of Paul's ministry.

No personal advantage involved for Paul manifests the divine nature of his miracle-power which is further magnified in a sequential miracle (16:25-30). That the prison doors are opened while Paul and Silas pray and sing praises to God signifies the divine presence and approval.[218] The miraculous deliverance and their non-escape force the jailer to recognise Paul's supernal authority and ask for the way to be saved.[219] The motif of salvation underlies both miracles. The slave-girl's true-yet-syncretic announcement of *a way of salvation* (16:17; note the absence of the article of ὁδόν) makes Paul's salvific message one among many others.[220] By calling on the name of Jesus for exorcism (16:18) Paul relates Jesus to God the Most High and his way of salvation. Furthermore, the jailer's sincere query (note the use of δεῖ; 16:30) allows Paul to explicate that faith in Jesus leads to salvation, that is, believing in Jesus is the way to believing in the one true God and receiving his salvation (16:31, 34).

In the narrative Jesus, as the core of the Word Paul proclaims, is increasingly highlighted in the second missionary journey. Although Paul's speech at Pisidian Antioch centres on God's salvation in Jesus (13:26), which elucidates the fundamental theme of Paul's proclamation, the Word in general is stressed throughout his ministry in the first missionary journey (13:5, 7, 44, 46, 48, 49; 14:3; cf. Jesus as the core teaching is only implied in 13:12, τῇ διδαχῇ τοῦ

---

[218] Brian Rapske, *The Book of Acts and Paul in Roman Custody* (Grand Rapids: Eerdmans, 1994) 418.

[219] Paul's non-escape greatly marks the preternatural event as a miracle because no personal advantage, rather the jailer's salvation, is the concern here. See Andy M. Reimer, 'Virtual Prison Breaks: Non-Escape Narratives and the Definition of "Magic"' in Klutz (ed.), *Magic in the Biblical World*, 125-39, citing 137.

[220] Marguerat, 'Magic,' 112-13; Klauck, *Paganism*, 68; Gaventa, *Acts*, 238; Polhill, *Acts*, 351; Paul R. Trebilco, 'Paul and Silas—"Servants of the Most High God" (Acts 16.16-18),' *JSNT* 36 (1989) 51-73, citing 64-65. Trebilco mainly argues that, for a pagan, ὁ θεός ὁ ὕψιστος, though common in the LXX, 'would simply suggest the creation of a hierarchy in their pantheon' (60) and God 'would be one of a number of other gods' (62). He contends that it is the *content* of the slave-girl's message, which leads to a syncretistic misunderstanding, that makes Paul exorcise the demon. The term, however, is applied to the Jews whose belief is widely known to be monotheism. It is more likely that the exorcism results from the *source* of the message; see F. Scott Spencer, 'Out of Mind, Out of Voice: Slave-Girls and Prophetic Daughters in Luke-Acts,' *BInt* 7 (1999) 133-55, citing 149.

κυρίου). The specification of Jesus as the essence of Paul's message is more accentuated in the second missionary journey (16:18, 31; cf. 17:3, 18; 18:5). This implies that Paul's proclamation of the Jewish God's salvation in Jesus is gradually recognised (17:4-7); this results in a close tie between Paul the messenger and Jesus the message. The further the westward mission goes, the closer the tie between Paul and Jesus and the more powerful Paul's authority. In other words, the one true God is made known in the Gentile polytheistic world as the Saviour Jesus is proclaimed.

During the Third Missionary Journey

The divine authority and power within Paul is strikingly amplified both among the disciples (19:1-6; 20:9-12) and the Gentiles (19:11-12; 28:5-10). Among the disciples, Paul's authority is enhanced in his raising up of Eutychus from death (20:10; see also his laying on of hands upon John's disciples for the descent of the Spirit; 19:6). At the great mission in Ephesus, Paul's authority is perceived in his effective proclamation of the Word spread out in Asia (19:8-10). Nonetheless, there Paul also encounters greater magical forces (19:13, 19). However, God's power is unfolded exceedingly in the miracles, especially the healings and the casting out of the evil spirits, performed through Paul (19:11-12; that God is the subject of the main clause emphasises that he is the author of these miracles). Accordingly, Paul's authority in proclaiming Jesus, although presented in a negative way, is widely recognised (19:13; see the failure of the Jewish exorcists' invoking of both Jesus' and Paul's names)[221] and Jesus' name is conspicuously magnified (19:15-17). It is not the formula of Jesus' name which bears the authority over the demon but the person who is given the authority to call on Jesus' name that casts out the demon (cf. Lk 10:17-19).[222] The evil spirit's overpowering of the Jewish exorcists who manipulate Jesus' name dramatically enhances the name and Paul's authority in calling on the name.[223] Again, a confrontation between divine and demonic power lies behind Paul's encounter with magic forces. The implicit acknowledgement of the power of Jesus' name, though by a demonic source, greatly

---

[221] The calling on Jesus' name may be viewed as a magical technique in the polytheistic world (Vos, 'Charge,' 59-60). Apparently, Sceva's seven sons adopt 'the name of the Lord Jesus' as a formula of exorcism (Garrett, *Demise*, 92, 97; Klauck, *Paganism*, 99).

[222] Garrett, *Demise*, 93; Strelan, *Strange Acts*, 112.

[223] Todd Klutz, *The Exorcism Stories in Luke-Acts* (SNTSMS 129; Cambridge: Cambridge University Press, 2004) 235. See also Scott Shauf, *Theology as History, History as Theology: Paul in Ephesus in Acts 19* (BZNW 133; Berlin: Walter de Gruyter, 2005) 224.

fortifies human faith and the Word (19:18-20).[224] The more Paul is empowered to proclaim the Word, the more his tie with Jesus and his authority are recognised. This tie features Paul as the Word-bearer and reveals that Paul, sharing the divine authority and power in the name of Jesus,[225] authoritatively and powerfully bears out God's Word. Paul is thus characterised as the authorised messenger of God the Most High;[226] his miracles 'exhibit the proclamation as an irresistible force'.[227] The characterisation of Paul further reflects the God whom he serves as the true deity who holds the supreme authority and power and mightily empowers his messenger.

Paul on Trial

At the trials, the Word-bearer Paul powerfully defends his proclamation against the Jews' accusation and his *suffering* for Jesus' sake serves as a witness to the Word. In fact, God's protection of Paul from the persecutors' hands is itself a 'miracle' (cf. 21:31-36; 23:12-24; 25:1-5) which not only safeguards the Word-bearer but reinforces the Word. On the way to Rome, the miraculous rescue from the shipwreck and from the viper bite manifest Paul as thoroughly under *God's protection* (27:21-28:6).[228] Moreover, the healing miracles on the island, with no indication of the proclamation of the Word, emphatically heighten the divine empowerment and Paul's authority (28:7-9). Overall, God's sovereignty undergirds Paul's trials and sea voyage. God's authority and power, having been revealed in the Word and miracles, now expose, in the ordinary life of the Word-bearer,[229] that which is unfolded in the divine protection and empowerment in times of Paul's suffering and distress. Actually, the emphasis on the divine care and Paul's authority from above whispers that wherever the divinely empowered Word-bearer goes, the Word is spread without hindrance (28:31). This further manifests God's invincible power and sovereignty.

In Paul's first itineracy, miracles keep God's Word in the spotlight. In his second itineracy, miracles allow Jesus' name to come into the spotlight as the

---

[224] The perfect participle πεπιστευκότων in 19:18 indicates that these people have been members of the faith community for some time already. The impact of the self-appointed exorcism (in a magical formula) further fortifies their faith (Klauck, *Paganism*, 101).

[225] Annette Weissenrieder, *Images of Illness in the Gospel of Luke* (Tübingen: Mohr Siebeck, 2003) 337.

[226] Jervell, *Unknown*, 87.

[227] Jervell, *Unknown*, 86.

[228] Polhill, *Acts*, 533; Strelan, *Strange Acts*, 285. Alexandru Neagoe asserts Acts 27-28 as Paul's 'trial' before the court of nature which signifies God's vindication of his innocence (*The Trial of the Gospel* [SNTSMS 116; Cambridge: Cambridge University Press, 2005] 207).

[229] Cf. Loveday C.A. Alexander, 'Reading Luke-Acts from Back to Front' in Verheyden (ed.), *Unity*, 419-46, citing 446.

essence of the Word of salvation. In his third itineracy, miracles let Paul the messenger and Jesus the message stand side by side in the spotlight to magnify God's authority and power. Finally, at the trials and on the way to Rome, miracles enable the Word-bearer Paul to remain alone in the spotlight to reflect God's supreme power and authority. As Paul's status as a powerful Word-bearer becomes prominent at this stage, miracles no longer closely accompany the proclamation of the Word but enhance Paul's authority. The multi-miracle in 14:3 accentuates *the divine witness* to the Word, in 19:11-12 it highlights *the divine power through Paul* to fortify the Word and, in 28:3-9, it simply amplifies *Paul's healing power*. Although the Word is less explicit during Paul's journey to Rome,[230] the concern of the Word never disappears from the narrative since Jesus is the very cause of the Word-bearer Paul's bondage and the core of his defence (Acts 22, 24, 26, 28b). Overall, Paul himself is a living witness to God and his Word.

To sum up, God's redemptive plan is the ultimate cause of Paul's heavenly encounters either with God's revelators or miracles. As the recipient of the revelators' directives and promises, Paul is piloted to each new stage of God's mission and strengthened to carry on God's saving plan. As the mediator of God's mighty deeds, Paul is given the miracle-power to proclaim powerfully the Word of salvation in Jesus. The Word, to which God himself testifies by performing miracles through Paul, is crucial for distinguishing miracles from magic. Miracles, in turn, characterise Paul as a divine, powerful Word-bearer by whom the Word of God is spread out irresistibly. Foremost, the growing of the Word, which is the kernel of God's mission plan, is ensured by God's own authority and power revealed in Paul's miracles and suffering. It is God himself who, by his authority, initiates the saving plan and who, by his power, guarantees the consummation of the plan. Therefore, in God's authority Paul is led by heavenly instructions to promote the divine mission; in God's power Paul's proclamation of the Word is empowered in order to accomplish the divine plan. In brief, Paul, characterised as a powerful-yet-suffering Word-bearer, not only reflects God's supreme power and authority upon him, but testifies to God's sovereignty in carrying out the divine redemptive plan and mission.

---

[230] With regard to the absence of the Word in relation to the miracles in 28:3-9, Polhill suggests that the pattern of miracle and witness throughout Acts would naturally make one assume that Paul was evangelising the natives (*Acts*, 533). The image of the powerful Word-bearer makes even clearer that Paul and the proclamation of the Word are unseparated, or at least the Word is attached to Paul, in the narrative. Whether or not there is an indication of the Word amid the miracles, the reader would carry the impression of Paul's proclamation of the Word.

Interpersonal Characterisation—
Interactions with Other Human Characters

Paul's human interactions provide a background for the advance of God's mission. The human context, which is 'primarily a web of relationships,'[231] is intricate and complex and can be roughly categorised into four groups (churches, Jews, Gentiles, Roman officials). The narrator creates a microcosm of society in which each collective character represents a particular point of view. This creates perspectives of depth in the narrative that make God's will profoundly realised. Moreover, the collective characters function as buttresses (actively) or triggers (passively) that promote God's mission. This section will investigate Paul's interaction with these groups. Each interaction presents a perspective in the complicated relationships and plays a distinct role in unfolding God's plan and contributing to the narrative plot, from which a more thorough portrait of God is drawn.

INTERACTIONS WITH THE CHURCHES IN JERUSALEM AND ANTIOCH

Paul is first introduced into the narrative as Saul who is standing in the background of the scene of Stephen's death (7:60). He then sporadically appears in the foreground as a violent persecutor of the church (8:3; 9:1-2). This hostile relationship is dramatically inverted on his way to Damascus where he encounters the risen Jesus and is converted (9:3-19). Paul, a persecutor of Jesus' followers, then becomes a persecuted witness of Jesus (9:23-25, 29; cf. 9:16). His relation to the church shifts from attack to defence. As the narrative develops, the nature of this new defensive relation changes accordingly as Paul vigorously interacts with the local churches in Jerusalem, Antioch and the mission field. There are two stages in Paul's relation to each local church. While each first-stage relation paves the way for its second, both the second-stage relations in Jerusalem and Antioch buttress Paul's Gentile mission. See the following chart for an indication of Paul's role and relation to the local churches in the narrative.

---

[231] Harvey, *Character*, 69.

By the Major Characters—Paul

JERUSALEM	ANTIOCH	MISSION FIELD
First Stage Saul is accepted into the church as a disciple ↓	*First Stage* Saul is introduced to the church as a minister ↓	
Second Stage The church confirms Paul's message and affirms him as an authorised preacher in the Gentile mission	*Second Stage* The church sends Saul out as a missionary	*First Stage* Paul as a church-planter establishes churches overseas ↓ *Second Stage* Paul as a fortifier strengthens the churches

Immediately after his conversion in Damascus and the reception by other disciples through Barnabas' introduction in Jerusalem, Saul stays with the disciples (9:19b, 26-28) yet his preaching of the theocentric Christology in Jesus (9:20, 22) provokes the Jews to want to kill him (9:23-24, 29). At this stage, Saul is portrayed as a powerful witness of Jesus among the disciples. Being sent to Tarsus because of the Jews' plot in Jerusalem (9:30), Saul is later brought to Antioch by Barnabas to co-shepherd the church (11:25-26). Both Barnabas and Saul then become the delegates of the Antioch church, where they serve as core leaders (13:1), to bring the famine-offering to the Jerusalem church (11:30). Saul's first stage-relation with the Jerusalem and Antioch churches is a preliminary in which he plays a minor role and gradually emerges onto the narrative arena. Thus far, the narrative provides the background of Saul's relation to Jesus and to the Jerusalem and Antioch churches. The former transforms his perspective of serving God; the latter paves the way for God's mission as assigned to him.

While Jesus' entering Saul's life draws him into the church, the Holy Spirit's stepping into the church's life drives Saul to God's worldwide mission. Obeying the Spirit's command, the Antioch church sends Barnabas and Saul out as missionaries (13:2-3). At the very first confrontation with magical forces in the missionary journeys, Saul's role in the arena shifts from minor character to major protagonist. Such a change in status is initiated in his name being changed to Paul since name changes in antiquity sometimes accompany a change in status (13:9).[232] When fully coming into the spotlight, Paul is portrayed as a powerful preacher of the Word of God.[233] Throughout the Gentile mission in the narrative Paul becomes the leading person to bring God's salvation to the Gentiles. In relation to the churches in the mission field he first appears as a church-planter who evangelises both Jews and Gentiles and makes them disciples (13:52; 14:1, 21a; 16:15, 31-34; 17:12, 34; 18:8; 19:9). At his second visit to these churches Paul as a fortifier strengthens the churches in God's Word (14:21b-23; 15:41; 16:4-5; 18:23; 20:1-35). The disciples/churches, in turn, protect him from the Jews' persecutions (17:10, 14; 19:30-31; cf. 21:1-14).

As Paul carries on the third stage of God's mission, the Antioch and Jerusalem churches become his strong backers. The Antioch church serves as a mother church which upholds Paul's overseas mission. After each missionary journey Paul returns to the Antioch church before launching out into another journey (14:26-28; 15:35-40; 18:22). The Jerusalem church functions as the headquarters of churches which acknowledges Paul as an authorised messenger by confirming his message and affirming his authority in preaching to the Gentiles.[234] Paul's controversial message about God's salvation in Jesus being apart from Mosaic convention is eventually corroborated by the Jerusalem church leaders (15:1-21). At the Jerusalem council the leaders affirm with positive regard what Paul has done for Jesus among the Gentiles (15:25b-26); at the end of the third missionary journey they recognise what God has done through Paul among the Gentiles yet with negative concern (21:19-26). With reference to the Gentile mission, the Antioch church is the citadel supporting the missionary Paul in his mission and the Jerusalem church, especially their leaders, is the stronghold backing up Paul's message and authority (cf. Acts 15).

Specifically speaking, Barnabas' introduction of Paul builds up Paul's relation with the churches in Jerusalem and Antioch. Both relations prepare and uphold him for the Gentile mission to which Jesus has called him (9:15). Either relation promotes God's universal mission plan. By sending partners with Paul, the front-line missionary, the Antioch church partakes in the Gentile mission; by confirming Paul's preachings and doings, the Jerusalem church fortifies the Gentile mission. Paul's relation with Jewish and Gentile churches communi-

---

[232] Garrett, *Demise*, 85; Klauck, *Paganism*, 55; Polhill, *Acts*, 295. See also the change of the name order between Barnabas and Paul. The change of name, however, may also signify that Paul (Saul's Roman name) is henceforth dealing with the Gentiles (Witherington, *Acts*, 401).

[233] Strauss asserts that Paul's sermon at Pisidian-Antioch makes him become 'the great diaspora missionary and the leading figure in Acts' (*Messiah*, 148). The leading image, however, is set up in the narrative prior to the giving of the sermon that would enhance Paul's authority in preaching.

[234] Alex T.M. Cheung, 'A Narrative Analysis of Acts 14:27-15:35: Literary Shaping in Luke's Account of the Jerusalem Council,' *WTJ* 55 (1993) 137-54, citing 153.

cates God as the God of the universe, who prepares the universal salvation in Jesus, and as the Lord of the churches, who makes his people one in Jesus.

INTERACTIONS WITH THE JEWS

Both the churches and the Jews, the subsidiary group-characters in the narrative structure, create a perspective of depth that provides emphasis and colour to Paul's ministry. The churches actively reinforce the Gentile mission assigned to Paul; the Jews passively give rise to the background that prompts the mission. While the individual Jews who are involved in magic provide a context for Paul's spiritual warfare with demonic power in the Gentile world (13:6-11; 19:13), the collective Jew who persecutes Paul presents the warfare in the physical realm.[235] Right after Paul turns his faith to Jesus, the Jews desperately want to kill him because of his powerful witness to Jesus (9:22-24, 29). Throughout Paul's mission the Jews, whether in Jerusalem or the dispersion, are the strongest opposition which blocks the Word Paul preaches.

In the dispersion, the synagogue is usually the first place Paul visits in a city (13:5, 14; 14:1; 17:1-3, 10; 18:19; 19:8). In the synagogues, Paul brings both Jews and Gentiles to faith in Jesus (13:43; 14:1; 17:4, 12; 19:8-9) yet the unbelieving Jews become the most dreadful force which opposes Paul and his proclamation. Their rejection of the Word, however, creates a perspective of depth through which the design of *God's worldwide mission* is unveiled and Paul's Gentile activities are justified. More specifically, the Jews' rejection of the Word results in Paul's turning to the Gentiles (13:46-47; 18:6; 28:28)[236] which corresponds with Jesus' commission to him (9:15; 22:21; 26:17). Simultaneously, the Jews' persecution, as a spur, drives Paul to evangelism in other cities and thus furthers the mission geographically (13:50; 17:13-15).

In Jerusalem, the opposition to Paul not only comes from the unbelieving Jews but also the believing law-keeping Jews (15:1-5; 21:21b-25). Both create a perspective of depth through which *God's Word of salvation in Jesus* is clarified and Paul's witness to Jesus extends to those of a higher social rank. That the Jewish law-keeping believers insist on Mosaic law as a part of salvation forces the Jerusalem church leaders to hold out for the purity and clarity of the

---

[235] Joseph B. Tyson, 'The Problem of Jewish Rejection in Acts' in Joseph B. Tyson (ed.), *Luke-Acts and the Jewish People* (Minneapolis: Augsburg Publishing House, 1988) 124-37, citing 131.

[236] Strauss indicates that 13:46-51 introduces a theme which makes the narrative climax in chapter 28 (*Messiah*, 149). He further explains, the Jews' rejection of the Word 'is not the fundamental motivation for the Gentile mission. Rather, Paul's pattern reflects the God-ordained *order* of mission: to the Jew first, then to the Gentile' (176-77). See also Robert C. Tannehill, 'Rejection by Jews and Turning to Gentiles: The Pattern of Paul's Mission in Acts' in Tyson (ed.), *Luke-Acts and the Jewish People*, 83-101, esp. 83-84; John J. Kilgallen, 'Hostility to Paul in Pisidian Antioch (Acts 13,45)—Why?' *Bib* 84 (2003) 1-15, citing 14.

Word (i.e. to constitute God's salvation in Jesus apart from Mosaic law; 15:1-29) and to keep the unity of the church (21:20-25). On the other hand, the unbelieving Jews conspire with their leaders to kill Paul by accusing him before the Roman officials (21:27-31; 22:30; 23:12-14; 24:1-9; 25:1-7). Ironically, their accusation makes Paul's witness to Jesus reach the Jewish leaders and the Gentile rulers (23:6; 24:1-21; 26:1-23; cf. 9:15). The trials unexpectedly advance the mission in social hierarchy.

Simply put, the Jews' opposition of Paul's message ironically paves the way for the clarification and confirmation of God's will of universal mission and salvation in Jesus alone; their persecution of Paul the messenger ironically promotes his proclamation and mission.[237] In the dispersion the opposition illuminates God's plan for the Gentile mission and enables the mission to expand geographically; in Jerusalem it challenges and clarifies the quintessence of the Word and allows the Word to be passed on to a higher social rank. Paul's relation with the Jews conveys a sovereign God who turns the opposed forces into a driving force for his purpose.

INTERACTIONS WITH THE GENTILES

Paul's interactions with the believing Gentiles magnify the effectiveness of his Gentile evangelism (13:48; 16:15, 34; 17:4, 34) and, thus, signify the breakthrough of God's universal mission. Paradoxically, the unbelieving Gentiles provide a contrasting counterpart to manifest Paul's message and authority. Those who syncretise Paul's preaching and actions implicitly acknowledge the conspicuity of his message and activities (14:11-13; 17:18-21; 28:6); those who persecute Paul for their economic loss tacitly confess his authority as being from a higher power which overpowers their own magical force (16:19-23; 19:23-32). Both the positive and negative response of the Gentiles illuminate that God's mission is undefeated and the Word with divine authority is irresistible.

Paul is also persecuted by the Gentiles who are associated with and manipulated by the diaspora Jews to persecute Paul and oppose his proclamation (13:50; 14:2, 5, 19; 17:5, 13).[238] By reinforcing the Jews' opposition to Paul, these Gentiles essentially boost the Jews' prompting forward of the Gentile mission. Although they are a part of the Jews' scheme to thwart Paul and the Word, their opposition ultimately develops into a part of God's universal mission plan. This reveals that no opposed force can prevent God from consummating his mission plan. On the contrary, under God's sovereign authority and

---

[237] John J. Kilgallen, 'Persecution in the Acts of the Apostles' in Gerald O'Collins and Gilberto Marconi (eds.), *Luke and Acts* (Mahwah: Paulist Press, 1993) 143-60, citing 155; Cunningham, *Tribulations*, 293-94.

[238] Richard J. Cassidy, 'The Non-Roman Opponents of Paul' in Richard (ed.), *New Views on Luke and Acts*, 150-62, citing 153-54.

power, all the opposition turns out to be a driving force to promote the Gentile mission (cf. 26:19-23).

INTERACTIONS WITH THE ROMAN OFFICIALS

Whereas Paul's active interaction with the officials furthers the mission, his passive association with them guards him from the persecution of Gentiles and Jews. The former explicitly manifests the power of the proclamation of the Word; the latter implicitly discloses God's sovereign authority over human persecution.

Introduced by miracles, Paul's proclamation of the Word powerfully convinces both the proconsul Sergius-Paulus (13:7-12; note the emphasis on the teaching of the Lord) and the jailer (16:25-34; note the emphasis on Jesus as the core of the word of the Lord). This communicates the breakthrough of the Gentile mission especially the reaching out to the Roman officials.

Besides such outreaching evangelism, Paul associates with other Roman officials on account of the attack and accusation of Gentiles or Jews. The persecutors' inner world is revealed to be one of self-interest (Jews' jealousy at Paul's success in proclamation, 13:45; 17:5; Gentiles' anger at their personal loss, 16:19; 19:24-27). Therefore, manipulating the power of people, they attack Paul by kindling a disturbance in the city which is the exact concern of the Roman officials (17:7; 19:40; 21:31-34). As a result of the two Gentile accusations (16:19-24; 19:23-41), while Paul is physically tortured in the first case (16:22-23), the officials in both cases eventually forgo a further hearing (16:35; 19:37). Although the Jews' accusation is judged to be a Jewish internal affair (18:14-15) which deserves no death or imprisonment (23:29; 25:18-19; 26:31), the officials still keep Paul in prison to please the Jews (24:27; 25:9). Their injustice makes them indirect participants in the Jews' persecution.

Nonetheless, as the Jews' persecution grows from taking Paul to court to intending to kill him (18:12-17; 21:31-36; 22:22; 23:13-15; 25:2-3), the Roman officials become his safeguard. In Corinth the proconsul Gallio's disregard of the Jews' accusation implicitly justifies Paul's proclamation (18:12-17). In Jerusalem, while the Jews desperately want to kill Paul, Paul's Roman citizenship makes the Roman officials give him safe passage to Rome (22:29; 23:27). In the light of the divine promise (23:11), Paul's bondage is God's means to safeguard him as well as God's providence to fulfil Paul's calling, that is, the outreach to kings and other dignitaries, both Jews and Gentiles (cf. 9:15-16; 26:19-23).[239] God's sovereignty and authority are conspicuously magnified in his overruling of the malignant conspiracy of Jews by making the Roman officials a divine means for protecting Paul. Neither the Jews' nor the Gentiles' evil schemes can deter the divine mission plan for the Word; on the contrary, they

---

[239] Witherington, *Acts*, 747.

provide a context to make manifest and amplify God's invincible authority and power.

Summary

The heavenly encounters steer and uphold Paul in God's mission, whereas the human interactions provide perspectives of depth to continually highlight God's power and authority over the mission. With regard to the divine initiative, the heavenly revelators shepherd the messenger Paul to implement the Gentile mission; miracles fortify his message, the Word, and his authority of proclamation. In respect of the human response, both the positive and negative reaction to Paul's witness makes the Word spread out significantly and God's mission is carried out irresistibly. The churches actively buttress the Gentile mission by standing alongside Paul and his proclamation of the Word. Passively, in contrast, the unbelieving Jews and Gentiles manifest God's authority over the Gentile mission. They stand side by side to oppose Paul and the Word yet God's sovereignty overrules their opposition and turns it into a driving force for God's mission plan. Although they intend to destroy Paul through Roman legal power, this power ultimately becomes God's means of protecting Paul from pernicious persecution and safeguarding him to Rome. God reigns over every human interest for his highest interest which concerns his saving plan for the world. The greater the opposed force over Paul's proclamation, the greater God's authority over that opposition. No human force can overturn God's mission plan which is secured in his sovereign authority and power.

Conclusion

In the Gentile polytheistic context, miraculous deeds hardly shape Paul's speeches and are more narrowly fitted into the narrative context (cf. the healing of the lame man which contributes little to his preaching, 14:8-18).[240] When asked to preach in the synagogue, Paul stresses God's plan of salvation in Jesus based upon the Davidic promise-fulfilment (13:16-41) and reveals God's salvation also for Gentiles after the Jews' rejection (13:46-47). Facing the Gentiles' confusion, Paul introduces the God of the universe who creates the world and rules over humankind (14:15-17; 17:22-31). In the farewell speech to the believers, Paul expresses his faithfulness in proclaiming the Word to Jews and Gentiles (20:18-35). At the trials before the unbelieving Jews and Roman officials, Paul asserts that both his witness to the risen Jesus and his Gentile mission conform to God's will (22:1-21; 24:10-21; 26:2-23). Unlike Peter's miracle-shaped speeches, Paul's speeches are essentially circumstance-driven; they are the response to human challenges, from which emerges a *God of the*

---

[240] Cf. Jervell, *Unknown*, 80.

universe, and through which *God's mission, the divine will of the universal saving plan*, is firmly realised.

Miracles may carry different implications in different cultures (14:11), thus, to avoid the danger of being syncretised into local beliefs,[241] Paul's proclamation of the Word mainly precedes his miracles and miracles simply attest to what Paul has proclaimed and invigorate people's faith in the Word (13:12). Therefore, miracles reinforce Paul's mission more directly than his speeches (cf. 15:12). Even the divine interventions concern the mission instead of the speeches (see divine vision/instructions and promises relating to Gentile mission, 13:2; 16:6-7; 18:9-10; 23:11). Importantly, the similarities between the miracles of Peter and Paul signify that the God who reveals his will of universal salvation is continuously and actively working for his plan of the universal mission of salvation.

Alongside his proclamation of the Word and performing of miracles, Paul is persecuted throughout his missionary ministry (13:50; 14:5, 19; 16:22; 17:5; 18:12; 19:29-31; 21:30ff.; cf. 9:22-25, 29). The greater persecution,[242] the less human support[243] and the less indication of the effectiveness of proclamation[244] all characterise Paul as a suffering witness as Jesus reveals (9:16).[245] Significantly, in the polytheistic world, the powerful Word-bearer's suffering for a salvific message distinguishes him from a magician and renders him a miracle-worker. Moreover, the suffering itself, excluding any personal advantage, becomes a powerful witness to the divine origin of the Word Paul preaches, in both the polytheistic and Jewish contexts. Both Paul's miracles, a positive witness, and suffering, a negative witness, powerfully fortify the Word through which God dynamically communicates his salvation in Jesus and consummates his salvific plan. Eventually, 'it is the Christian proclamation that wins

---

[241] William Barclay, 'A Comparison of Paul's Missionary Preaching and Preaching to the Church' in Gasque and Martin (eds.), *Apostolic History and the Gospel*, 165-75, citing 171-72.

[242] While the persecution of Peter only comes from the Jewish leaders, Paul's persecutors arise from all sides (the unbelieving Jews and Gentiles, the Jewish leaders and even the law-keeping believers).

[243] Although persecuted, Peter, together with other apostles, is intimately upheld by the Jewish crowd and the faith community in Jerusalem (4:5-35; 5:19-26). In contrast, Paul mainly faces the persecution alone or with only his mission partner (13:51; 14:19; 16:22-23; 18:12; 21:31ff.). Although undergirded by the Jerusalem and Antioch church, their distant support was unlikely to reach to the overseas missionary and the local believers do not help much because of the forceful persecution.

[244] Instead of specifying a great number of converts (cf. 2:41; 4:4), the narrative underlines individual converts in Paul's mission (13:12; 16:15, 34; 17:34; 18:8) and a large number of converts is only indicated generally (13:43; 14:1; 17:4; 18:8; even in the great Ephesus mission mass converts are merely implied, 19:10-20).

[245] Wilson, *Gentiles*, 168.

the trial of strength, relying not so much on a superior miraculous power, but rather on the message of salvation which it brings.'[246]

Foremost, through heavenly revelators God is active in carrying out his mission plan and never leaves his messenger alone. The heavenly Jesus calls Paul into God's mission; the Spirit directs him to the second stage of Gentile mission—a consummate step with geographical concern. Divine promises come forth to Paul individually in times of distress (18:9-10; 23:11; 27:23-24; yet none to Peter). The less the human support in public; the more the divine invigoration in private. Even though the divine safekeeping of Paul is mainly through other human forces (18:14-15; 21:31-32; 23:12-24; 27:43), God's promises never fail. Paul's life testifies to the torrents of divine power overwhelming all human forces and the strings of the divine plan coiling around and triumphing over all human schemes. God arms Paul with his authoritative power in accordance with his sovereign plan. Throughout Paul's life in the narrative (speeches and actions) God is characterised as a sovereign Lord of the universe, who through his heavenly agents authoritatively calls his human agents into the divine mission of universal salvation, and who powerfully overrules human forces for his salvific purpose. God's redemptive plan for the world and protection of his Word-bearers also unveil his sovereign love and care.

---

[246] Klauck, *Paganism*, 54.

CHAPTER 5

The Characterisation of God by Minor Characters

The narrative world of Acts is constructed of sequential events which are woven together by complex interrelationships of characters. Such relationships and interactions make up, to some extent, the contextual knowledge of each character. In addition to the major characters in Acts, certain characters and groups deserve exploration in relation to the characterisation of God since they not only serve to reveal the major characters but to develop the plot. These are minor characters who carry a variety of functions in the narrative world. They should not be confused with background characters who primarily function as foils to the major characters. While both groups provide human contexts for the social setting in which the major characters are realised in depth, minor characters are delineated in a more individual way than background characters.[1] The interactions between the minor characters and the major characters present a further development of the plot while purely background characters 'may be merely useful cogs in the mechanism of the plot, collectively they may establish themselves as a chorus to the main action... or may exist simply to establish the density of society in which the protagonists must move if they are to have any depth of realization.'[2] Thus, according to the importance of characters' parts to the plot in Acts, the minor characters can be categorised into groups, for example, the believers, the God-fearers and the opponents. They are either associated directly with God or closely interact with the major characters, Peter and Paul, who witness God's activities. While examining each group, the minor and background characters will first be briefly clarified to provide a lucid structure of the deployment of characters. Thereafter, within this human context the individual or collective minor characters will be investigated thoroughly to explore their presentation of God.

The Believers: The Believers as a Whole, Stephen, Philip, Barnabas, James

The believers are presented as a collective character for the main action at the beginning of certain episodes. Nevertheless, as the story develops, the image of a collective character fades into the backcloth and certain believers are named individually and introduced laconically to the reader before their contribution

---

[1] Harvey, *Character*, 56-58.
[2] Harvey, *Character*, 56.

to the plot (or their main performance) later in the narrative. Among these are Stephen and Philip (listed among the seven in 6:5), Barnabas (introduced in 4:36-37), James (indicated in 12:17), Mark (indicated in 12:12, 25), Silas (introduced in 15:22) and Timothy (introduced in 16:1-3).[3] While Stephen, Philip, Barnabas and James play crucial roles in the plot progression (as minor characters), Mark, Silas and Timothy provide social settings for the story (as background characters). Mark provides the context of the sharp argument between Paul and Barnabas and provides the very cause of the division of the first overseas mission team. Both Silas and Timothy partner with Paul on his itinerant mission without any individual speaking part. Their accompaniment of Paul, as John with Peter, seems to follow Jesus' pattern of sending out the disciples two by two (cf. Lk 10:1). Overall, Paul is the leading actor in these scenes. Silas and Timothy serve as the human context enabling Paul to be realised in depth.

The witness of the believers as a whole is particularly prominent in the first five chapters of Acts and crucial in chapters 11 and 13. They are mostly presented as a background character (in a collective sense) to provide a social context or as a chorus to the main action. Their prayer to God, however, reveals their perception of God's activities. By their interactions with the apostles in the faith community God is reflected in a new way to the Jewish community. Stephen, the first martyr whose ministry provokes the Jews' persecution of the believers in Jerusalem, presents the most lengthy speech in Acts and his God-centred discourse is undoubtedly crucial to the portrait of God. Philip, the first believer who evangelises the Samaritans and Gentiles (8:40), geographically widens the boundary of the faith community[4] and makes known the will of God. At first sight, Barnabas' role is similar to that of Silas and Timothy in the narrative. Nevertheless, unlike Silas and Timothy being chosen by Paul to be his assistants (15:40; 16:3), Barnabas is a key person introducing Paul to the

---

[3] Ananias, another key disciple known by name, although playing an important part in Paul's conversion, mainly characterises Paul and Jesus (9:10-17). He is Jesus' agent to light up Paul's new understanding of Jesus, the Son of God (9:17, 20). Such perception leads Paul to a new perspective of God. Basically, Ananias' role in the narrative serves to provide a social context for Paul's conversion. Thus, he will not be discussed in this section.

[4] To contend that Peter is the legitimate founder of the Gentile mission, Haenchen argues that the Ethiopian eunuch is simply an official under a foreign ruler (*eunuch* is a mere title of office and the text does not indicate the eunuch is a Gentile) and that his conversion serves as 'a stepping-stone between those of the Samaritans and the Gentiles' (*Acts*, 314). However, without such a presumption it is rather natural to regard the Ethiopian eunuch as a Gentile. Cf. Bernd Kollmann, arguing from a redactional perspective, examines all the traditional sources used by Luke and concludes that the traditional sources assign to Philip a greater role than the role Luke himself sets for Philip ('Philippus der Evangelist und die Anfänge der Heidenmission,' *Bib* 81 [2000] 551-65).

faith community and is Paul's associate. Both are called by the Holy Spirit and sent by the Antioch church for the Gentile mission (13:2-3). James, the likely chairman of the Jerusalem council, is mentioned by name three times (12:17; 15:13; 21:18). His only individual speaking part serves the vital point of accepting the Gentiles into the faith community; this is a difficult issue for Jewish believers who have been nurtured under Jewish laws and conventions but it is crucial for the unity of the church which embraces both Jews and Gentiles as the new people of God. The above sketch shows the significance of these minor characters' important role in God's mission. Their presentation of God thus merits further investigation.

Conceptual Characterisation

As Berlin asserts that 'biblical narrative makes extensive use of the speech and actions of characters to further the plot and to create characterisation,'[5] the believers' speeches with reference to God definitely move along the characterisation of God (their actions will be investigated in the next section). There is no personal speech for Philip and Barnabas. Philip's preaching is summarised by the narrator as Christ-centred proclamation which relates to the kingdom of God (8:12).[6] Barnabas' only voice joins in Paul's defence of the nature of God to the pagan Gentiles (14:15-17). Nonetheless, there are three speeches crucial to the portrayal of God—the accordant prayer of the believers (4:24-30),[7] Stephen's God-centred speech (7:2-53) and James' speech indicating God's plan for his people (15:13-21). These speeches present the believers' image of God which reinforce the major characters' portrait of God since minor characters serve to enhance major characters in the plot.

THE ACCORDANT PRAYER OF THE BELIEVERS AS A WHOLE (4:24-30)

After hearing of the two apostles' confrontation with the Jewish authorities, the believers appeal to God with one mind.[8] See the following sketch to highlight their acknowledgement of God's sovereignty.

---

[5] Berlin, *Biblical Narrative*, 38.
[6] F. Scott Spencer argues that Philip's proclamation is Jesus-centred. Regarding Jesus' relation to God's kingdom, he indicates that 'the Jesus who is the "kingdom-preacher par excellence" in Luke's Gospel becomes the focus of the church's kingdom-proclamation in the book of Acts' (*The Portrait of Philip in Acts* [JSNTSup 67; Sheffield: Sheffield Academic Press, 1992] 40-41).
[7] Acts 1:24-25 is another voice of the believers as a whole. No matter whether the object of κύριε refers to God or Jesus, the prayer serves to justify the choosing of Matthias rather than to reveal God in the light of the ongoing divine mission.
[8] The term ὁμοθυμαδόν is often translated 'together' (cf. Haenchen, *Acts*, 225; Witherington, *Acts*, 201; Conzelmann, *Acts*, 34). Nevertheless, in surveying the favourite adverb ὁμοθυμαδόν in Acts (occurring 11 times in the NT: 10 in Acts and the only

Δέσποτα, Recognition of God's Sovereign Lordship (4:24-28)
> God Sovereign over the Universe (v. 24)
> God Sovereign over Human History (vv. 25-28)

Κύριε, Petition to the Authoritative Lord (4:29-30)
> Strengthening God's Servants for Their Witness to the Word (v. 29)
> Confirming the Word with Signs and Wonders (v. 30)

The first part of the prayer (4:24-28), which is prefaced with the vocative δέσποτα (Sovereign Lord), reveals their recognition of God's absolute authority. The two substantival participles function as appositions of σύ which refers to δέσποτα (4:24-25) and introduce the very nature of God. The first phrase points out God's relationship with the cosmos (4:24b); God is the Creator who brought the whole universe into being. The second phrase indicates God's relationship with humankind; God takes the initiative to reveal himself to humankind. His revelation is by means of the Holy Spirit and through the mouth of his servant David (4:25a). Such a revelation bears the prophetic nature which foretells the future events recorded in Psalm 2:1-2 (4:25b-26). Two scenes are presented in the quotation which correspond to the historical event (4:27-28). The first scene accentuates the gathering of the hostile force of earthly authorities and people against God and his anointed One.[9] Acts 4:27 points out who they are: Herod, Pontius Pilate, the Gentiles and the people of Israel. The second scene declares that their plot runs fruitlessly (4:25b). Their conspiracy, which is now regarded as that against Jesus, God's anointed One, ultimately furthers God's predestined plan (4:28). Προορίζω stresses that God determines

---

other occurrence in Rom 15:6), we see it emphasises 'the oneness of spirit' (Marshall, *Acts*, 104) as suggested by the semantic meaning of the word ('with one mind,' cf. L&N, §31.23; BDAG, 706). Barrett further discusses the use of ὁμοθυμαδόν in the LXX. Ὁμοθυμαδόν means, simply, 'together' in the Hebrew translation and is interchangeable with Greek words or phrases, e.g. ὅμα, ἐπὶ τὸ αὐτό, κατὰ τὸ αὐτό which also mean simply 'together.' The etymological meaning (with one accord), however, suggests the unity of the individuals as a corporate whole (cf. Barrett, *Acts*, 1: 88-89). By and large, the oneness and unity of the believers are in view. See also Steve Walton, "Ὁμοθυμαδόν in Acts: Co-location, Common Action or "Of One Heart and Mind"?' in P.J. Williams, Andrew D. Clarke, Peter M. Head and David Instone-Brewer (eds.), *The New Testament in Its First Century Setting* (Grand Rapids: Eerdmans, 2004) 89-105.

9 Two verbs (παρίστημι and συνάγω) and a phrase (ἐπὶ τὸ αὐτό) enforce the assembly despite the motive of each individual. Παρίστημι means 'to stand near or alongside of someone, either with friendly or hostile intent' (L&N, §17.3). The idea of gathering further echoes in the word συνάγω together with the phrase ἐπὶ τὸ αὐτό. It reinforces the main thought that, no matter how strong earthly power and might are, God on high sovereignly governs human affairs.

history beforehand.[10] It is, thus, futile to machinate against the God who creates humankind and foreknows human intrigue.[11] Not only does God have the whole universe well in hand (4:24), nor merely does he initially reveal his will to people (4:25-26), but he dominates human history, even overruling human vile schemes, to his end (4:27-28).

Based on such comprehension of God, the second part of the prayer, which is introduced by the vocative κύριε, presents the believers' supplication to God. Κύριος reveals the believers' acknowledgement of God's powerful control of every circumstance so that they come to him with full confidence. They solicit God to behold their intimidators and to grant them the boldness to proclaim his Word under intimidating circumstances (4:29). God is recognised as both the judge of their intimidators and the source of their boldness.[12] Moreover, they beseech God's confirmation of their preaching of the Word by stretching out his mighty hand for healing and by performing signs and wonders through Jesus' name (4:30).[13] God is recognised as the source and cause of the miraculous works which occur only through the name of Jesus.

Throughout the prayer the repetitious use of σου and παῖς serve as two key words to disclose the unspoken thought of the believers.[14] That the eight occurrences of σου in seven verses are dense in use indicates the intensive notion of the word (4:25, Δαυὶδ παιδός σου; 4:27, τὸν ἅγιον παῖδά σου Ἰησοῦν; 4:28, ἡ χείρ σου; 4:28, ἡ βουλή σου; 4:29b, τοῖς δούλοις σου; 4:29b, τὸν λόγον σου; 4:30a, τὴν χεῖρά σου; 4:30b, τοῦ ἁγίου παιδός σου Ἰησοῦ). This emphasises not only the relationships between God and his servants (David and Jesus, cf. παῖς in 4:25; 27,30) and between God and the believers (4:29b, δοῦλοι) but also God's ownership over them. All these people belonging to God

---

[10] L&N, §30.84; see also Squires, *Plan*, 99, 171-72.

[11] Marshall, *Acts*, 105.

[12] The boldness of Peter and John is seen clearly in their confrontation with the Jewish authorities. The desire for greater boldness to proclaim the word does not evince that they lack such boldness but rather it implies that they know the boldness is of God and only he can bestow it increasingly upon them. Furthermore, it is argued that the meaning of παρρησία implies a prophetic quality (Johnson, *Acts*, 85) or speaking with tongues (Richard, 'Pentecost,' 135-36). Nevertheless, as the narrator indicates the answer of the believers' prayer in 4:31, παρρησία is better regarded as simply the boldness to witness, as Peter and John do, to the hostile world in the context.

[13] The use of the image of God's hand indicates God's mighty power (Marshall, *Acts*, 106). Miracles accompanying God's word are considered as God's confirmation of his own word. It is from this perspective that Witherington indicates that miracles 'are seen to have an apologetic function in Acts' (*Acts*, 204). Moreover, while the two imperatives (ἔπιδε and δός) in 4:29 introduce the content of the believers' supplication, the ἐν τῷ clause with two infinitives (ἐκτείνειν and γίνεσθαι) indicates how their petition for the boldness to proclaim the word can be done (4:30).

[14] Bar-Efrat, *Narrative Art*, 212.

are in the different stages of the history to do God's will by his power (4:28, 29, 30). David is intended to be God's mouthpiece, Jesus God's anointed One and the believers God's witnesses. While David prospectively declares what would happen to God's anointed One, the believers retrospectively proclaim what God has done through his anointed One. Jesus is the centre of God's plan in human history and the essence of God's Word in this age (4:29b). On the one hand, the possessive pronoun σου points out God's proprietorship and thus implies his unchallenged sovereignty; on the other hand, it indicates the source of the divine plan and power and thus highlights God's unchangeable authority over his servants in relation to his will in human events.

Παῖς is employed to depict the relationship between God and both David and Jesus. It means 'a slave, possibly serving as a personal servant and thus with the implication of kindly regard.'[15] It also indicates Christ in his relation to God that 'in this connection it has the meaning servant, because of the identification of "servant of God" of certain OT passages with the Messiah.'[16] While both David and Jesus are God's distinctively appointed ones, Jesus is further portrayed as ὁ ἅγιος παῖς σου. The use of ἅγιος makes Jesus the unique servant of God who brings God's holy will and plan to realisation. The believers, however, do not apply παιδές to themselves but use δοῦλοι instead which indicates slaves 'in the sense of becoming the property of an owner.'[17] The slight difference between παῖς and δοῦλος (the former is a servant in a more personal sense and the latter in a more inferior sense) signifies the believers' regard of themselves as God's slaves who submit themselves utterly to his authority. Conzelmann points out that 'the counterpart to δέσποτα is not παῖς, "child, servant," but δοῦλος, "slave".'[18] The use of παῖς and δοῦλος signifies the believers' understanding that all human agents are God's servants to do his will and make manifest his plan. Even Jesus, the very word of their proclamation, is God's servant. By such recognition they realise themselves as deserving a more subservient status towards God.

In short, the single-minded prayer essentially unveils the believers' fundamental notion of God. By their acknowledgement of God in human history, God the sovereign Lord (δεσπότης) is perceived as the Creator of the universe (4:24), the Revealer of future events (4:25-6) and the Governor of human history (4:27-8). By the supplication towards God in their intimidation, God the authoritative Lord (κύριος) is recognised as the judge/discerner of human schemes (4:29a), the fortifier of human strength (4:29b) and the justifier/confirmer of his own Word (4:30). Overall, the undergirding thought of the

---

[15] L&N, §87.77.

[16] BDAG, 604. Soards points out that the term 'provides information indirectly about the theological identity of Jesus (see 2:36)' (*Speeches*, 49).

[17] L&N, §87.76.

[18] Conzelmann, *Acts*, 34.

prayer makes clear the absolute sovereignty, authority, omnipotence and omniscience of God over the event of Jesus in human history.

STEPHEN'S SPEECH (7:2-53)

The accusation of Stephen in Acts 6:11, 13 and 14 reveals two items of the charge, the Temple and the Law, which are related to the worship of God and which Jesus is going to destroy and change.[19] To Stephen, the accusation comes not from his inadequacy of presenting Jesus but from the Jews' disobedience and hardness of hearts. His speech, given at the trial before the Sanhedrin, which recounts God's participation in Israel's history and Israel's response to God, manifests the essence of worshipping God[20] and the nature of the Jews' opposition. See the outline of the speech with particular regard to the interactions between God and his people.

From Abraham Comes God's People (7:2-8)
    God calls out Abraham and promises him descendants (vv. 2-5)
    God makes them a people of worship and covenant (vv. 6-8)

Through Joseph Comes God's Deliverance (7:9-16)
    God delivers Joseph by being with him in Egypt (vv. 9-10)
    God delivers his people by moving them to Egypt through Joseph (vv. 11-16)

Through Moses Comes God's Salvation (7:17-43)
    God saves Moses (vv. 17-22)
    Moses is rejected by his people (vv. 23-29)
    God makes Moses a saviour (vv. 30-37)
    People of Israel again reject Moses and God (vv. 38-43)

Along with His People Comes God's Presence (7:44-53)
    Israel regards the Tabernacle and Temple as God's presence (vv. 44-47)
    God cannot be confined to any location (vv. 48-50)
    The rejection of God characterises the people of Israel (vv. 51-53)

---

[19] The word *Temple* does not appear in the accusation; however, the concept of the Temple and worship is evident throughout Stephen's speech (7:4, 7, 41-50). The juxtaposition of God (6:11), the holy place (6:13) and this place (6:14) signifies that the Jews have laid a close connection between God and the Temple (7:48). See Marshall, *Acts*, 128, 132; Dennis D. Sylva, 'The Meaning and Function of Acts 7:46-50,' *JBL* 106 (1987) 261-75, citing 268-69; cf. Craig C. Hill, 'Acts 6.1-8.4: Division or Diversity?' in Witherington (ed.), *History, Literature, and Society*, 129-53, esp. 143-44; N.H. Taylor, 'Stephen, the Temple, and Early Christian Eschatology,' *RB* 110 (2003) 62-85, citing 75-77. Neagoe further indicates that the temple and the law are 'two major identity markers of the people of God' (*Trial*, 162).

[20] Dennis Hamm, 'The Tamid Service in Luke-Acts: The Cultic Background behind Luke's Theology of Worship,' *CBQ* 65 (2003) 215-31, citing 227-28.

Two story-lines run through Stephen's speech—God's plan for Israel and Israel's rejection of God. The divine initiative in 'Israel's life as a nation'[21] is highlighted in God's interactions with Israel. God takes the initial step into human history and finds favour in Abraham, the founder-forefather of Israel.[22] God promises him land and descendants and makes him a distinct people of worship and covenant (7:2-8). Later, God becomes the saviour of Joseph and Moses and makes them saviours for his people (7:9-36). In Stephen's speech, God is active in the life of the individual forefathers; God's saving plan for his people to worship him is the thematic concern. Throughout God's interactions with Israel's forefathers, God's presence and sovereign care are not confined geographically to the promised land.[23] Rather, the omnipresent God is with and cares for his people wherever they are, even in Egypt.

Instead of being a people of worship, Israel, characterised as a people of hardness with recalcitrant hearts, rejects God and his chosen ones.[24] Joseph is first rejected by his brothers, the forefathers of Israel (7:9a); Moses is rejected by his people (7:25-28, 39-40). Their rejection of God's appointed saviours is ultimately the rejection of God (7:41-43).[25] Stephen, speaking at length about Moses, emphasises his crucial role in God's saving plan and reveals the nature of Israel's opposition.[26] The opposition results from their misapprehension of the worship of God—the worship of a visible image and in a fixed location. Such misconception causes their disobedience and recalcitrance which is also the central issue of the Jews who accuse Stephen (7:51).

The desire to worship a visible god leads Israel to apostasy and idolatry (7:40), which also indicates their disobedience to the Law.[27] They know Moses but do not truly know Moses' God; thus, they desire only a visible guide but cannot see in faith the most powerful guide behind Moses. In responding to their idolatry, God turns away from them, gives them over to further idol wor-

---

[21] Martin-Asensio, *Foregrounding*, 97.

[22] In introducing the beginning of Israel's history, Stephen places Abraham in a very passive role. God is always the subject in Abraham episode. The only verse which seemingly depicts Abraham taking an action is 7:4a; however, this still describes his obedience to God's command.

[23] Neagoe, *Trial*, 163.

[24] John J. Kilgallen, *The Stephen Speech* (AB 67; Rome: Biblical Institute Press, 1976) 112; Martin William Mittelstadt, *The Spirit and Suffering in Luke-Acts* (JPTSup 26; London: T & T Clark, 2004) 105-10; Neagoe, *Trial*, 164.

[25] John J. Kilgallen, 'The Function of Stephen's Speech,' *Bib* 70 (1989) 173-193, citing 189.

[26] Tannehill, *Narrative Unity*, 2:85.

[27] Sylva, 'Acts 7,' 269.

ship and sends them into exile (7:42-43).[28] What then does *worship* mean according to God? Or, what is Stephen's understanding of *worshipping God*? There are two words for worship in Stephen's speech: λατρεύω (7:7, 42) and προσκυνέω (7:43). Both are terms pertaining to religious activities. Λατρεύω conveys the idea of religious practice to 'perform religious rites as a part of worship.'[29] Προσκυνέω signifies 'one's complete dependence on or submission to a high authority figure' which is expressed in attitude or, possibly, in position.[30] Specifically, λατρεύω involves certain religious rites in worship and προσκυνέω emphasises the attitude of a worshipper. The word for calling Abraham out to *worship* God (7:7) and giving Israel over to *worship* heavenly bodies (7:42) is λατρεύω which possibly implies the observation of certain religious rites.[31] While citing God's utterance in Amos 5:25-27, the use of προσκυνέω for the Israelites' worshipping of handmade gods elucidates God's judgement for their wrong motive and attitude (7:43). The context of these words indicates that the object of worship is God alone (7:7)[32] and that true worship demands both right attitude toward and right relationship with God.

Besides their misconception of the very essence of worship, the Israelites also have a wrong notion for the place of worship. Stephen's identification of God's promised land with his accusers' alleged *the holy place* (compare 7:7 τῷ τόπῳ τούτῳ with 6:13 τοῦ τόπου τοῦ ἁγίου and 6:14 τὸν τόπον τοῦτον) paves the way for his further elucidation of worship and his later denunciation of his accusers (cf. 7:51-53).[33] The true nature of the holy place is spelt out by God's voice in 7:32-33. The place is holy because God is present;[34] in other words, where there is the presence of God, there is the holy place. It is made clear that even in Israel's desert-wandering wherever the tent for worship is, there is God's presence (7:44-45). As to the building of the Temple for worship, the indication of David ὃς εὗρεν χάριν ἐνώπιον τοῦ θεοῦ exposes that Stephen

---

[28] That God withdraws himself and keeps his favour from his people is the greatest judgement upon them since without his grace and mercy they are not able to turn to him and enjoy his presence and abundant blessings.

[29] L&N, §53.14.

[30] BDAG, 882; cf. L&N, §53.56.

[31] It is obviously true that God did instruct them in the way of worship (7:44; Exod 25-30).

[32] Throughout the Abraham episode, God is positioned by Stephen as the subject of the main clauses. Acts 7:7b is the only occurrence that God is in the position of an object (cf. also Gen 15:13-14; Exod 12:3).

[33] Calling out Abraham, God instructs him to τὴν γῆν ἥν ἄν σοι δείξω (7:3). Stephen further identifies the unspecified location of God's promised land τὴν γῆν ταύτην εἰς ἣν ὑμεῖς νῦν κατοικεῖτε (7:4) and then explains that God's people will worship him in τῷ τόπῳ τούτῳ (7:7).

[34] Cf. Heinz-Werner Neudorfer, 'The Speech of Stephen' in Marshall and Peterson (eds.), *Witness*, 275-94, citing 285.

regards the relationship between God and his people as fundamental and essential rather than the visible and tangible temple (7:46). The citation of Isaiah 66:1-2 precisely expresses Stephen's understanding of God being transcendent spatially over all creation (7:48-50).[35] It evinces 'not that God's presence can't be found in the temple, but that God's presence can't be confined there, nor can God be controlled or manipulated by the building of a temple.'[36] Therefore, where there is true worship of God, there is the holy place with the presence of God.

Whereas Stephen's major concern is *worship of God*, the Jews' interest is *this place*.[37] *This place* is related to God's promise, a gracious gift, to Abraham who is fully in a passive role while receiving God's promises of either the descendants or the land.[38] Yet, worshipping God is associated with God's purpose, divine will and plan.[39] While the promise of the land is connected with God's benevolent bestowal, the purpose of worshipping God is linked with God himself. The promise of God invites one to believe and receive without human merit; the worship of God demands one's full submission to and exaltation of God. As God's promises bring salvation for his people, the God of glory is worthy of their worship and honour. In brief, Stephen's notion of *worshipping God* is to submit oneself to God's authority, enjoy his presence and honour him with one's full trust and obedience. Instead of letting God be God and worshipping him wholeheartedly, the Israelites lay their focus on God's blessings rather than God himself and desire to have authority over God by making themselves handmade gods. Therefore, while Abraham's obedience moves him to the promised land, Israel's disobedience stops them short of the land. Only in true worship of God can Israel inherit God's promise since worship is the divine purpose to keep God's people in his presence and thus in his sovereign care. See the following chart for Stephen's overall understanding of God's perspective of worship; this contradicts that of the Israelites.

---

[35] Cf. Huub van de Sandt, 'The Presence and Transcendence of God: An Investigation of Acts 7,44-50 in the Light of the LXX,' *ETL* 80/1 (2004) 30-59, esp. 55.

[36] Witherington, *Acts*, 273; also Sylva, 'Acts 7,' 267-78.

[37] Cf. David Seccombe, 'The New People of God' in Marshall and Peterson (eds.), *Witness*, 349-72, citing 357.

[38] While in the promised land, Abraham has no son (7:5); after God gives him a covenant of circumcision as a confirmation of his promise, Abraham begets Isaac. Οὕτως in 7:8 implies the giving of birth to Isaac is of God's covenant (cf. Gen 17:10-13; Barrett, *Acts*, 1:346). Also, God is the subject in both 7:7 and 7:45. God not only judges the nation which enslaves his people but drives out, for his people, the nations in the promised land.

[39] The purpose of God's salvation, as it is presented consistently in the Bible, is to worship God. See Exodus 3:12, the deliverance from Egypt is to worship God; Luke 1:74, Jesus' salvation is to enable us to worship God; Romans 12:1, standing in God's salvation (Rom 1-11), we are to offer him spiritual worship.

Viewpoint of God[1]	God	Worshippers	Israel's Plight
Nature (Being)	The one true God with all divine attributes [Invisible & intangible]	Glorify God as who he is	Desire visible and tangible gods
Deeds (Doing)	The salvation of God The fulfilment of his promises[2] [Visible & tasted]	Glorify God for what he has done	Cannot recognise the work of God [Spiritually blind]
Place of Worship	The presence of God [Not being confined spatio-temporally]	Wherever the true worship of God is [The right attitude toward and relationship with God]	The Temple (7:48) [The dwelling place of God]
Attitude towards the Counterpart of Worship	God is faithful to the salvation of his people [1. Sends his chosen ones to be saviours 2. Reveals his will]	Trust and obey [Submit themselves to God's chosen ones and his words given through them]	Disbelieve and disobey (7:51) [Reject God's chosen ones and his words (7:52-53)]

[1] Worship involves two parties: the recipient of worship, God, and the worshipper, Israel. The above chart shows God's perspective of the two parties concerning the acknowledgement of God (his being and doing) and the concept of worship (the place and attitude of worship). The misinterpretation of God definitely leads to pseudo-worship of him.

[2] God's promise and salvation are the benevolence of his attributes. Only by his gracious deeds are the divine attributes known to his people. God's salvation fulfils his promise which serves his purpose. God's saving plan tells of his faithfulness and lovingkindness.

Israel's desire for blessings from a tangible God leads to their misapprehension of the worship of God. Throughout Stephen's account, the essence of true worship is gradually disclosed and the nature of the Jews' opposition exposed (7:51). In contrast to the Jews' rebellious nature, God's sovereign faithfulness in consummating his purpose stands out.[40] Throughout Israel's history, God's

[40] The omniscient God has his perfect timing to carry out his promises and plan (7:17; 34). Without waiting for God's commission and timing, Moses' first appearance to

people pass by generation after generation and their inhabitancy is moved from place to place. What remains unchanged is that the omnipresent God is always with his people wherever they are, working for their salvation and building up for himself a people of worship. Those who stay in true worship live in God's supreme presence and sovereign care. From Stephen's speech appears a supreme and faithful God, who sovereignly chooses and cares for his people; an omnipresent God, who is with his people wherever they go; an omniscient God, who looks at his people's innermost being; and a forbearing God, who endures his people's constant rebellion.

JAMES' SPEECH (15:13-21)

The criteria for accepting the Gentile believers into the faith community diverge within the Jewish believers (15:1-2). A council is held in Jerusalem to resolve whether circumcision should be required of Gentile Christians, where faith is rooted in Judaism. The issue is crucial for the unity of the faith community since it determines whether Gentile believers can be fully accepted by Jewish believers and thus participants in one fellowship. After a long dispute including the witnesses of Peter, Barnabas and Paul, James elucidates his perception of God's will. His God-centred speech provides a solution for the debate (15:13-21). Two subjects appear in the speech: God's work and will among the Gentiles (15:13-18); James' suggestion of their response to God's will (15:19-21).

Appealing for a hearing, James depicts God's will to the Gentiles by citing Simon's declaration of God's activities among the Gentiles at present[41] and the scriptural revelation of God's plan for the Gentiles foretold in the ancient time (15:13-18). James first points out that it is God taking the initiative (πρῶτον) to make himself a people from the Gentiles (15:14).[42] The two verbs ἐπεσκέψατο

---

his people, which is of his own passion, accomplishes nothing (7:23-29). It is not by human might or power but God alone who fulfils the divine plan.

[41] The name Simeon obviously refers to Peter Simon in the context (15:7-11). Bruce gives a clear explanation that 'Συμεών is the LXX rendering of Heb. *sim'ôn*, the ε representing the Heb. *'ayin* (which has no equivalent in the hellenized Σίμων)' (*Acts*, 3rd edn., 339). It is appropriate for a Palestinian Jew to address his fellow Jew Συμεών, which is in Semitic form (cf. 2 Pet 1:1), see also Marshall, *Acts*, 251; Haenchen, *Acts*, 447; Witherington, *Acts*, 458.

[42] Soards considers πρῶτον in its temporal qualification which echoes ἀφ' ἡμερῶν ἀρχαίων in Peter's speech in 15:7 (*Speeches*, 93; cf. also *Haenchen, Acts*, 447; Conzelmann, *Acts*, 117). While most commentators are silent about the significance of πρῶτον in the text (e.g. Marshall, Bruce, Witherington, Johnson), Dunn subtly implies the ordinal qualification of πρῶτον as he denotes that 'God has taken an initiative' (*Acts*, 203). According to BDAG (893-4), the adverb πρῶτον may refer to time (before, earlier), sequence (first) or degree (in the first place, above all, especially). Since James' speech is a final solution to the debate, 15:14 is not a repetition

λαβεῖν, which 'dramatises the divine action being reported and adds emphasis to God's action in relation to the Gentiles,'[43] reinforce God's care for the Gentiles and his will to embrace them as his own.[44] The vocabulary and phrases ἐπισκέπτομαι (*to care for* with the implication of continuous responsibility), λαμβάνω (*to take* with the implication of taking into one's possession)[45] and λαὸν τῷ ὀνόματι αὐτοῦ (*people for him* with the indication of God's people)[46]

---

of what Peter said but rather an exegesis of its gist. That Peter presents God in an active role (God is the subject throughout 15:7-9) impresses upon James that God has taken the initiative to reach Gentiles. Thus, πρῶτον is better understood in its ordinal meaning.

With regard to *for his name*, N.A. Dahl points out that the phrase 'is found neither in the Hebrew Bible nor in the Septuagint.' By studies of the phrase used in the old Palestinian Targum and the Old Testament, Dahl concludes that 'the phrase "a people for His (My, the LORD's) name" is a standard idiom of the old Palestinian Targum, where it is regularly used to render the Hebrew לִי (לְיהוה, לִי) לְעַם ('"A People for His Name" [Acts xv.14],' *NTS* 4 [1957-58] 319-27, citing 321). Here τῷ ὀνόματι αὐτοῦ may be a targumic replacement for *for himself* (cf. Deut 7:6; Isa 43:21; also Bruce, *Acts*, 3rd edn., 340). J. Dupont further expounds a vertical relationship between God and his people which is the result of free initiative by which God chose for himself men and women to consecrate them for his name ('Un Peuple d'entre les Nations [Acts 15:14],' *NTS* 31 [1985] 321-35, citing 329).

[43] Soards, *Speeches*, 93. Dupont indicates that it is of God's 'benevolent initiative' that Gentiles become the people of God ('Peuple,' 328).

[44] Most commentators translate ἐπεσκέψατο 'he visited' (Bruce, *Acts*, 339; Conzelmann, *Acts*, 117; Johnson, *Acts*, 264; Marshall, *Acts*, 251; Soards, *Speeches*, 93) which conveys the idea of going to see a person on the basis of friendship and with helpful intent (L&N, §34.50; BDAG, 378). Another possible translation for ἐπισκέπτομαι is 'to look after, care for' with the implication of continuous responsibility (L&N, §35.39; BDAG, 378). Based on Peter's speech of God making no distinction between Jews and Gentiles (15:9), the theme of James' speech does not simply indicate God's visit to the Gentiles (which is more concerned with the whole event) but further signifies God's care for them (which is more regarding God's favour). Just as God cared for Abraham's descendants and made them his own people, so God is now giving the same favour to the Gentiles. The latter expression makes James' argument more forceful and convincing because God's will and sovereignty are highlighted.

[45] BDAG, 583.

[46] Λαός in relation to God often refers to Israel as the people of God who belong to God alone (Exod 19:5; Deut 7:6; 14:2). Dahl further contends that 'the plural עַמִּים = λαοί is often used as a synonym of גּוֹיִם = ἔθνη, and the singular frequently means Israel as a totality.' Exploring the general use of the two words in the OT, he concludes that God takes 'a group of people out of Gentile nations' for his own (15:14). 'The point is not that this group is "a people" in the sense of "a nation" or "a cultural unit," but that it now belongs to God in the same way as Israel does' ('People,' 325-26).

remind the Jewish audiences of God's early election and favour of them. It is now this same God, who made them his own and whom they believe, who is actively working among the Gentiles. He takes a people by faith (cf. 15:9) from the Gentiles to join in the people of God. The faith community is no longer made up of Jews but also Gentiles. Both are of God's initiating care; both are taken for God's own; both are in God's plan.[47]

James' annotation of Peter's witness is reinforced by the Prophets (15:15).[48] His quotation of Amos 9:11-12 asserts that what God is doing among the Gentiles is God's plan announced early (15:16-17).[49] The quotation, which follows the LXX rather than the Masoretic Hebrew text, refers to a restoration of Israel with a view to their possession of the remnant of Edom and all the nations called by God's name (Amos 9:12). The LXX, however, differing from the Hebrew text in places, indicates that the purpose (ὅπως) of God's restoration of David's fallen tent is for the Gentiles who are called by God's name to seek the Lord (15:16-17).[50] In his citation James adds τὸν κύριον to make his contention clear, that is, in the time of rebuilding David's tent the Gentiles will seek after God. In the context of the Jerusalem council, it is obvious that James refers what God has done through Jesus by the Spirit (cf. 15:7-8) to Amos' declaration of the restoration. He considers that God is now at work among Gentiles to build up a new people, made up of Jews and Gentiles, for himself (cf. 15:7-12). The new element is not in the sense of contrasting Israel as the old people of God but of a new recognition that God's people also includes Gentiles. The conversion of the Gentiles is the realisation of God's early revelation of what he would do among the Gentiles (15:17b-18). Founded on Peter's and

---

[47] Walter C. Kaiser, 'The Davidic Promise and the Inclusion of the Gentiles (Amos 9:9-15 and Acts 15:13-18): A Test Passage for Theological Systems,' *JETS* 20 (1977) 97-111, citing 108.

[48] The plural προφητῶν may refer to the collection of the Twelve Prophets (Johnson, *Acts*, 264; Bruce, *Acts*, 3rd edn., 340; Marshall, *Acts*, 252).

[49] Some commentators argue that the quotation is 'essentially Amos 9:11-12, with the opening phrase (μετὰ ταῦτα ἀναστρέψω) possibly drawn from Jer 12:15 and the closing phrase (ποιῶν ταῦτα) from Isa 45:21' (Dunn, *Acts*, 203; cf. Soards, *Speeches*, 94). For further discussion on the author's source of the quotation see Marshall, *Acts*, 252-53; Tannehill, *Narrative Unity*, 2: 187-89; Witherington, *Acts*, 457-58; Jostein Ådna, 'Die Heilige Schrift als Zeuge der Heidenmission. Die Rezeption von Amos 9,11-12 in Apg 15,16-18' in Jostein Ådna, Scott J. Hafemann und Otfried Hofius (eds.), *Evangelium-Schriftauslegung-Kirche* (Göttingen: Vandenhoech & Ruprecht, 1997) 1-23; Huub van de Sandt, 'An Explanation of Acts 15:6-21 in the Light of Deuteronomy 4:29-35 (LXX),' *JSNT* 46 (1992) 73-97.

[50] For detailed discussion on the OT quotation see Richard Bauckham, 'James and the Gentiles (Acts 15.13-21)' in Witherington (ed), *History, Literature, and Society*, 154-84, esp. 156-70.

the prophet's witnesses, James powerfully contends that Gentile salvation is ultimately and utterly of God.[51]

Once God's will and plan are confirmed, James sets forth his judgement for the present debate. To Jewish believers, James proposes that they should not burden or 'cause extra difficulty' (παρενοχλεῖν)[52] for those Gentiles who turn to God (15:19, cf. 15:10) because their salvation is of God's will. To Gentile believers, James' proposal (15:20, four prohibitions; cf. Lev 17-18)[53] is to break down social barriers between Jewish and Gentile believers and then merge two people into one people of God. An eclectic way is found in practice in order to remain allegiant and compliant to God's will and to placate the conventional and unalterable notion of the Jewish Christians.[54] As James exalts God's will over the issue, God's people are kept as one and God's plan is carried on. The omniscient God, knowing the obstacle of embracing the Gentile as his own, subdues the Jews' obstinacy by foretelling his will through the prophet and by initiating and upholding the Gentile mission through Jesus' witnesses.

By and large, the believers' conception of God is no more than that of the Jews except for their recognition of God's plan in Jesus and towards Gentiles. The *one* true God, the sovereign Lord, has authority and power over the universe and humankind as well as goodness and benevolence for humankind. He provides for human needs by sustaining the operation of the universe; he directs human history by revealing his will to his servants and by governing human affairs toward his purpose; he cares for humanity by offering them salvation and calling a people under his special care (first Jews then Gentiles). God's omnipotence, omnipresence and omniscience assure the consummation of his plan; his grace and lovingkindness ensures the best for his people. Above all,

---

[51] Cf. Earl Richard, 'The Divine Purpose: The Jews and the Gentile Mission (Acts 15),' *SBLSP* 19 (1980) 267-82, esp. 273.

[52] L&N, §22.25.

[53] For further discussion on the background of the 'Jerusalem decrees' see S.G. Wilson, *Luke and Law* (SNTSMS 50; Cambridge: Cambridge University, 1983) 84-102; M. Klinghardt, *Gesetz und Volk Gottes* (Tübingen: Mohr/Siebeck, 1988) 185-86; Terrance Callan, 'The Background of the Apostolic Decree (Acts 15:20, 29; 21:25),' *CBQ* 55 (1993) 284-97, esp. 284-89; Justin Taylor, 'The Jerusalem Decrees (Acts 15:20, 29 and 21:25) and the Incident at Antioch (Gal 2:11-14),' *NTS* 47 (2001) 372-80; Etienne Nodet and Justin Taylor, *The Origins of Christianity: An Exploration* (Collegeville: The Liturgical Press, 1998) 218-29; Markus Bockmuehl, 'The Noachide Commandments and New Testament Ethics, With Special Reference to Acts 15 and Pauline Halakha,' *RB* 102 (1995) 72-101; Richard Bauckham, 'James and the Jerusalem Church' in Bauckham (ed.), *Acts in Its Palestinian Setting*, 415-480, esp. 462-67; Bauckham, 'James,' 172-78.

[54] Cf. Timothy Wiarda, 'The Jerusalem Council and the Theological Task,' *JETS* 46 (2003) 233-48, esp. 245.

God's initiative allows people to share the true knowledge of himself and invites people to participate in his plan.

Personal/Interpersonal Characterisation

Besides their words, both collective and individual believers' interactions with others concerning God's plan will also be examined in order to explore their characterisation of God in deeds. The believers as a whole will first enter into discussion to provide an overall picture of their role in God's mission. Then the individual believers will be taken into consideration in order to disclose their critical role in God's mission plan. While Stephen and Philip as pioneers, indirectly or directly, break through the Gentile mission, Barnabas and James, as the representatives of the believers, open their arms to embrace Gentile believers as one people of God.

INTERPERSONAL WITNESS OF THE BELIEVERS AS A WHOLE

The believers are presented as a collective character in Jerusalem (Acts 1-5) where they witness God's mighty deeds. They first witness Jesus' resurrection and ascension and choose Judas' successor to be Jesus' witness (Acts 1). Witnessing the descent of the Spirit and being filled with the Spirit, they bear witness to God's great deeds (2:11). As Peter expounds the significance of the Pentecost phenomena (2:14-36), the believers increase in number and live a life distinct from that of Jews. The message about Jesus and the baptism of the Spirit lead the believers to a deeper and fresher comprehension of God which determine their attitude and response towards God. Their accordant prayer, as the climax to the episode of healing the lame man and a finale of the whole event (3:1ff.),[55] explicitly highlights their oneness in spirit (4:24-30).[56] The earthquake and divine empowerment following their prayer signifies God's presence and approval of their acknowledgement of him.[57] The characteristics of their lives are depicted in 2:42-47; 4:32-35 and 5:12-16. They devote themselves to the apostles' teaching, share all things in common and live in unity (2:42, 44; 4:32; 5:12). The community, characterised by their faith (2:44; 4:32; 5:14; cf. 3:16), is full of extreme gladness (2:46) and great grace (4:33); the apostles, especially, are full of power in performing miracles (2:43; 5:12) and witnessing to Jesus' resurrection (4:33). The number of believers is constantly added to by God (2:47; 5:14). Their lifestyle whispers of God powerfully working in the midst of the community. As miraculous signs explicitly tell of the

---

[55] Barrett, *Acts*, 1:241; Dunn, *Acts*, 55.

[56] Marshall, *Acts*, 104.

[57] Marshall points out that the earthquake is 'one of the signs which indicated a theophany in the Old Testament (Exod 19:18; Isa 6:4), and it would have been regarded as indicating a divine response to prayer' (*Acts*, 107).

presence of God, the life of the faith community implicitly testifies to a new thing done by God at present. The external wonders among the believers and the internal renewal in them enhance their preaching of God's will in Jesus.

The choosing of the Seven to share the apostles' administrative responsibility is the first time that two groups—the apostles and the disciples—within the faith community are indicated (6:1-2). In Jerusalem, the faith community is well nurtured by God through the apostles. The disciples serve as a silent and satellitic witness (in their distinct lifestyle) which reinforces the apostles' witness of God to the Jews (note their preaching of the Word is also fortified by miracles). As the Jews' persecution intensifies in Jerusalem, the disciples are scattered throughout Judea and Samaria (8:1). Wherever they go, they preach the Word (8:4) as far as Phoenicia, Cyprus and Antioch, and expand God's mission (11:19-21). The apostles become the disciples' backers as they outreach for God. In the narrative, the individual believers' witness indicates the cause and the first step of outreach to Gentiles (e.g. Stephen's martyrdom and Philip's evangelism); the collective believers scattered from Jerusalem establish the Gentile church (particularly those with a Hellenistic background, 11:20-22). In the Antioch church, a stronghold for God's overseas commission, the collective believers function as an arrow carrying out God's plan of Gentile mission; in the Jerusalem church, the headquarters of God's mission, the faith community acting as a bow strengthens the Gentile mission. The believers as a whole serve as a human context which reinforces the major characters' witness to God and magnifies God's expanding mission. Through the life of the faith community God is perceived as a sovereign Lord, whose will the believers commit themselves to, even to the point they may suffer for it, and who empowers his persecuted people, turning the persecuting forces towards the divine purpose.

PERSONAL WITNESS OF STEPHEN

The Spirit-filled Stephen, one of the Seven, powerfully bears witness to Jesus and is fiercely accused by the Jews (6:8-15). While his speech testifies to God at work throughout Israel's history and at present, his life fortifies his witness of God. Moreover, God's appearing to him in vision vindicates his witness and strengthens him for his culminating witness to God and Jesus.[58] Seeing the glory of God (7:55-56), 'practically equivalent to God himself,'[59] Stephen is assured by the presence of the God of glory (7:2). God in heaven corroborates Stephen's contention of his transcendency (7:48-50); Jesus' standing at the right hand of God notarises Stephen's reprobation of the Jews' killing of Jesus (7:52).[60] This heavenly vision of God is God's verification for Stephen's whole presentation of him. More significantly, Stephen's final prayer, which resem-

---

[58] Barrett, *Acts*, 1:383; Soards, *Speeches*, 69; Neagoe, *Trial*, 170.
[59] Barrett, *Acts*, 1:383.
[60] Neagoe, *Trial*, 170.

bles Jesus', manifests God's plan of saving his people for his glory and for their good (7:60).[61] Stephen's speech, functioning 'as a prophecy for the narrative,'[62] foreshadows the Jews' ongoing opposition in the narrative.[63] His faith makes his martyrdom a living witness which continuously impacts the narrative world; death cannot stop God's saving purpose.[64]

Stephen acts as he believes and God fulfils what he believes. Stephen believes the God of glory and sees the glory of God; he believes in a God of transcendency and sees God in heaven. His martyrdom serves as a final witness to his argument—that which people reject, God will turn to become a blessing according to his plan.[65] Stephen's death, which causes great persecution in Jerusalem, opens the door for a new milestone of spreading the Gospel (cf. 8:1; 11:19-26).[66] That God is with his persecuted people and empowers them wherever they go further affirms Stephen's contention of God's omnipresence (8:6; 11:21). God's people will pass away generation by generation, yet God is still working in history and speaking through history. What God has spoken through human history is another way of God's self-characterisation (with his deeds in history as Stephen presented). Stephen's life enhances his preaching of God as sovereign, omnipresent and invincible.

PERSONAL WITNESS OF PHILIP

Philip, one of the Seven with four unmarried daughters who prophesy (6:5; 21:8-9), is characterised as 'the evangelist' (21:8) who is full of the Spirit and wisdom (6:3) and performs miraculous healings (8:6-7). He appears four times in the narrative (6:5-6; 8:5-13, 26-40; 21:8-9) and his Moses/Elijah-like characteristics are often noted.[67] His roles in the first and the last scenes function as an assistant to the apostles (6:5-6) and as Paul's host (21:8-9). In both scenes

---

[61] Soards, *Speeches*, 70.
[62] Luke T. Johnson, *The Literary Function of Possessions in Luke-Acts* (SBLDS 39; Missoula: Scholars Press, 1977) 76.
[63] Hill, 'Division,' 146.
[64] Mittelstadt, *Spirit and Suffering*, 112.
[65] Martin-Asensio, *Foregrounding*, 110.
[66] Tannehill further indicates that 'there is an ironic turn. The efforts of the Sanhedrin to halt the preaching of the word, carried to an extreme in the stoning of Stephen, result in the spread of the word in Judea, Samaria, and Antioch' (*Narrative Unity*, 2:101).
[67] Philip's relationship with Simon Magus is viewed as that of Moses with Pharaoh's magicians (Spencer, *Philip*, 107-15). The parallels between Philip and Elijah are also noticed: both are associated with Samaria (8:5; 1 Kgs 18-21); both are directed by a divine source (8:26, 29; 1 Kgs 17:8-9); both run fast enough to follow a chariot (8:27; 1 Kgs 18:46); both are snatched away (8:39-40; 2 Kgs 2:11). Rick Strelan further contends that Philip's running is a spirit-compelled movement which is of similar ilk to Elijah ('The Running Prophet,' *NovT* 43 [2001] 31-38, citing 34-36).

Philip is only a background character, providing a social context for the major characters and thus they do not merit further discussion. Philip's major performance, however, is in Acts 8 where he makes a clear breakthrough to the mission in Samaria (location) and to the Gentile (object).

Among the disciples scattered from Jerusalem (8:1), Philip gets the spotlight in the narrative. Though miracles characterise his evangelism, the Spirit's instruction and intervention highlight his Gentile ministry (8:29, 39). The concise and lucid narration of Philip's activities in Samaria speaks of his great success in the Samaritans' turning to God's Word, fortified by miracles (8:5-13). God's power is further amplified by the conversion of Simon, a sorcerer, who amazes people with sorcery and is called the 'Great Power of God' (8:10-11). Nevertheless, when the secular 'Great Power of God' encounters the divine Great Power of God, it becomes 'great power of god' which is no longer great. Nonetheless, no matter how great God's power is, God sovereignly withholds the outpouring of the Spirit.[68] This signifies that God holds the power above all human powers and has the authority to execute that power. Although the Jews' persecution intended to destroy the church, God makes the crisis an opportunity to extend the church. The Word of God is now spread to Samaritans (semi-Jews) in Samaria (the second stage of Jesus' commission, cf. 1:8).

Furthermore, it is through Philip that 'from a people (Samaritans) stationed socially within a vague, marginal realm between Jews and Gentiles, the Christian mission now extends to an individual who, despite his attraction to Judaism, is no Jew at all but rather a full-fledged Gentile from a far-flung land.'[69] The divine agents conduct this crucial breakthrough by directing Philip to the Ethiopian eunuch on his way towards Gaza (8:26, 29).[70] The passive role of Philip throughout the Ethiopian episode (he is directed by an angel and the Spirit, asked by the Ethiopian and finally snatched away by the Spirit) clearly

---

[68] The Philip-Simon scene (8:9-13) serves as an introduction to the Peter-Simon scene (8:14-24). The former is in narration form (a silent performance with the narrator's voice in third person); the latter is in dialogue form (a vivid performance by the characters in second person expression). This draws the attention of the whole event to the latter.

[69] Spencer, *Philip*, 186.

[70] Μεσημβρία lexically means *midday, noon* (of time) or *south* (of place), cf. BDAG, 634. Κατὰ μεσημβρίαν in 8:26, thus, could mean either *about noon* or *toward the south*. Opinions on the meaning differ among scholars. It may indicate the time at which Philip is to depart or the direction to which Philip is to go. Either fits into the context. The former stresses the debatable command of God's angel since there would be no one in such a hot desert district and thus reinforces Philip's obedience and God's supernatural guidance. The latter depicts God's sending out of Philip from Jerusalem or Samaria and thus accentuates God's will of reaching out to people geographically. No matter which view it is, the following indication αὕτη ἐστὶν ἔρημος points out that Philip is directed to a desolate place and without any question

indicates that he is absolutely God's agent called to accomplish God's will. Divine intervention plays a significant role in Philip's mission to the Ethiopian.[71] Moreover, Philip's obedience implies God's authority over him and enables him to experience God's extraordinary guidance and provision.[72] It is utterly God's initiative that Philip becomes the pioneer missionary to Gentiles. God's mission is now extended, through Philip, to a eunuch (a Gentile) from Ethiopia (a place viewed as on the southern edge of the earth).[73]

The Spirit-filled Philip evangelises wherever he goes and wherever God leads him (8:40). His love of sharing the Word is accompanied with God's mighty presence; his full submission to God's will makes him a sheer channel of divine power. God's will (salvation for all) and plan (the worldwide mission) are implemented through Philip's commitment to his mission. In the Samaritan episode, God's mission is achieved by Philip's powerful preaching which is fortified by God's mighty deeds. In the Ethiopian episode, the mission is carried out by the divine guidance and Philip's compliance. Philip therefore becomes an initiator of the Samaritan mission and a pioneer of the Gentile mission.[74] The Gentile mission is of God, yet God invites the cooperation of human agents. Whereas Stephen, as the cause, prompts God's expanding mission, Philip takes the first step of God's Gentile mission. Philip's life, thus, reflects God's sovereignty, authority and omnipotence.

PERSONAL WITNESS OF BARNABAS

Barnabas, a Levite of Cyprus, named Joseph and called *son of encouragement*,[75] plays a quiet yet significant role throughout his performance in the nar-

---

or hesitation he goes. Taking the phrase in the temporal meaning, Spencer argues that the absurd and supernatural guidance (8:26; 9:10-16; 10:9-16) 'binds together the conversions of the Ethiopian eunuch, Saul and Cornelius as divinely engineered events critical to the development of the Gentile mission' (*Philip*, 158).

[71] R.F. O'Toole, 'Philip and the Ethiopian Eunuch (Acts viii 25-40),' *JSNT* 17 (1983) 25-34, citing 29.

[72] God not only enables Philip to run after a chariot but also provides him with the *divine transportation* to Azotus (8:30, 40).

[73] Ethiopia is the Nubian Kingdom, the land south of Egypt, known in the Bible as the ancient land of Cush (Gen 2:13) whose capital is Meroe, which is today's Sudan. Ethiopia was widely viewed as on the southern edge of the earth. See Witherington, *Acts*, 295; Johnson, *Acts*, 154; Gaventa, *Light*, 103-4; Carl G. Rasmussen, *The NIV Atlas of the Bible* (London: Marshall-Pickering, 1989) 57, 59.

[74] Tannehill, *Narrative Unity*, 2:110; Spencer, *Philip*, 273; Andrew C. Clark, *Parallel Lives* (Carlisle: Paternoster Press, 2001) 290; Kollmann, 'Philippus,' 565.

[75] Besides the explicit characterisation of Barnabas in the narrative, Jenny Read-Heimerdinger argues that Codex Bezae identifies Barnabas with the biblical figure of Joseph in Acts 1:23 ('Barnabas in Acts: A Study of His Role in the Text of Codex Bezae,' *JSNT* 72 [1998] 23-66).

rative. Introduced onto the stage as a fully devoted believer (4:36-37), Barnabas plays the role as a mediator and a partner to Paul (9:27; 11:25-30; 12:25-15:39) and a delegate of both the Jerusalem and Antioch churches (11:22, 30). In Jerusalem and Antioch, Barnabas as an arrowhead invigorates God's mission by introducing Paul first to the Jerusalem church (9:27) then to the Antioch church (11:25-6). Moreover, Barnabas is first sent by the Jerusalem church to encourage Gentile believers (11:22) and later, with Paul, is sent by the Antioch church to extend the great Gentile mission (13:3). It is his attribute of encouraging others that makes him a channel whereby the people of God are welcomed, and that offers him a chance to witness God's power over Paul and the Gentile mission. His Hellenistic background enables him to nurture the Antioch church, a citadel of Gentile mission; his high reputation in the churches allows him to pave the way for the crucial person Paul, a key leader of Gentile mission; his benevolent and magnanimous characteristics make him *a bridge figure* in God's mission (a bridge between the Jerusalem and Antioch churches and between the Apostles and Paul).[76] Barnabas' life delineates God's invincible mission of salvation, and images God as a supreme Lord worthy of his all, to whom he offers all of his possessions, to whose sovereign will of universal salvation he devotes himself, and who powerfully and authoritatively calls people to his salvation and mission.

PERSONAL WITNESS OF JAMES

James functions as a linchpin to tie in the Gentile and Jewish believers as one people of God. The dissension about the criteria of being the people of God challenges the mutually-supported relationship between the Jewish (Jerusalem) and Gentile (Antioch) churches (11:22, 29). The core debate lies in whether the Mosaic custom, especially circumcision, is a prerequisite for salvation (12:1, 5). Both the representative of the apostles (Peter) and the delegates of the Antioch church (Barnabas and Paul) accentuate God's initiative in the Gentile mission (15:7-9, 12). James, the leader of the Jerusalem church (cf. 12:17; 15:13; 21:18),[77] then concludes the debate by highlighting what God is doing at present and what he has said in the past (15:14-8). James' utterance as the decisive voice in the discussion resolves the most intractable issue of embracing Gentile believers into the people of God.[78] The first Christian community therefore is able to keep its loyalty to God's will and rightly applies it to a new historical

---

[76] Clark, *Parallel Lives*, 294; Bauckham, 'Jerusalem Church,' 450.

[77] Dupont indicates that Peter is the spokesman of the apostles and James of the elders in the Jerusalem council ('Peuple,' 322).

[78] Marshall indicates that James' increasing role as the foremost leader in the church (12:17) and his more conservative attitude and Jewish outlook (cf. Gal 2:12) make his voice critical and decisive (*Acts*, 243, 251).

epoch.[79] As Barnabas paves the way for sending God's delegate to reach Gentiles, James establishes the foundation for welcoming Gentiles into the people of God. That James acknowledges God's sovereign will revealed in his words and deeds reflects a faithful and authoritative God, who is at work on the fulfilment of his former promise and the transformation of his people's understanding of his will.

Concisely speaking, the collective believers in Jerusalem are the backers of the apostles' witness to God's Word and the patrons of Gentile mission; those in Antioch are the promoters of God's worldwide mission. Among the individual believers, Stephen witnesses to God and Jesus with his life and God makes his martyrdom a living witness; Philip witnesses to God with his commitment to preaching the Word and with his submission to God's will and God makes him a pioneer of Gentile mission; Barnabas witnesses to God with his gift of encouragement in strengthening the new believers and God makes him a bridge figure in God's expanding mission; James witnesses to God with his honouring of God's will and God makes him a linchpin figure in keeping one people of God. The overall role of the believers as a whole is to carry out the first stage of outreach and pave the way for the second stage of God's worldwide mission. Through the implied author's deployment of God's human agents in carrying out his redemptive plan, the implied readers may image God as the sovereign Lord of human history, as well as the one universal church, who powerfully and authoritatively calls, guides and transforms his people to do his will.

Summary

As the minor characters come alongside the major characters to further the plot progression, God's saving plan of universal mission appears to be the common concern among them. The speeches and actions of the minor characters, thus, reinforce the major characters' presentation of God as well as promote the plot. The believers' accordant prayer professes God's sovereignty and power over human affairs. Their prayer for boldly preaching God's Word under persecution is answered as they carry out the first stage of God's mission. Stephen's speech acknowledges God's supreme presence remaining with those who truly worship him in full submission to his authority. Philip and Barnabas testify to God's authoritative power, as elucidated in Stephen's exegesis of God that God's powerful presence never withdraws from them while they fully comply with God's will. James' speech honours God's sovereign will of Gentile salvation; this keeps the two people of God in one while the great Gentile mission is carried on.

In Jerusalem, the apostles are empowered to be the witnesses of God; the disciples eyewitness God's mighty deeds through the apostles and they them-

---

[79] Kesich, 'Apostolic Council,' 114.

selves also become a living witness in reinforcing the apostles' witness. In Samaria and Judea, the disciples are strengthened to boldly bear witness to God's Word; the apostles turn to become their backers in God's outreach mission. In Antioch, the believers send out missionaries for God's universal mission. After acting out their tasks in this intermediary stage of God's mission, the believers move to the background of the narrative stage. Whichever mission-stage and whatever role God's messengers are in, God is always with them, empowering them for the tasks assigned to them. The overall presentation of the believers represents the glorious and gracious God, who initiates the mission of salvation, powerfully and faithfully keeps and enables his people, for his supreme and sovereign purpose, to be a people of mission and a people of sharing the Word of life (cf. 3:15; 5:20).

The God-Fearers: Cornelius, the Ethiopian Eunuch, Lydia

Two adjectives (εὐλαβής, εὐσεβής) and two participles (σεβόμενος, φοβούμενος) are employed to indicate *God-fearer* in Acts.[80] Only εὐλαβής is applied to the devout Jews (2:5; 8:2; 22:12) and the rest refer to the devout Gentiles who are either associated with the synagogue or are worshippers of God.[81] The devout Jews are background characters who provide a context and social setting for the main characters:[82] they are the audience of Peter's speech (2:5), the finale of Stephen's story (8:2) and the channel of Paul's restoration (22:12). Also, there are background characters among the devout Gentiles, particularly those with the Jews in synagogues (13:16, 26, 43, 50; 17:4, 17) and the individual worshipper of God, who have no phraseological presentation (i.e. no speaking part, 18:7) and contribute only to round out the presentation of the major character Paul. Both the devout Jews and Gentiles (in a collective sense), functioning as foils for the implied author's interest in main characters, do not directly characterise God but, rather, main characters and thus will not be taken into further consideration.

---

[80] For more details on the words indicating God-fearer see Appendix Two; Martinus C. de Boer, 'God-Fearers in Luke-Acts' in Tuckett (ed.), *Luke's Literary Achievement*, 50-71; Sanders, *Jews in Luke-Acts*, 137-40.

[81] See the devout Gentiles in the synagogue (13:16, 26, 43, 50; 17:4, 17) and the individual worshippers of God (the Ethiopian eunuch, 8:27-28; Cornelius, 10:2, 7, 22, 35; Lydia, 16:14; Titus Justus, 18:7). In Acts, it is this group of Gentiles who respond to the mission; cf. Christoph W. Stenschke, *Luke's Portrait of Gentiles Prior to Their Coming to Faith* (WUNT 2/108; Tübingen: Mohr Siebeck, 1999) 312; Jacob Jervell, 'The Church of Jews and Godfearers' in Tyson (ed.), *Jewish People*, 11-20.

[82] Harvey, *Character*, 56.

There are individual devout Gentiles—the Ethiopian eunuch,[83] Cornelius and Lydia—whose function is weighted more in promoting the plot than in characterising main characters. Together with main characters, they provide the human contexts for the narrative world in which God's saving plan is manifested. Their presentation, thus, will be investigated in order to explore their characterisation of God. Cornelius, playing an important role in God's revelation of Gentile salvation, deserves a thorough scrutiny. The Ethiopian eunuch and Lydia will be examined in the section of personal characterisation since through their interactions with main characters God's will towards Gentile mission is enhanced.

Conceptual Characterisation

The interlocution between Cornelius and God's angel, and Cornelius and Peter reveals a progressive development in Cornelius' perception of God and God's plan. Along with the narrator's account, Cornelius' encounter with God's angel discloses God's mindset of one's piety; his encounter with Peter tells of God actively and impartially interacting with those who truly worship him.

CORNELIUS' ENCOUNTER WITH GOD'S ANGEL

While the narrator characterises Cornelius from two strata (his being—being devout and fearing God; his doing—giving alms and keeping prayer, 10:2), the angel indicates only his doings (10:4). That God prizes Cornelius' doings without mention of his being need not be understood as God's negligence of his being. Rather it is a subtle way of disclosing God's mindset toward one's piety. The introduction of Cornelius by the narrator impresses the reader that Cornelius is typically devout according to Jewish piety.[84] In the repetition of Cornelius' vision, depicted by his messengers to Peter (10:22), an emphasis on Cornelius' being and status is given in a way which lays a foundation for the narra-

---

[83] While Cornelius and Lydia are explicitly indicated as God-fearers, the Ethiopian eunuch is implicitly characterised as a God-fearer not by the narrator's *telling* but by his *showing* as Dunn articulates his piety: 'his degree of commitment had been shown by his journey; his degree of enthusiasm was shown by his purchase of a no doubt expensive scroll' (*Acts*, 114).

[84] Almsgiving and prayer are characteristic marks of Jewish piety. Barrett indicates that 'in Aramaic מצותא, literally (the fulfilling of a) *commandment* came to mean *charity*, a clear pointer to the fact that charity, almsgiving, was regarded as the greatest of all commandments.... Prayer in the sense of communion with God is evidently a central religious practice; it was connected with almsgiving' (*Acts*, 1:501; also Dunn, *Acts*, 135; Geir Otto Holmås, '"My house shall be a house of prayer": Regarding the Temple as a Place of Prayer in Acts within the Context of Luke's Apologetical Objective,' *JSNT* 27 [2005] 393-416, esp. 412-13).

tive presentation of a God-fearer's piety.[85] Based upon such recognition, Cornelius' doings are remembered by God (10:4); this is also Cornelius' understanding as he reiterates the vision to Peter (10:31). Finally, God's mindset toward the devout is made clear by Peter's words (10:35). God is pleased not only by one's being but his doing (ὁ φοβούμενος αὐτὸν καὶ ἐργαζόμενος δικαιοσύνην). The one article with two substantival participles indicates that both one's being and doing are keys to pleasing God and being accepted by him.[86] God discerns one's innermost parts which lead to outward deeds as God has commanded. In other words, genuine piety before God is to fear God and to live accordingly.

CORNELIUS' ENCOUNTER WITH PETER

The interlocution between Cornelius and Peter reveals God as omnipotent, sovereign and faithful in responding to those truly worshipping him. God's purpose in the two visions is unfolded as the two characters, unknown to each other and ignorant of the implications of God's commands to them, encounter each other (10:25-48). In Cornelius' reiteration of the angel's instruction, two slight variations in between shed light on Cornelius' characterisation of God.[87]

First, the angel spells out that Cornelius' piety now becomes a memorial before God (10:4; εἰς μνημόσυνον ἔμπροσθεν τοῦ θεοῦ). The preposition εἰς indicates 'the result of an action or condition.'[88] God's remembrance of him is a result of his prayer and almsgiving which are as a memorial offering before God. In his utterance to Peter, Cornelius uses the inferential conjunction οὖν (which, while in commands and invitations, carries not only inferential result but intensive force, 10:32)[89] instead of the temporal adverb νῦν (which makes the angel's command more authoritative, 10:5) to convey his understanding that his piety has caused God's remembrance of him. This explains why Cornelius indicates his prayer time at the ninth hour (10:30), one of the traditional prayer hours for the pious Jews.[90] What Cornelius perceives is that God re-

---

[85] Kurz indicates that one of the acknowledged effects of repetitions is producing emphasis ('Effects,' 570).

[86] The word δεκτός conveys the idea of that 'which is pleasing in view of its being acceptable' (L&N, §25.85).

[87] Witherup asserts that 'what appeared to be merely repetitious details of slight variation were actually part of a narrative strategy of functional redundancy which intimately connected characterisation and plot' ('Over and Over,' 47; also Kurz, 'Effects,' 571; Sternberg, *Biblical Narrative*, 390-93).

[88] BDAG, 290 (in subdivision *e*); also L&N, §89.48 indicates εἰς as 'a mark of result, with the probable implication of a preceding process.'

[89] BDAG, 736; in subdivision b: in commands and invitations, with intensive force.

[90] Bruce, *Acts*, 3rd edn., 136.

members those, whether Jews or Gentiles, with sincere faith and piety before him.

Second, the concept of *memorial* is changed from noun (10:4, μνημόσυνον) to verb (10:31, μιμνῃσκομαι). The angel's discourse elucidates Cornelius being in a state of pleasing God (10:4, αἱ προσευχαί σου καὶ αἱ ἐλεημοσύναι σου ἀνέβησαν εἰς μνημόσυνον ἔμπροσθεν τοῦ θεοῦ). Cornelius, however, emphasises that God responds individually to his prayer and almsgiving (10:31, εἰσηκούσθη σου ἡ προσευχὴ καὶ αἱ ἐλεημοσύναι σου ἐμνήσθησαν ἐνώπιον τοῦ θεοῦ). While the noun μνημόσυνον indicates an offering that presents a worshipper to God,[91] the verb μιμνῃσκομαι conveys the idea of calling attention to something or someone.[92] The former underlines Cornelius' prayer and almsgiving as a cause of God's remembrance of him;[93] the latter accentuates how God, being aware of Cornelius' plight, responds in an appropriate manner.[94] This stylistic variation places the emphasis on God's response to Cornelius,[95] which presents Cornelius' understanding of God as a God of action. Cornelius' notion is reinforced by the addition of εἰσηκούσθη, which indicates listening to someone, with the implication of heeding and responding.[96] For Cornelius, God is a God who takes initiative in responding to a devout Gentile.

In short, by encounter with God's angel and Peter, Cornelius profoundly perceives God looking at one's innermost being, and remembering and responding to those, whether Jews or Gentiles, who have genuine faith in him. In the Cornelius episode, God is recognised as sovereign and omnipotent in giving visions and commands to people in order to accomplish his divine plan. God is impartial as he takes the initiative to visit and provides salvation for both Jews and Gentiles.

Personal Characterisation

Being the only episode fully developed among those of the God-fearers, the Cornelius episode serves to amplify the essential motifs common in God-fearer scenes. By exploring the similarities of these episodes, the Gentile mission is confirmed as God's will. By probing into the interactions between God-fearers and main characters sent by God in each episode, God is vividly characterised by their witness in life.

---

[91] BDAG, 655.
[92] BDAG, 652.
[93] L&N, §29.12.
[94] L&N, §29.16.
[95] Johnson, *Acts*, 190.
[96] L&N, §24.60; BDAG, 293.

PERSONAL WITNESS OF CORNELIUS

As Cornelius, coming from a Gentile polytheistic background, monotheistically calls God *the Lord*, his confession is shown in words as well as in actions. He lives a life as God would have one live. In responding to Cornelius' piety, God visits and grants him the favour which brings salvation. Cornelius' piety is further seen in his immediate obedience to the angel's command, even without knowing its purpose, and in his faith that there is a message of God, via Peter, for himself and his household.[97] The story terminates at God's great deeds among the Gentiles—the outpouring of the Spirit and the baptism of Cornelius' household. Yet the story is silent about Cornelius' reaction to God's remarkable deeds. Such silence indicates that Cornelius, having achieved the plot, 'fades into the background.'[98] This allows the major character Peter to continue the plot by stepping up into another episode in which he contends for God's will of Gentile salvation unfolded in the Cornelius incident.

In the Cornelius episode, a preparatory step for Gentile mission,[99] the supernatural interventions accentuate 'the divine initiative that guides the story's developments.'[100] Through an angel and Peter, what God has done among Gentiles is the interest point of view in the whole story and its aftermath (Acts 11, 15). Throughout the episode, God's sovereignty, authority and power in carrying out his plan of Gentile salvation are striking and unwavering; God's justice and impartiality stand out as salvation is for both the Jews and Gentiles who believe in him.

PERSONAL WITNESS OF THE ETHIOPIAN EUNUCH

The Ethiopian eunuch's piety is shown in his marvellously long journey to worship God in Jerusalem and his eager desire to know God's words (8:27-28). That no name is given to him leaves the focus on his status—a Gentile eunuch

---

[97] As the word μεταπέμπω conveys the idea of sending someone to obtain something or someone (L&N, §13.73), Cornelius knows that God has something to tell him through a man called Peter. Thus, while reiterating the utterance of the angel to Peter, he uses the word μετακαλέω (10:32), which simply means *to summon someone* (L&N, §33.311), instead of μεταπέμπω (10:5). The idea of obtaining something from Peter is clearly expressed in his concluding words (10:33).

[98] Witherup, 'Over and Over,' 64; cf. Alter, *Biblical Narrative*, 79.

[99] Irina Levinskaya, *The Book of Acts in Its Diaspora Setting* (Grand Rapids: Eerdmans, 1996) 121.

[100] Walter T. Wilson, 'Urban Legends: Acts 10:1-11:18 and the Strategies of Greco-Roman Foundation Narratives,' *JBL* 120 (2001) 77-99, citing 88. Significantly, as the story develops, Peter's role gradually grows from passive (10:17, 29) to active (10:34-43, 47-48) while Cornelius' declines from active (10:7-8) to passive (10:33). See Witherup, 'Over and Over,' 56-57.

and an important official in Ethiopia.[101] Being 'mutilated,' he is excluded from the assembly of the Lord according to Deuteronomy 23:1. No matter how passionate and enthusiastic his desire to worship God in the Temple (8:27), he is unable to participate in all parts of worship with God's people.[102] By an angel's instruction God brings together Philip and the Ethiopian. This very encounter becomes the turning-point of the Ethiopian's life and brings hope to his plight.[103] Instead of formulating Philip's speech, the narrator indicates only its theme (8:35). This leaves the focus of the scene on the interactions between the Ethiopian and God's intention, for which Philip plays only the role of God's agent.

The three questions raised by the Ethiopian, which expose his inner life, are the keys for the development of the plot in this episode (8:31, 34, 36).[104] The first question regards his ignorance of the Scriptures (8:31); this reveals what he has been reading (cf. Isa 53:7-8). The second question indicates his desire to understand the Scriptures (8:34); this brings out Philip's preaching of Jesus (8:35). The narrator's summary of Philip's speech in one word *Jesus* highlights the gist of Philip's preaching—God's salvation. The third question, which is a plea for baptism, deals with the most pressing issue in the Ethiopian's life, namely, to be a part of God's people. Such a desire is now fulfilled through the baptism of Philip; this is the apex of the episode. As for the Ethiopian, the baptism is an act of confession to his faith and the point of becoming a member of God's people (cf. 2:38-42). As for God, the snatching away of Philip by the Spirit alludes to the fact that the baptism is with the promised divine approval (cf. Isa 56:3-5).[105]

Although God does not explicitly take part in the scene, his activities, via an angel and the Spirit, are perceived throughout the story. The whole episode is

---

[101] For thorough discussion on the social status of the Ethiopian see Spencer, *Philip*, 158-73.

[102] As investigated in Stephen's speech, προσκυνέω accentuates the attitude of a worshipper while λατρεύω heightens the performance of religious rites as a part of worship. Here the use of προσκυνέω for worship rather λατρεύω alludes to the fact that the Ethiopian is a sincere worshipper. However, whether or not he is able to participate in the religious activities in the Temple remains unknown and his status suggests the answer is no. Gaventa clearly states that 'worshipping in Jerusalem merely indicates the receptivity of this particular individual' (*Light*, 104).

[103] Gaventa, *Light*, 105.

[104] O'Toole considers that the Ethiopian's three questions with Philip's one question constitute the central section ('Philip,' 28-29).

[105] There is no mention of the outpouring of the Spirit upon the Ethiopian which is a sign of God's approval in Acts. Nevertheless, the guidance of Philip's coming and leaving by the Spirit is evidently another way of showing God's approval (8:29, 39). For God's approval see Marguerat, *Historian*, 104; for the OT promise see Tannehill, *Narrative Unity*, 2:109; Barrett, *Acts*, 1:425.

well constructed by the narration and dialogue. Alter indicates that one of the functions served by the narration which is woven around dialogue is 'the conveying of actions essential to the unfolding of the plot which could not be easily or adequately indicated in dialogue.'[106] The Ethiopian's three lines of dialogue in the narration are the subtle techniques of the implied author which unfold the Ethiopian's inner life (his desire, confusion and resolution) and God's intention (he sovereignly intervenes to provide a way, incredibly guides to give salvation and unconditionally accepts to fulfil his promise).[107] From the episode of the Ethiopian eunuch emerges an omniscient and compassionate God who discerns one's genuine desire of seeking to know him, and who powerfully and sovereignly makes himself known through his agents. Looking at the episode from a lager angle, the reader further perceives God's sovereignty and authority in his mightily carrying out his universal salvation.

PERSONAL WITNESS OF LYDIA

Lydia, a woman called by her personal name and with considerable means, is a person of high station.[108] She may have already been attracted to Judaism while staying in Thyatira (16:14).[109] Her presence with other women in a place of prayer (προσκυνή) indicates that there is no synagogue in Philippi (16:13).[110] By divine intervention, Paul, going to Macedonia by the Spirit's prohibition and the guidance through a vision (16:6-10), encounters Lydia and Lydia's heart is opened up to perceive and receive Paul's teaching (16:14, the Lord God

---

[106] Alter, *Biblical Narrative*, 77.

[107] Paul Elbert indicates that questions are used by a narrator to 'present further information through his characters that is of didactic value to his readers' ('An Observation on Luke's Composition and Narrative Style of Questions,' *CBQ* 66 [2004] 98-109, citing 104).

[108] Witherington contends that Lydia is 'a person of some status, since it was normal in such a Greco-Roman setting not to mention women by personal name in public unless they were either notable or notorious.' He further argues that the reference to Lydia's house and household suggest she is one of the notable ones (*Acts*, 492; also Ivoni Richter Reimer, *Women in the Acts of the Apostles: A Feminist Liberation Perspective* [Minneapolis: Fortress Press, 1995] 97).

[109] The participial phrase σεβομένη τὸν θεόν may refer to the appositional phrase πορφυρόπωλις πόλεως Θυατείρων of τις γυνή and be understood as 'a dealer in purple cloth from the city of Thyatira, who feared God' which serves as the characterisation of Lydia (cf. Dunn, *Acts*, 219).

[110] Johnson asserts that 'in Hellenistic Jewish literature, the term προσκυνή is virtually synonymous with συναγωγή' (*Acts*, 292). However, throughout Acts the implied author employs συναγωγή for synagogue. It is unlikely that he would only use προσκυνή for the synagogue in Philippi. Bruce elucidates that 'there is no thought of a synagogue congregation here, since women only are mentioned. A synagogue service traditionally requires a quorum of ten men. When used of a building, προσκυνή is a synonym for συναγωγή' (*Acts*, 358; also Dunn, *Acts*, 219).

opened her heart).[111] Later, Lydia's hospitality gives way to a new Christian community (16:40, where brothers are present). The Lydia episode is the briefest of the three God-fearer episodes. Yet it still conveys a rough pattern of God's work towards the God-fearers. Like the episodes concerning Cornelius and the Ethiopian, the divine intervention and initiative are emphasised. The Word is carried into the Gentile world under God's super-guidance in conformity to his plan. The Lydia episode, thus, enhances the image of God that the reader draws from the previous God-fearer episodes.

Summary

In these God-fearer episodes God is never the focus of the stories. The reader's attention, however, remains on God because God's activities, via heavenly and human agents, are always in view. The divine intervention and initiative in the beginning of each episode make the reader ponder what God is going to do. Therefore, even though God is offstage, his intention is the common interest of these episodes. The God-fearers' or even the apostles' or disciples' performance is significant only in their implications for God's purpose.

The significant similarities in the God-fearer episodes—divine intervention and initiative—disclose and accentuate God's will for Gentile salvation. In his sovereignty and authority God unmistakably directs his human agents to evangelise the Gentile God-fearers. Knowing the deepest desires of those who seek him, God incredibly satisfies the longings of the God-fearers. Cornelius has merely partial status of the Jewish religious assembly; the Ethiopian eunuch cannot fully participate in the assembly of the Lord; and Lydia has no proper place to worship God with God's people. Now, by God's mighty work and in his mercy and grace, they are all embraced into the people of God. God's unconditional acceptance of the believing Gentiles as the people of God manifests his justice and love as his salvation is impartially offered to both Jews and Gentiles. Overall, in the narrative plot the God-fearer episodes provide the settings for the breakthrough of God's worldwide mission and tell of God's will of universal salvation, from which, again, God's sovereignty, authority, and power stand out.

The Opponents

Along the line of the development of God's mission, there comes an opposing force arising from four collective characters. These are the believers who fully adhere to the Mosaic law, the Jews who disbelieve the Word, the Gentiles who reject Paul's preaching, and the Roman officials who join in the Jews' and Gentiles' opposition. Whereas the disciples and the God-fearers (as a positive force) promote God's mission, the opponents (as a negative force) drive it. As

---

[111] Marguerat, *Historian*, 248.

antagonists these four groups serve to amplify the protagonists' performance that are closely connected with God's mission of universal salvation. Therefore, an in-depth knowledge of their opposition will reinforce the protagonists' presentation of God's redemptive plan.

Conceptual Characterisation—The Speech of Gamaliel (5:35-39)

Most of the opponents' speeches present their dissension or enmity toward the main characters. Only Gamaliel's speech in preventing the Sanhedrin from killing the apostles reflects his Jewish notion of God (5:35-39). He uses two conditional clauses to express his view on the apostolic movement which could be of humans or of God. Aligning it with other turbulences, Gamaliel points out that the movement could be another wave of human uproar (note the subjunctive in the third class conditional clause indicating a probability, 5:38b). Yet acknowledging God's sovereign authority over human affairs, he advises the Sanhedrin to 'wait and see' and leave the apostles alone (note the indicative in the first class conditional clause conveying an 'temporary' assumption of truth, 5:39).[112] 'It is richly ironic that here a leader of a group that has "rejected the will of God for themselves"... advises others on how not to oppose the will of God concerning the early believers in Christ.'[113] More importantly, Gamaliel's argument lies in the fact that he links the recognition of God's will with the destiny of Jesus' witnesses.[114] As learned in the narrative that the apostles' witness is of God and their mission is of his plan, Gamaliel's assertion of no one being able to stand against God's plan ironically serves as a *witness* to the apostles' proclamation and as an indicator to God's invincible mission.[115] Without giving his personal judgement, the high-reputed Gamaliel presents an objective view on the apostolic movement which not only safeguards the apostles but testifies to God's sovereignty over the movement and foreshadows God's expanding mission.

---

[112] Wallace, *Beyond*, 450, 470; Johnson, *Acts*, 100; cf. Peter J. Tomson, 'Gamaliel's Counsel and the Apologetic Strategy of Luke-Acts' in Verheyden (ed.), *Unity*, 585-604, citing 603. For further discussion on Gamaliel's principle see William John Lyons, 'The Words of Gamaliel (Acts 5.38-39) and the Irony of Indeterminacy,' *JSNT* 68 (1997) 23-49.

[113] Darr, *Character Building*, 119.

[114] Aletti, *Luc raconte*, 59; Daniel Marguerat, 'The God of the Book of Acts' in G.J. Brooke and J.-D. Kaestli (eds.), *Narrativity in Biblical and Related Texts* (BETL 149; Leuven: Leuven University Press, 2000) 159-81, citing 166.

[115] Guy D. Nave, *The Role and Function of Repentance in Luke-Acts* (SBLAB 4; Atlanta: Society of Biblical Literature, 2002) 18; cf. Bruce W. Longenecker, 'Rome's Victory and God's Honour: The Jerusalem Temple and the Spirit of God in Lukan Theodicy' in Stanton et al. (eds.), *Christian Origins*, 90-102, esp. 102; Marguerat, 'God,' 167.

Interpersonal Characterisation

By negative parallel, the opponents' interaction with Jesus' witnesses boosts God's mission plan of universal salvation. The examination of their roles in regard to God's mission will therefore provide an in-depth understanding for the overall picture of God. Since the opponents' interactions with major and minor characters have been investigated, here the emphasis will be laid on the function of their roles in the plot with regard to God's mission plan, which also sheds light on the characterisation of God from the negative angle.

INTERNAL OPPOSITION

Although characterised by its unity (1:14; 2:44; 4:24, 32), the faith community 'remains riddled with divisions and tensions.'[116] While the apostles' authority in proclaiming the Word is enhanced as they deal with the conflict of personal affairs within the community (5:1-11; 6:1-4),[117] their solution for the internal dissension over Gentile salvation manifests God's sovereign authority and power. The issue of whether God's salvation is also offered to Gentiles is first raised by Jewish believers after Peter evangelises the Cornelius household (11:1-18). Later, as Paul carries on the Gentile mission, the law-keeping believers dispute greatly with him on how the Gentiles can receive salvation (15:1-21; cf. 21:18-22). By this internal opposition the church is shaken to ponder God's will for Gentile salvation. In solving both controversial issues, the divine initiative throughout the Gentile mission is strongly emphasised.[118] The internal opposition to Gentile mission, thus, serves to offer a setting for further clarification and confirmation of both God's universal salvation in Jesus alone and God's plan of worldwide mission.[119] That God's initiative in Gentile mission calms the internal conflict within the faith community evinces God's omniscience (in knowing the obstacle of the Gentile mission), omnipotence (in initiating the Gentile mission in crucial events), and authority (seen in the apostles' submission to the divine will).

JEWISH OPPOSITION

Although Judaism as a whole is divided by the proclamation of the Word, the narrative lays the emphasis on the majority who reject the message.[120]

---

[116] Andrianjatovo Rakotoharintsifa, 'Luke and the Internal Divisions in the Early Church' in Tuckett (ed.), *Luke's Literary Achievement*, 165-77, citing 176.
[117] Walworth, *Narrator*, 111.
[118] Rapske, 'Opposition,' 240, 242.
[119] Walworth, *Narrator*, 110.
[120] Cunningham, *Tribulations*, 229.

Near the beginning of the story, the Jewish-Christian community is viewed with favor by all people (2:47). But as the narrative continues, this favorable situation subsides. First the temple authorities (4:1-2; 5:17-18), then the diaspora Jews in Jerusalem (6:9-14) and finally the Jewish people in general (6:12) are aroused to instigate a great persecution of the Christian community (8:1).[121]

The disbelieving Jews, whether the Jewish leaders or crowd, or the Jews in Jerusalem or in the Diaspora (especially in Asia), or even both,[122] are the main force opposed to the believers in Acts.[123] Their opposition grows in increasing intensity;[124] this climaxes at the attempts to kill Jesus' witnesses (5:33; 7:57-60; 9:29; 14:19; 21:31; 23:12). The cause of opposition and persecution is attributed to the witnesses' preaching of Jesus' resurrection (5:27-32; 25:19)[125] and the Jews' jealousy of the great number of converts (5:17; 13:45; 17:5).[126] In the narrative, the Jews' rejection of the Word is 'both the *occasion* for the turning to τὰ ἔθνη and a contributory *cause*... to why the gospel went to Gentiles.'[127] Their rejection does not change God's saving plan but causes them to miss God's invitation of participating in his mighty work. Nonetheless, their opposition is eventually woven into the divine plan[128] and overruled by God as a divine means of promoting the Gentile mission.[129] By and large, the Jewish opposition, playing a structural role in the narrative, offers a setting for the profound realisation of God's worldwide mission of salvation, against which God's sovereign authority and power over human intrigue and persecution stand out.

GENTILE OPPOSITION

Paul's preaching of the Word to Gentiles also inevitably causes division among them. The opposition of the unbelieving Gentiles appears in two ways: some

---

[121] Powell, *About Acts*, 103-4.
[122] For further discussion on the term οἱ Ἰουδαῖοι see Augusto Barbi, 'The Use and Meaning of *(Hoi) Ioudaioi* in Acts' in O'Collins and Marconi (eds.), *Luke and Acts*, 123-42; Robert L. Brawley, *Luke-Acts and the Jews: Conflict, Apology, and Conciliation* (SBLMS 33; Atlanta: Scholars Press, 1987) 133-54; Sanders, *Jews*, 37-83; Joseph B. Tyson, 'The Jewish Public in Luke-Acts,' *NTS* 30 (1984) 574-83.
[123] Cunningham, *Tribulations*, 248 n.210; Barbi, '*Ioudaioi*,' 141.
[124] Walworth, *Narrator*, 119.
[125] Ernst Bammel, 'Jewish Activity against Christians in Palestine according to Acts' in Bauckham (ed.), *Acts in Its Palestinian Setting*, 357-64, citing 358.
[126] Kilgallen, 'Hostility,' 5. For further discussion on the Jews' jealousy see Bruce W. Longenecker, 'Moral Character and Divine Generosiy: Acts 13:13-52 and the Narrative Dynamics of Luke-Acts' in Donaldson and Sailors (eds.), *Exegesis*, 141-64.
[127] Cunningham, *Tribulations*, 249; Johnson, *Acts*, 241.
[128] Aletti, *Luc raconte*, 65.
[129] McBride, *Emmaus*, 197.

actively persecute Paul because his powerful ministry results in their economic loss and threatens their livelihood (16:19-24; 19:24-27); some passively persecute Paul because of the Jews' instigation (13:50; 14:2, 19; 17:5, 13).[130] The former ironically testifies that God's authority and power, on which Paul acts, is greater than other spiritual forces (e.g. the fortunetelling spirit and Ephesian goddess) by which the Gentiles make a living. The latter manifests God's plan to be higher than human intrigue since God overrules human schemes for his purpose. In general, the Gentile opponents, playing only a minor technical role in the narrative structure, create a background for the characterisation of Paul as a suffering witness and as a powerful missionary for God's mission. Against this background God's sovereign authority and power are magnified since no force can impede his expanding mission.

ROMAN OPPOSITION

The Roman officials oppose major characters by being directly or indirectly involved in persecution. To please the Jews, Herod kills the apostle James and puts Peter in prison for later execution (12:1-2). Other Roman officials are often associated with Paul as he is accused by Jews and Gentiles. Though judging Paul innocent (18:12-17; 19:35-41; 24:22; 25:24-27), they still keep him in prison to do the Jews a favour (24:27; 25:9). The direct opposition is overturned by God's mighty power (12:23); the indirect opposition turns into a divine means of safeguarding Paul from the Jews' killing scheme and for the ongoing mission (21:31-36; 23:16-24; 27:43). God's authority and power, surpassing that of human authorities, are greatly revealed in his delivering and protecting of his witnesses. God's sovereignty is magnified by his overruling of human injustice for his good end. Similar to the Gentiles' minor technical role, the Roman officials offer the backdrop of intensifying persecution against which God's supreme authority and power and his plan of universal mission are amplified.

Summary

Overall, the opposing force is overruled by God as a driving force to promote God's mission plan. The internal opposition, though challenging the unity of the church, impels it to validate the Gentile salvation and mission. The external opposition, though testing the faith of Jesus' witnesses, brings along God's mighty care and enables the witnesses to carry on God's mission. Among the three types of external opposition, the Jewish opposition is the dominant impulse with the Gentile and Roman opposition as its aid. The Jews actively and constantly persecute the witnesses throughout the narrative. The Gentiles and Roman officials actively persecute the witnesses for their own advantage; they

---

[130] Cunningham, *Tribulations*, 249.

passively partake in persecuting Paul while being urged by the Jews. God's sovereignty, authority and omnipotence stand from his powerfully riding over all human opposition and turning it into an impulse for his mission plan.

Conclusion

The function of minor characters appears in their relationships with major characters and in their contribution to the plot. In relation to major characters, the collective believers function as a living witness to the apostles' proclamation in Jerusalem and as a backing in Antioch to Paul's overseas mission; the individual believers continue the apostolic ministry and initiate the breakthrough of Gentile evangelism. In the plot the ministry of believers serves as a bridge between that of major characters. The God-fearers are those first reached as the Gentile mission is carried out; they function as a bridge between the mission to Jews and that to Gentiles. Both believers and God-fearers stand in the intermediary stage which manifests God's plan of universal salvation and thus connects the ministry of Peter and Paul as one ministry of God as well as the mission to Jews and Gentiles as one mission of God. In contrast, as a negative parallel, the opponents as a whole interact with major characters throughout the narrative. By their opposition God's mission plan is fortified as God's sovereignty overrules all human opposition for his highest purpose. By and large, the minor characters provide a setting to profoundly realise the transition of God's mission and to testify to God's authority and power as the controlling force behind all characters and incidents. The overall presentation of the minor characters reinforces the major characters' representation of God as the sovereign God, who authoritatively and powerfully dominates the narrative characters and events for his supreme redemptive purpose and mission.

PART II

THEMATIC CHARACTERISATION OF GOD—TELLING AND PLOT

CHAPTER 6

The Characterisation of God by the Narrator

The narrator is one of the most important structural features in narrative who exists alongside the characters and gives them life in the narrative world.[1] In the preceding chapters, from the characters' speeches and actions (i.e. the narrator's *showing*) emerges the mimetic characterisation of God; herein appears a common concern among characters, that is, *God's universal saving will and mission plan realised in Jesus and carried out by the Spirit-empowered witnesses of Jesus*. Such a divine purpose functions as the controlling thread which weaves together characters and incidents.[2] Importantly, no single character acting throughout the narrative suggests that the characterisation in Acts is plot-oriented instead of character-centred.[3] When characters are mostly a function of the plot they promote the plot within which they have determinate functions.[4] The narrator often uses narrative themes as plot devices.[5] Along such a plot line characters dance to bring out the thematic concerns of the narrative. The purpose of this chapter is to investigate God's role in the plot, i.e. the thematic characterisation of God. Both mimetic and thematic strata of characterisation are progressively developed and, more or less, coalesced. However, the thematic characterisation examines God's role in the narrative as a whole (macro-narrative) while the mimetic one does so in each episode (micro-narrative).

Repetition is a powerful literary technique for conveying the narrative theme, especially in Acts. Although there are other stylistic devices (e.g. metaphor, simile, irony, etc.), they mainly add colour and emphasis to the individual scenes rather than the whole picture of the narrative. Yet the repetition of cer-

---

[1] Bar-Efrat, *Narrative Art*, 13.

[2] Tannehill asserts that God's saving purpose stands behind the events of Luke-Acts (*Unity*, 2:7); also, Charles H. Talbert, *Reading Luke-Acts in its Mediterranean Milieu* (Leiden: Brill, 2003) 164. Examining the cultural belief, Talbert asserts that '[t]he belief that a divine necessity controls human history, shaping the course of its events, was a widespread assumption in Mediterranean antiquity' (165).

[3] Walworth, *Narrator*, 80-81; Darr, *Character Building*, 39; Charles Wade Bibb, *The Characterization of God in Luke-Acts* (unpublished PhD dissertation, Southern Baptist Theological Seminary, 1996) 299; Robert C. Tannehill, *The Narrative Unity of Luke-Acts*, vol. 1 (Philadelphia: Fortress Press, 1986) 1.

[4] Walworth, *Narrator*, 80; Shepherd, *Spirit*, 56-57.

[5] Steven M. Sheeley, *Narrative Asides in Luke-Acts* (JSNTSup 72; Sheffield: Sheffield Academic Press, 1992) 139.

tain key-terms and key-patterns not only continues the theme but promotes the plot.[6] To examine God's role in the plot, the repeated key-terms from the overt narrator's voice concerning God and his interest will first be investigated in order to grasp the narrator's fundamental notion of God in the narrative. The covert narrator's presentation of God along the plot line will then be explored. The thematic characterisation reflects the narrator's most panoramic view of the portrayal of God, in which the narrative highlight of God's status and their corresponding applications are unfolded.[7]

Overt Narrator's Distinctive *Telling* of God

To unearth the narrator's ingrained notion in his *telling*, it is important to first distinguish two basic kinds of voice in the narrative: the characters' and the narrator's. The speeches given in the Acts narrative are from the characters' voice, introduced by the narrator (see *he said, he asked*, etc.), through which the implied author may communicate his viewpoint. The rest of the narration is in the narrator's voice, in which two types of narration can be further classified: the description of incidents; the summary of, or remark on, the overall happenings.[8] The former, predominant over the narrative, narrates the development of the story, presenting 'the actions in such a way as to give the illusion that they are recurring before the reader's eyes and ears' (i.e. the narrator's literary technique of *showing*).[9] The latter embraces the narrator's keen interest in the narrative and therefore is the focal study of this section. See the following list for the narrator's nine summaries/remarks and their gist.[10]

---

[6] George W. Savran, *Telling and Retelling: Quotation in Biblical Narrative* (Bloomington & Indianapolis: Indiana University Press, 1988) 30; Robert C. Culley, *Themes and Variations: A Study of Action in Biblical Narrative* (Atlanta: Scholars Press, 1992) 47. See also the narrative rhetoric of characterisation, in which Paul L. Danove elucidates that 'repetition of words with God as the referent of a particular argument not only highlights and reinforces particular positive actions and attributes of God but directly relates God positively or negatively to other characters referenced by the same argument of the same words and imposes a positive or negative evaluation of those characters' actions and attributes' (*The Rhetoric of Characterization of God, Jesus, and Jesus' Disciples in the Gospel of Mark* [JSNTSup 290; New York: T & T Clark, 2005] 35).

[7] Phelan defines any attribute of a character as a *dimension* and a particular application of that attribute as a *function* (*Reading People*, 9).

[8] For the references for the narrative voice see Appendix Three.

[9] Funk, *Poetics*, 135.

[10] There are also remarks on certain settings (1:12; 4:36-37; 8:1a; etc.) and summaries of the characters' proclamation (8:5; 9:20; 17:3; etc.) in the narrator's depiction of incidents. Yet they are part of the story to realise the incidents in depth. The summary/remark on the overall events conveys the narrator's evaluation about the

1:1-3	Narrator's previous book regarding Jesus' story and his teaching concerning the kingdom of God
2:43-47	Dynamic and unified life of the faith community (singling out the apostles' miracles)
4:32-35	Dynamic and unified life of the faith community (singling out the apostles' witness to the Lord Jesus' resurrection)
6:7	The Word of God grows and the number of disciples multiplies
9:31	The church in Judea, Galilee and Samaria grows
12:24	The Word of God grows and increases
16:5	The churches are strengthened in faith and grow in number
19:20	The Word of the Lord grows and is strong
28:30-31	Paul proclaims the kingdom of God and the Lord Jesus Christ without hindrance

To fully grasp the narrator's vital interest in the portrayal of God, the significance of the repeated key-terms regarding God in these succinct accounts (κύριος, ὁ λόγος τοῦ θεοῦ and ἡ βασιλεία τοῦ θεοῦ) will be scrutinised together with their other occurrences and other relevant terms in the narrative. Significantly, all these terms appear in the reliable voices in the narrative (i.e. those of Peter, Paul and the disciples) which may convey the implied author's viewpoint (ultimately, the whole narrative is his literary work). From the above list appear two significant points concerning the narrator's notion of God: his exclusive use of the epithet κύριος for God,[11] shared by Jesus; his interest in God's kingdom, Word and church.

Exclusive Use of Epithet for God

Epithet, which denotes a term, adjective or adjectival phrase defining the distinctive nature of a person,[12] is the most explicit and authoritative indicator for introducing God.[13] Κύριος is the only epithet for God coming from the narrator's voice, either in his description or summary, as well as the only one shared by other reliable voices.[14] This reveals that κύριος conveys the narrator's fun-

---

ongoing movement. Brian S. Rosner notes that the summaries in 6:7; 9:31; 12:24; 16:5; 19:20; 28:30-31 report a central theme—the progress of the gospel—in Acts ('The Progress of the Word' in Marshall and Peterson [eds.], *Witness*, 215-33, citing 221). See also Henry J. Cadbury, 'The Summaries in Acts,' *Beg*, 5:392-402; Maria Anicia Co, 'The Major Summaries in Acts,' *ETL* 68/1 (1992) 49-85.

[11] Though the referent of κυρίου in 19:20 may refer to God or Jesus, a comparison with its parallels in 6:7 and 12:24 reveals that κυρίου probably refers to God.

[12] Abrams, *Literary Terms*, 82; David B. Gowler, 'Characterization in Luke: A Socio-Narratological Approach,' *BTB* 19 (1989) 54-62, citing 56.

[13] Sternberg, *Biblical Narrative*, 325.

[14] For the occurrences of the epithet for God see Appendix Four.

damental notion of God in the narrative. While referring to a transcendent being, κύριος, a title for God, speaks of the one 'who exercises supernatural authority over mankind.'[15] The referent of κύριος, whether God or Jesus, is sometimes ambiguous.[16] From those definitely referring to God emerges an authoritative self-disclosed God (7:31-32) who creates and transcends the world (7:48-50; 17:24), who foretells and preordains human history (2:20-21, 39; 3:20-22; 4:26; 13:47; 15:17), who supervises human events in conformity to his plan (5:19; 8:26, 39; 10:33; 12:7, 11, 17, 23; 13:11; 14:3) and who hears human prayers (1:24; 4:29; 7:33-34).

Basically, God is the authoritative Lord over the world and humans. Such an image is reinforced by God's other two titles uttered by the disciples: δεσπότης and ὕψιστος. Δεσπότης denotes a person 'who holds complete power or authority over another.'[17] In 4:24, it signifies God's sovereign control over all human affairs.[18] Ὕψιστος indicates a person who has the most supreme status.[19] In 7:48, its context reveals that the supreme God is transcendent over the whole universe (cf. 16:17). The three titles of God highlight God as the sovereign and supreme Lord who is in powerful control of the universe and humankind and is authoritatively and actively working in human life.

As God's three titles reveal his innate status (the sovereign and supreme Lord), its application, which expresses God's relational status, is disclosed in the epithets indicating God's relationship with the believers, the Jews and the universe.[20] Πατήρ, the term with which Peter addresses God while following Jesus' example, signifies that the loving Father of Jesus is now the Father of the believers (1:4, 7; 2:33). The supreme God in his sovereign lordship intimately builds up the loving relationship of Father-son with the believers of Jesus. Such a fatherhood refers to 'a relationship of trust and to the promise of faithfulness. God's trustworthiness and faithfulness are central to understanding God as Father.'[21] The phrases, such as ὁ θεὸς τῶν πατέρων ἡμῶν, are employed by the believers to emphasise that the God who now acts powerfully through Jesus is the same God of the Jewish patriarchs (3:13; 5:30; 7:32; 22:14; cf. 2:39;

---

[15] L&N, §12.9; BDAG, 577.

[16] For the referent of κύριος see Appendix Five.

[17] L&N, §37.63; BDAG, 220.

[18] Marshall comments that 'the title Sovereign Lord (δεσπότης) is comparatively infrequent in the New Testament (and also in the LXX) perhaps because the word suggested a despotic, arbitrary kind of lordship. Here, however, it is appropriately used to stress the powerful control exerted by God' (*Acts*, 105).

[19] L&N, §12.4; BDAG, 1045.

[20] Beside the epithets conveying God's status, there are other epithets of God which demonstrate God's attributes expressed by attributive modifiers or inferred from God's deeds (see Appendix Six).

[21] Marianne Meye Thompson, *The Promise of the Father* (Louisville: Westminster John Knox Press, 2000) 183.

13:17; 24:14).²² The repeated highlighting of the collective identification of God (a God of 'Abraham, Isaac, and Jacob' and 'our fathers') stresses not only the same origin of the faith of believers and Jews but 'the ongoing nature of the pledge' of God.²³ The supreme God in his sovereign lordship gives a new revelation in Jesus regarding his old promise to his people Israel. The adjectival participles (ὁ θεὸς ὁ ποιήσας...) speak of God's relationship with the universe as the Creator (4:24; 17:24; cf. 14:15). Such thought pervades Judaism and permeates every single Jew;²⁴ underneath this is the belief in one true God whose sovereignty, power and grace are over all creation and humankind. Overall, God's lordship is recognised over his relationship with the universe as the Creator, with his people Israel as the self-Revealer and with the believers as Father-to-sons.

In summary, the narrator's exclusive use of the epithet κύριος for God exposes his undergirding notion of God (the sovereign and supreme Lord) having authority and power over the universe and humankind. The relational epithets specify God's lordship over various relationships which amplify God's supremacy and sovereignty over the ongoing events and his absolute reign over the circumstances the characters are in (3:13; 4:24; 5:30; etc.). Such a divine lordship is shared by Jesus because of his central role in carrying out God's very interest—human salvation—as other repeated terms in the summary accounts reveal.

Especial Indication of God's 'Interest' ²⁵

The two repeated terms ὁ λόγος τοῦ θεοῦ and ἡ βασιλεία τοῦ θεοῦ in the summary accounts unveil the narrator's focal concern in the narrative. Moreover, the formula of noun+θεοῦ, which indicates the divine ownership or origin of a noun, signifies that the narrator's concerns are also God's. Significantly, of the forty occurrences of this formula,²⁶ twenty-nine directly relate to God's interest in the saving plan, five to God's power or majesty²⁷ and six to God's agents.²⁸ Among the twenty-nine references to God's saving plan, ὁ λόγος τοῦ

---

[22] Barrett, *Acts*, 1:194; Dunn, *Acts*, 44; Marshall, *Acts*, 90-91.
[23] Savran, *Retelling*, 53.
[24] God as Creator is seen throughout the OT (Gen 1-2; 14:19; Ex 20:11; 2 Kgs 19:15; Neh 9:6; Ps 135:4-6; 146:6; Isa 37:16; Jer 31:35).
[25] In this chapter, the phrase 'God's interest' or 'God's concern' is used in a sense related to the *interest point of view* (see Chatman, *Story and Discourse*, 152), which signifies the interest of both God and the narrator.
[26] There are other three occurrences which refer to a god other than the God of Israel (7:43; 8:10; 12:22).
[27] See τὰ μεγαλεῖα τοῦ θεοῦ in 2:11; ἡ δεξιός τοῦ θεοῦ in 2:33; 7:55, 56; δόξα θεοῦ in 7:55.
[28] See 10:3; 16:17; 17:29; 22:3; 23:4; 27:23.

θεοῦ and ἡ βασιλεία τοῦ θεοῦ occur most frequently and are almost always in the narrator's voice. As noted, God's interest serves as a controlling thread weaving through the narrative. These two phrases therefore are crucial in grasping the narrator's essential notion of God as well as the undergirding themes of the narrative.

Ὁ λόγος τοῦ θεοῦ occurs eleven times in which nine are of the narrator's voice.[29] Its parallel phrase ὁ λόγος τοῦ κυρίου is also almost invariably from the narrator's voice.[30] Both phrases greatly reflect the narrator's interest in the divine origin of the Word.[31] The singular λόγος serves as terminology to express God's saving will made known in the significance of Jesus' death and resurrection, the focal point of Peter's and Paul's speeches to the Jews and God-fearers.[32] By singling out these phrases the narrator aligns his interest with God's.[33] Furthermore, other qualifiers of λόγος, bearing a salvific implication (see σωτηρίας, εὐαγγελίου, χάριτος; 13:26; 14:3; 15:7; 20:32), reinforce the saving force of the Word. For the *attributive* qualifiers, σωτηρία defines the innate quality of λόγος as the message concerning God's salvation manifest in Jesus (13:26).[34] Εὐαγγέλιον specifies λόγος as God's good news to human beings (15:7), namely, the gospel about Jesus.[35] Both qualifiers clarify what God's will in Jesus is. For the qualifier functioning as *genitive of producer*, χάρις indicates the λόγος being produced by God's grace and as gracious deeds wrought by God in Christ (note that χάρις in both 14:3 and 20:32 is modified by αὐτοῦ which refers to God; cf. 20:24, τὸ εὐαγγέλιον τῆς χάριτος τοῦ θεοῦ).[36] In other words, the Word/gospel originates from 'the loving favour of

---

[29] Those from the narrator's voice are 4:31; 6:7; 8:14; 11:1; 12:24; 13:5, 7; 17:13; 18:11. Those from the characters' voice in dialogue form are 6:2; 13:46.

[30] Eight out of the nine occurrences of ὁ λόγος τοῦ κυρίου are of the narrator (8:25; 13:44, 48, 49; 15:35; 16:32; 19:10, 20) and one is the narrator's deliberate use of Paul's voice (15:36).

[31] The genitive θεοῦ or κυρίου in the terminological phrases may function as genitive of source (i.e. λόγος derives from or depends on God/Lord) or producer (i.e. λόγος is produced by God/Lord). Either signifies the divine origin of the Word (cf. Wallace, *Beyond*, 104-5, 109).

[32] See 2:14-36; 3:12-26; 4:9-12; 5:29-32; 10:34-43; 13:16-41.

[33] There are thirty-five terminological uses of λόγος (twenty-five in the accusative, 4:4, 29, 31; 6:2; 8:4, 14, 25; 10:36, 44; 11:1, 19; 13:5, 7, 44, 46, 48; 14:25; 15:7, 35, 36; 16:6, 32; 17:11; 18:11; 19:10; six in the nominative, 6:7; 12:24; 13:26, 49; 17:13; 19:20; four in oblique cases, 6:4; 14:3; 18:5; 20:32) in which twenty are modified by θεοῦ or κυρίου. Of these seventeen are in the narrator's voice.

[34] Wallace, *Beyond*, 86. Note that σωτηρία is a word with focus on the transcendent aspect (BDAG, 986); cf. L&N, §21.26; Haenchen, *Acts*, 410; Johnson, *Acts*, 233; Barrett, *Acts*, 1:638; Witherington, *Acts*, 411.

[35] BDAG, 402; L&N, §33.217.

[36] BDAG, 1079-80; Marshall, *Acts*, 335; Polhill, *Acts*, 428-29.

God'[37] and this grace is the basis of God's salvation in Jesus. Overall, the qualifiers of λόγος introduce the essence of the Word which communicates a message about God's salvific will and gracious deeds done in Jesus. That the narrator highly regards the divine origin of the Word signifies the supremacy and authority of the Word since it conveys God's sovereign will of salvation.

Ἡ βασιλεία τοῦ θεοῦ occurs six times and is again a term nearly exclusive to the narrator (1:3; 8:12; 19:8; 28:23, 31; also the narrator's artful use of Paul's voice in 14:22; cf. 20:25). While the phrase in 14:22 may refer to the future realm of God's rule,[38] others convey the idea of God's sovereign reign with complete authority.[39] The latter further signifies God's lordship over his people.[40] In the beginning of the narrative, the narrator summarises Jesus' proclamation concerning the kingdom of God (1:1-3). Hence the subject of God's kingdom is whispered throughout the narrative. This signifies that 'God's kingdom is a central concern of Acts,'[41] which closely relates to the Word (see the preaching of Jesus coming alongside proclamation of the kingdom of God in 8:12; 19:8; 28:23, 31).[42] The narrator adopts the phrase to summarise the believers' proclamation, having the Word as its central message (i.e. the Christian belief).[43] The narrator ends his story 'not on Paul but on the gospel, on the message of the kingdom. The word of God in Christ—not Peter, not Paul—is the real hero of Acts.'[44] The ongoing concern for God's kingdom and for its message, God's Word, makes God's saving interest the common concern

---

[37] Barrett, *Acts*, 1:670.

[38] Marshall, *Acts*, 241; John Nolland, 'Salvation-History and Eschatology' in Marshall and Peterson (eds.), *Witness*, 63-81, citing 70.

[39] L&N, §37.64; Polhill, *Acts*, 82; Bruce, *Acts*, 100. While βασιλεία may also refer to the sphere of God's reign, Caragounis elucidates that βασιλεία 'is abstract and dynamic, that is, "sovereignty" or "royal rule." This is almost always the case in the OT and Jewish literature when the term is applied to God. The sense of realm—a territorial kingdom—is secondary, arising out of the necessity for a definite locus as the sphere for the exercise of sovereignty.' Jesus also shares this conception of the OT. See Chrys C. Caragounis, 'Kingdom of God/Kingdom of Heaven' in Joel B. Green and Scot McKnight (eds.), *Dictionary of Jesus and the Gospels* (Leicester: InterVarsity Press, 1992) 417-30, citing 417, 420.

[40] Robert L. Brawley, *Centering on God* (Louisville: Westminster/John Knox Press, 1990) 120.

[41] Polhill, *Acts*, 82; cf. Maddox, *Purpose*, 133; Spencer, *Philip*, 40.

[42] Peterson, 'Fulfilment,' 94; Rosner, 'Progress,' 224; Agustín Del Agua, 'The Lucan Narrative of the "Evangelization of the Kingdom of God"' in Verheyden (ed.), *Unity*, 639-661, citing 655, 659; Robert O'Toole, 'The Kingdom of God in Luke-Acts' in Wendell Willis (ed.), *The Kingdom of God in 20th-Century Interpretation* (Peabody: Hendrickson Publishers, 1987) 147-62, citing 153-54.

[43] Barrett, *Acts*, 1:408; idem, 'The End of Acts' in Lichtenberger (ed.), *Geschichte*, 3:545-55, citing 552; Fitzmyer, *Acts*, 311; Salmeier, *Ordainer*, 94-95.

[44] Polhill, *Acts*, 548.

among characters and thus keeps God always in the reader's mind, whether on stage or off.

Additionally, other relevant phrases in the formula of noun+θεοῦ reinforce God's saving plan as his special interest. By God's mighty acts (τὰ μεγαλεῖα τοῦ θεοῦ, 2:11; cf. 13:17-23) salvation comes to all through Jesus, God's Son (ὁ υἱὸς τοῦ θεοῦ, 9:20), and the Spirit, God's gift (ἡ δωρεὰ τοῦ θεοῦ, 8:20; cf. 11:17). God's Word communicated in Jesus is fundamentally rooted upon God's plan (ἡ βουλὴ τοῦ θεοῦ, 2:23; 20:27) and God's worldwide Word-mission is buttressed by God's grace (ἡ χάρις τοῦ θεοῦ, 11:23; 13:43; 14:26; note the narrator's voice in these references). It is by his grace and in his plan that God's salvation prevails (τὸ σωτήριον τοῦ θεοῦ, 28:28; cf. 13:26; 20:24) and God calls a people for himself, namely the church of God (ἡ ἐκκλησία τοῦ θεοῦ, 20:28; cf. 15:14). Their 'specification of teaching and manner of life relating to Jesus Christ'[45] is known as God's Way (ἡ ὁδὸς τοῦ θεοῦ, 18:26; cf. 9:2; 19:9, 23; 22:4; 24:14, 22). As shown in the summary accounts, the dynamic life of the church is also the narrator's concern which expresses God's reign among his people.

Overall, the narrator's distinctive indication of God's interest discloses God's inner world which centres on his saving plan. Salvation originates only from divine initiative. Founded on his loving grace and sovereign plan, God's salvation comes into reality with the participation of Jesus and the Spirit. Whereas God's Word in Jesus is the key to receiving salvation and becoming the people/church of God, God's kingdom is the ultimate concern of the redemptive plan and the Word-mission. As God's mission expands and the Word grows, God's kingdom extends and his sovereignty and authority reign.

Summary

The narrator's exclusive use of κύριος for God highlights God's innate status as supreme and sovereign Lord, perceived in his lordship over a threefold relationship: God as the Creator of the universe, the self-Revealer to the people Israel and the Father of Jesus' believers. The narrator's typical use of the phrases ὁ λόγος τοῦ θεοῦ and ἡ βασιλεία τοῦ θεοῦ indicates God's interest in involving himself in human salvation and in involving people in his kingdom. Human salvation is utterly of God's plan (that he promised salvation) and by his grace (that he gave Jesus and the Spirit), by which God builds up his universal church for his kingdom. In brief, the narrator represents a Lord God who supremely transcends humankind yet sovereignly participates in human history to authoritatively and powerfully share his gracious salvation.

By and large, in *telling*, the narrator's distinctive use of repeated terms singles out not only the fundamental notion of who God is and what his interest is

---

[45] BDAG, 692.

but the controlling theme of the narrative. The narrative underscores God's status as the sovereign Lord; God's sovereignty is made manifest through his supreme plan of salvation in relation to God's kingdom. Yet the *telling* simply sketches a static image of God. Therefore, a thorough and animated picture of God's activity for the universal mission of salvation requires an investigation of the covert narrator's deployment of the whole narrative whereby the sovereign God's actions in order to carry out his redemptive plan come to light.

Covert Narrator's Presentation of God in the Plot

Along the narrative theme (God's saving plan) the narrator, taking the point of view of God's interest in each episode as shown in the previous chapters via a zoom-in lens, presents that 'God, the super-agent who remains unseen, controls the action from offstage.'[46] This mimetic characterisation of God reveals God's authoritative and powerful deeds in Israel's history, in Jesus' life and in the lives of Jesus' witnesses. How this super-agent is characterised thematically, however, requires a scrutiny of God's role in the plot.[47] To this end, the role of God's interest in the plot will first be investigated to confirm its controlling function in the narrative as shown in the mimetic portrayal of God. Then, God's activities working around his interest will be explored in order to detect the narrator's highlighting of how God acts in plot devices. Finally, God's promotion of the thematic plot will be examined. In other words, the implied author adopts the literary technique of the *interest point of view* in the mimetic stratum of the narrative, which keeps the invisible God's redemptive plan (the divine interest) always in view. Moreover, through the narrative plot of making God's interest the narrative theme, the implied author aligns his interest with God's. This thematic characterisation of God bears a dynamic force governing the development of the narrative and reflects the narrator's ultimate concern in his overall literary work.

The Role of God's 'Interest' in the Plot

As noted, God's saving will expressed in the Word (λόγος) is a common concern throughout the narrative. This section will scrutinise the role of λόγος in

---

[46] John A. Darr, 'Narrator as Character: Mapping a Reader-Oriented Approach to Narration in Luke-Acts,' *Semeia* 63 (1993) 43-60, citing 55.

[47] With respect to the significance of biblical narrative in the plot level, Grant R. Osborne indicates: 'Narrative does not merely inform; it acts. The illocutionary force takes place via plot, characterization, and a point of view that invites readers to share its world. As such there are at least two aspects that are communicated, the historical event told in the story and its theological interpretation accomplished by the imaginative reconstruction of the author' ('Historical Narrative and Truth in the Bible,' *JETS* 48 [2005] 673-88, citing 684).

the plot which is embedded in its syntactical use as the direct object and the subject of active verbs in the literary work. The syntactical significance of λόγος confirms its centrality in the narrative theme.

ΛΟΓΟΣ AS A DIRECT OBJECT

Mostly, λόγος serves as the direct object of a clause (i.e. the receiver of the action of a verb). Even three of the six nominatives of λόγος, occurring with passive verbs, function as the direct object in meaning (13:26, 49; 17:13). Predominantly, the human character is the producer of the action of the verb associated with λόγος while only a few relate to the divine character. Depending on the meaning of the verb, three types of relation exist between the subject (character) and the object (λόγος). Each sheds light on God's will in the Word and profoundly brings out God's mission.

The relation most frequently appearing is between the believers and λόγος (fifteen occurrences);[48] the linking verbs are λαλέω, εὐαγγελίζομαι, διαμαρτύρομαι, καταγγέλλω and διδάσκω which basically convey the idea of making known and proclaiming. These verbs signify the narrator's great interest in the proclamation of λόγος by the believers. Another relation is between the unbelievers and λόγος (nine occurrences);[49] the connecting verbs are ἀκούω and δέχομαι which further relate to *believe* (4:4; 15:7). This elucidates the need for λόγος to be heard so that the unbeliever may receive and believe it. The relation appearing least, yet the most fundamental, is between God and λόγος (occurring twice);[50] the associated verbs are cognate (ἀποστέλλω or ἐξαποστέλλω) which signify the divine sending. This implies a divine mission via Jesus, initiated by God. More significantly, λόγος interconnects narrative characters, which reveals a divine design about God's mission. See the following diagram for clarification of the central role of λόγος in God's mission.

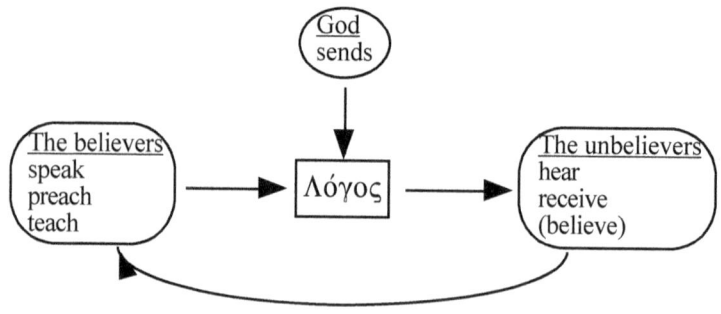

---

[48] For λόγος with active verbs see 4:29, 31; 8:4, 25; 11:19; 13:5; 14:25; 15:35, 36; 16:6, 32; 18:11. For those with passive verbs see 13:46, 49; 17:13.
[49] See 4:4; 8:14; 10:44; 11:1; 13:7, 44; 15:7; 17:11; 19:10.
[50] See 10:36 (with active verb); 13:26 (with passive verb).

Λόγος, though passive on the surface, plays a central role as the narrative characters relate to it. God initiates his mission by sending the Word to humans through Jesus. The Word, God's will, then stands as a division between believers and unbelievers. To proclaim the Word of salvation is the common interest of the believers as well as the narrator. The hearers' response to the Word, receiving or opposing, leads to conflict incidents between the believing and disbelieving groups (which will soon be explored in the ministry pattern). The positive impact of the Word signals the expansion of God's mission which is specified in the subjective use of λόγος.

ΛΟΓΟΣ AS A SUBJECT

The most significant yet often ignored use of λόγος is its function as the subject of an active verb ($λόγος^{nom}$+$verb^{act}$). There are only three occurrences in Acts which appear in the succinct summary of the growth of the Word (6:7; 12:24; 19:20). To grasp the significance of λόγος first requires an investigation of the verbs in these verses.

6:7   ὁ λόγος τοῦ θεοῦ ηὔξανεν καὶ
      ἐπληθύνετο ὁ ἀριθμὸς τῶν μαθητῶν ἐν Ἰερουσαλὴμ σφόδρα

12:24 ὁ λόγος τοῦ θεοῦ ηὔξανεν καὶ ἐπληθύνετο

19:20 κατὰ κράτος τοῦ κυρίου ὁ λόγος ηὔξανεν καὶ ἴσχυεν

All the verbs are progressive imperfect which highlights the ongoing growth of the Word. Three verbs are employed to express the growth of the Word: αὐξάνω, πληθύνω and ἰσχύω. Αὐξάνω, appearing in all three verses, is the key word employed for the growth. Yet its meaning is ambiguous since it may refer to an increase in size, extent, status, quality or the degree of a state. Nonetheless, its parallel verbs, πληθύνω and ἰσχύω, clarify it. Πληθύνω in 6:7[51] unambiguously shows the increase in the number of the disciples which can also be applied to 12:24.[52] Ἰσχύω in 19:20, on the other hand, points out another con-

---

[51] Note ἀριθμός, the subject of πληθύνω, indicates 'the sum or total of a numbered quantity' (L&N, §60.2).

[52] The formula of αὐξάνω καὶ πληθύνω is used in the LXX 'to express the promise and realization of the growth and expansion of God's covenant people' (Jerome Kodell, '"The Word of God Grew" — The Ecclesial Tendency of Λόγος in Acts 6,7; 12,24; 19,20,' *Bib* 55 [1974] 505-19, citing 511; cf. also O'Reilly, *Word*, 82-83). Examining the fourteen occurrences of this formula in the LXX reveals that God is the only cause of the growth and multiplication which come from God's promise (see the future tense in Gen 17:20; 48:4; Lev 26:9; Jer 23:3) and his blessing (Gen 1:22, 28; 9:1) or indication (Gen 8:17; 9:7; 35:11; Jer 3:16). Even human blessing (Gen 28:3) and the narrator's account (Gen 47:27; Exod 1:7) bear the recognition of God as the source of αὐξάνω καὶ πληθύνω.

notation of αὐξάνω. Ἰσχύω is a word used to indicate the possession of power.[53] The phrase κατὰ κράτος, in which κράτος expresses innate strength[54] with the implication of supernatural force,[55] makes clear that such a power is both from within and from God.[56] Accordingly, the Word's mighty growth is intimately connected with its innately dynamic power.[57] Overall, the numerical growth of the Word is an outward growth which is seen in the spread of the Word from Jerusalem to Gentile cities and in the growing number of the faith community. The growth of the Word in power is an inward one shown in the messengers' committing of themselves to the Word (6:2, 4; 18:5) and their powerful proclamation of the Word in the midst of opposition and persecution.[58]

Importantly, the dynamic power in the Word signifies the presence of God since the Word bears the divine will.[59] God sends Jesus to accomplish his will (3:26) and remains with him by anointing him with the Spirit and power (10:38).[60] Similarly, God sends the Word to fulfil his will (10:36) and God's presence is therefore assured and power ensured (cf. miracles accompany the Word). Explicitly, the Word which communicates the significance of Jesus' life is ultimately the substitute for Jesus[61] since it represents the presence of Jesus (cf. the Word is glorified as Jesus is, 3:13; 13:48; the believer is entrusted to the

---

[53] BDAG, 484; L&N, §74.9.

[54] BDAG, 565.

[55] L&N, §76.7.

[56] Wilhelm Michaelis, 'κράτος' in *TDNT* 3:905-10, citing 907.

[57] David W. Pao, *Acts and the Isaianic New Exodus* (Tübingen: Mohr Siebeck, 2000) 162-63; O'Reilly, *Word*, 207; cf. William H. Willimon, '"Eyewitnesses and Ministers of the Word": Preaching in Acts,' *Int* 42 (1988) 158-70, esp. 161, 166.

[58] Cf. O'Reilly, *Word*, 85-87.

[59] Though indicating that the Word represents the divine will, Pao, based on the use of αὐξάνω in 6:7; 12:24; 19:20, δοξάζω in 13:48 and οἰκοδομέω in 20:32, argues that λόγος is the active agent of God. It is the active force of the Word in these verses which makes Pao infer the Word as a being/reality that represents the divine will (*New Exodus*, 160-61; cf. O'Reilly, *Word*, 73). In response to the unexpected use of λόγος with active force, Barrett indicates that it is ultimately God in the Word (*Acts*, 1:658; 2:981). As investigated, while pertaining to the narrative characters, most uses of λόγος are in the passive sense as they are used terminologically for the divine message made manifest through Jesus. The active force of the Word can be understood in the light of the presence of God revealed by the power of the Spirit and in the name of Jesus.

[60] Note that χρίω signifies 'an anointing by God setting a person apart for special service under divine direction' (BDAG, 1091; cf. L&N, §37.107).

[61] O'Reilly pinpoints that the Word which has Jesus both as subject and object (i.e. the Saviour and the Word of salvation) is identified with Jesus himself (*Word*, 221). Cf. Paul S. Minear, 'Dear Theo: The Kerygmatic Intention and Claim of the Book of Acts,' *Int* 27 (1973) 131-50, esp. 141.

care of the Word as to that of Jesus, 14:23; 20:32).[62] As those who believe in Jesus receive salvation, so do those who believe the Word. As the earthly Jesus' followers commit themselves to his teaching, so do the heavenly Jesus' believers to the teaching about Jesus himself (the Word).[63] The divine presence of God, Jesus, or especially the Spirit[64] is the foundation of the dynamic power in the Word which further causes the growth of the faith community, i.e. the church, the new people of God (cf. 15:14). Turner rightly comments: 'the church is very much a community the quality of whose life is profoundly shaped by the presence of God (and of Christ) in the charismatic Spirit.'[65] Accordingly, the growth of the Word is the signal of the church's growth,[66] either in number (quantity) or in power (quality). It is an ongoing growth, without hindrance, since the divine power resides in the Word (note the progressive imperfect of the verbs).

More significantly, it is in the midst of conflict and at the end of each stage of God's mission that the victory of the Word is marked to magnify the invincible power of the Word[67] and the supremacy of God's will. The first summary is recorded following the conflicts within and without the faith community; this is also the end of the first stage of God's mission under the leadership of Peter and the other apostles in Jerusalem (6:7).[68] The second summary follows the conflict between King Herod's persecution of the apostles and the angel's bringing forth of divine deliverance and punishment (12:24); this happens at the end of the second stage of God's mission launched by the disciples with Peter as their backer. The narrator's emphasis on the region of Judea signifies his concern regarding the growth of the Word in Jerusalem, Samaria and Judea

---

[62] Cf. Pao, *New Exodus*, 161; O'Reilly, *Word*, 120. In Acts, the object of the five occurrences of δοξάζω is either God (4:21; 11:18; 21:20) or Jesus (3:13). The Word as the object of δοξάζω in 13:48a is unique. Its immediate context shows that those who believe the Word are granted eternal life (13:48b). As the witness to Jesus is featured as 'the words of this life' (5:20), the Word in 13:48 definitely refers to Jesus who brings salvation (cf. 4:12; 15:11). Παρατίθημι which means entrusting someone to the care of someone else only occurs twice in Acts (14:23; 20:32). In 14:23, the believers are entrusted to the Lord whom they have believed (i.e. Jesus); in 20:32, they are entrusted to God and the Word of his grace. Again, that the Word signifies Jesus who brings the gospel of God's grace is clear (15:7; 20:24).

[63] Kodell, 'Word,' 512.

[64] O'Reilly, *Word*, 53, 214. See also the Spirit's close relationship with the proclamation of the Word (4:8, 31; 10:44; 16:6). Moreover, together with the believers, the Spirit co-witnesses to Jesus (5:32).

[65] Turner, *Power*, 406.

[66] Cf. Pao, *New Exodus*, 173; Kodell, 'Word,' 511; O'Reilly, *Word*, 83.

[67] Pao, *New Exodus*, 150-55; O'Reilly, *Word*, 208.

[68] 6:8-8:3 paves the way for the second stage of God's mission in which the incident leading to the reaching-out is introduced.

(11:29; 12:19).[69] The third summary is given at the end of Paul's great Ephesian evangelism (full of various conflicts);[70] this is at the end of Paul's overseas missionary journeys (19:20).[71] Not only does the narrator's significant remark on the Word's victory elucidate the supremacy and invincibility of God's sovereign will over all opposed forces but it also signifies the consummation of God's saving plan in each stage.

In its syntactical use, the object λόγος communicates God's saving will in the Word and functions as a controlling thread weaving together characters and incidents. The subject λόγος announces God's invincible power within the Word and signals the narrative development. Both evince God's saving interest playing a central role in the narrative.[72]

God's Activities in Plot Devices

In order to disclose the narrative emphasis on how God carries out his saving interest, God's activities working around the Word will be investigated. In the light of the implied author's literary technique of repetition, certain patterns of God's activities are found in the plot devices. With regard to the plot device, Bar-Efrat lucidly points out, '[t]he principal relations between the various units are those of cause and effect, parallelism and contrast.... At the centre of the plot there is almost always a conflict or collision between two forces.'[73] In the light of these plot devices, God's mission for salvation is introduced by the pattern of divine cause-effect; that is, the divine initiative inaugurates each stage of God's Word-mission by sending Jesus' witnesses to it. Thereafter, the divine-human cooperation leads to a conflict between two human forces (the believers of the Word and their opponents); in other words, from the viewpoint of Jesus' witnesses, their Word-miracle ministry causes their Word-suffering ministry. This section aims to examine God's activities in the repeated patterns

---

[69] In the light of 11:30 and 12:25, the events concerning the Antioch church's contribution and Herod's persecution happen in Jerusalem. Yet the narrator's geographical concern is still in Judea as a whole (note that he twice uses Judea instead of Jerusalem; 11:29; 12:19).

[70] Cf. the unbeliever's enmity, 19:9; the exorcists' confusion, 19:13; and the disturbance later in the city provoked by the silversmith, 19:23-34.

[71] Paul's ministry in Acts 20 is mainly to the believers and that in Acts 21-28 is mainly defensive in nature rather than evangelistic.

[72] Bolt regards the whole Acts narrative as the Word of God ('Mission and Witness,' 214).

[73] Bar-Efrat, *Narrative Art*, 93-94; cf. Forster, *Aspects*, 87; Sternberg, *Biblical Narrative*, 366.

By the Narrator

of divine-initiating promise-fulfilment, Word-miracle and Word-suffering ministry.[74]

THE PATTERN OF DIVINE INITIATIVE IN PROMISE-FULFILMENT

Fundamentally speaking, the Acts narrative is a story about God's redemptive plan which undergirds the promise-fulfilment motif in the narrative,[75] which is utterly divine-initiating and which tells of God's sovereignty and faithfulness.[76] This is elucidated in the major characters' speeches, especially in their use of the Old Testament,[77] and manifested in the ongoing mission depicted in the narrative.[78] That is, both Peter and Paul emphasise that the salvation in Jesus is the fulfilment of God's former promise; both consider their missions as God's continuous fulfilment of his promised salvation. By means of divine agents, personal and impersonal, God's mission plan for salvation is manifested unequivocally. The divine initiative determines the development of God's

---

[74] Interestingly, God's actions are vividly introduced almost entirely through characters whereas the narrator primarily provides summaries of God's work among Gentiles through the missionaries (14:27; 15:4, 12; 19:11; 21:19; also 16:10, God's calling for Gentile evangelism). This reveals the narrator's interest in what God is doing at the narrative time. Significantly, the repeated patterns of God's activities shown in the believers' lives greatly draw the reader's attention to their parallel lives in Acts. This is the effect of the patterns of repetition which not only continue thematic assertions (Alter, *Biblical Narrative*, 91; Scholes and Kellogg, *Nature*, 208) but intimately connect characterisation and plot (Witherup, 'Over and Over,' 47).

[75] Marshall, *Luke: Historian*, 106; Jacob Jervell, 'The Future of the Past: Luke's Vision of Salvation History and Its Bearing on His Writing of History' in Witherington (ed.), *History, Literature, and Society*, 104-26, citing 107-8. John Squires indicates three levels of perceiving the Acts narrative. The surface level is presented 'within an understanding that everything takes place under the guidance of God.' The second level reveals narrative themes—the Spirit's guidance, the fulfilment of OT prophecy, divine interventions by divine agents and miracles. The third level conveys a more fundamental theological theme—the plan of God ('The Plan of God in the Acts of the Apostles' in Marshall and Peterson [eds.], *Witness*, 19-39, citing 22-23, 37).

[76] Powell, *About Acts*, 41; Peterson, 'Fulfilment,' 100; Salmeier, *Ordainer*, 169, 203, 249; cf. Plunkett, 'Ethnocentricity,' 473.

[77] Joseph A. Fitzmyer, 'The Use of the Old Testament in Luke-Acts,' *SBLSP* 31 (1992) 524-38, citing 536-38.

[78] Squires, 'Plan,' 26-27; cf. Steve Walton, 'Where Does the Beginning of Acts End?' in Verheyden (ed.), *Unity*, 447-67, esp. 454. Peterson asserts: '[i]n the flow of the narrative, what happens is clearly a fulfilment of Jesus' prediction [1:8] as well as a fulfilment of Old Testament prophecy' ('Fulfilment,' 95-96). Reasoner even contends the story in Luke-Acts as 'a composite fulfilment of divine necessity' ('Divine Necessity,' 637, 656-58).

Word-mission.[79] Divine personal agents (i.e. the heavenly revelators) give divine instructions and promises which steer Jesus' witnesses to God's mission and invigorate them to carry it on. Divine impersonal agents (e.g. miracles and visions) inspire believers concerning God's will of universal salvation and mission and buttress their witness to Jesus.

The heavenly revelators play a regular and so decisive role in revealing God's saving will and in piloting the witnesses to carry out God's mission. They commission, guide, instruct and protect the witnesses, especially the major characters of Peter and Paul, to take part in God's redemptive plan. Jesus' commissioning of them to be his witnesses opens up the page of God's mission in their lives (1:8; 9:15-16; 22:21). No matter whether the calling is from the earthly or heavenly risen Jesus, or whether the call is to Jews or Gentiles, divine initiative and purpose remain the same and are fundamental to the witnesses' further ministry. Alongside the commission are Jesus' promises (1:8; 18:9-10; 23:11) which not only strengthen the witnesses to carry on God's saving mission but play a crucial part in the ongoing fulfilment of God's christocentric promise.

Then the Spirit, whose guidance occurs at critical points of God's universal saving plan,[80] sets off each new step of God's mission in connection with Gentile evangelism. God's gift of the Spirit upon the Jewish believers inaugurates the new epoch of God's salvation (2:4), and upon the Gentile God-fearers it announces God's salvation also for Gentiles (10:44). Moreover, the Spirit empowers the believers for witness (2:4; 4:8; 6:5; 13:9) and actively directs them to Gentile mission (8:29, 39; 10:19-20; 13:2; 16:6-7). This is also enhanced by visions (10:9-16; 16:9) and an angel (8:26). To ensure God's mission is accomplished in accordance with his plan, angels not only instruct people to do God's will (8:26; 10:3-6) but they safeguard Jesus' witnesses for the mission (5:19; 12:7-11; cf. 27:23-24).

By miracles and visions, God's will of universal salvation and mission is enhanced and buttressed. As miracles are for the authentication of the prophets' declaration of God's will they also attest to the believers' proclamation of the Word since miracles are 'the continuous activity of God'[81] as well as 'God's stamp of legitimation upon the message.'[82] Likewise, visions communicate God's will and serve as a pilot lamp, converting Peter to God's will of universal salvation (Acts 10-11) and directing Paul to God's worldwide evangelism

---

[79] Cf. Marguerat, 'God,' 165.

[80] Cf. Robert Banks, 'The Role of Charismatic and Noncharismatic Factors in Determining Paul's Movements in Acts' in Stanton et al. (eds.), *Christian Origins*, 117-30, esp. 129.

[81] G.W.H. Lampe, 'Miracles in the Acts of the Apostles' in C.F.D. Moule (ed.), *Miracles* (London: A.R. Mowbray, 1965) 165-78, citing 166.

[82] A.J. Mattill, 'The Jesus-Paul Parallels and the Purpose of Luke-Acts: H.H. Evans Reconsidered,' *NovT* 17 (1975) 15-46, citing 28.

(16:9-10; cf. 22:17-21). Whereas visions specifically illuminate God's will of universal salvation and evangelism,[83] miracles reinforce God's Word and promote God's mission accordingly (2:42-43; 5:12-16; 6:8-10; 8:5-7; 9:32-42; 13:11-12; 16:25-34; 19:10-12).

Throughout the Acts narrative God is 'the overarching initiator of the action.'[84] The divine interventions in the crucial moment of God's mission disclose a God-designed and God-driven mission, which signifies God's *faithfulness* to the ongoing divine-initiating fulfilment of the promised salvation, and which manifests God's *sovereign authority* over the mission and the witnesses, thus assuring the consummation of God's supreme mission plan for salvation.[85]

THE PATTERN OF WORD-MIRACLE MINISTRY

As revealed in the pattern of divine initiative, God upholds his witnesses with miracles which authenticate the messengers sent by him to deliver the divine message.[86] The parallels between the miracles of Peter and Paul are stunning.[87] Both heal a lame man (3:1-10; 14:8-10), execute miraculous punishment (5:1-10; 13:6-12), exorcise (5:16; 16:16-18), raise the dead (9:36-41; 20:9-12) and, extraordinarily, perform multiple healings (5:15-16; 19:11-12; cf. 9:32-34;

---

[83] Bart J. Koet, 'Divine Communication in Luke-Acts' in Verheyden (ed.), *Unity*, 745-57, citing 757.

[84] Gaventa, 'Initiatives,' 82. Salmeier specifies that '[d]ivine involvement is intrinsic to the plot' (*Ordainer*, 167). Shauf elucidates that '[d]ivine activity is not isolated as the discrete actions of divine beings, but rather divine activity is woven into the fabric of human history so that human events themselves are infused with divine significance' (*Theology as History*, 299).

[85] Charles H. Cosgrove, 'The Divine Δεῖ in Luke-Acts,' *NovT* 26 (1984) 168-90, citing 187. Noting that God is involved everywhere and shapes and directs the plot, Salmeier does not single out the divine interventions crucial to the plot progression (*Ordainer*, 169-72, 212-17, 252-58).

[86] Latourelle, *Miracles*, 284. Note that the multiple miracles greatly increase the apostles' reputation among the Jews (2:43; 5:12-13).

[87] The Peter-Paul parallels are often compared with that of Jesus-Peter and Jesus-Paul. For further discussion on this triangular parallelism, especially Jesus-Paul, in Luke-Acts see Susan Marie Praeder, 'Jesus-Paul, Peter-Paul, and Jesus-Peter Parallelisms in Luke-Acts: A History of Reader Response,' *SBLSP* 23 (1984) 23-39; S.M. Praeder, 'Miracle Worker and Missionary: Paul in the Acts of the Apostles,' *SBLSP* 22 (1983) 107-29, esp. 114-20; Mattill, 'Jesus-Paul Parallels,' 15-46; R.F. O'Toole, 'Parallels between Jesus and His Disciples in Luke-Acts: A Further Study,' *BZ* 27/2 (1983) 195-212; David P. Moessner, '"The Christ Must Suffer": New Light on the Jesus–Peter, Stephen, Paul Parallels in Luke-Acts,' *NovT* 28 (1986) 220-56; Walter Radl, *Paulus und Jesus im lukanischen Doppelwerk: Untersuchungen zu Parallelmotiven im Lukasevangelium und in der Apostelgeschichte* (Europäische Hochschulschriften 23/49; Bern/Frankfurt: Lang, 1975), focusing on suffering; Gudrun Muhlack, *Die Parallelen von Lukas-Evangelium und Apostelgeschichte* (Theologie

28:8-9). Both are agents for the Spirit's descent on those simply receiving the water-baptism of either Jesus or John (8:17; 19:6). Through miracles both powerfully and authoritatively proclaim the Word. These parallels emphasise the continuity of God's saving will and 'the unity of the missions to Israel and to the Gentiles.'[88]

Whereas God initiates the mission for salvation, its consummation is divinely designed to rely on divine-human cooperation.[89] Through the Spirit the witnesses are strengthened inwardly to proclaim the Word; in the name of Jesus their proclamation is undergirded by public signs. By their commitment to proclaiming the Word, Peter and Paul share divine authority and power in Jesus' name (3:6; 16:18; cf. Jesus' sharing of God's lordship, 2:36) and through the Spirit (note the empowerment of the Spirit at the beginning of their ministry, 2:4; 4:8; 6:3; 13:9). By this divinely authorised Word-miracle ministry, God's mission plan of universal salvation in Jesus is realised. To be specific, by miracles, God's will of universal salvation is comprehended first in the Word expounded by Peter (see his miracle-shaped speeches in Chapter Three) then in the Gentile mission taken on and extended by Paul. By miracles God's mighty power over the proclamation and with the witnesses is manifested. The divine deeds throughout the mission greatly evince that 'at every significant point in the transitions of Christianity from its Jewish origins in Jerusalem to its Gentile outreaching to Rome itself, the hand of God is evident in the form of public miraculous confirmation.'[90] Miracles thus testify that the Word-mission and the Word-bearers are God-vindicated and God-empowered, which again assure the consummation of God's mission plan, and which makes known God's *sovereign power*.

THE PATTERN OF WORD-SUFFERING MINISTRY

Nevertheless, the proclamation of the Word inevitably leads to division among people,[91] either receiving the Word or opposing the witnesses. While confronting the opponents of the Word, the witnesses' proclamation of the Word is in-

---

und Wirklichkeit 8; Frankfurt: Lang, 1979) 15-38, 55-71; Charles H. Talbert, *Literary Patterns, Theological Themes, and the Genre of Luke-Acts* (SBLMS 20; Missoula: Scholars Press, 1974) 15-65; M.D. Goulder, *Type and History in Acts* (London: S.P.C.K., 1964) 65-110; Frans Neirynck, 'The Miracle Stories in the Acts of the Apostles' in J. Kremer (ed.), *Les Actes des Apôtres: Traditions, rédaction, théologie* (BETL 48; Gembloux: J. Duculot, 1979) 169-213, esp. 172-88; Joel B. Green, 'Internal Repetition in Luke-Acts: Contemporary Narratology and Lucan Historiography' in Witherington (ed.), *History, Literature and Society*, 283-99; Aletti, *Luc raconte*, 69-112; Clark, *Parallel Lives*, 150-260.

[88] Clark, 'Apostles,' 169.
[89] Cosgrove, 'Divine Δεῖ,' 190; Gaventa, 'Initiatives,' 79-89.
[90] Kee, *Miracle*, 220.
[91] O'Reilly, *Word*, 76, 199.

tertwined with their suffering for the Word.[92] When persecuted, the witnesses' perseverance in suffering and their persistence in witnessing testify to the divine power within them. When imprisoned, the divine deliverance of the witnesses evinces that God's power overrules, sovereignly, all human opposition forces.[93] In times of suffering, by God's power from within, Jesus' witnesses are strengthened to proclaim the Word; by God's power from without, they are emboldened to carry on the proclamation.

Furthermore, the differences in suffering between the two major characters reinforce the narrator's interest in God's sovereign authority over his witnesses. Although both are empowered to undergo persecution, Paul's suffering is much more tenacious and fierce than Peter's in the narrative. Whereas suffering is a result of Peter's witness to Jesus (5:41), suffering itself is part of Paul's witness and makes Paul a living witness for Jesus (see Paul's suffering-shaped ministry in Chapter Four).[94] The spotlight on Paul's serious suffering reflects the programmatic implication indicated in Jesus' commission of him (9:15-16)[95] and reflects God's sovereign plan over him in carrying out the mission (26:19-23). In other words, Paul's imprisonment amplifies the degree of his suffering and represents new environments for his proclamation which enable his witness to reach Roman officials.[96] Therefore, Paul's suffering for Jesus' name, which intimately connects him with Jesus,[97] is the fulfilment of God's plan for him

---

[92] Richard J. Dillon, *From Eye-Witnesses to Ministers of the Word: Tradition and Composition in Luke 24* (AB 82; Rome: Biblical Institute Press, 1978) 296; Cunningham, *Tribulations*, 198; Rapske, 'Opposition,' 246.

[93] The angelic deliverance of the apostles from the Sanhedrin's imprisonment amplifies God's power over that of the religious leaders (4:16; 5:19). In Herod's imprisoning of Peter, the angelic deliverance of Peter and the angelic killing of Herod greatly magnify God's power over that of the earthly king. Similarly, the miraculous deliverance of Paul from prison magnifies God's power over that of the Roman official (16:26).

[94] Note that ὁ ὁδός which signifies the believer's teaching and lifestyle is mainly applied to Paul; see Appendix Seven.

[95] Cunningham, *Tribulations*, 242.

[96] Matthew L. Skinner, *Locating Paul: Places of Custody as Narrative Settings in Acts 21-28* (SBLAB 13; Atlanta: Society of Biblical Literature, 2003) 171.

[97] The divine δεῖ often refers to Jesus' suffering as a necessity in God's plan (Lk 9:22; 13:33; 17:25; 22:37; 24:7, 26, 44). The parallels of suffering between Jesus and Paul (e.g. the prediction of their passion, their journeys to Jerusalem and their trials before the Sanhedrin and a Roman procurator) lead many to argue that the narrator intends to portray Paul as following the pattern of Jesus' suffering. For Paul as a suffering witness parallel to Jesus see Mattill, 'Jesus-Paul Parallels,' 30-36; O'Toole, 'Parallels,' 207-9; Radl, *Doppelwerk*, 68-294; Cunningham, *Tribulations*, 285-87; Kilgallen, 'Persecution,' 157-59; Johnson, *Acts*, 357; Moessner, 'Pattern,' 209-12; Moessner, 'Parallels,' 249-52; Glenn R. Jacobson, 'Paul in Luke-Acts: The Savior

(see the divine δεῖ in 9:16; cf. 22:14; Lk 21:12-19).⁹⁸ As Jesus' suffering brings God's Word of salvation, Paul's suffering occasions God's universal mission of the Word. Suffering thus turns into a part of the divine plan in accomplishing God's salvific purpose.⁹⁹

In general, God's authority and power are demonstrated directly in the witnesses' Word-miracle ministry and indirectly in their Word-suffering ministry. Miracles signify God's public confirmation of the Word and its mission;¹⁰⁰ victory over persecution is itself a powerful attestation to the persecuted witnesses' message, the Word.¹⁰¹ Through both the Word-miracle and Word-suffering ministry of human agents, God's sovereign authority and power over his witnesses and mission of the Word are amplified. The major task assigned to Peter is to make known to the Jews God's will of universal salvation in Jesus, which is enhanced by Peter's Word-miracle ministry and which is the fulfilment of God's promised salvation. The major task assigned to Paul is to expand God's universal mission of the saving Word, which is advanced in Paul's Word-suffering ministry (persecution moves Paul forward) and which is the ongoing fulfilment of God's redemptive plan. It is God's salvific purpose that introduces miracles and overrules persecution for God's Word-mission.

SIGNIFICANCE OF THE WORD-MIRACLE-SUFFERING MINISTRY PATTERN

Based on the governing force of the Word in God's mission plan, the Word-miracle-suffering ministry pattern is essential to the development not only of salvation history expounded in the characters' speeches but of the Acts narrative recounted by the narrator. In the speeches, this ministry pattern is applied to prophets and to Jesus. It is spelt out that Jesus is the focal point of the witness of the prophets in the Old Testament (2:21, 30-31; 3:18; 10:43; 13:27-29; 26:22-23; cf. Lk 24:44). Later, Jesus himself also partakes in this prophetic ministry as he is considered to be the prophet, like Moses (3:22; 7:37), 'mighty

---

Who is Present,' *SBLSP* 22 (1983) 131-46. As the concern of this study, the discussion here centres on the significance of Paul's sharing of Jesus' suffering.

⁹⁸ Reasoner, 'Divine Necessity,' 657.

⁹⁹ Trites, *Witness*, 131; David P. Moessner, 'The "Script" of the Scriptures in Acts: Suffering as God's "Plan" (Βουλή) for the World for the "Release of Sins"' in Witherington (ed.), *History, Literature, and Society*, 218-50, citing 249; idem, '"The Christ Must Suffer," The Church Must Suffer: Rethinking the Theology of the Cross in Luke-Acts,' *SBLSP* 29 (1990) 165-95, esp. 183, 195; cf. Beverly Roberts Gaventa, 'Toward a Theology of Acts' *Int* 42 (1988) 146-57.

¹⁰⁰ O'Reilly, *Word*, 134, 200.

¹⁰¹ Charles H. Talbert indicates that martyrdom from persecution serves 'as part of the confirmation of the Christian message. Its persuasiveness was that of a selfless commitment on the part of stable persons' ('Martyrdom in Luke-Acts and the Lukan Social Ethic' in Richard J. Cassidy and Philip J. Scharper (eds.), *Political Issues in Luke-Acts* [Maryknoll: Orbis Books, 1983] 99-110, citing 106).

in deed and word who is sent to redeem his people but who is rejected by them.'[102] Jesus comes in power to proclaim and become, implicitly, the saving Word (2:22; 10:36-38) yet suffers unto death in accordance with God's plan (2:23). Embracing the framework of promise-fulfilment,[103] the believers testify that God is at work in delivering a message of salvation throughout the history of Israel;[104] by his prophets, through the Spirit, God foretold his will (4:25; 28:25) then by Jesus, through the Spirit, God makes his will realised (10:38).[105] The prophets and Jesus, however, are persecuted by and suffer from the opponents of their message (7:52). In the story, the narrator presents that Jesus' witnesses continue the prophetic ministry of the Mosaic pattern.[106] Similarly, Jesus is the core of their witness (4:33; 8:5; 9:20; 17:3) and they, empowered by the Spirit and encouraged by the divine promise-fulfilment at present, proclaim the Word and suffer for their proclamation. This prophetic ministry pattern is characterised by the Christocentric message, the divine empowerment and the re-

---

[102] O'Reilly, *Word*, 214; cf. also E.L. Allen, 'Jesus and Moses in the New Testament,' *ExpT* 67 (1955-56) 104-6; John T. Carroll, 'The Use of Scripture in Acts,' *SBLSP* 29 (1990) 512-28, esp. 520-21; J. Severino Croatto, 'Jesus, Prophet Like Elijah, and Prophet-Teacher Like Moses in Luke-Acts,' *JBL* 124 (2005) 451-465.

[103] The pattern of promise-fulfilment may be regarded as the pattern of prophecy-fulfilment (Brigid Curtin Frein, 'Narrative Predictions, Old Testament Prophecies and Luke's Sense of Fulfilment,' *NTS* 40 [1994] 22-37).

[104] Arnold rightly indicates that the OT quotations in the speeches 'establish continuity and cohesion between past and present' and concludes that Luke's phraseological use of OT expressions makes his characters (Peter, Stephen, Paul and himself the narrator) 'ideological extensions of the Old Testament story, participating in and continuing that salvation history' ('Characterizing,' 321, 323).

[105] Max Turner points out a consensus on Luke's pneumatology: 'for Luke the Spirit is largely the "Spirit of prophecy"; in Acts especially as an "empowering for mission"' ('The Spirit and Salvation in Luke-Acts' in Stanton et al. [eds.], *Christian Origins*, 103-16, citing 105).

[106] Reasoner, 'Divine Necessity,' 649; Cunningham, *Tribulations*, 208; O'Reilly, *Word*, 159, 190; cf. McBride, *Emmaus*, 200; Johnson, *Acts*, 237; O'Toole, 'Parallels,' 211; Dennis Hamm, 'Acts 3,1-10: The Healing of the Temple Beggar as Lucan Theology,' *Bib* 67 (1986) 305-19, esp. 318; Anitra Bingham Kolenkow, 'Relationships between Miracle and Prophecy in the Greco-Roman World and Early Christianity' in *ANRW* II.23.2 (1980) 1470-1506, esp. 1495; Otto Betz, 'The Kerygma of Luke,' *Int* 22 (1968) 131-46, esp. 142; Robert P. Menzies, *Empowered for Witness* (JPTSup 6; Sheffield: Sheffield Academic Press, 1991) 202-25; Kenneth Duncan Litwak, *Echoes of Scripture in Luke-Acts: Telling the History of God's People Intertextually* (JSNTSup 282; London: T & T Clark, 2005) 170-71. Although the focus of the prophetic witness in different ages remains the same, the witness of the OT prophets is prospective (cf. the predictive office of a prophet, i.e. prophesy, foretelling God's will) whilst that of Jesus' witnesses is retrospective (cf. the didactic office of a prophet, i.e. exhort people to do God's will).

jected messenger. God's salvific message is delivered in Jesus and through the Spirit and is backed up by miracles. God's messengers, though undergirded by divine empowerment, often encounter the rejection of their message and suffer the persecution of their opponents.

From the Word-miracle aspect, the divine origin and confirmation of the Word signify the unity and continuity of God's will in two dimensions—historical continuity and contemporary unity. The Word-miracle ministry pattern speaks of a God at work in human history, who actively works through the Spirit, whose will is revealed in Jesus, and who continuously invites human cooperation in carrying out his will. As the prophetic witness in the Old Testament is given by God's Spirit through the prophets (1:16; 3:18; 28:25), so does that at present by the Spirit through Jesus' witnesses.[107] The same Spirit of God indicates a continuation of the prophetic ministry from the ancient to the present time. While Jesus' witnesses stand in the foreground, striving on behalf of the mission of the Word, divine empowerment, especially revealed in the concrete form of miracle, continues. Although Peter is a witness mainly to the Jews and Paul to all people, the similarities between their miracles not only signify the same origin of their authority and power in carrying out God's Word-mission but reinforce the unity and continuity of the mission. This weaves the two missions to Jews and Gentiles into one mission of God and the two sagas of Peter and Paul into one story of God. In short, throughout all ages, Jesus is the same focus of God's message and the Spirit the same agent of God's power; this signifies the unity and continuity of God's will, historically between the old and present ages and synchronically between Peter and Paul.

From the Word-suffering aspect, persecution coming from the opponents of the Word carries twofold significance—christological identification and missiological function.[108] The christocentric proclamation provokes the Jews' persecution of the witnesses; yet persecution resulting from the powerful proclamation of God's will connects the ministry of Peter-Paul-Stephen with the prophetic ministry of Jesus-Moses, full of divine power and human opposition.[109] By sharing the Christ-suffering, the witnesses are identified with Jesus (9:5).[110]

---

[107] Cf. Paul S. Minear, *To Heal and To Reveal* (New York: Seabury Press, 1976) 144-47, where Minear particularly argues for a prophetic witness in Gentile mission under the Spirit's guidance and at Pentecost with the Spirit's presence.

[108] Similarly, Cunningham indicates a twofold foundation (christological and missiological) of Luke's understanding of the persecution of the disciples (*Tribulations*, 292).

[109] David P. Moessner, 'Paul and the Pattern of the Prophet like Moses in Acts,' *SBLSP* 22 (1983) 202-12, citing 211; Moessner, 'Parallels,' 247; Radl, *Doppelwerk*, 285; Mittelstadt, *Spirit and Suffering*, 114; Roger Stronstad, *The Prophethood of All Believers* (JPTSup 16; Sheffield: Sheffield Academic Press, 1999) 89.

[110] In the light of Luke 21:12-19, the persecution of the witnesses is the programmatic prophecy of Jesus (Mittelstadt, *Spirit and Suffering*, 98).

By identifying with Jesus, the witnesses experience the divine presence and share divine power.[111] In turn, by sharing divine power, they are strengthened powerfully to preach the Word and undergo persecution. More importantly, suffering functions as a confessional witness[112] that prompts God's mission of the Word.[113] God's overruling plan and purpose make suffering a divine means for the growth of the Word. Suffering thus signifies a divine necessity in God's mission of salvation and serves as a catalyst which furthers the mission.[114] The missiological function of suffering manifests tactfully God's sovereign authority and power over all opposed forces and therefore guarantees the victory of the Word and the consummation of its mission.

In the divine-initiating prophetic ministry, God's sovereign lordship is perceived in his overturning of all opposed forces for the divine purpose and in the continuity and unity of his salvific will and plan throughout the ages and in each epoch. By elucidating God's saving work in history, Jesus' witnesses testify to God the Lord of history whose authority and power directs human history towards his ends. By depicting God's work at the present time, the narrator testifies to God as a Lord who changes and reigns over human life for his own purposes. Whereas God's redemptive will is the controlling thread throughout history and the narrative, the prophetic ministry pattern unfolds how God progresses his saving plan in history and the narrative. How the narrator presents God along the narrative progression, which is also part of the historical progression, provides the most comprehensive portrayal of God. To this we now turn.

God's Function in the Plot Progression

As 'the plot of Acts moves forward through the development of thematic plot devices,'[115] this section will first examine how God's working patterns contribute to the plot progression, then God's role in the narrative development, from which the thematic portrait of God along the plot progression will emerge.

---

[111] Cf. Minear, *Reveal*, 121.

[112] Dillon, *Eye-Witnesses*, 282. Suffering throughout Paul's ministry serves as an affirmation of his witness to Jesus' suffering prophesied long before (17:2-3; 26:22-23). Also, the Jews' rejection makes Paul turn to the Gentile evangelism (13:46; 18:6; 28:26-28) which consequently expands God's mission. The suffering of persecution not only cannot impede God's plan of universal mission but becomes a divine means (i.e. divine necessity) to prompt God's mission.

[113] Paul R. House, 'Suffering and the Purpose of Acts,' *JETS* 33 (1990) 317-30, citing 320-21.

[114] Cunningham, *Tribulations*, 214; Mittelstadt, *Spirit and Suffering*, 116; Talbert, *Mediterranean*, 110.

[115] Sheeley, *Asides*, 144.

GOD'S WORKING PATTERN IN THE PLOT PROGRESSION

Founded on the prophetic ministry pattern, a circular relation of cause-effect connects the proclamation of the Word, the Word-miracle-suffering ministry and the growth of the Word. For the tri-relation mission pattern see the following diagram.

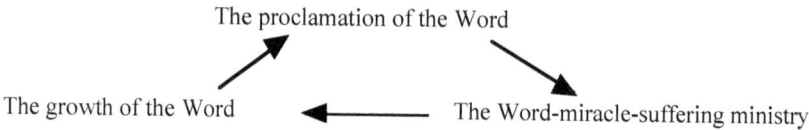

This cycle, having the Word as its central concern, serves as an undergirding pattern that weaves together the narrative units throughout.[116] The smallest narrative units are the incidents;[117] this circular relation of cause-effect more or less interconnects the incidents in Acts. Yet a narrative unit may be defined by one incident, one tri-relation mission pattern or a topical or geographical concern, etc.

Remarkably, the narrative units in the first half of Acts are determined by the incidents connected by the cause-effect relation underlying the tri-relation mission pattern (Acts 1-12). Turning to the second half of the narrative (Acts 13-28), though present in almost every incident, this tri-relation pattern contributes mainly to the geographical progression of Gentile mission rather the combination of incidents into one unit. The narrative units, thus, are better delimited by Paul's missionary journeys. The different ways in which the narrative units are shaped shed light on the plot progression. As revealed in the narrator's *showing* of God through divine and human agents, Peter's ministry focuses on God's will for universal salvation while Paul's centres on God's worldwide mission for salvation. Acts 1-12 takes a close look at the incidents which depict divine deeds and/or their significance and allows God's will and plan for universal salvation in Jesus to be perceived in depth. While taking a close-up look at certain significant incidents, Acts 13-28 also gives a panorama of Paul's missionary journeys that provides a more comprehensive background for his mission and enables God's expanding worldwide mission to be understood in depth. God's works in the plot progression will be highly appreciated as the relations between narrative units are scrutinised. See the following layout for a sketch of the narrative development.[118]

---

[116] Cf. Tannehill, *Narrative Unity*, 1:4; 2:6.

[117] Bar-Efrat also indicates the multiple purposes of the narrative units in biblical narrative: 'as components of the plot, as a means of characterizing the protagonists and as ways of expressing meaning' (*Narrative Art*, 95).

[118] For additional details to this chart, especially the cause-effect relation, see Appendix Eight.

Part One: The Recognition of God's Will of Universal Salvation (Acts 1-12)	Section One: Peter's Exegesis of God's Saving Will in Jesus (Acts 1:1-6:7) [In Jerusalem]	Unit One: Introduction of God's Promise-Fulfilment of Salvation (chs 1-2)
		Unit Two: Realisation of God's Saving Power in Jesus (chs 3-4)
		Unit Three: Manifestation of God's Saving Power over His People (5:1-6:7)
	Section Two: The Making Known of God's Universal Mission Plan for Salvation (Acts 6:8-12:25) [In all Judea and Samaria]	Unit Four: The Jews' Persecution in Jerusalem Kindles the First Stage of Gentile Mission (6:8-8:40)
		Unit Five: God Prepares His People for the Epoch of Gentile Mission (9:1-11:18)
		Unit Six: The Jews' Rejection in Judea Launches the Second Stage of Gentile Mission (11:19-12:25)
Part Two: The Realisation of God's Universal Mission of Salvation (Acts 13-28)	Section Three: The Fulfilment Stage of Gentile Mission (Acts 13-28) [To the Ends of the Earth]	Unit Seven: Paul's First Missionary Journey in Galatia (chs 13-14)
		Unit Eight: The Jerusalem Council (ch 15)
		Unit Nine: Paul's Second and Third Missionary Journeys in Macedonia, Achaia and Asia (chs 16-20)
		Unit Ten: Paul's Trials unto Rome (chs 21-28)

GOD'S ROLE IN THE NARRATIVE DEVELOPMENT

God's promise-fulfilment of salvation, behind which lies God's purpose and plan,[119] is brought into focus by Jesus and the Spirit and becomes the foundation and signpost for the rest of the narrative (Acts 1-2).[120] The saving power of God is concretised and authenticated by God's healing power working in the

---

[119] Talbert, *Mediterranean*, 167.
[120] Richard, 'Pentecost,' 145.

name of Jesus, through the apostles, as Jesus shares God's lordship and authority (Acts 3-5; note the narrator's subtle use of σῴζω for healing in 4:9).[121] God's mighty deeds cause conflict between the apostles and the Jewish leaders over their authority in declaring who Jesus is (4:17; 5:28). Meanwhile, God's saving power also works through the Spirit or angels in purifying the church (5:1-11; in a negative sense), in safeguarding the witnesses (5:19-20; in a positive sense) and in bestowing wisdom upon those who serve God (6:1-6; in an applied sense). In this way God's saving will is greatly manifested by the dynamic power of the apostles' witness and by the negative force of the leaders' opposition. In Jerusalem, God's will of Word-mission wins invincibly its first victory as revealed in the narrator's remark on the growth of God's Word (6:7).

God's Word-mission expands while the disciples, as relay runners, take over the baton of the main responsibility of evangelism from the apostles; correspondingly, the opposed force extends from the Jewish leaders to the Jews (Acts 6-9). Yet the dynamic power through the Word is with the Word-bearers either in time of persecution or proclamation (Acts 6-8). Moreover, through Jesus, the Spirit and angels, God, overruling the persecuting force for his universal mission (especially God's overturning of the persecutor Saul to the persecuted Paul),[122] sovereignly directs and prepares his witnesses for the Gentile Word-mission (Acts 8-11). This is the first stage of God's outreach mission in Samaria and Judea, which is the outgrowth of the church's witness under persecution, with the Jerusalem church as its stronghold (8:1; 11:19-10).[123] This is also a transitional stage in which God, transforming his chosen ones (Peter and Paul), equips the Jerusalem church (Acts 11, 15) and prepares the leading Gentile missionary for the next stage of God's universal mission (Acts 9). As the Jerusalem church expands in witnesses, in geography and in ethnic groups, the persecution of the church also extends from the Jews (religious) to king Herod (political). However, the conflict between the church and Herod (his killing of its leaders) is eventually a conflict between the earthly king and the heavenly King (Acts 12). The angelic deliverance of Peter and the killing of Herod manifest God's sovereign authority and power over Herod. Though under greater persecution, God's sovereignty ensures his mission is invincibly carried out from Jerusalem to Judea and from Jews to Gentiles. Again, the narrator's remark on the growth of God's Word declares the victory of the second stage of God's Word-mission in Judea (12:24).[124]

---

[121] Cf. Neagoe, *Trial*, 150; Ben Witherington, 'Salvation and Health in Christian Antiquity: The Soteriology of Luke-Acts in Its First Century Setting' in Marshall and Peterson (eds.), *Witness*, 145-66, citing 153-54.

[122] Mittelstadt, *Spirit and Suffering*, 99.

[123] The Jerusalem church sends out its representatives (Peter, John and Barnabas) to strengthen the disciples' ministry in Samaria and Judea.

[124] The sequence of the famine visit (11:27-30) and the events in chapter 12 is disputed. Although the exact time of the famine relief is uncertain, the famine took place

Whereas the killing of Stephen signifies the Jews' rejection of the Word in Jerusalem[125] and occasions the first stage of non-Jewish mission in Samaria and Judea (Acts 8-12), the killing of James implies their rejection of the Word in Judea and introduces the second stage of the Gentile mission (Acts 13-19).[126] Paul is the key figure, another relay-runner taking over the baton of the main responsibility of Gentile mission from the disciples, continuing the race for God's Word-mission. Under the lead of the Spirit (13:2; 16:6-7) and the promise of Jesus (18:9-10) Paul, like Peter, is empowered in the Word-miracle witness for the Gentile mission; however, a long-standing conflict lies between him and unbelieving Jews and Gentiles (Acts 13-28). Persecution, moreover, drives Paul to keep moving forward and thus to promote the mission. The expansion of God's universal Word-mission is singled out by the narrator's literary technique of creating a sense of progress in geography, that is, the high frequency of the tri-relation mission pattern and the route-account. While the narrative entirely turns to the Gentile mission, the cause-effect relation underlying the mission pattern no longer merges incidents into one unit but permeates almost every incident. This emphasises Paul's advancing ministry as he is driven from place to place by his opponents. With regard to the route-account, Bar-Efrat comments:

---

around AD 46-48 (Marshall, *Acts*, 204; Barrett, *Acts*, 1:563; Haenchen, *Acts*, 374). As Herod died in AD 44, it is likely that Peter's arrest occurs before the famine (Barrett, *Acts*, 1:592). However, a consecutive reading of the text suggests that all the events happen about at the same time (cf. 11:30; 12:25) and implies a particular purpose behind the narrator's literary skill here. Barrett further indicates this as the implied author 'winds up one part of his book and prepares the way for another' (*Acts*, 1:572).

[125] Talbert, *Mediterranean*, 110.

[126] The persecution which extends from religious to political force signifies the Jews' rejection of the Word in Judea. Instead of singling out the city Jerusalem, the narrator emphasises the region of Judea (11:29; 12:19); also, Herod Agrippa I was the king over Judea and all Palestine (A.D. 41-44), cf. H. Wayne House, *Chronological and Background Charts of the New Testament* (Grand Rapids: Zondervan, 1982) 66; Barrett, *Acts*, 1:573; F.F. Bruce, *New Testament History* (London: Pickering & Inglis, 1982) 244; Joseph A. Fitzmyer, *The Acts of the Apostles* (New York: Doubleday, 1998) 486. Dean P. Bechard specifies that Judea may indicate the political geography of the client king's expansive domain ('The Theological Significance of Judaea in Luke-Acts' in Verheyden [ed.], *Unity*, 675-91, citing 683). Foremost, the cause of persecuting the apostles, the leaders of the faith community, being indicated as to please the Jewish people reinforces the Jews' rejection (cf. 12:3, 11). While arguing 11:27-12:25 as a transitional chain-link, Bruce W. Longenecker also points out that Acts 12 brings the 'opposition to the twelve to its zenith' ('Lukan Aversion to Humps and Hollows: The Case of Acts 11.27-12.25,' *NTS* 50 [2004] 185-204, citing 198).

> In biblical narratives space is shaped primarily through the movement of characters and the reference to places. Both these features are often used together; the characters go on journeys, during the course of which the names of the places from which they set out and to which they are going or which they pass on the way are mentioned.[127]

The narrator's account of Paul's journeys between incidents, thus, creates for the reader a sense of Paul's movement in space and amplifies the ongoing expansion of God's worldwide mission.[128] No matter how tenacious the persecution, God's authority and power working through Paul are far greater; even the opposed force is overturned into a divine means for furthering God's mission. God's sovereign will and plan, therefore, overrules the narrative characters and incidents. Once again, the narrator announces the victory of the third stage of God's Word-mission, which is also the second stage of Gentile mission, with the remark *the Word grows mightily* (19:20).

God's will of universal salvation accompanying his sovereign authority and power is invincibly and cooperatively carried out by his witnesses' commitment to it. Throughout the narrative, the more the Word of God is honoured and proclaimed, the more the power of the Word emanates;[129] the more powerful the Word-mission is, the bigger and stronger the church grows. Likewise, the more Paul commits himself as a suffering witness to God's will and testifies to God's Word,[130] the more God's saving plan is carried out through him (Acts 20-28).[131] The rest of the narrative is controlled by the Spirit's and Jesus'

---

[127] Bar-Efrat, *Narrative Art*, 185.

[128] Comparing the coincidence of sea voyages and first person plural narration in Acts with the literature in Mediterranean antiquity (16:10-17; 20:5-15; 21:1-18; 27:1-28:16), Vernon K. Robbins contends that '[t]he first person plural sea voyages furnish the dynamic for the movement through space, and the careful structuring of the episodes relates Paul's mission to Jerusalem and Rome' ('By Land and by Sea: A Study in Acts 13-28,' *SBLSP* 10 [1976] 381-96, citing 391).

[129] The more Jesus' witnesses commit themselves to the proclamation of the Word, the more the power of the Word is revealed in their proclamation. The power is not merely revealed to Peter and Paul but to every proclaimer of the Word (see the scattered disciples from Jerusalem [8:1-40; 11:19-26] and those in dispersion [18:24-28]). Even at the conflict within the church, the apostles' setting of the Word as their first priority in ministry brings in the growth of the Word and the community (6:1-7).

[130] Regardless of the Spirit's revelation of his bondage in Jerusalem and the other disciples' restraining him from going, Paul insists on going to Jerusalem in God's will (20:23-24; 21:4, 12-13).

[131] Salmeier indicates that the characterisation of Paul in 19:21-28:31 'concentrates on his piety, obedience and innocence. Thus, we should expect that the portrayal of God will be used to support Paul, but the overall image continues to focus on divine control over all things' (*Ordainer*, 221).

prophecy of Paul's coming bondage and safe arrival in Rome (20:23; 23:11).[132] Although Paul is greatly persecuted by the Jews, and even the divine care comes to him in an ordinary way, God still overrules the opposition and turns the Jews' accusation into part of the divine means to safeguard Paul to Rome. The lengthy narration of Paul's imprisonment reinforces the ultimate victory of God and his Word. In the light of 'Jerusalem and Rome as the symbols of Jew and Gentile,'[133] Paul's arrival at Rome, the opposite pole to Jerusalem and the centre of the Gentile world, may signify the Word reaching to 'the end of the earth' (1:8).[134] This is reinforced by the narrator's final remark at 28:31 which gives an open-ended presentation of the Word-mission (which invites speculation on its future development)[135] and thus declares the fulfilment stage of the ongoing triumph of God's universal Word-mission for the kingdom of God.[136]

THE PORTRAIT OF GOD ALONG THE PLOT PROGRESSION

The plot progression conveys also the development of God's Word-mission in which the sovereign lordship of God is fully manifested. After divine initiative inaugurates or introduces each crucial step of God's Word-mission, God's sovereign authority is seen in conducting human agents for his Word-mission plan; God's sovereign power is perceived in upholding his witnesses for the tasks assigned to them and in overruling all opposing forces for the mission. Throughout the narrative God's supreme will of the saving Word governs the interactions among characters and the movement of incidents and thus deter-

---

[132] Talbert, *Mediterranean*, 190.

[133] John J. Bimson (ed.), *Illustrated Encyclopedia of Bible Places* (Leicester: Inter-Varsity Press, 1995) 268.

[134] Parsons, *Departure*, 157-58; Alexander, 'From Back to Front,' 426; Jervell, *Theology*, 105. For those who disagree that Rome is a reference to 'the ends of the earth' see Rosner, 'Progress,' 218; Brawley, *Jews*, 32-33.

[135] Shepherd, *Spirit*, 78. It is also suggested, from the reader's perspective, that the open-ending in a narrative serves as 'an attempt to allow the reader to continue not a fiction but the history of his or her own life' (Docherty, *Character*, 110; cf. Daniel Marguerat, 'The End of Acts [28:16-31] and the Rhetoric of Silence' in Porter and Olbricht [eds.], *Rhetoric*, 74-89, citing 89).

[136] Scholes and Kellogg indicate that '[o]nce an autobiography continues beyond the moment in which the author comes to terms with his vocation, its interest turns outward and its form becomes open-ended' (*Nature*, 215). This suggests that the kingdom and the Word of God, rather than the story of Paul, are the implied author's ultimate interest. Rosner specifies that the open-ending signifies the 'unending progress of the word' and 'functions to include the reader in the task of spreading the word' ('Progress,' 230, 233; cf. Marie-Eloise Rosenblatt, *Paul the Accused* [Collegeville: Litergical Press, 1995] 91). For the invincible triumph of God's reign see also the use of ἀκωλύτως in D.L. Mealand, 'The Close of Acts and Its Hellenistic Greek Vocabulary,' *NTS* 36 (1990) 583-97, esp. 589-96.

mines the development of the narrative. Overall, God is characterised as a supreme and sovereign Lord who authoritatively and omnipotently acts in human history in order to faithfully bring salvation for his people concerning his kingdom, just as he promised.

Summary

In the Acts narrative, the plot which organises characters and incidents for thematic interest is mainly based on the devices of repetition, cause-effect and conflict. The repeated pattern of divine initiative functions as the cause which brings out the Word-miracle-suffering ministry pattern in which lies a conflict between two forces. In the plot, God's saving Word plays a controlling role. Divine initiative which occurs at each crucial step of God's Word-mission expresses a God-designed and God-driven mission and magnifies God's sovereign authority over the mission and the witnesses. The Word-miracle-suffering ministry speaks of a God-vindicated and God-empowered mission and amplifies God's sovereign power over the mission plan as God strengthens the witnesses for proclamation and in persecution and overturns all opposing forces into a driving force for the mission.

In the explication of God's salvific plan, these repeated patterns appear in two time modes. Historically, God's working pattern throughout ages is indicated by the main characters as the divine-initiating prophetic ministry; synchronically, this prophetic ministry is now applied to Jesus' witnesses as presented by the narrator. The historical and synchronal repetition of the ministry pattern signifies the continuity and unity of God's saving will throughout the ages and throughout the narrative. God's saving Word is the pivotal link in the story of Jesus and his witnesses, especially Peter and Paul (see their parallel lives).[137] Nevertheless, the dissimilarities, which add colour to underline certain thematic points, between the ministry of Peter and Paul convey the development of the theme. The highlighting of Peter as a Word-miracle witness fortifies Peter's interpretation of God's salvific will in Jesus and through the Spirit; the emphasis of Paul as a Word-suffering witness testifies to God's invincible Word-mission through his living witness. In tracing God in the vertical and horizontal time zones, one perceives that the supreme and transcendent Lord God, a dominant figure in human history, actively involves himself in human lives working for their highest interest, through his divine and human agents, and sovereignly overrules all human events for his highest purpose.

---

[137] For detailed discussion on parallels among Jesus' witnesses see Clark, *Parallel Lives*, 209-93. See also footnote 87 in this chapter.

Conclusion

As the functions of epithet reveal,[138] the narrator, employing the epithet κύριος for God, explicitly characterises God as a sovereign and supreme Lord; implicitly, κύριος foreshadows God's sovereignty as the very cause of the narrative development. The entire Acts narrative is about the saving acts of this sovereign God; such a thematic line is reinforced by the literary technique of repetition. The repeated key-terms, like a zoom-in lens giving a close-up, highlight the central point of the narrative theme. The repeated key-patterns, as a zoom-out lens providing a wide angle, allow the reader to grasp the narrator's notion which is embedded in the theme. The deployment in the plot, resembling a panoramic screen showing the whole picture, enables the reader to perceive the flow of the theme. Specifically speaking, the key-terms reflect *what* God's salvific will is; the key-patterns project *how* God's redemptive plan is carried out; the deployment discloses God's crucial role in the plot progression which depicts the thematic portrayal of God from the narrator's all-inclusive view.

The repeated term ὁ λόγος τοῦ θεοῦ communicates God's saving will in Jesus and serves as a key signal to the plot progression. The Word is a manifestation of God's presence as well as a mark of God's people; its dynamic power is the source and guarantee of the victory of God's Word-mission. With respect to the repeated patterns, divine initiative signifies that the Word-mission for salvation is completely of God; the prophetic (Word-miracle-suffering) ministry interconnects God's saving activities historically and syncronically, through divine-human cooperation, and thus attests to the continuity and unity of God's salvific plan. Significantly, in the prophetic ministry the conflict between Jesus' witnesses and their opponents never ceases; this is, in nature, a clash in authority and power and a clash of personal interests. Eventually, it is a conflict between the authority and power of God and that of Satan (26:18; cf. 5:3)[139] and is, in nature, a conflict between the kingdoms of God and Satan (1:3; 28:31; note that God's kingdom is the ultimate concern of the proclamation, cf. another repeated key-term ἡ βασιλεία τοῦ θεοῦ in 8:12; 19:8; 20:25; 28:23).

The movement of the Word, signalling the plot progression, signifies the victory of the Word as well as the triumph of God's Word-mission.[140] This

---

[138] In the light of Sternberg's two functions of epithet, the epithets of God directly characterise God and indirectly promote the plot. The former, an explicit characterisation, renders a static feature of God. The latter implicitly bears a twofold dynamic force, a foreshadowing device and a developmental factor, which presents an active trait of God. The foreshadowing device shapes the readers' expectations of God's actions since they are informed who God is. The developmental factor shapes the sequence of narrative events since God's deeds serve as a cause that brings about a certain effect in the narrative (*Biblical Narrative*, 337-38).

[139] Gaventa, 'Initiatives,' 85; idem, *Acts*, 99.

[140] 'Point of view introduces a dynamic element into a text: every one of the points of view in a text makes claims to be the truth and struggles to assert itself in the conf-

manifests God's supreme will and sovereign authority and power in consummating his redemptive plan and in bringing to himself a new people (including Gentiles). Behind God's sovereignty over the provision of salvation lies God's magnanimity. To provide salvation, God shares his supreme lordship with Jesus and makes Jesus the promised Saviour (2:36; 5:31; 13:23). Then Jesus' commission of his witnesses serves as a divine invitation for them to partake in God's universal Word-mission by which they share divine authority and power in the name of Jesus and through the Spirit (but not divine lordship). By the witnesses' sharing of the Word, God's mission is carried out; a people of sharing is built for God's kingdom. Based on his sharing nature, God's salvific plan is consummated by his own authority and power coming through Jesus and Jesus' witnesses via the Spirit.

Throughout Acts the narrator emphasises 'God's plan and sovereign hand guiding the circumstances in the life of Jesus and then in the life of the church,'[141] and 'underscores his understanding that historical events have proceeded under divine guidance and themselves served an underlying aim – namely God's salvific purpose.'[142] The narrative deployment reinforces the narrator's 'larger purpose of speaking of the communication and realisation of God's purpose behind and within human history.'[143] Along the plot line God bears various functions in relation to the theme of *God's universal saving will and plan realised in Jesus and consummated through the Spirit-empowered witnesses of Jesus*. In the main characters' speeches (the interpretation of God's action in history), God's salvific plan is presented with christocentric realisation embedded in the theocentric programme (i.e. the promise-fulfilment base, cf. Acts 2, 13).[144] In the narrator's depiction, the witnesses' mission is the christocentric ministry upheld by the theocentric reinforcement (which is perceived in the ongoing promise-fulfilment,[145] cf. Acts 20, and the divine promises to Paul). God's supreme will and plan promote the thematic point of God's sovereignty over history and the individual; God's sovereign authority and power promote the thematic point of God's reign over incidents and characters.

---

lict with the opposing ones' (Lotman, 'Point of View,' 352). It is the ultimate victory of the Word in the midst of conflict that attests to the witnesses' proclamation of God's saving Word to be the truth.

[141] Witherington, *Acts*, 416; cf. Soards, *Speeches*, 184.

[142] Green, 'Internal Repetition,' 294.

[143] Green, 'Internal Repetition,' 295.

[144] Marguerat, 'God,' 175; cf. Sheeley, *Asides*, 147; Brawley, *God*, 57; Chen, *Father*, 6; W. Ward Gasque, 'A Fruitful Field: Recent Study of the Acts of the Apostles,' *Int* 42 (1988) 117-31, citing 125.

[145] Cosgrove indicates that God's presence in the ministry of Jesus and the church 'is viewed consistently in terms of the work of the Spirit and under the heading of "promise and fulfilment"' ('Divine Δεῖ,' 190).

God's redemptive plan, which is the narrative concern, makes God, the invisible and offstage figure, the dominant character who aligns human history with the divine purpose and who invites people to share his salvation and to partake in his invincible mission for salvation. By this God is the sovereign Lord of history and of every individual. He is so authoritative and powerful, there can be no hindrance nor defeat of his kingdom (i.e. his reign).

CHAPTER 7

Conclusion

As noted in Chapter Two, the communication between the narrator and the reader resembles a dot-to-dot picture in which the narrator deploys the dots (i.e. characters and incidents) to communicate his message. Throughout Acts, God 'never appears onstage as an actor'[1] yet is the only *constant* primary character 'who is consistently acting and engaging with the other characters of the narrative world.'[2] To manifestly present the hidden God, the narrator distributes the indicators along the textual continuum[3] which shape the reader's image of God. By the narrator's multiple-angle of characterisation a distinctive portrait of God appears in Acts.

Characteristics of the Characterisation of God

Characterisation is quite complex and varied because of the multiple points of view for presenting a character. In the narrative the narrator portrays God in double-stratum representation (mimetic and thematic) and through double-orbit presentation (via divine and human agents). Behind the narrative lies the hand of the implied author who characterises God in double-track characterisation (*showing* and *telling*) and through double-lens characterisation (via zoom-in and zoom-out lens).

Double-Stratum Representation

In the plot-oriented narrative of Acts, God can be tracked through the indicators laid by the narrator in two strata. In the mimetic stratum God, presented from various characters' perspectives, is primarily perceived as a character who is sovereign, authoritative and omnipotent, and whose interest—universal salvation in Jesus—is the common concern among characters. In the thematic stratum God's interest plays a crucial role in the narrative development as his Word functions as the controlling thread in the plot and divine initiative is the major cause for plot progression. The overall narrative does not carry one single focal point but a diffused area containing several thematic points. God's supreme salvific will and mission plan and his sovereign authority and power

---

[1] Shepherd, *Spirit*, 255; cf. Darr, *Character Building*, 51.
[2] Bibb, *God*, 295; cf. Wilk, 'Licht,' 606.
[3] Fred W. Burnett, 'Characterization and Reader Construction of Characters in the Gospels,' *Semeia* 63 (1993) 3-28, citing 5.

are shown to run parallel in order faithfully to carry out his promised salvation; their interplay is manifest throughout the narrative as God opens up a new page for his redemptive plan. To consummate his salvific purpose, God sovereignly reigns over humankind, historically and synchronically, governing the development of human history and human affairs.[4] The images of God emerging from both strata correspond to each other, and thus amplify the primary attributes of God. In this double-stratum representation God appears to be the supreme and sovereign Lord of salvation, who authoritatively, powerfully and faithfully carried out his redemptive plan in human history.

Double-Orbit Presentation

In the narrative the invisible God can also be traced out from two orbits: by his vertical relationship through heavenly revelators to human characters and by his horizontal relationship with each revelator. While the horizontal relationships reveal God's will of universal salvation and mission, the vertical relationships elucidate God's saving plan and the realisation of God's Word-mission. In Jesus God fulfils his promise of salvation; by the Spirit God makes manifest his universal salvation and mission; through angels God enforces his will and ensures his people do it. Divine interventions inspire the witnesses of God's saving will, direct them to the mission in line with God's plan and assure its consummation. Through his human agents, who are commissioned by Jesus, empowered by the Spirit and escorted by angels to be Jesus' witnesses, God's universal Word-mission is carried out and realised. Main characters proclaim God's redemptive plan, throughout the ages and at present, in Jesus; their bold witness to Jesus expands God's Word-mission. Both orbits of relationship weave a web of interrelationships, which communicates God's determined providence of universal salvation and his authoritative faithfulness in fulfilling his promise of salvation, from which the portrait of a sovereign, omnipotent and gracious God emerges.

Double-Track Characterisation

The offstage God is made known by the implied author through the literary techniques of characterisation—*telling* and *showing*. In *showing*, the narrator, adopting various characters' points of view, unfolds God's mission plan for salvation. Main characters play a major role in carrying out God's saving mission while heavenly revelators act in a minor yet pivotal role in determining the movement of the mission. On the stage the theocentric speeches of main characters reveal God's inner world (i.e. the divine interest in human salvation);[5] by

---

[4] Jervell, 'Salvation History,' 106.
[5] Cf. Johnson, 'Portrait,' 160.

characters' telling of God's will revealed in the divine deeds throughout the ages the narrator shows God's will both in history and at present. Furthermore, characters' interactions with God's will reveal a God who, through divine agents, actively participates in human lives working for their salvation. In the name of Jesus and through the Spirit, people are invited to share God's salvation and to partake in his universal Word-mission. In *telling*, the narrator subtly highlights God's supreme and sovereign lordship, the dynamic saving power of God's Word and God's working pattern, concealed in the plot, among his people. Both tracks of characterisation portray God as a super director whose sovereignty determines the movement of characters and the development of incidents.[6]

Double-Lens Characterisation

Throughout the narrative it is the narrator's use of the *interest point of view* that keeps this offstage God remaining on stage invisibly. There are two ways of bringing God's interest, as well as the narrator's, into focus. As through a zoom-in lens, the narrator presents a close-up at crucial interactions between heavenly revelators and human characters which unfold the vital points of God's saving plan. Through a zoom-out lens the narrator presents a long shot of a certain corner or angle of the theocentric world which provides an overall picture of the progressive development of God's plan. The main characters' speeches are parts of the close-up whilst they simultaneously provide a panorama for the theocentric world. The most panoramic shot is the narrator's. Both views are adopted chiastically to elucidate God still at work. More specifically, the focal point of a close-up falls on God's sovereign authority and power over his universal salvation;[7] that of a wide-angle stays on God's invincible mission plan for salvation. The former portrays, in the foreground, a Lord God who is the sovereign and omnipotent Saviour of all; the latter sketches, in the background, a Lord God who is the gracious and faithful ruler of the heavenly kingdom.

---

[6] Salmeier, *Ordainer*, 173, 217, 258; Bibb, *God*, 287.

[7] One may infer that divine love initiates the saving plan and inaugurates the mission of God; divine sovereignty and power assures its consummation. Surprisingly, love is never the concern in the narrative (cf. no occurrence of ἀγάπη, ἀγαπάω, φιλία or φιλέω in Acts). While divine authority and power prevail throughout the narrative, divine love is simply sensed in its whisper behind the divine saving plan, deliverance, protection and invigoration. The absence of the explicit expression of divine love removes the ultimate cause of God's saving purpose from the spotlight and leaves the focus on divine authority. This magnifies God's supremacy and omnipotence and thus firmly assures the consummation of his mission plan.

Distinctive Portrait of God

A seemingly paradoxical portrait of God appears from the multiple-angle characterisation: God is 'offstage' yet perceived as an invisible onstage character; God dominates human lives for his divine purpose yet humans are invited to participate in the sovereign plan; God's salvific plan remains unchanged yet the way for salvation is transformed.

Invisible-yet-Perceivable

God, though never stepping onto the stage of the Acts narrative, hardly ever disappears from the narrative stage. Marguerat also indicates that the God in Acts is 'a God who allows himself to be known, while at the same time hiding, in the events of history. "God" does not speak, he is brought to expression by the word of witness.'[8] It is the heavenly revelators who make God known, 'a unique and enigmatic power, knowable only through his incursions into history,'[9] to the believers. God is brought into focus (by the implied author's literary technique of the *interest point of view*) because his will and purpose are always the concern in the sequential incidents. By means of the multiple-angle characterisation, the narrator impressively characterises God as an invisible-yet-perceivable character, who supremely transcends humankind yet sovereignly participates in human history to bring forth salvation, and whose plan is a governing cause that moves human history toward his end. Accordingly, this invisible God is perceived as a super-conductor who from offstage controls the onstage characters and incidents.

Dominant-yet-Cogent

God's predominant interventions in history cause Haenchen to contend that the human characters are almost divine puppets.[10] His assertion, which solely focuses on God's invincible authority and interventions, is understandable. It is, however, inadequate in that it overlooks the interactions between heavenly revelators and human characters.[11] Encouraged by the divine deliverance and promise and refortified by the consecutive divine instructions, the witnesses are convinced of God's will and thus commit themselves to it. Instead of interpreting the witnesses' full submission as a twitching of human puppets, it is, rather, the divinely authoritative care and the impressively divine interventions which bring a full conviction of human faith.[12] Such unwavering faith in God leads to

---

[8] Marguerat, *Historian*, 103.
[9] Sternberg, *Biblical Narrative*, 323.
[10] Haenchen, *Acts*, 362.
[11] Aletti, *Luc raconte*, 65; cf. Marguerat, 'God,' 179.
[12] Cf. Gaventa, 'Initiatives,' 88-89.

unreserved submission to the divine directives which are given without indicating the reason. The withholding of the whole picture of God's will certainly invites human trust and obedience; human desire to do God's will excludes the autocratic reign of God. Instead, it portrays a sovereign God who, authoritatively, sets up his plan for human salvation and powerfully invites human participation with it, and a supreme God who convinces his people of his will and faithfully strengthens them to accomplish it.

Continuous-yet-Changing

As the narrative develops, the reader's understanding of God is progressively deepened and reinforced as the background settings change. The descent of the Spirit gives birth to the church in Jerusalem, amongst Jews and in a monotheistic environment.[13] As God's mission marches on, these three settings change significantly. First, the geographical progression is striking. The Jews' rejection of the Word in Jerusalem occasions God's mission in Samaria and Judea, whereas that in Judea moves God's mission westwards towards Rome. Second, the breaking of Jewish ethnic purity and the embracing of Gentiles redefines who the people of God are. Third, the requirements for God's people are shifted from observance of Jewish law simply to faith in Jesus alone. All the changes enhance that 'the God of Israel becomes the God of all.'[14] Essentially, the Acts narrative is 'a narrative description of a historical movement,'[15] regarding the continuity and change of God's way for salvation which leads to 'an image of God that changes and is transformed.'[16] Throughout Acts it is emphasised that God fulfils his old promise of salvation in Jesus. This new revelation and its impact among God's people renew and reshape the reader's perspective of God.

Concluding Remark

As a concluding remark, we are ready to answer concisely the questions indicated in the statement of purpose: Who is God? What is his interest? How does he act? Is the Acts narrative God-centred or character-centred? According to our overall investigation, the invisible God is the sovereign and supreme Lord over human history and over every individual; he is the Lord of salvation will-

---

[13] Cf. Joseph B. Tyson, 'The Emerging Church and the Problem of Authority in Acts,' *Int* 42 (1988) 132-45, esp. 135.

[14] Marguerat, *Historian*, 37; cf. Francois Bovon, 'The God of Luke' in idem, *New Testament Traditions and Apocryphal Narratives* (PTMS 36; Allison Park: Pickwick Publications, 1995) 67-80, esp. 78.

[15] Tyson, 'Emerging Church,' 132.

[16] Marguerat, *Historian*, 36.

ingly revealing himself through his divine and human agents. God's interest is exposed in his plan for human salvation which is set off by Jesus and the Spirit and carried on by Jesus' witnesses; God is building a people for his kingdom. God authoritatively and powerfully reigns over humans and events for his salvific purpose; he graciously invites people to share his salvation by faith in Jesus; he further invites the believers to participate in his mission plan by sharing with them his own authority and power in the name of Jesus and through the Spirit. The overall portrayal of God, emphasising God's sovereign authority and power in fulfilling his redemptive plan and God's faithful empowerment and care in protecting his witnesses, suggests the implied reader is in need of being encouraged, and is expected, to stay in the faith in Jesus or to bear witness to this faith in times of opposition.

Ostensibly, the major characters and, occasionally, individual minor characters are put in the spotlight on the narrative stage. Yet, when they step down from the stage, what remains on the stage is God's saving will and Word-mission.[17] This is the continued interest of the narrative: Peter is put in the spotlight while declaring God's saving will; the disciples are in the spotlight as they continue the proclamation of God's Word; Paul is in the spotlight as he carries on God's Word-mission. At the end of the narrative, though, Paul stays on the stage, the narrator's voice pinpoints the exact interest of the narrative as introduced in the beginning of the narrative—God's kingdom and his saving Word. Significantly, when the major characters' viewpoints are evaluated from the more dominant one (i.e. the narrator's) they, as the subject characterising God, become the object characterised by God. That is, by participating in God's mission, the main characters, on the one hand, authoritatively and powerfully bear witness to God's salvific will and, on the other, they themselves are characterised as God's authoritative and powerful messengers. More specifically, on the surface of the narrative (mimetic stratum), characters characterise God in ways by their interaction with God's will. Along the narrative interest (thematic stratum), characters are characterised by God since they exist to make God's will known. From the *interest point of view*, God's will for human salvation interweaves the narrative characters and incidents to tell of the new development of God's redemptive plan with respect to God's kingdom. In Acts, God's kingdom is like a patchwork quilt sewn by God in his authoritative love. Each stage in human history is uniquely interwoven with God's plan; each step in the divine plan is carried out as the threads of God's divine and human agents are tightly stitched together to bring forth salvation powerfully to all throughout the ages. God's lordship is supreme and sovereign; God's kingdom is everlasting.

---

[17] Skinner, *Locating Paul*, 169.

APPENDIX 1

The Lukan Use of Πατήρ

Although the phrase ὁ πατήρ μου is found nowhere in Mark, it is often used by Jesus to address God the Father; this is true particularly in Matthew (16 times) and John (25 times) yet less often in Luke (4 times). The mere phrase ὁ πατήρ μου in John accentuates the Father-Son relationship (2:16; 5:17, 43; 6:32, 40; etc.); in Matthew another phrase, ὁ οὐράνιος or ἐν τοῖς οὐρανοῖς, is constantly added to ὁ πατήρ μου to highlight additionally the supremacy of the Father (7:21; 10:32, 33; 12:50; 15:13; 16:17; 18:10, 19, 35); all the phrases in Luke are set within the twofold relationship: the Father and Jesus; Jesus and the believers (2:49; 10:22; 22:29; 24:49).

In Luke, only Jesus addresses God as the Father (2:49; 9:26; 10:21, 22; 11:2, 13; 12:30, 32; 22:29, 42; 23:34, 46; 24:49). Scrutinising these verses, one finds a slightly different stress on the Father. Out of the sixteen occurrences (twice in 10:21 and three times in 10:22) six are vocative, directly and lucidly accentuating the Father-Son relation, in Jesus' prayers to the Father (10:21 twice; 11:2; 22:42; 23:34, 46); six with personal pronouns particularly highlight a certain relationship (four with μου stressing the Father-Son relationship, cf. 2:49; 10:22; 22:29; 24:49; two with ὑμῶν stressing the Father-son relationship, cf. 12:30, 32); the remaining four, with explicit or inexplicit reference to heaven (9:26; 10:21-2; 11:13), lay emphasis merely on the supreme status of the Father and thus assure what Jesus says.

In Acts, while indicating the descent of the Holy Spirit (1:4-5; cf. 1:8), Jesus twice speaks of the promise of God the Father (1:4, 7). Later, Peter elucidates its fulfilment through Jesus' death and resurrection (2:33). In comparison with Jesus' parallel saying of the Father's promise of the Spirit in Luke (Lk 24:49; τὴν ἐπαγγελίαν τοῦ πατρός μου), the personal pronoun μου is lacking in Acts. This leaves the focus on the Father, accentuating the Father's authority, and thus assures the fulfilment of the promise.

APPENDIX 2

The Words Indicating God-Fearer

The God-fearers,[1] belonging neither to the Jews nor to the disciples,[2] stand in the tension between them. Their response to the Word throughout Acts, negative or positive, subtly contributes to the plot. In the Jewish community, their

---

[1] Max Wilcox argues that the expression of the *God-fearer* in Acts lays its emphasis on piety rather than on a distinct group ('The "God-Fearers" in Acts—A Reconsideration,' *JSNT* 13 [1981] 102-22). However, in arguing that these terms refer not to the membership of a class but the piety itself, Wilcox, throughout his presentation, fails to provide explicit, forceful and convincing support for his contention. Thomas M. Finn's article on 'The God-fearers Reconsidered' (*CBQ* 47 [1985] 75-84) furthers Wilcox's argument. Based on A.T. Kraabel's argument ('The Disappearance of the "God-Fearers",' *Numen* 28 [1981] 113-26), which not only supports Wilcox's view but contends for God-fearers as the proselytes among the native-born Jews from the study of archaeological and literary evidence, Finn mainly concludes: 'the phenomenon of Gentiles attached to Judaism had not by the time of Acts given birth to tecnnical terminology... the literary evidence in Juvenal, Josephus, and Philo tends to corroborate Acts at least to the extent that these authors, roughly contemporary with Acts, reveal the existence of Gentiles in a variety of places who, short of conversion, were drawn to Jewish belief and practice' ('God-fearers Reconsidered,' 83; cf. John G. Gager, 'Jews, Gentiles, and Synagogues in the Book of Acts,' *HTR* 79/1-3 [1986] 91-99; J. Andrew Overman, 'The God-Fearers: Some Neglected Features,' *JSNT* 32 [1988] 17-26; Louis H. Feldman, 'The Omnipresence of the God-Fearers,' *BAR* 12/5 [1986] 58-69).

The recent excavations at Aphrodite shed new light on the God-fearers. Conrad H. Gempf offers a concise and essential introduction and evaluation to both the Aphrodisias find and Kraabel's contention ('The God-fearers' in Colin J. Hemer [ed.], *The Book of Acts in the Setting of Hellenistic History* [Tübingen: J.C.B. Mohr, 1989] 444-47; cf. Robert F. Tannenbaum, 'Jews and God-Fearers in the Holy City of Aphrodite,' *BAR* 12/5 [1986] 54-57; Jerome Murphy-O'Connor, 'Lots of God-Fearers? *Theosebeis* in the Aphrodisias Inscription,' *RB* 99/2 [1992] 418-24). Barrett also provides a brief discussion of the term (*Acts*, 1:499-501). While the terms employed for the *God-fearers* evidently indicate the attributes of the persons as the terms themselves suggest, they are apparently regarded as a distinct group because of the parallel use between them and the Jews (Acts 13:16, 26, 43; 17:17). Whatever usage the term has, the fact is, in the text itself, that 'some Gentiles were attracted to Jewish ethics, theology, and worship, but did not become proselytes... such Gentiles presented a great opportunity to Christian evangelists' (Barrett, *Acts*, 1:501).

[2] The occurrence of the God-fearers (οἱ σεβόμενοι or φοβούμενοι τὸν θεόν) together with the Jews in the synagogue (Acts 13:16, 26, 43; 17:17) and its connection with

positive response to the Word provokes the Jews' jealousy and persecution of the disciples (13:43, 50; 17:4). Fundamentally speaking, the God-fearers, as they appear in Acts, are associated with Jewish synagogues. Four terms are employed to address the God-fearers in Acts: two adjectives (εὐλαβής, εὐσεβής) and two verbs in participle form (σεβόμενος, φοβούμενος).

The word φοβέω, in general, indicates a state of fearing.³ Only if God is the object of the verb does the participle phrase οἱ φοβούμενοι τὸν θεόν indicate the God-fearers (10:2, 22, 35; 13:16, 26). The phrase in Acts 10 enunciates Cornelius' piety but refers to a distinct group other than the Jews in Acts 13.⁴

Σέβομαι expresses 'in attitude and ritual one's allegiance to and regard for deity — to worship, to venerate.'⁵ Occurring in participle form, functioning either as an adjective (13:43, 50; 17:4) or a substantive (17:17), σέβομαι carries the meaning of *devout*. While taking τὸν θεόν as its object, regardless of whether it is a substantival participle (16:14; 18:7) or a verb in infinitive (18:13) or indicative form (19:27, though referring to foreign deity), it conveys the meaning of *worship*. It is also obvious that *devout* not only indicates the attitude of the person but refers to those of a Gentile background.⁶ Being introduced as worshippers of God, Lydia and Titus Justus are also of Gentile background (16:14; 18:7).

In Acts, the adjective εὐλαβής refers solely to devout Jews (2:5; 8:2; 22:12) while εὐσεβής applies only to the Gentile Cornelius (10:2, 7). The former expresses a religious attitude—devout, God-fearing;⁷ the latter implies one's rela-

---

the Gentiles (Acts 10:2, 22, 35; 16:14; 17:4) suggests that they are a group of people who are of the Gentile background yet attracted to Judaism and associated with the Jews.

3   L&N, §25.252.
4   It is clearly depicted in L&N, §53.58 that 'in Ac 13:16 the phrase "those who fear God" is essentially a technical phrase to identify non-Jews who worshipped the God of the Jews. These would have been Gentiles who were "God-fearers" or "worshipers of God".' Barrett elucidates the term as an alternative designation of 'a specific class of persons, not Jews, and not proselytes, but attached to the synagogue by their acceptance of Jewish religious and ethical principles and general sympathy with the Jewish way of life' (*Acts*, 1:500).
5   L&N, §53.53.
6   It is seen in Ac 13:43 and 17:4 that σεβομένων describes the Gentile. The expression of 'the Jews and the devout in the synagogue' (17:17) also suggests that the devout is a distinct group of people other than the Jews. It is clearly depicted in BDAG that the middle voice of σέβομαι with τὸν θεόν, indicating God-fearers or worshippers of God, 'is a term applied to former polytheists who accepted the ethical monotheism of Israel and attended the synagogue, but who did not obligate themselves to keep the whole Mosaic law; in particular, the males did not submit to circumcision' (917-18).
7   BDAG, 407.

tion to God—being profoundly reverent or respectful.[8] The word εὐσεβής even further indicates a proper expression of religious beliefs, conveying the concept of 'living a God-fearers life' as 'God would have one live.'[9] Thus, as this word εὐσεβής is employed to depict Cornelius' piety, in addition to his attitude toward God (10:2; φοβούμενος τὸν θεόν), the way of his life is further introduced (10:2; he gave alms liberally to the people and prayed constantly to God).

---

[8] BDAG, 413.
[9] L&N, §53.6.

APPENDIX 3

References for the Narrative Voices

Characters' Voices	The Narrator's Voice	
References for Characters' Formal Speeches	References for Description of Incidents (Characters' Actions and Dialogue)	References for Summary of or Remark on the Overall Events
1:16-22 2:14-36 3:12-26 4:8-12, 24-31 5:29-32, 35-39 7:2-53 10:34-43 11:4-17 13:16-41 14:14-17 15:7-11, 14-21, 23-29 17:22-31 20:18-35 22:1-21 23:25-30 24:3-21 25:14-21, 24-27 26:1-23 28:17-22, 25-29	1:4-15, 23-26 2:1-13, 37-42 3:1-11 4:1-7, 13-23 5:1-28, 33-34, 40-42 6:1-6, 8-15 7:1, 54-60 8:1-40 9:1-30, 32-43 10:1-33, 44-48 11:1-3, 18-30 12:1-23, 25 13:1-15, 42-52 14:1-13, 18-28 15:1-6, 12-13, 22, 30-41 16:1-4, 6-40 17:1-21, 32-34 18:1-28 19:1-19, 21-40 20:1-17, 36-38 21:1-40 22:22-30 23:1-24, 31-35 24:1-2, 22-27 25:1-13, 22-23 26:24-32 27:1-44 28:1-16, 23-24	1:1-3 2:43-47 4:32-35 6:7 9:31 12:24 16:5 19:20 28:30-31

APPENDIX 4

The Epithets Applied to God

All epithets applied to God are uttered by the reliable voices in Acts.

Peter
1. πατήρ (2:33)
2. κύριος (2:20, 21, 25, 34, 39; 3:20, 22, etc.)
3. ὁ θεὸς τῶν πατέρων ἡμῶν (3:13; 5:30; cf. 2:39)
4. οὐκ προσωπολήμπτης (10:34)
5. ὁ καρδιογνώστης (15:8)

The disciples as a whole
1. δέσποτα (4:24)
2. ὁ ποιήσας τὸν οὐρανὸν καὶ τὴν γῆν καὶ τὴν θάλασσαν καὶ πάντα τὰ ἐν αὐτοῖς (4:24)
3. ὁ... διὰ πνεύματος ἁγίου... εἰπών (4:25)
4. κύριος (4:29)

Stephen
1. ὁ θεὸς τῆς δόξης (7:2)
2. κύριος (7:31)
3. ὁ θεὸς τῶν πατέρων σου, ὁ θεὸς Ἀβραὰμ καὶ Ἰσαὰκ καὶ Ἰακώβ (7:32)
4. ὁ ὕψιστος (7:48)

James
1. κύριος ποιῶν ταῦτα (15:17)

Paul
1. ὁ θεὸς τοῦ λαοῦ τούτου Ἰσραήλ (13:17)
2. θεὸν ζῶντα (14:15)
3. ὁ θεὸς ὁ ποιήσας τὸν κόσμον καὶ πάντα τὰ ἐν αὐτῷ (17:24)
4. οὐρανοῦ καὶ γῆς... κύριος (17:24; see also 13:47)
5. ὁ θεὸς τῶν πατέρων ἡμῶν (22:14)
6. τῷ πατρῴῳ θεῷ (24:14)

The narrator
1. κύριος (2:47; 5:19; 8:26, 39; etc.)

APPENDIX 5

The Referent of Κύριος

There are 107 occurrences of κύριος in Acts, among which four refer to human masters (16:16, 19, 30; 25:26), three to supernatural beings (10:4, 14; 11:18) and the rest to either God or Jesus. An analysis of the narrator's use of κύριος for God or Jesus in Acts sheds light on his notion of the divine lordship.[1]

There are three points observed from the analysis:
1. Κύριος as God occurs intensively in Acts 1-7, then gradually decreases (except in Acts 12) and disappears from Acts 18 onwards. God's lordship frequently relates to OT quotations.
2. Κύριος as Jesus occurs evenly in both parts of Acts yet with emphasis on Acts 9 and 18-20. Jesus' name is frequently attached to κύριος in the second half of Acts.
3. The ambiguous referent of κύριος slightly and gradually increases. The ambiguity appears mainly in the phrase of ὁ λόγος τοῦ κυρίου (8:25; 13:44, 48, 49; 15:35, 36; 16:32; 19:10; cf. 13:10), in the indication of a number of believers added or turning to the Lord (5:14; 9:35; 11:21b, 24) and in the cases where κύριος is the object of one's trust (8:22, 24; 9:31; 11:23; 15:40) and the conductor of one's life (16:14; 21:14).

The diagram exposes the narrator's progressive highlighting of Jesus' divine lordship. Together with the deliberately ambiguous use of κύριος for God and Jesus, the narrator believes Jesus shares the divine lordship of God and becomes the Lord of the believers' ministry for God's mission. This also supports the different emphases on the missions of Peter and Paul: Peter in his theocentric speeches which attest to God's saving will in Jesus; Paul in his christocentric ministry which carries out God's universal mission of salvation.

---

[1] The referent of κύριος is sometimes ambiguous and scholars may hold different views (cf. Schneider, 'Kyrios,' 162-66; Dunn, *Christology*, 245-48).

God		Jesus		Ambiguity		God		Jesus		Ambiguity	
OVs	NV	OVs	NV	OVs	NV	OVs	NV	OVs	NV	OVs	NV
		1:6									
		1:21°				8:26					
1:24						8:39					
2:20*									9:1		
2:21* †								9:5			
2:25*								9:10b	9:10a		
2:34a*		2:34b*							9:11		
		2:36						9:13			
2:39									9:15		
	2:47?							9:17			
3:20									9:27		
3:22*									9:28		
4:26*											9:31
4:29											9:35
			4:33°						9:42		
5:9						10:33					
					5:14			10:36			
	5:19							11:16			
7:31								11:17°			
7:33									11:20°		
7:49*							11:21a				11:21b
		7:59°									11:23
		7:60									11:24
			8:16°				12:7				
				8:22		12:11					
				8:24			12:17				
					8:25		12:23				

Appendixes

God		Jesus		Ambiguity		God		Jesus		Ambiguity	
OVs	NV	OVs	NV	OVs	NV	OVs	NV	OVs	NV	OVs	NV
					13:2				18:8		
				13:10					18:9		
13:11									18:25		
			13:12						19:5°		
					13:44						19:10
13:47†									19:13°		
					13:48				19:17°		
					13:49		19:20?				
	14:3								20:19		
			14:23						20:21°		
		15:11°							20:24°		
15:17a.b*									20:35°		
			15:26°						21:13°		
					15:35						21:14
					15:36			22:8			
					15:40				22:10a.b		
					16:14			22:19			
		16:15							23:11		
			16:31°					26:15a.b			
					16:32				28:31°		
17:24											

OVs   Other voices
NV   The narrator's voice

* Κύριος occurs in the OT quotation.
° Κύριος occurs with the name of Jesus.
† Though κύριος refers to God, the implied author might have Jesus in mind.
? Κύριος probably refers to God while compared with other parallel uses.

APPENDIX 6

Epithets Conveying God's Attributes

These epithets of God demonstrate the attributes of God as expressed by attributive modifiers or inferred from God's deeds. Καρδιογνώστης (a heart-knower), the apposition of God, spells out that God is omniscient and hence discerns one's interior dispositions (1:24; 15:8).[1] Οὐκ προσωπολήμπτης, the negative predicative of God, points out the attribute of a just God who shows no favouritism between Jews and Gentiles receiving his salvation.[2] In the phrase ὁ θεὸς τῆς δόξης (7:2), the attributive genitive δόξα emphasises the glorious attribute of God[3] who is majestic, sublime and honourable.[4] It also signifies 'a benevolent supernatural power deserving respect and honor'[5] as implied in how God revealed himself to, and what he did for, the people Israel (7:2ff.). In the phrase θεὸς ζῶν (14:15), the anarthrous θεός and the attributive participle ζῶν accentuate the essential attribute of God as living,[6] who is not subject to death.[7] By contrast to the vain things in the context (i.e. idolatry), the living God gives meaning to all existence while the futile idols return to emptiness and worthlessness.[8]

God's attributes also underlie his deeds as specified by two participial epithets. The adjectival participial phrase in 4:25 indicates that by the mouth of

---

[1] L&N, §28.12; BDAG, 509; Marshall, *Acts*, 249-50; Johnson, *Acts*, 262. Haenchen further indicates that *God knowing all hearts* is 'a favourite expression of post-apostolic Christendom' (*Acts*, 162).

[2] Haenchen, *Acts*, 351.

[3] Wallace, *Beyond*, 86-87.

[4] BDAG, 257.

[5] L&N, §12.49.

[6] Robertson, *Grammar of the Greek New Testament*, 794. The anarthrous θεὸς ζῶν conveys the qualitative force. Moreover, the other objects of the phrase ἐπιστρέφειν ἐπί (either the Lord or God) in Acts have an article (9:35; 11:21; 15:19; 26:18, 20). Here the exceptional use obviously signifies the very nature of God, namely, the *living* God.

[7] BDAG, 425.

[8] The word μάταιος conveys the idea of 'being useless on the basis of being futile and lacking in content' (L&N, §65.37). By contrast God is understood to be the significance and meaning of all.

David God speaks through the Holy Spirit.[9] Both divine and human agents are involved in God's revelation. Though the Spirit speaks through human agents (1:16; 28:25), God is the ultimate source of the revelatory words. Such divine origin endorses the realisation and consummation of the words which evinces the attribute of God as faithful. God's faithfulness is further revealed in another adjectival participial phrase in 15:17. Ποιῶν ταῦτα (the rebuilding of David's fallen tent and the Gentiles' seeking after God, 15:16-17) and γνωστὰ ἀπ' αἰῶνος (known for ages, 15:18) elucidate 'God's active role in revealing divine purposes.'[10] Not only does God make his intention known through the prophets but he faithfully carries out his plan in due course. God's revelatory nature and faithfulness are largely exposed throughout his interactions with his people.

As God's overall attributes reveal, though transcendent, ever-living and majestic in being, the Creator God first reveals and relates himself to his people and then actively participates in their lives. Being omniscient and just in nature, the Revealer God makes no discrimination—salvation is offered to all. Being faithful and loving in essence, the Father God keeps his promise of salvation and consummates his saving plan.

---

[9] The awkward expression of the phrase causes different renderings among the MSS. According to 'the golden rule of textual criticism,' the most difficult reading is probably closer to the original one since the rest may have been raised to smooth the readings. Thus, our text here, also with the support of more reliable MSS P⁷⁴, B and ℵ, is probably the best reading. Regardless of the textual variations, which arise to resolve the difficulty and confusion of the sentence, the text conveys two agents by which God speaks.

[10] Soards, *Speeches*, 94.

APPENDIX 7

Λόγος Compared with Ῥῆμα and Ὁδός

There are two words which may indicate a message about Jesus in addition to λόγος: ῥῆμα and ὁδός. Ῥῆμα in Acts, mainly in plural form, may refer to the message/words about Jesus (2:14; 5:20; 10:44; 11:14) or the events/things concerning Jesus (5:32). Also, ῥῆμα in certain contexts may carry the above twofold meaning (10:37; 13:42).[1] When indicating the words about Jesus, ῥῆμα parallels the terminological use of λόγος. Yet it emphasises the *oral witness* to Jesus since ῥῆμα is often employed for the spoken words of a narrative character.[2] Ὁδός (the Way) is the term which 'succinctly describes the form of Christianity.'[3] In its indication of particular patterns of behaviour,[4] ὁδός signifies the 'specification of teaching and manner of life relating to Jesus Christ' (9:2; 18:25, 26; 19:9, 23; 22:4; 24:14, 22).[5] In such a use ὁδός appears in singular form and with an article. It combines the believer's teaching and lifestyle (i.e. ethic)[6] which serves as a *living witness* to Jesus. Ὁδός is characterised by christocentric teaching (18:25, cf. the terminological use of λόγος)[7] and by the

---

[1] For further discussion on the twofold use of ῥῆμα see Christoph Burchard, 'A Note on Ῥῆμα in Josas 17:1f.; Luke 2:15, 17; Acts 10:37,' *NovT* 27/4 (1985) 281-95. For ῥῆμα as the message about Jesus in these two verses see Marshall, *Acts*, 229; Witherington, *Acts*, 358, 414; Gaventa, *Acts*, 171. For ῥῆμα as the events about Jesus see BDAG, 905; Haenchen, *Acts*, 352, 413; Polhill, *Acts*, 306.

[2] Note ῥῆμα is closely connected to λαλέω (5:20; 6:11, 13; 10:44; 11:14; 13:42).

[3] Joseph A. Fitzmyer, 'Jewish Christianity in Acts in Light of the Qumran Scrolls' in Keck and Martyn (eds.), *Studies in Luke-Acts*, 233-57, citing 240; cf. J. Pathrapankal, 'Christianity as a "Way" according to the Acts of the Apostles' in J. Kremer (ed.), *Les Actes des Apôtres: Traditions, rédaction, théologie* (BETL 48; Gembloux: J. Duculot, 1979) 533-39, citing 535. Fitzmyer further indicates that Christianity's absolute use of ὁδός for itself, in contrast to αἵρεσις used by unbelieving Jews (24:14), parallels what the Qumran community indicates itself (240-41), though in eschatological sense. Cf. Haenchen, *Acts*, 352 n. 1; Marshall, *Acts*, 168-69; Witherington, *Acts*, 316; Pao, *New Exodus*, 59-60; Pathrapankal, 'Christianity,' 537.

[4] L&N, § 41.35.

[5] BDAG, 692.

[6] Pao, *New Exodus*, 68. Cf. Bruce J. Malina and Jerome H. Neyrey, 'First-Century Personality: Dyadic, Not Individualistic' in Jerome H. Neyrey (ed.), *The Social World of Luke-Acts: Models for Interpretation* (Peabody: Hendrickson Publishers, 1991) 92.

[7] The emphasis on the Word-aspect of ὁδός in 18:25, 26 causes many scholars to exclude these two verses from the technical meaning of ὁδός.

believers' commitment to the life of the community (cf. 2:42-47; 4:32-35). Therefore, ὁδός becomes an identity marker that signifies 'the early Christians over against the claims of the Jews.'[8] Those who devote themselves to the Way often encounter opposition and persecution. Ironically, their undergoing of persecution turns into a powerful living witness to Jesus (e.g. suffering divorces Paul's miracles from magic and marks the divine power within him).

Interestingly, among the words adopted to convey God's will of salvation in Jesus, λόγος appears in the narratives both of Peter and Paul but ῥῆμα is mainly applied to Peter and ὁδός to Paul. Λόγος highlights the essence of God's will/message, ῥῆμα its oral witness and ὁδός its living witness. To make God's will (λόγος) fully known is the main concern throughout the narrative. God's will is intensively disclosed in Peter's speeches (ῥῆμα) then through Paul's commitment to the Way (ὁδός). Through the narrator's use of vocabulary, a development on the mission of the Word emerges. The Word is first elucidated and clarified by Peter in his convincing speeches of theocentric Christology then is carried on and reinforced by Paul in his christocentric ministry of suffering.

---

[8] Pao, *New Exodus*, 65.

APPENDIX 8

Development of Narrative Units
(See Chart on page 215)

Unit One—Acts 1-2
Introduction of God's Promise-Fulfilment of Salvation

Acts 1 serves as an introduction, reminding the disciples of God's and Jesus' promise of the Spirit (the assurance of salvation, 1:4), supplying a sketch for the narrative theme (i.e. the Spirit-empowered disciples are to carry out a mission of witnessing to Jesus, 1:8), introducing the first protagonist Peter (his leading status among the faith community, 1:15) and providing information about the primitive faith community (its unity in prayer, 1:14, 24-26). In Acts 2, the descent of the Spirit fulfils the divine promise and initiates the mission of witnessing about Jesus. In his speech on theocentric Christology, Peter explains God's salvation in the name of Jesus and through the Spirit to the Jewish pilgrims (2:14-39); his witness brings about the first growth of the faith community (2:40-47). As one narrative unit, the relationship between Acts 1 and Acts 2 rests on the promise-fulfilment motif, another expression of the cause-effect relation.

Unit Two—Acts 3-4
Realisation of God's Saving Power in Jesus

Acts 3 reinforces this divine fulfilment. Of the apostles' powerful ministries (2:43), Peter's healing miracle is singled out to evince the healing power in the name of Jesus (3:16) by which the saving power in Jesus is amplified since healing is a concrete expression of salvation (note the narrator's subtle use of σῴζω for healing in 4:9). The cause-effect relationship between Acts 3 and Acts 4 explicates the tri-relation mission pattern. Peter's speech leads to the opposition of the Jewish religious authorities. Yet not only are they impotent to debar the apostles from proclaiming Jesus (4:18-22) but also the faith community keeps growing larger and stronger (4:4, 32-35). Both unit one and two offer a definite elucidation of God's saving will in Jesus and a succinct depiction of the life of the growing faith community. Meanwhile, Barnabas, a positive example of the disciples' sharing of personal property, is introduced to

Appendixes

pave the way for the next unit for contrast and for his later appearance as well (5:36-37; cf. 9:27).[1]

Unit Three—Acts 5:1-6:7
Manifestation of God's Saving Power over His People

Unit three, narrating a testing time for the church, turns to the negative side of the community life and depicts the Jewish leaders' continued persecution increasing in degree. The unit is framed by the problems arising within the community and has the persecution as its centrepiece. Again, the cause-effect relation underlying the tri-relation mission pattern links these three incidents. The sharing aspect of community life tests the purity of the disciples' motives. God's awesome power in the episode of the death of Ananias and Sapphira (the negative examples of property-sharing) and in signs and wonders through the apostles occasions another wave of growth in the church (5:5, 10, 12-16). This incites the Jewish leaders to try to kill the apostles (5:33). Yet the angelic deliverance and Gamaliel's advice rescue them (5:19, 34-40). This brings in further proclamation (5:25, 29-32, 42). As a result of the ongoing growth, an issue of care emerges from the communal life of the community (6:1). While making God's Word their first priority in ministry, the apostles keep the unity of the community by choosing the Seven (note the introduction of Stephen and Philip onto the stage in preparation for their later performance). As God and his Word are highly regarded, the apostles are greatly empowered to vanquish the crises from within and without the church. Each crisis serves as an opportunity to manifest God's saving power which inevitably brings the growth of the Word (6:7). Whereas units one and two expounded God's saving power in Jesus, unit three explicates its manifestation in the church.

Unit Four—Acts 6:8-8:40
The Jews' Persecution in Jerusalem
Kindles the First Stage of Gentile Mission

Unit four presents a very significant tri-relation mission pattern, which expresses the expansion of the Word in three aspects (i.e. the spread of the Word in its witnesses, recipients and in geography). The choosing of the Seven signifies not only the growth of the church in Jerusalem but also the increase of Jesus' witnesses in public. Both Stephen and Philip, like the apostles, are empowered to perform miracles and bear witness to Jesus (6:8-10; 8:5-8). As the

---

[1] This is a common narrative technique of the implied author to introduce characters who are crucial to the later plot. For example, Stephen is first encountered in 6:5, then performs in 6:8-7:60; Philip in 6:5 and 8:4-40; Paul in 7:60; 9:1-30 and 11:25-30; 12:25-28:31; Mark in 12:25; 13:13 and 15:36-41, etc.

body of Jesus' witnesses extends from the apostles to the disciples, the persecutors of the witnesses also extend from the Jewish leaders to the people and so do those persecuted from the apostles to the disciples (8:1). Stephen, taking the lead among the disciples, encounters the persecution of the Hellenistic Jews and becomes the first martyr. This implies the Jews' rejection of the Word in Jerusalem. In the narrative plot, Stephen's martyrdom leads onto the next two narrative units, introducing Saul to the reader for his later performance (7:60; 9:1ff.) and providing the background for the birth of the Antioch church (11:19ff.). More importantly, Stephen's martyrdom kindles the great persecution in Jerusalem which engenders the spread of the Word geographically and to other ethnic groups. In the narrative Philip undertakes the mission and evangelises the Samaritan and the Gentile in Samaria and Judea. This unit delineates the first expansion of God's worldwide mission carried out by the disciples.

Unit Five—Acts 9:1-11:18
God Prepares His People for the Epoch of Gentile Mission

Alongside the first reaching-out, God prepares his people for the next stage of outreach in three ways. Through Jesus God first chooses and converts Saul from a persecutor to a persecuted witness of Jesus and entrusts him with the Gentile mission (9:1-30). Then through divine deeds in Judea, Galilee and Samaria (9:31-43) and, particularly, the Spirit's presence in the Cornelius incident (10:1-48), Peter is prepared and transformed to the divine perspective concerning universal salvation. Later, through Peter, the Jerusalem church is attuned to the divine will for Gentile salvation (11:1-18; 15:7-21). This unit centres on transforming God's people to God's will for Gentile salvation and thus prepares them for the coming epoch of the Gentile mission.

Unit Six—Acts 11:19-12:25
The Jews' Rejection in Judea
Launches the Second Stage of Gentile Mission

In this unit, though the incidents fit into the framework of the tri-relation pattern, its cause-effect relation does not exist between the incidents. The disciples' witness which led to the birth of the Antioch church is a result of the Stephen incident (11:19). Though the killing of James and the intent to kill Peter recalls Stephen's martyrdom which was part of the result of the growth of the Jerusalem church, king Herod's political persecution of the apostles has no connection with the growth of the Antioch church. The two incidents are deployed in one unit with a geographical connection in order to create for the reader an impression of a tri-relation pattern parallel to that in the Stephen incident and guide the reader to the next stage of outreach (see the narrator's concluding note on the growth of God's Word, 12:24; also, the incident of Herod's persecution is framed with Barnabas' and Saul's visit to the Jerusalem church and their return to the Antioch church which is immediately followed by the second stage of Gentile mission). The relationship between the newly-born Antioch church, the citadel of Gentile mission, and the Jerusalem church via Barnabas and Saul connotes that the Jerusalem church has a share in Gentile mission.

Unit Seven—Acts 13-14
Paul's First Missionary Journey in the Region of Galatia

The pattern of the Jews' rejection of the Word leading to another step of outreach is singled out in Paul's three missionary journeys. It justifies, from the narrative, Paul's viewpoint and promotes, from the flow of the narrative plot, the Gentile mission. Correspondingly, the contribution of the tri-relation pattern is shifted from connecting the incidents and/or units, which convey the divine deeds and their interpretation which progressively make recognised God's universal saving will, to introducing each step of God's expanding mission driven by persecution, which makes God's universal Word-mission realised. Introduced onto the narrative stage, the Antioch church sends out the missionaries, Barnabas and Paul, for God's worldwide mission in accordance with the Spirit's directive (13:2). In the narrative, Paul's first missionary journey contains four incidents (13:6-12, 14-52; 14:1-4, 8-23). The connecting thread between the incidents is the persecution of the Jews and the account of the missionary route (13:4-5, 13, 51; 14:5-7, 24-26). The region for this primitive overseas mission is Galatia.

Unit Eight—Acts 15
The Jerusalem Council

This unit provides a full exegesis and application of God's will for universal salvation. Though in unit five the Jerusalem church recognised God's will to save the Gentiles, the question of how to unite the Gentiles with the Jews into one people of God is a practical issue. From James' interpretation of God's works among the Gentiles, reported by Peter and Paul, the church council legitimates that believing Gentiles are also people of God apart from the Law. This declaration maintains a single people of God while embracing the Gentiles.[2] Though not every Jewish believer would fully appreciate the approval (21:20-22), this settlement presents the standpoint of the church as a whole. Significantly, it is a step that separates the believers from Judaism

---

[2] Maloney, *God Had Done*, 157.

(Christians are called a sect by the Jews, 24:14) yet a step that truly opens the door of salvation to the Gentiles.

Unit Nine—Acts 16-20
Paul's Second and Third Missionary Journeys in Macedonia, Achaia and Asia

Similar to his first missionary journey, the mission in Paul's second and third missionary journeys is driven by persecution; his movements from city to city is linked by the route-accounts.[3] Again, the narrative of Paul's westward journey inspires the reader for the expanding mission. Whereas the persecuting force in his first journey is mainly from the Jews, in this stage it comes from both the Jews and the Gentiles. The more the persecution, the more the divine empowerment and the more widespread the mission. In his second missionary journey, Paul is divinely guided to Macedonia (16:6-10) where he preaches in the cities of Philippi, Thessalonica and Berea (16:13-17:12) and is compelled to Achaia by the Jews' persecution (17:13-15) where he preaches in Athens and Corinth (17:16-18:11). In his third missionary journey, the focus of Paul's ministry is in Ephesus (19:1-20). At the end of Paul's overseas evangelism, the narrator concludes that *the Word grows mightily* (19:20). Paul's powerful mission is amplified by the uproar of Ephesus since it causes 'damage to the trade in cult objects which was one source of the prosperity of Ephesus' (19:21-41).[4] The rest of Paul's missionary journey is for the strengthening of the disciples in Macedonia, Greece and Asia (20:1-38). God's mission is spread by Paul's itineracy, either for evangelism or discipleship. Wherever Paul goes, the Word spreads and grows because God is with him.

Unit Ten—Acts 21-28
Paul's Trials unto Rome

This unit highlights the Jews' rejection of God's Word and manifests Jesus' programmatic calling of Paul to be a suffering witness. It presents Paul's full commitment to God's will and reveals how God escorts Paul to Rome in the midst of the Jews' tenacious persecution. That Paul's trials are narrated at length and that the divine protection of him comes in an ordinary way greatly reinforce his suffering.

---

[3] If all incidents are grouped into one segment according to city, then there are nine segments in these two missionary journeys—16:1-5, 13-40; 17:2-9, 11-12, 16-34; 18:2-17; 18:24-19:41; 20:7-12, 17-38. For the route-accounts between cities see 16:6-12; 17:1, 10, 13-15; 18:1, 18-23; 20:1-6, 13-16.

[4] Bimson (ed.), *Illustrated Encyclopaedia of Bible Places*, 130.

BIBLIOGRAPHY

Abrahams, I., *Studies in Pharisaism and the Gospels*, 2nd Series. New York: Ktav Publishing House, 1967.

Abrams, M. H., *A Glossary of Literary Terms*, 7th edn. Fort Worth: Harcourt Brace College Publishers, 1999.

Ådna, Jostein, 'Die Heilige Schrift als Zeuge der Heidenmission. Die Rezeption von Amos 9,11-12 in Apg 15,16-18' in Jostein Ådna, Scott J. Hafemann und Otfried Hofius (eds.), *Evangelium-Schriftauslegung-Kirche*. Göttingen: Vandenhoech & Ruprecht, 1997, 1-23.

Agua, Agustín Del, 'The Lucan Narrative of the "Evangelization of the Kingdom of God": A Contribution to the Unity of Luke-Acts' in J. Verheyden (ed.), *The Unity of Luke-Acts*. BETL 142; Leuven: Leuven University Press, 1999, 639-661.

Aletti, Jean-Noël, *Quand Luc raconte. Le récit comme théologie*. Lire la Bible 115; Paris: Cerf, 1998.

Alexander, Loveday C. A., 'Fact, Fiction and the Genre of Acts.' *NTS* 44 (1998) 380-99.

___. 'Reading Luke-Acts from Back to Front' in J. Verheyden (ed.), *The Unity of Luke-Acts*. BETL 142; Leuven: Leuven University Press, 1999, 419-46.

Allen, E. L., 'Jesus and Moses in the New Testament.' *ExpT* 67 (1955-56) 104-6.

Allen, Leslie C., 'The Old Testament Background of (ΠΡΟ)ʹΟΡΙΖΕΙΝ in the New Testament.' *NTS* 17 (1970-71) 104-8.

Alter, Robert, *The Art of Biblical Narrative*. London: George Allen & Unwin, 1981.

Arnold, Bill T., 'Luke's Characterizing Use of the Old Testament in the Book of Acts' in Ben Witherington, III (ed.), *History, Literature and Society in the Book of Acts*. Cambridge: Cambridge University Press, 1996, 300-23.

Arrington, French L., *The Acts of the Apostles*. Peabody: Hendrickson Publishers, 1988.

Assis, Elie, 'Chiasmus in Biblical Narrative: Rhetoric of Characterization.' *Prooftexts* 22 (2002) 273-304.

Aune, David E., 'Magic in Early Christianity' in *ANRW* II.23.2, 1980, 1507-57.

Avery-Peck, Alan J., 'Miracles in Judaism, the Classical Statement' in Jacob Neusner, Alan J. Avery-Peck and William Scott Green (eds.), *The Encyclopaedia of Judaism*. Leiden: Brill, 2000, 888-97.

Balch, David L., 'The Areopagus Speech: An Appeal to the Stoic Historian Posidonius against Later Stoics and the Epicureans' in David L. Balch, Everett Ferguson and Wayne A. Meeks, *Greeks, Romans, and Christians*. Minneapolis: Fortress Press, 1990, 52-79.

Baltzer, Klaus, *A Commentary on Isaiah 40-55*. Minneapolis: Fortress Press, 2001.

Bammel, Ernst, 'Jewish Activity against Christians in Palestine according to Acts' in Richard Bauckham (ed.), *The Book of Acts in Its Palestinian Setting*. Grand Rapids: Eerdmans, 1995, 357-64.

Banks, Robert, 'The Role of Charismatic and Noncharismatic Factors in Determining Paul's Movements in Acts' in Graham N. Stanton, Bruce W. Longenecker and Stephen C. Barton (eds.), *The Holy Spirit and Christian Origins: Essays in Honor of James D. G. Dunn*. Grand Rapids: Eerdmans, 2004, 117-30.

Barclay, William, 'A Comparison of Paul's Missionary Preaching and Preaching to the Church' in W. Ward Gasque and Ralph P. Martin (eds.), *Apostolic History and the Gospel: Biblical and Historical Essays presented to F. F. Bruce on his 60th Birthday*. Exeter: Paternoster Press, 1970, 165-94.

Barbi, Augusto, 'The Use and Meaning of *(Hoi) Ioudaioi* in Acts' in Gerald O'Collins and Gilberto Marconi (eds.), *Luke and Acts*. Mahwah: Paulist Press, 1991, 123-42.

Bar-Efrat, Shimon, *Narrative Art in the Bible*. JSOTSup 70; Sheffield: Sheffield Academic Press, 2000.

Barrett, Charles Kingsley, 'Paul's Address to the Ephesian Elders' in Jacob Jervell and Wayne A. Meeks (eds.), *God's Christ and His People*. Oslo-Bergen-Tromsö: Universitetsforlaget, 1977, 107-21.

___. *The Acts of the Apostles*, vol. I. ICC; Edinburgh: T & T Clark, 1994.

___. *The Acts of the Apostles*, vol. II. ICC; Edinburgh: T & T Clark, 1998.

___. 'The End of Acts' in Hermann Lichtenberger (ed.), *Geschichte — Tradition — Reflexion: Festschrift für Martin Hengel zum 70. Geburtstag*, vol. 3. Frühes Christentum, Tübingen: J.C.B. Mohr (Paul Siebeck), 1996, 545-55.

Bassler, Jouette M., 'Luke and Paul on Impartiality.' *Bib* 66/4 (1985) 546-52.

Bauckham, Richard, 'James and the Gentiles (Acts 15.13-21)' in Ben Witherington, III (ed.), *History, Literature and Society in the Book of Acts*. Cambridge: Cambridge University Press, 1996, 154-84.

___. 'James and the Jerusalem Church' in Richard Bauckham (ed.), *The Book of Acts in Its Palestinian Setting*. Grand Rapids: Eerdmans, 1995, 415-480.

___. 'Kerygmatic Summaries in the Speeches of Acts' in Ben Witherington, III (ed.), *History, Literature and Society in the Book of Acts*. Cambridge: Cambridge University Press, 1996, 185-217.

Bayer, Hans F., 'The Preaching of Peter in Acts' in I. Howard Marshall and David Peterson (eds.), *Witness to the Gospel*. Grand Rapids: Eerdmans, 1998, 257-74.

Béchard, Dean P., 'Paul Among the Rustics: The Lystran Episode (Acts 14:8-20) and Lucan Apologetic.' *CBQ* 63/1 (2001) 84-101.

___. 'The Theological Significance of Judaea in Luke-Acts' in J. Verheyden (ed.), *The Unity of Luke-Acts*. BETL 142; Leuven: Leuven University Press, 1999, 675-91.

Beck, Norman A., 'The Lukan Writer's Stories about the Call of Paul.' *SBLSP* 22 (1983) 213-18.

Berlin, Adele, *Poetics and Interpretation of Biblical Narrative*. Winona Lake: Eisenbrauns, 1994.

___. 'Point of View in Biblical Narrative' in *A Sense of Text: The Art of Language in the Study of Biblical Literature*. Eisenbrauns: Dropsie College, 1983, 71-113.

Betz, Otto, 'The Kerygma of Luke.' *Int* 22/2 (1968) 131-46.

___. *What Do We Know about Jesus?* London: SCM Press, 1968.

Bibb, Charles Wade, *The Characterization of God in Luke-Acts*. Unpublished PhD dissertation; Southern Baptist Theological Seminary, 1996.

Bietenhard, Hans, '"Ονομα' in *TDNT*, 5:242-81.

Bimson, John J. (ed.), *Illustrated Encyclopaedia of Bible Places*. Leicester: Inter-Varsity Press, 1995.

Bock, Darrell L., *Acts*. Baker Exegetical Commentary on the New Testament; Grand Rapids: Baker Academic, 2007.

___. 'Jesus as Lord in Acts and in the Gospel Message.' *BSac* 143 (1986) 146-54.

___. *Proclamation from Prophecy and Pattern: Lucan Old Testament Christology*. JSNTSup 12; Sheffield: Sheffield Academic Press, 1987.

___. 'Scripture and the Realisation of God's Promises' in I. Howard Marshall and David Peterson (eds.). *Witness to the Gospel: The Theology of Acts*. Grand Rapids: Eerdmans, 1998, 41-62.

Bockmuehl, Markus, 'The Noachide Commandments and New Testament Ethics, With Special Reference to Acts 15 and Pauline Halakha.' *RB* 102 (1995) 72-101.

Boer, Martinus C. de, 'God-Fearers in Luke-Acts' in C. M. Tuckett (ed.), *Luke's Literary Achievement*. JSNTSup 116; Sheffield: Sheffield Academic Press, 1995, 50-71.

Bolt, Peter G., 'Mission and Witness' in I. Howard Marshall and David Peterson (eds.), *Witness to the Gospel*. Grand Rapids: Eerdmans, 1998, 191-214.

Bovon, Francois, 'The God of Luke' in idem, *New Testament Traditions and Apocryphal Narratives*. PTMS 36; Allison Park: Pickwick Publications, 1995, 67-80.

Bowker, J. W., 'Speeches in Acts: A Study in Proem and Yelammedenu Form.' *NTS* 14 (1967-68) 96-111.

Brawley, Robert L., 'Abrahamic Covenant Traditions and the Characterization of God in Luke-Acts' in J. Verheyden (ed.), *The Unity of Luke-Acts*. BETL 142; Leuven: Leuven University Press, 1999, 109-132.

___. *Centering on God: Method and Message in Luke-Acts*. Louisville: Westminster/John Knox Press, 1990.

___. *Luke-Acts and the Jews: Conflict, Apology, and Conciliation*. SBLMS 33; Atlanta: Scholars Press, 1987.

Brooks, James A. and Winbery, Carlton L., *Syntax of New Testament Greek*. Washington: University Press of America, 1979.

Bruce, F. F., *New Testament History*. London: Pickering & Inglis, 1982.

___. *The Acts of the Apostles: Greek Text with Introduction and Commentary*, 3rd edn. Grand Rapids/Leicester: Eerdmans/Apollos, 1990.

___. 'The Holy Spirit in the Acts of the Apostles.' *Int* 27 (1973) 166-83.

Büchsel, Herntrich, 'Κρίνω' in *TDNT* 3:935.

Buckwalter, H. Douglas, *The Character and Purpose of Luke's Christology*. SNTSMS 89; Cambridge: Cambridge University Press, 1996.

___. 'The Divine Saviour' in I. Howard Marshall and David Peterson (eds.), *Witness to the Gospel*. Grand Rapids: Eerdmans, 1998, 107-23.

Burchard, Christoph, 'A Note on Ῥῆμα in Josas 17:1f.; Luke 2:15, 17; Acts 10:37.' *NovT* 27/4 (1985) 281-95.

Burnett, Fred W., 'Characterization and Reader Construction of Characters in the Gospels.' *Semeia* 63 (1993) 3-28.

Cadbury, Henry J., 'The Summaries in Acts.' *Beg*, 5:392-402.

Callan, Terrance, 'The Background of the Apostolic Decree (Acts 15:20, 29; 21:25).' *CBQ* 55/2 (1993) 284-97.

Caragounis, Chrys C., 'Kingdom of God/Kingdom of Heaven' in Joel B. Green, Scot McKnight and I. Howard Marshall (eds.), *Dictionary of Jesus and the Gospels*. Downers Grove/Leicester: InterVarsity Press, 1992, 417-30.

Carroll, John T., 'The Use of Scripture in Acts.' *SBLSP* 29 (1990) 512-28.

Cassidy, Richard J., 'The Non-Roman Opponents of Paul' in Earl Richard (ed.), *New Views on Luke and Acts*. Collegeville: The Liturgical Press, 1990, 150-62.

Charlesworth, James H., 'From Jewish Messianology to Christian Christology Some Caveats and Perspectives' in Jacob Neusner, William S. Green and Ernest Frerichs (eds.), *Judaisms and Their Messiahs at the Turn of the Christian Era*. Cambridge: Cambridge University Press, 1987, 225-64.

___ (ed.), *The Messiah: Developments in Earliest Judaism and Christianity*. Minneapolis : Fortress Press, 1992.

Chatman, Seymour, 'On the Formalist-Structuralist Theory of Character.' *JLS* 1 (1972) 57-79.

___. *Story and Discourse*. Ithaca: Cornell University Press, 1980.

Chen, Diane G., *God as Father in Luke-Acts*. SBL 92; New York: Peter Lang Publishing, 2006.

Cheung, Alex T. M., 'A Narrative Analysis of Acts 14:27-15:35: Literary Shaping in Luke's Account of the Jerusalem Council.' *WTJ* 55 (1993) 137-54.

Childs, Brevard S., *Isaiah*. Louisville: Westminster John Knox Press, 2001.

Clark, Andrew Charles, *Parallel Lives: The Relation of Paul to the Apostles in the Lucan Perspective*. Carlisle: Paternoster Press, 2001.

___. 'The Role of the Apostles' in I. Howard Marshall and David Peterson (eds.), *Witness to the Gospel*. Grand Rapids: Eerdmans, 1998, 169-90.

Co, Maria Anicia, 'The Major Summaries in Acts—Acts 2,42-47; 4,32-35; 5,12-16— Linguistic and Literary Relationship.' *ETL* 68/1 (1992) 49-85.

Collins, John J., 'Jesus and the Messiahs of Israel' in Hermann Lichtenberger (ed.), *Geschichte — Tradition — Reflexion: Festschrift für Martin Hengel zum 70. Geburtstag*, vol. 3. Frühes Christentum, Tübingen: J.C.B. Mohr (Paul Siebeck), 1996, 287-302.

Conzelmann, Hans, *Acts of the Apostles*. Philadelphia: Fortress Press, 1987.

___. 'The Address of Paul on the Areopagus' in Leander E. Keck and J. Louis Martyn (eds.), *Studies in Luke-Acts*. London: SPCK, 1968, 217-30.

___. *The Theology of St Luke*. London: Faber and Faber, 1960.

Cosgrove, Charles H., 'The Divine Δεῖ in Luke-Acts: Investigations into the Lukan Understanding of God's Providence.' *NovT* 26/2 (1984) 168-90.

Croatto, J. Severino, 'Jesus, Prophet Like Elijah, and Prophet-Teacher Like Moses in Luke-Acts.' *JBL* 124/3 (2005) 451-465.

Croy, N. Clayton, 'Hellenistic Philosophies and the Preaching of the Resurrection (Acts 17:18, 32).' *NovT* 39 (1997) 21-39.

Culley, Robert C., *Themes and Variations: A Study of Action in Biblical Narrative*. Atlanta: Scholars Press, 1992.

Culpepper, R. Alan, *Anatomy of the Fourth Gospel*. Philadelphia: Fortress Press, 1983.

Culy, Martin M. and Parsons, Mikeal C., *Acts: A Handbook on the Greek Text*. Waco: Baylor University Press, 2003.

Cunningham, Scott, *'Through Many Tribulations' The Theology of Persecution in Luke-Acts*. JSNTSup 142; Sheffield: Sheffield Academic Press, 1997.

Dahl, Nils A., '"A People for His Name" (Acts xv. 14).' *NTS* (1957-58) 319-27.

___. 'The Story of Abraham in Luke-Acts' in Leander E. Keck and J. Louis Martyn (eds.), *Studies in Luke-Acts*. London: SPCK, 1968, 139-58.

Danove, Paul L., 'The Narrative Function of Mark's Characterization of God.' *NovT* 43/1 (2001) 12-30.

___. *The Rhetoric of Characterization of God, Jesus, and Jesus' Disciples in the Gospel of Mark*. JSNTSup 290; New York: T & T Clark, 2005.

Darr, John A., 'Narrator as Character: Mapping a Reader-Oriented Approach to Narration in Luke-Acts.' *Semeia* 63 (1993) 43-60.

___. *On Character Building: The Reader and the Rhetoric of Characterization in Luke-Acts*. Louisville: Westminster/John knox Press, 1992.

Dawsey, James M., 'Characteristics of Folk-Epic in Acts.' *SBLSP* 28 (1989) 317-25.

Davidson, M. J., 'Angels' in Joel B. Green, Scot McKnight and I. Howard Marshall (eds.), *Dictionary of Jesus and the Gospels*. Downers Grove/ Leicester: InterVarsity Press, 1992, 8-11.

Dibelius, Martin, *Studies in the Acts of the Apostles*, Heinrich Greeven (ed.). London: SCM Press, 1956.

Dillon, Richard J., *From Eye-Witnesses to Ministers of the Word: Tradition and Composition in Luke 24*. AB 82; Rome: Biblical Institute Press, 1978.

Docherty, Thomas, *Reading (Absent) Character: Towards A Theory of Characterization in Fiction*. Oxford: Clarendon Press, 1983.

Downing, F. Gerald, 'Magic and Scepticism in and around the First Christian Century' in Todd E. Klutz (ed.), *Magic in the Biblical World*. JSNTSup 245; London: T & T Clark, 2003, 86-99.

Dunn, James D. G., *The Acts of the Apostles*. Peterborough: Epworth Press, 1996.

___. *The Christ and the Spirit: Christology*, vol. 1. Edinburgh: T & T Clark, 1998.

Dupont, Jacques, 'The Conversion of Paul and Its Influence on His Understanding of Salvation by Faith' in W. Ward Gasque and Ralph P. Martin (eds.), *Apostolic History and the Gospel: Biblical and Historical Essays presented to F. F. Bruce on his 60th Birthday*. Exeter: Paternoster Press, 1970, 176-94.

___. 'Un Peuple d'entre les Nations (Acts 15:14).' *NTS* 31 (1985) 321-35.

Egan, Kieran, 'What is a Plot?' *NLH* 9 (1978) 455-73.

Elbert, Paul, 'An Observation on Luke's Composition and Narrative Style of Questions.' *CBQ* 66 (2004) 98-109.

Evans, C. F., '"Speeches" in Acts' in Albert Descamps and André de Halleux (eds.), *Mélanges Bibliques*. Gembloux: Éditions J. Duculot, 1970, 287-302.

Eynde, Sabine van den, 'Children of the Promise: On the ΔΙΑΘΗΚΗ-Promise to Abraham in Lk 1,72 and Acts 3,25' in J. Verheyden (ed.), *The Unity of Luke-Acts*. BETL 142; Leuven: Leuven University Press, 1999, 469-82.

Feldman, Louis H., 'The Omnipresence of the God-Fearers.' *BAR* 12/5 (1986) 58-69.

Fiensy, David A., 'The Composition of the Jerusalem Church' in Richard Bauckham (ed.), *The Book of Acts in Its Palestinian Setting*. Grand Rapids: Eerdmans, 1995, 213-36.

Finn, Thomas M., 'The God-fearers Reconsidered.' *CBQ* 47 (1985) 75-84.

Fitzmyer, Joseph A., 'David, "Being Therefore a Prophet …".' *CBQ* 34 (1972) 332-39.

___. 'Jewish Christianity in Acts in Light of the Qumran Scrolls' in Leander E. Keck and J. Louis Martyn (eds.), *Studies in Luke-Acts*. London: SPCK, 1968, 233-57.

___. *The Acts of the Apostles*. The Anchor Bible 31; New York: Doubleday, 1998.

___. 'The Role of the Spirit in Luke-Acts' in J. Verheyden (ed.), *The Unity of Luke-Acts*. BETL 142; Leuven: Leuven University Press, 1999, 165-83.

___. 'The Use of the Old Testament in Luke-Acts.' *SBLSP* 31 (1992) 524-38.

Flemming, Dean, 'Contextualizing the Gospel in Athens: Paul's Areopagus Address as a Paradigm for Missionary Communication.' *Missiology* 30/2 (2002) 199-214.

Forster, Edward Morgan, *Aspects of the Novel*. London: Penguin Books, 1990.

Foulkes, Irene W., 'Two Semantic Problems in the Translation of Acts 4.5-20.' *BT* 29/1 (1978) 121-25.
Franklin, Eric, *Christ the Lord: A Study in the Purpose and Theology of Luke-Acts*. London: SPCK, 1975.
___. 'The Ascension and the Eschatology of Luke-Acts.' *SJT* 23 (1970) 191-200.
Frein, Brigid Curtin, 'Narrative Predictions, Old Testament Prophecies and Luke's Sense of Fulfilment.' *NTS* 40 (1994) 22-37.
Funk, Robert W., *The Poetics of Biblical Narrative*. Sonoma: Polebridge Press, 1988.
Gager, John G., 'Jews, Gentiles, and Synagogues in the Book of Acts.' *HTR* 79/1-3 (1986) 91-99.
Garrett, Susan R., *The Demise of the Devil: Magic and the Demonic in Luke's Writings*. Minneapolis: Fortress Press, 1989.
Gärtner, Bertil, *The Areopagus Speech and Natural Revelation*. Lund: Gleerup, 1955.
Garvey, James, 'Characterization in Narrative.' *Poetics* 7 (1978) 63-78.
Gasque, W. Ward, 'A Fruitful Field: Recent Study of the Acts of the Apostles.' *Int* 42 (1988) 117-31.
Gaventa, Beverly Roberts, *From Darkness to Light: Aspects of Conversion in the New Testament*. Philadelphia: Fortress Press, 1986.
___. 'Initiatives Divine and Human in the Lukan Story World' in Graham N. Stanton, Bruce W. Longenecker and Stephen C. Barton (eds.), *The Holy Spirit and Christian Origins: Essays in Honor of James D. G. Dunn*. Grand Rapids: Eerdmans, 2004, 79-89.
___. *The Acts of the Apostles*. Abingdon New Testament Commentaries; Nashville: Abingdon Press, 2003.
___. 'Theology and Ecclesiology in the Miletus Speech: Reflections on Content and Context.' *NTS* 50/1 (2004) 36-52.
___. 'Toward a Theology of Acts.' *Int* 42 (1988) 146-57.
Geller, Stephen A., 'Through Windows and Mirrors into the Bible: History, Literature and Language in the Study of Text' in *A Sense of Text: The Art of Language in the Study of Biblical Literature*. Eisenbrauns: Dropsie College, 1983, 3-40.
Gempf, Conrad, 'Athens, Paul at' in Gerald F. Hawthorne and Ralph P. Martin (eds.), *Dictionary of Paul and His Letters*. Downers Grove/Leicester: Inter-Varsity Press, 1993, 51-54.
___. 'Mission and Misunderstanding: Barnabas and Paul in Lystra (Acts 14:8-20)' in Antony Billington, et al. (eds.), *Mission and Meaning*. Carlisle: Paternoster Press, 1995, 56-69.
___. 'The God-fearers' in Colin J. Hemer, *The Book of Acts in the Setting of Hellenistic History*. Tübingen: J.C.B. Mohr (Paul Siebeck), 1989, 444-47.
Genette, Gérard, *Narrative Discourse: An Essay in Method*. Ithaca: Cornell University Press, 1995.

Giles, K. N., 'Luke's Use of the term Ἐκκλησία with special reference to Acts 20.28 and 9.31.' *NTS* 31 (1985) 135-42.
Gordon, Robert P., 'Targumic Parallels to Acts XIII 18 and Didache XIV 3.' *NovT* 16 (1974) 285-89.
Goulder, M. D., *Type and History in Acts*. London: S.P.C.K., 1964.
Gowler, David B., 'Characterization in Luke: A Socio-Narratological Approach.' *BTB* 19 (1989) 54-62.
Green, Joel B., 'Internal Repetition in Luke-Acts: Contemporary Narratology and Lucan Historiography' in Ben Witherington, III (ed.), *History, Literature and Society in the Book of Acts*. Cambridge: Cambridge University Press, 1996, 283-99.
___. 'Salvation to the End of the Earth: God as Saviour in the Acts of the Apostles' in I. Howard Marshall and David Peterson (eds.), *Witness to the Gospel*. Grand Rapids: Eerdmans, 1998, 83-106.
Green, William Scott, 'Messiah in Judaism: Rethinking the Question' in Jacob Neusner, William S. Green and Ernest Frerichs (eds.), *Judaisms and Their Messiahs at the Turn of the Christian Era*. Cambridge: Cambridge University Press, 1987, 1-13.
Green, William Scott and Silverstain, Jed, 'The Doctrine of the Messiah' in Jacob Neusner and Alan J. Avery-Peck (eds.), *The Blackwell Companion to Judaism*. Malden: Blackwell Publishers, 2000, 247-67.
Guthrie, Donald, *New Testament Theology*. Leicester: Inter-Varsity Press, 1981.
Haenchen, Ernst, *The Acts of the Apostles*. Oxford: Basil Blackwell, 1971.
Hamm, Dennis, 'Acts 3,1-10: The Healing of the Temple Beggar as Lucan Theology.' *Bib* 67 (1986) 305-19.
___. 'Paul's Blindness and Its Healing: Clues to Symbolic Intent (Acts 9, 22 and 26).' *Bib* 71 (1990) 63-72.
___. 'The Tamid Service in Luke-Acts: The Cultic Background behind Luke's Theology of Worship (Luke 1:5-25; 18:9-14; 24:50-53; Acts 3:1; 10:3, 30).' *CBQ* 65/2 (2003) 215-31.
Hansen, Walter, 'The Preaching and Defence of Paul' in I. Howard Marshall and David Peterson (eds.), *Witness to the Gospel*. Grand Rapids: Eerdmans, 1998, 295-324.
Harris, Murray J., *Jesus as God: The New Testament Use of Theos in Reference to Jesus*. Grand Rapids: Baker Book House, 1992.
Hartman, Lars, '"Into the Name of Jesus:" A Suggestion concerning the Earliest Meaning of the Phrase.' *NTS* 20 (1974) 432-40.
Harvey, A. E., *Jesus and the Constraints of History*. London: Duckworth, 1982.
Harvey, W. J., *Character and the Novel*. London: Chatto & Windus, 1970.
Hemer, Colin J., 'The Speeches of Acts II. The Areopagus Address.' *TynB* 40 (1989) 239-59.
Hengel, Martin, *Between Jesus and Paul: Studies in the Earliest History of Christianity*. London: SCM Press, 1983.

___. 'The Geography of Palestine in Acts' in Richard Bauckham (ed.), *The Book of Acts in Its Palestinian Setting*. Grand Rapids: Eerdmans, 1995, 27-78.

Hill, Craig C., 'Acts 6.1-8.4: Division or Diversity?' in Ben Witherington, III (ed.), *History, Literature, and Society in the Book of Acts*. Cambridge: Cambridge University Press, 1996, 129-53.

___. *Hellenists and Hebrews: Reappraising Division within the Earliest Church*. Minneapolis: Fortress Press, 1992.

Hochman, Baruch, *Character in Literature*. London: Cornell University Press, 1985.

Holmås, Geir Otto, '"My House Shall be a House of Prayer": Regarding the Temple as a Place of Prayer in Acts within the Context of Luke's Apologetical Objective.' *JSNT* 27/4 (2005) 393-416.

Horbury, William, *Jewish Messianism and the Cult of Christ*. London: SCM Press, 1998.

Horst, Pieter W. van der, 'A New Altar of a Godfearer?' (*Journal of Jewish Studies* 43 [1992] 32-37) in van der Horst (ed.), *Hellenism – Judaism – Christianity: Essays on Their Interaction*, 2nd edn. Leuven: Peeters Press, 1998, 65-71.

___. 'The Altar of the "Unknown God" in Athens (Acts 17:23) and the Cult of "Unknown Gods" in the Graeco-Roman World' (*Aufstieg und Niedergang der Römischen Welt* II 18, 2, Berlin-New Work 1989, 1426-1456) in P. W. van der Horst (ed.), *Hellenism – Judaism – Christianity: Essays on Their Interaction*, 2nd edn. Leuven: Peeters Press, 1998, 187-220.

House, H. Wayne, *Chronological and Background Charts of the New Testament*. Grand Rapids: Zondervan, 1982.

House, Paul R., 'Suffering and the Purpose of Acts.' *JETS* 33/3 (1990) 317-30.

Hultgren, Arland J., 'Paul's Pre-Christian Persecutions of the Church: Their Purpose, Locale and Nature.' *JBL* 95 (1976) 97-111.

Hur, Ju, *A Dynamic Reading of the Holy Spirit in Luke-Acts*. JSNTSup 211; Sheffield: Sheffield Academic Press, 2001.

Hurtado, Larry W., *Lord Jesus Christ*. Grand Rapids: Eerdmans, 2003.

___. *One God, One Lord*. Edinburgh: T & T Clark, 1998.

Jacobson, Glenn R., 'Paul in Luke-Acts: The Savior Who is Present.' *SBLSP* 22 (1983) 131-46.

Jervell, Jacob, *Die Apostelgeschichte*. Göttingen: Vandenhoech & Ruprecht, 1998.

___. 'The Church of Jews and Godfearers' in Joseph B. Tyson (ed.), *Luke-Acts and the Jewish People*. Minneapolis: Augsburg Publishing House, 1988, 11-20.

___. 'The Future of the Past: Luke's Vision of Salvation History and Its Bearing on His Writing of History' in Ben Witherington, III (ed.), *History, Literature, and Society in the Book of Acts*. Cambridge: Camgridge University Press, 1996, 104-26.

___. *The Theology of the Acts of the Apostles*. Cambridge: Cambridge University Press, 1996.

___. *The Unknown Paul: Essays on Luke-Acts and Early Christian History*. Minneapolis: Augsburg Publishing House, 1984.

Johnson, Andy, 'Resurrection, Ascension and the Developing Portrait of the God of Israel in Acts.' *SJT* 57/2 (2004) 146-62.

Johnson, Luke Timothy, *The Acts of the Apostles*. Collegeville: The Liturgical Press, 1992.

___. *The Literary Function of Possessions in Luke-Acts*. SBLDS 39; Missoula: Scholars Press, 1977.

Kahl, Werner, *New Testament Miracle Stories in Their Religious-Historical Setting*. Göttingen: Vandenhoeck & Ruprecht, 1994.

Kaiser, Walter C., 'The Davidic Promise and the Inclusion of the Gentiles (Amos 9:9-15 and Acts 15:13-18): A Test Passage for Theological Systems.' *JETS* 20/2 (1977) 97-111.

Karris, Robert J., 'Windows and Mirrors: Literary Criticism and Luke's Sitz im Leben.' *SBLSP* 16 (1979) 47-58.

Kaufmann, Yehezkel, *Christianity and Judaism: Two Covenants*. Jerusalem: The Magnes Press, 1988.

Keck, Leander E. and Martyn, J. Louis (eds.), *Studies in Luke-Acts*. London: SPCK, 1968.

Kee, Howard Clark, *Medicine, Miracle and Magic in New Testament Times*. SNTSMS 55; Cambridge: Cambridge University Press, 1986.

___. *Miracle in the Early Christian World: A Study in Sociohistorical Method*. New Haven: Yale University Press, 1983.

___. *To Every Nation under Heaven: The Acts of the Apostles*. Harrisburg: Trinity Press International, 1997.

Kennedy, George A., *New Testament Interpretation through Rhetorical Criticism*. Chapel Hill: The University of North Carolina Press, 1984.

Kesich, Veselin, 'The Apostolic Council at Jerusalem.' *VSQ* 6/3 (1962) 108-17.

Kilgallen, John J., 'Acts 13,38-39: Culmination of Paul's Speech in Pisidia.' *Bib* 69 (1988) 480-506.

___. 'Hostility to Paul in Pisidian Antioch (Acts 13,45)—Why?' *Bib* 84/1 (2003) 1-15.

___. 'Persecution in the Acts of the Apostles' in Gerald O'Collins and Gilberto Marconi (eds.), *Luke and Acts*. Mahwah: Paulist Press, 1991, 143-60.

___. 'The Function of Stephen's Speech (Acts 7:2-53).' *Bib* 70 (1989) 173-193.

___. *The Stephen Speech: A Literary and Redactional Study of Acts 7:2-53*. AB 67; Rome: Biblical Institute Press, 1976.

Klauck, Hans-Josef, *Magic and Paganism in Early Christianity: The World of the Acts of the Apostles*. Edinburgh: T & T Clark, 2000.

Klinghardt, M., *Gesetz und Volk Gottes*. Tübingen: Mohr/Siebeck, 1988.

Klutz, Todd E., *The Exorcism Stories in Luke-Acts: A Sociostylistic Reading*. SNTSMS 129; Cambridge: Cambridge University Press, 2004.

Kodell, Jerome, '"The Word of God Grew" — The Ecclesial Tendency of Λό γος in Acts 6,7; 12,24; 19,20.' *Bib* 55 (1974) 505-19.

Koet, Bart J., 'Divine Communication in Luke-Acts' in J. Verheyden (ed.), *The Unity of Luke-Acts*. BETL 142; Leuven: Leuven University Press, 1999, 745-57.

Kolenkow, Anitra Bingham, 'Relationships between Miracle and Prophecy in the Greco-Roman World and Early Christianity' in *ANRW* II.23.2, 1980, 1470-1506.

Kollmann, Bernd, 'Philippus der Evangelist und die Anfänge der Heidenmission.' *Bib* 81/4 (2000) 551-65.

Kraabel, A. T., 'The Disappearance of the "God-Fearers".' *Numen* 28 (1981) 113-26.

Kurz, William S., 'Effects of Variant Narrators in Acts 10-11.' *NTS* 43 (1997) 570-86.

___. *Reading Luke-Acts: Dynamics of Biblical Narrative*. Louisville: Westminster/John Knox Press, 1993.

Lampe, Geoffrey W. H., *God as Spirit*. Oxford: Clarendon Press, 1977.

___. 'Miracles in the Acts of the Apostles' in C. F. D. Moule (ed.), *Miracles: Cambridge Studies in their Philosophy and History*. London: A. R. Mowbray & Co Ltd, 1965, 165-78.

___. 'The Holy Spirit in the Writings of St. Luke' in D. E. Nineham (ed.), *Studies in the Gospels*. Oxford: Basil Blackwell, 1957, 159-200.

___. 'The Lucan Portrait of Christ.' *NTS* 2 (1955-56) 160-75.

Lanser, Susan Sniader, *The Narrative Act: Point of View in Prose Fiction*. Princeton: Princeton University Press, 1981.

Larkin, William J., 'The Spirit and Jesus "on Mission" in the Postresurrection and Postascension Stages of Salvation History: The Impact of the Pneumatology of Acts on Its Christology' in Amy M. Donaldson and Timothy B. Sailors (eds.), *New Testament Greek and Exegesis: Essays in Honor of Gerald F. Hawthorne*. Grand Rapids: Eerdmans, 2003, 121-39.

Latourelle, René, *The Miracles of Jesus and the Theology of Miracles*. New York/Mahwah: Paulist Press, 1988.

Léonas, Alexis, 'A Note on Acts 3,25-26: The Meaning of Peter's Genesis Quotation.' *ETL* 76/1 (2000) 149-61.

Levinskaya, Irina, *The Book of Acts in Its Diaspora Setting*. Grand Rapids: Eerdmans, 1996.

Litwak, Kenneth Duncan, *Echoes of Scripture in Luke-Acts: Telling the History of God's People Intertextually*. JSNTSup 282; London: T & T Clark, 2005.

___. 'Israel's Prophets Meet Athens' Philosophers: Scriptural Echoes in Acts 17,22-31.' *Bib* 85/2 (2004) 199-216.

Long, William R., 'The Paulusbild in the Trial of Paul in Acts.' *SBLSP* 22 (1983) 87-105.

Longenecker, Bruce W., 'Lukan Aversion to Humps and Hollows: The Case of Acts 11.27-12.25.' *NTS* 50/2 (2004) 185-204.

___. 'Moral Character and Divine Generosity: Acts 13:13-52 and the Narrative Dynamics of Luke-Acts' in Amy M. Donaldson and Timothy B. Sailors (eds.), *New Testament Greek and Exegesis: Essays in Honor of Gerald F. Hawthorne*. Grand Rapids: Eerdmans, 2003, 141-64.

___. 'Rome's Victory and God's Honour: The Jerusalem Temple and the Spirit of God in Lukan Theodicy' in Graham N. Stanton, Bruce W. Longenecker and Stephen C. Barton (eds.), *The Holy Spirit and Christian Origins: Essays in Honor of James D. G. Dunn*. Grand Rapids: Eerdmans, 2004, 90-102.

Longenecker, Richard N., 'The Acts of the Apostles' in Frank E. Gaebelein (ed.), *The Expositor's Bible Commentary*, vol. IX. Grand Rapids: Zondervan, 1981, 207-573.

Lotman, J. M., 'Point of View in a Text.' *NLH* 6 (1975) 339-52.

Lövestam, Evald, *Son and Saviour: A Study of Acts 13, 32-37*. Lund: CWK Gleerup, 1961.

Lyons, William John, 'The Words of Gamaliel (Acts 5.38-39) and the Irony of Indeterminacy.' *JSNT* 68 (1997) 23-49.

MacRae, George W., '"Whom Heaven Must Receive Until the Time": Reflections on the Christology of Act.' *Int* 27 (1973) 151-65.

Maddox, Robert, *The Purpose of Luke-Acts*, John Riches (ed.). Edinburgh: T. & T. Clark, 1982.

Mair, Lucy, *An Introduction to Social Anthropology*, 2nd edn. Oxford: Clarendon Press, 1992.

Malbon, Elizabeth Struthers and Berlin, Adele (eds.), *Characterisation in Biblical Literature. Semeia* 63; Atlanta: Scholars Press, 1993.

Malina, Bruce J. and Neyrey, Jerome H., 'First-Century Personality: Dyadic, Not Individualistic' in Jerome H. Neyrey (ed.), *The Social World of Luke-Acts: Models for Interpretation*. Peabody: Hendrickson Publishers, 1991.

Maloney, Linda M., *'All that God Had Done with Them': The Narration of the Works of God in the Early Christian Community as Described in the Acts of the Apostles*. American University Studies, Series VII, Theology and Religion 91; New York: Peter Lang, 1991.

Marcus, Joel, 'Paul at the Areopagus: Window on the Hellenistic World.' *BTB* 18 (1988) 143-48.

Marguerat, Daniel and Bourquin, Yvan, *How to Read Bible Stories*. London: SCM Press, 1999.

Marguerat, Daniel, 'Magic and Miracle in the Acts of the Apostles' in Todd E. Klutz (ed.), *Magic in the Biblical World: From the Rod of Aaron to the Ring of Solomon*. JSNTSup 245; London: T & T Clark, 2003, 100-24.

___. 'Saul's Conversion (Acts 9, 22, 26) and the Multiplication of Narrative in Acts' in C. M. Tuckett (ed.), *Luke's Literary Achievement*. JSNTSup 116; Sheffield: Sheffield Academic Press, 1995, 127-55.

___. 'The End of Acts (28:16-31) and the Rhetoric of Silence' in Stanley E. Porter and Thomas H. Olbricht (eds.), *Rhetoric and the New Testament: Es-*

says from the 1992 Heidelberg Conference. JSNTSup 90; Sheffield: JSOT Press, 1993, 74-89.

___. *The First Christian Historian*. SNTSMS 121; Cambridge: Cambridge University Press, 2002.

___. 'The God of the Book of Acts' in G.J. Brooke and J.-D. Kaestli (eds.), *Narrativity in Biblical and Related Texts*. BETL 149; Leuven: Leuven University Press, 2000, 159-81.

Marshall, I. Howard, *Luke: Historian and Theologian*. London: Paternoster Press, 1997.

___. *The Acts of the Apostles*. Leicester: Inter-Varsity Press, 1980.

Marshall, I. Howard and Peterson, David (eds.), *Witness to the Gospel: The Theology of Acts*. Grand Rapids: Eerdmans, 1998.

Martens, Karen, '"With a Strong Hand and an Outstretched Arm" The Meaning of the Expression ביד חזקה ובזרוע נטויה.' *SJOT* 15/1 (2001) 123-41.

Martin-Asensio, Gustavo, *Transitivity-Based Foregrounding in the Acts of the Apostles: A Functional-Grammatical Approach to the Lukan Perspective*. JSNTSup 202; SNTG 8; Sheffield: Sheffield Academic Press, 2000.

Mattill, A. J., 'The Jesus-Paul Parallels and the Purpose of Luke-Acts: H. H. Evans Reconsidered.' *NovT* 17/1 (1975) 15-46.

McBride, Denis, *Emmaus:The Gracious Visit of God according to Luke*. Dublin: Dominican Publications, 1991.

McDonald, J. Ian H., 'Rhetorical Issue and Rhetorical Strategy in Luke 10.25-37 and Acts 10.1-11.18' in Stanley E. Porter and Thomas H. Olbricht (eds.), *Rhetoric and the New Testament: Essays from the 1992 Heldelberg Conference*. JSNPSup 90; Sheffield: JSOT Press, 1993, 59-73.

Mealand, D. L., 'The Close of Acts and Its Hellenistic Greek Vocabulary.' *NTS* 36 (1990) 583-97.

Ménard, Jacques, '*Pais Theou* as Messianic Title in the Book of Acts.' *CBQ* 19 (1957) 83-92.

Menzies, Robert P., *Empowered for Witness: The Spirit in Luke-Acts*. JPTSup 6; Sheffield: Sheffield Academic Press, 1994.

___. *The Development of Early Christian Pneumatology: With Special Reference to Luke-Acts*. JSNTSup 54; Sheffield: JSOT Press, 1991.

Merenlahti, Petri and Hakola, Raimo, 'Reconceiving Narrative Criticism' in David Rhoads and Kari Syreeni (eds.), *Characterization in the Gospel: Reconceiving Narrative Criticism*. JSNTSup 184; Sheffield: Sheffield Academic Press, 1999, 13-48.

Metzger, Bruce M., *A Textual Commentary on the Greek New Testament*, 2nd edn. Stuttgart: Deutsche Bibelgesellschaft, 1994.

Michaelis, Wilhelm, 'Κράτος' in *TDNT*, 3:905-10.

Miller, John B. F., *Convinced that God had Called Us: Dreams, Visions, and the Perception of God's Will in Luke-Acts*. Biblical Interpretation Series 85; Leiden: Brill, 2007.

Minear, Paul S., 'Dear Theo: The Kerygmatic Intention and Claim of the Book of Acts.' *Int* 27/2 (1973) 131-50.

___. *To Heal and To Reveal: The Prophetic Vocation according to Luke.* New York: Seabury Press, 1976.

Mittelstadt, Martin William, *The Spirit and Suffering in Luke-Acts: Implications for a Pentecostal Pneumatology.* JPTSup 26; London: T & T Clark, 2004.

Moessner, David P., 'Paul and the Pattern of the Prophet like Moses in Acts.' *SBLSP* 22 (1983) 202-12.

___. '"The Christ Must Suffer": New Light on the Jesus–Peter, Stephen, Paul Parallels in Luke-Acts.' *NovT* 28/3 (1986) 220-56.

___. '"The Christ Must Suffer," The Church Must Suffer: Rethinking the Theology of the Cross in Luke-Acts.' *SBLSP* 29 (1990) 165-95.

___. 'The "Script" of the Scriptures in Acts: Suffering as God's "Plan" (Βουλή) for the World for the "Release of Sins"' in Ben Witherington, III (ed.), *History, Literature, and Society in the Book of Acts.* Cambridge: Cambridge University Press, 1996, 218-50.

Morris, Leon, *New Testament Theology.* Grand Rapids: Zondervan, 1986.

Motyer, J. Alec, *The Prophecy of Isaiah.* Leicester: Inter-Varsity Press, 1993.

Moule, C. F. D., 'Once More, Who Were the Hellenists?' *ExpT* 70 (1958-59) 100-102.

___. 'The Christology of Acts' in Leander E. Keck and J. Louis Martyn (eds.), *Studies in Luke-Acts.* London: SPCK, 1968, 159-85.

___. *The Origin of Christology.* Cambridge: Cambridge University Press, 1977.

Moulton, James Hope, *A Grammar of New Testament Greek, vol. 1: Prolegomena.* Edinburgh: T & T Clark, 1930.

Moulton, James Hope and Howard, Wilbert Francis, *A Grammar of New Testament Greek, vol. 2: Accidence and Word-Formation.* Edinburgh: T. & T. Clark, 1929.

Mowery, Robert L., 'Direct Statements Concerning God's Activity in Acts.' *SBLSP* 29 (1990) 196-211.

___. 'The Divine Hand and the Divine Plan in the Lukan Passion.' *SBLSP* 30 (1991) 558-75.

___. 'God the Father in Luke-Acts' in Earl Richard (ed.), *New Views on Luke and Acts.* Collegevill: The Liturgical Press, 1990.

___. 'Lord, God, and Father, Theological Language in Luke-Acts.' *SBLSP* 34 (1995) 82-101.

Muhlack, Gudrun, *Die Parallelen von Lukas-Evangelium und Apostelgeschichte.* Theologie und Wirklichkeit 8; Frankfurt: Lang, 1979.

Murphy-O'Connor, Jerome, 'Lots of God-Fearers? *Theosebeis* in the Aphrodisias Inscription.' *RB* 99/2 (1992) 418-24.

Nave, Guy D., *The Role and Function of Repentance in Luke-Acts.* SBLAB 4; Atlanta: Society of Biblical Literature, 2002.

Neagoe, Alexandru, *The Trial of the Gospel: An Apologetic Reading of Luke's Trial Narratives*. SNTSMS 116; Cambridge: Cambridge University Press, 2005.

Neirynck, Frans, 'The Miracle Stories in the Acts of the Apostles' in J. Kremer (ed.), *Les Actes des Apôtres: Traditions, rédaction, théologie*. BETL 48; Gembloux: J. Duculot, 1979, 169-213.

Neudorfer, Heinz-Werner, 'The Speech of Stephen' in I. Howard Marshall and David Peterson (eds.), *Witness to the Gospel*. Grand Rapids: Eerdmans, 1998, 275-94.

Neusner, Jacob, Green, William S. and Frerichs, Ernest (eds.), *Judaisms and Their Messiahs at the Turn of the Christian Era*. Cambridge: Cambridge University Press, 1987.

Newman, Barclay M. and Nida, Eugene A., *A Translator's Handbook on the Acts of the Apostles*. London: United Bible Societies, 1972.

Nock, Arthur Darby, 'Paul and the Magus' in *Beg*, 5:164-88.

Nodet, Etienne and Taylor, Justin, *The Origins of Christianity: An Exploration*. Collegeville: The Liturgical Press, 1998.

Nolland, John, 'A Fresh Look at Acts 15.10.' *NTS* 27 (1981) 105-15.

___. 'Salvation-History and Eschatology' in I. Howard Marshall and David Peterson (eds.), *Witness to the Gospel*. Grand Rapids: Eerdmans, 1998, 63-81.

O'Neill, John Cochrane, 'The Use of *Kyrios* in the Book of Acts.' *SJT* 8 (1955) 155-74.

O'Reilly, Leo, *Word and Sign in the Acts of the Apostles: A Study in Lucan Theology*. Analecta Gregoriana 243; Roma: Editrice Pontificia Università Gregoriana, 1987.

Osborne, Grant R., 'Historical Narrative and Truth in the Bible.' *JETS* 48/4 (2005) 673-88.

Oswalt, John N., *The Book of Isaiah Chapters 40-66*. Grand Rapids: Eerdmans, 1998.

O'Toole, Robert F., 'Activity of the Risen Jesus in Luke-Acts.' *Bib* 62 (1981) 471-98.

___. 'Acts 2:30 and the Davidic Covenant of Pentecost.' *JBL* 102/2 (1983) 245-58.

___. 'Parallels between Jesus and His Disciples in Luke-Acts: A Further Study.' *BZ* 27/2 (1983) 195-212.

___. 'Philip and the Ethiopian Eunuch (Acts viii 25-40).' *JSNT* 17 (1983) 25-34.

___. *The Christological Climax of Paul's Defense: Acts 26*. AB 78; Rome: Biblical Institute Press, 1978.

___. 'The Kingdom of God in Luke-Acts' in Wendell Willis (ed.), *The Kingdom of God in 20th-Century Interpretation*. Peabody: Hendrickson Publishers, 1987, 147-62.

___. 'You Did Not Lie to Us (Human Beings) but to God (Acts 5,4c).' *Bib* 76 (1995) 182-209.
Overman, J. Andrew, 'The God-Fearers: Some Neglected Features.' *JSNT* 32 (1988) 17-26.
Owen, H. P., 'The Scope of Natural Revelation in Rom. I and Acts XVII.' *NTS* 5 (1958-59) 133-43.
Pao, David W., *Acts and the Isaianic New Exodus*. Tübingen: Mohr Siebeck, 2000.
Parsons, Mikeal C., *The Departure of Jesus in Luke-Acts: The Ascension Narratives in Context*. JSNTSup 21; Sheffield: JSOT Press, 1987.
Pathrapankal, J., 'Christianity as a "Way" according to the Acts of the Apostles' in J. Kremer (ed.), *Les Actes des Apôtres: Traditions, rédaction, théologie*. BETL 48; Gembloux: J. Duculot, 1979, 533-39.
Pervo, Richard I., *Profit with Delight: The Literary Genre of the Acts of the Apostles*. Philadelphia: Fortress Press, 1987.
Pesch, Rudolf, *Die Apostelgeschichte*, 1. Teilbd. Apg 1-12. Zürich: Benziger Verlag, 1986.
___. *Die Apostelgeschichte*, 2. Teilbd. Apg 13-28. Zürich: Benziger Verlag, 1986.
Petersen, Norman R., *Literary Criticism for New Testament Critics*. Philadelphia: Fortress Press, 1978.
Peterson, David, 'The Motif of Fulfilment and the Purpose of Luke-Acts' in Bruce W. Winter and Andrew D. Clarke (eds.), *The Book of Acts in Its Ancient Literary Setting*. Grand Rapids: Eerdmans, 1993, 83-104.
___. 'The Worship of the New Community' in I. Howard Marshall and David Peterson (eds.), *Witness to the Gospel*. Grand Rapids: Eerdmans, 1998, 373-95.
Phelan, James, *Reading People, Reading Plots: Character, Progression, and the Interpretation of Narrative*. Chicago: University of Chicago Press, 1989.
Pillai, C. A. Joachim, *Apostolic Interpretation of History: A Commentary on Acts 13:16-41*. Hicksville: Exposition Press, 1980.
Plevnik, Joseph, 'The Center of Pauline Theology.' *CBQ* 51/3 (1989) 461-78.
___. 'The Understanding of God at the Basis of Pauline Theology.' *CBQ* 65/4 (2003) 554-67.
Plunkett, Mark A., 'Ethnocentricity and Salvation History in the Cornelius Episode (Acts 10:1-11:18).' *SBLSP* 24 (1985) 465-79.
Polhill, John B., *Acts*. NAC 26; Nashville: Broadman Press, 1992.
Porter, Stanley E., 'Scripture Justifies Mission: The Use of the Old Testament in Luke-Acts' in idem (ed.), *Hearing the Old Testament in the New Testament*. Grand Rapids: Eerdmans, 2006, 104-126.
___. *The Paul of Acts: Essays in Literary Criticism, Rhetoric and Theology*. Tübingen: Mohr Siebeck, 1999.
Powell, Mark Allan, *What Are They Saying about Acts?* New York/Mahwah: Paulist Press, 1991.

___. *What is Narrative Criticism?* Minneapolis: Fortress Press, 1990.

Praeder, Susan Marie, 'Jesus-Paul, Peter-Paul, and Jesus-Peter Parallelisms in Luke-Acts: A History of Reader Response.' *SBLSP* 23 (1984) 23-39.

___. 'Luke-Acts and the Ancient Novel.' *SBLSP* 20 (1981) 269-92.

___. 'Miracle Worker and Missionary: Paul in the Acts of the Apostles.' *SBLSP* 22 (1983) 107-29.

Radl, Walter, *Paulus und Jesus im lukanischen Doppelwerk: Untersuchungen zu Parallelmotiven im Lukasevangelium und in der Apostelgeschichte*. Europäische Hochschulschriften 23/49; Bern/Frankfurt: Lang, 1975.

Rakotoharintsifa, Andrianjatovo, 'Luke and the Internal Divisions in the Early Church' in C. M. Tuckett (ed.), *Luke's Literary Achievement*. JSNTSup 116; Sheffield: Sheffield Academic Press, 1995, 165-77.

Rapske, Brian, 'Opposition to the Plan of God and Persecution' in I. Howard Marshall and David Peterson (eds.), *Witness to the Gospel*. Grand Rapids: Eerdmans, 1998, 235-56.

___. *The Book of Acts and Paul in Roman Roman Custody*. Grand Rapids: Eerdmans, 1994.

Rasmussen, Carl G., *The NIV Atlas of the Bible*. London: Marshall-Pickering, 1989.

Read-Heimerdinger, Jenny, 'Barnabas in Acts: A Study of His Role in the Text of Codex Bezae.' *JSNT* 72 (1998) 23-66.

Reasoner, Mark, 'The Theme of Acts: Institutional History or Divine Necessity in History?' *JBL* 118/4 (1999) 635-59.

Reimer, Andy M., *Miracle and Magic: A Study in the Acts of the Apostles and the Life of Apollonius of Tyana*. JSNTSup 235; Sheffield: Sheffield Academic Press, 2002.

___. 'Virtual Prison Breaks: Non-Escape Narratives and the Definition of "Magic"' in Todd Klutz (ed.), *Magic in the Biblical World*. JSNTSup 245; London: T & T Clark, 2003, 125-39.

Reimer, Ivoni Richter, *Women in the Acts of the Apostles: A Feminist Liberation Perspective*. Minneapolis: Fortress Press, 1995.

Rese, Martin, *Alttestamentliche Motive in der Christologie des Lukas*. Gerd Mohn: Gütersloher Verlagshaus, 1969.

Rhoads, David and Syreeni, Kari (eds.), *Characterizaion in the Gospels: Reconceiving Narrative Criticism*. JSNTSup 184; Sheffield: Sheffield Academic Press, 1999.

Richard, Earl, 'Pentecost as a Recurrent Theme in Luke-Acts,' in Earl Richard (ed.), *New Views on Luke and Acts*. Collegeville: The Liturgical Press, 1990, 133-49.

___. 'The Divine Purpose: The Jews and the Gentile Mission (Acts 15).' *SBLSP* 19 (1980) 267-82.

___. 'The Polemical Character of the Joseph Episode in Acts 7.' *JBL* 98/2 (1979) 255-67.

Rimmon-Kenan, Shlomith, *Narrative Fiction: Contemporary Poetics*, 2nd edn. London: Routledge, 2003.

Robbins, Vernon K., 'By Land and by Sea: A Study in Acts 13-28.' *SBLSP* 10 (1976) 381-96.

Robertson, A. T., *A Grammar of the Greek New Testament in the Light of Historical Research*. Nashville: Broadman Press, 1934.

Rosenblatt, Marie-Eloise, *Paul the Accused: His Portrait in the Acts of the Apostles*. Collegeville: Litergical Press, 1995.

___. 'Recurrent Narration as a Lukan Literary Convention in Acts: Paul's Jerusalem Speech in Acts 22:1-21' in Earl Richard (ed.), *New Views on Luke and Acts*. Collegeville: The Liturgical Press, 1990, 94-105.

Rosner, Brian S., 'Idolatry' in T. Desmond Alexander and Brian S. Rosner (eds.), *New Dictionary of Biblical Theology*. Leicester/Downers Grove: Inter-Varsity Press, 2003, 569-75.

___. 'The Progress of the Word' in I. Howard Marshall and David Peterson (eds.), *Witness to the Gospel*. Grand Rapids: Eerdmans, 1998, 215-33.

Rowe, C. Kavin, 'Luke-Acts and the Imperial Cult: A Way Through the Conundrum?' *JSNT* 27/3 (2005) 279-300.

Salmeier, Michael Allen, *'Ordainer of Times and Seasons': The Portrayal of God in the Book of the Acts of the Apostles*. Unpublished D.Phil. Thesis; Linacre College of Oxford University, 2005.

Sanders, Jack T., *The Jews in Luke-Acts*. London: SCM Press, 1987.

Sandnes, Karl Olav, 'Paul and Socrates: The Aim of Paul's Areopagus Speech.' *JSNT* 50 (1993) 13-26.

Sandt, Huub van de, 'An Explanation of Acts 15:6-21 in the Light of Deuteronomy 4:29-35 (LXX).' *JSNT* 46 (1992) 73-97.

___. 'The Fate of the Gentiles in Joel and Acts 2: An Intertextual Study.' *ETL* 66/1 (1990) 56-77.

___. 'The Presence and Transcendence of God: An Investigation of Acts 7,44-50 in the Light of the LXX.' *ETL* 80/1 (2004) 30-59.

___. 'The Quotations in Acts 13,32-52 as a Reflection of Luke's LXX Interpretation.' *Bib* 75 (1994) 26-58.

Savran, George W., *Telling and Retelling: Quotation in Biblical Narrative*. Bloomington & Indianapolis: Indiana University Press, 1988.

___. 'The Character as Narrator in Biblical Narrative.' *Prooftexts* 5 (1985) 1-17.

Schiffman, Lawrence H., 'The Concept of the Messiah in Second Temple and Rabbinic Literature.' *RE* 84/2 (1987) 235-46.

Schneider, Von Gerhard, *Die Apostelgeschichte*, 2 vols. Freiburg: Herder, 1980.

___. 'Gott und Christus als ΚΥΡΙΟΣ nach der Apostelgeschichte' in Josef Zmijewski and Ernst Nellessen (eds.), *Begegnung mit dem Wort: Festschrift für Heinrich Zimmermann*. Bonn: Hanstein, 1980, 161-74.

___. 'Καθεξῆς' in *EDNT* 2:221.

Scholes, Robert and Kellogg, Robert, *The Nature of Narrative*. New York: Oxford University Press, 1966.

Schubert, Paul, 'The Place of the Areopagus Speech in the Composition of Acts' in J. Coert Rylaarsdam (ed.), *Transitions in Biblical Scholarship*. Chicago: University of Chicago Press, 1968, 235-61.

Schwartz, Daniel R., 'The End of the ΓΗ (Acts 1:8): Beginning or End of the Christian Vision?' *JBL* 105/4 (1986) 669-76.

Schweizer, Eduard, 'Concerning the Speeches in Acts' in Leander E. Keck and J. Louis Martyn (eds.), *Studies in Luke-Acts*. London: SPCK, 1968, 208-16.

___. 'The Concept of the Davidic "Son of God" in Acts and Its Old Testament Background' in Leander E. Keck and J. Louis Martyn (eds.), *Studies in Luke-Acts*. London: SPCK, 1968, 186-93.

Seccombe, David, 'The New People of God' in I. Howard Marshall and David Peterson (eds.), *Witness to the Gospel*. Grand Rapids: Eerdmans, 1998, 349-72.

Segal, Alan F., 'Hellenistic Magic: Some Questions of Definition' in R. van den Broek and M. J. Vermaseren (eds.), *Studies in Gnosticism and Hellenistic Religions*. Leiden: E.J. Brill, 1981, 349-75.

Shauf, Scott, *Theology as History, History as Theology: Paul in Ephesus in Acts 19*. BZNW 133; Berlin: Walter de Gruyter, 2005.

Sheeley, Steven M., *Narrative Asides in Luke-Acts*. JSNTSup 72; Sheffield: Sheffield Academic Press, 1992.

Shelton, James B., *Mighty in Word and Deed: The Role of the Holy Spirit in Luke-Acts*. Peabody: Hendrickson Publishers, 1991.

Shepherd, William H., *The Narrative Function of the Holy Spirit as a Character in Luke-Acts*. SBLDS 147; Atlanta: Scholars Press, 1994.

Sieber, John H., 'The Spirit as the "Promise of My Father" in Luke 24:49' in Daniel Durken (ed.), *Sin, Salvation, and the Spirit*. Collegevill: The Liturgical Press, 1979.

Skinner, Matthew L., *Locating Paul: Places of Custody as Narrative Settings in Acts 21-28*. SBLAB 13; Atlanta: Society of Biblical Literature, 2003.

Soards, Marion L., *The Speeches in Acts: Their Content, Context, and Concerns*. Louisville: Westminster/John Knox Press, 1994.

Spencer, F. Scott, *Acts*. Sheffield: Sheffield Academic Press, 1997.

___. 'Out of Mind, Out of Voice: Slave-Girls and Prophetic Daughters in Luke-Acts.' *BInt* 7/2 (1999) 133-55.

___. *The Portrait of Philip in Acts*. JSNTSup 67; Sheffield: Sheffield Academic Press, 1992.

Spitaler, Peter, 'Διακρίνεσθαι in Mt. 21:21, Mk. 11:23, Acts 10:20, Rom. 4:20, 14:23, Jas. 1:6, and Jude 22—the "Semantic Shift" That Went Unnoticed by Patristic Authors,' *Nov T* 49/1 (2007) 1-39.

Squires, John T., *The Plan of God in Luke-Acts*. SNTSMS 76; Cambridge: Cambridge University Press, 1993.

___. 'The Plan of God in the Acts of the Apostles' in I. Howard Marshall and David Peterson (eds.), *Witness to the Gospel*. Grand Rapids: Eerdmans, 1998, 19-39.

Stählin, G., 'Τὸ πνεῦμα Ἰησοῦ (Apostelgeschichte 16:7)' in Barnabas Lindars and Stephen S. Smalley (eds.), *Christ and Spirit in the New Testament: Studies in Honour of C. F. D. Moule*. Cambridge: Cambridge University Press, 1973, 229-52.

Stanzel, Franz Karl, *A Theory of Narrative*. Cambridge: Cambridge University Press, 1988.

___. 'Teller-Characters and Reflector-Characters in Narrative Theory.' *PT* 2/2 (1981) 5-15.

Stenschke, Christoph W., *Luke's Portrait of Gentiles Prior to Their Coming to Faith*. WUNT 2/108; Tübingen: Mohr Siebeck, 1999.

Sternberg, Meir, *The Poetics of Biblical Narrative: Ideological Literature and Drama of Reading*. Bloomington: Indiana University Press, 1987.

Strauss, Mark L., *The Davidic Messiah in Luke-Acts: The Promise and Its Fulfillment in Lukan Christology*. JSNTSup 110; Sheffield: Sheffield Academic Press, 1995.

Strelan, Rick, *Strange Acts: Studies in the Cultural World of the Acts of the Apostles*. BZNW 126; Berlin: Walter de Gruyter, 2004.

___. 'The Running Prophet,' *NovT* 43/1 (2001) 31-38.

Stronstad, Roger, *The Prophethood of All Believers: A Study in Luke's Charismatic Theology*. JPTSup 16; Sheffield: Sheffield Academic Press, 1999.

Sylva, Dennis D., 'The Meaning and Function of Acts 7:46-50.' *JBL* 106/2 (1987) 261-275.

Tajra, Harry W., *The Trial of St. Paul*. WUNT: Reihe 2, 35; Tübingen: J.C.B. Mohr (Paul Siebeck), 1989.

Talbert, Charles H., *Literary Patterns, Theological Themes, and the Genre of Luke-Acts*. SBLMS 20; Missoula: Scholars Press, 1974.

___. 'Martyrdom in Luke-Acts and the Lukan Social Ethic' in Richard J. Cassidy and Philip J. Scharper (eds.), *Political Issues in Luke-Acts*. Maryknoll: Orbis Books, 1983, 99-110.

___. *Reading Luke-Acts in its Mediterranean Milieu*. Supplements to Novum Testamentum CVII; Leiden: Brill, 2003.

Tannehill, Robert C., 'The Composition of Acts 3-5: Narrative Development and Echo Effect' in *SBLSP* 23 (1984) 217-240.

___. 'The Functions of Peter's Mission Speeches in the Narrative of Acts.' *NTS* 37 (1991) 400-14.

___. *The Narrative Unity of Luke-Acts: A Literary Interpretation*, vol. 1. Philadelphia: Fortress Press, 1986.

___. *The Narrative Unity of Luke-Acts: A Literary Interpretation*, vol. 2. Minneapolis: Fortress Press, 1990.

___. 'Rejection by Jews and Turning to Gentiles: The Pattern of Paul's Mission in Acts' in Joseph B. Tyson (ed.), *Luke-Acts and the Jewish People*. Minneapolis: Augsburg Publishing House, 1988, 83-101.

Tannenbaum, Robert F., 'Jews and God-Fearers in the Holy City of Aphrodite.' *BAR* 12/5 (1986) 54-57.

Taylor, Justin, 'The Jerusalem Decrees (Acts 15:20, 29 and 21:25) and the Incident at Antioch (Gal 2:11-14).' *NTS* 47/3 (2001) 372-80.

Taylor, N. H., 'Stephen, the Temple, and Early Christian Eschatology.' *RB* 110/1 (2003) 62-85.

Thompson, Marianne Meye, '"God's Voice You Have Never Heard, God's Form You Have Never Seen": The Characterization of God in the Gospel of John.' *Semeia* 63 (1993) 177-204.

___. *The Promise of the Father: Jesus and God in the New Testament*. Louisville: Westminster John Knox Press, 2000.

Tolmie, D. Francois, 'The Characterization of God in the Fourth Gospel.' *JSNT* 69 (1998) 57-75.

Tomson, Peter J., 'Gamaliel's Counsel and the Apologetic Strategy of Luke-Acts' in J. Verheyden (ed.), *The Unity of Luke-Acts*. BETL 142; Leuven: Leuven University Press, 1999, 585-604.

Trebilco, Paul R., 'Paul and Silas—"Servants of the Most High God" (Acts 16.16-18).' *JSNT* 36 (1989) 51-73.

Trites, Allison A., *The New Testament Concept of Witness*. SNTSMS 31; Cambridge: Cambridge University Press, 1977.

Tuckett, Christopher M., 'The Christology of Luke-Acts' in J. Verheyden (ed.), *The Unity of Luke-Acts*. BETL 142; Leuven: Leuven University Press, 1999, 133-64.

Turner, Max, 'Jesus and the Spirit in Lucan Perspective.' *TynB* 32 (1981) 3-42.

___. *Power from on High: The Spirit in Israel's Restoration and Witness in Luke-Acts*. JPTSup 9; Sheffield: Sheffield Academic Press, 2000.

___. 'Spirit Endowment in Luke-Acts: Some Linguistic Consideration.' *VoxE* 12 (1981) 45-63.

___. 'The Spirit and Salvation in Luke-Acts' in Graham N. Stanton, Bruce W. Longenecker and Stephen C. Barton (eds.), *The Holy Spirit and Christian Origins: Essays in Honor of James D. G. Dunn*. Grand Rapids: Eerdmans, 2004, 103-16.

___. 'The Spirit of Christ and Christology' in Harold H. Rowdon (ed.), *Christ the Lord: Studies in Christology presented to Donald Guthrie*. Leicester: Inter-Varsity Press, 1982, 168-90.

___. 'The Spirit of Christ and "Divine" Christology' in Joel B. Green and Max Turner (eds.), *Jesus of Nazareth Lord and Christ: Essays on the Historical Jesus and New Testament Christology*. Grand Rapids/Carlisle: Eerdmans/Paternoster Press, 1994, 413-36.

___. 'The Spirit of Prophecy and the Power of Authoritative Preaching in Luke-Acts: A Question of Origins.' *NTS* 38 (1992) 66-88.

___. 'The "Spirit of Prophecy" as the Power of Israel's Restoration and Witness' in I. Howard Marshall and David Peterson (eds.), *Witness to the Gospel*. Grand Rapids: Eerdmans, 1998, 327-48.
Tyson, Joseph B., 'The Emerging Church and the Problem of Authority in Acts.' *Int* 42 (1988) 132-45.
___. 'The Jewish Public in Luke-Acts.' *NTS* 30 (1984) 574-83.
___. 'The Problem of Jewish Rejection in Acts' in Joseph B. Tyson (ed.), *Luke-Acts and the Jewish People: Eight Critical Perspectives*. Minneapolis: Augsburg Publishing House, 1988, 124-37.
Uspensky, Boris, *A Poetics of Composition: The Structure of the Artistic Text and Typology of a Compositional Form*. Valentina Zavarin and Susan Wittig (trans.); Los Angeles: University of California Press, 1983.
Veltman, Fred, 'The Defense Speeches of Paul in Acts' in Charles H. Talbert (ed.), *Perspectives on Luke-Acts*. Edinburgh: T & T Clark, 1978, 243-56.
Verheyden, J. (ed.), *The Unity of Luke-Acts*. BETL 142; Leuven: Leuven University Press, 1999.
Vos, Craig S. de, 'Finding a Charge that Fits: The Accusation against Paul and Silas at Philippi (Acts 16.19-21).' *JSNT* 74 (1999) 51-63.
Wallace, Daniel B., *Greek Grammar Beyond the Basics*. Grand Rapids: Zondervan, 1996.
Walsh, Richard, 'Who Is the Narrator?' *PT* 18/4 (1997) 495-513.
Walton, Steve, *Leadership and Lifestyle: The Portrait of Paul in the Miletus Speech and 1 Thessalonians*. SNTSMS 108; Cambridge: Cambridge University Press, 2000.
___. ' Ὁμοθυμαδόν in Acts: Co-location, Common Action or "Of One Heart and Mind"?' in P. J. Williams, Andrew D. Clarke, Peter M. Head and David Instone-Brewer (eds.), *The New Testament in Its First Century Setting*. Grand Rapids: Eerdmans, 2004, 89-105.
___. 'Where Does the Beginning of Acts End?' in J. Verheyden (ed.), *The Unity of Luke-Acts*. BETL 142; Leuven: Leuven University Press, 1999, 447-67.
Walworth, Allen James, *The Narrator of Acts*. Unpublished PhD dissertation; Southern Baptist Theological Seminary, 1984.
Warrington, Keith, 'Acts and the Healing Narratives: Why?' *Journal of Pentecostal Theology* 14/2 (2006) 189-217.
Watson, Duane F., 'Paul's Speech to the Ephesian Elders (Acts 20.17-38): Epideictic Rhetoric of Farewell' in Duane F. Watson (ed.), *Persuasive Artistry: Studies in New Testament Rhetoric in Honor of George A. Kennedy*. JSNTSup 50; Sheffield: JSOT Press, 1991, 184-208.
Watts, James W., 'The Legal Characterization of God in the Pentateuch.' *HUCA* 67 (1996) 1-14.
Weissenrieder, Annette, *Images of Illness in the Gospel of Luke*. Tübingen: Mohr Siebeck, 2003.
Westcott, Brooke Foss and Hort, Fenton John Anthony, *The New Testament in the Original Greek*. London: Macmillan, 1909.

Westermann, Claus, *Isaiah 40-66*. London: SCM Press, 1969.
Whitsett, Christopher G., 'Son of God, Seed of David: Paul's Messianic Exegesis in Romans 1:3-4.' *JBL* 119/4 (2000) 661-681.
Wiarda, Timothy, 'The Jerusalem Council and the Theological Task.' *JETS* 46/2 (2003) 233-48.
Wilckens, Ulrich, *Die Missionsreden der Apostelgeschichte: Form- und Traditionsgeschichtliche Untersuchungen*. Neukirchen-Vluyn: Neukirchener Verlag des Erziehungsvereins, 1963.
Wilcox, Max, 'The "God-Fearers" in Acts — A Reconsideration.' *JSNT* 13 (1981) 102-22.
___. 'The Promise of the "Seed" in the New Testament and the Targumim.' *JSNT* 5 (1979) 2-20.
Wilk, Florian, 'Apg 10,1-11,18 im Licht der lukanischen Erzählung vom Wirken Jesu' in J. Verheyden (ed.), *The Unity of Luke-Acts*. BETL 142; Leuven: Leuven University Press, 1999, 605-17.
Willimon, William H., '"Eyewitnesses and Ministers of the Word": Preaching in Acts.' *Int* 42 (1988) 158-70.
Wilson, Stephen G., *Luke and Law*. SNTSMS 50; Cambridge: Cambridge University, 1983.
___. *The Gentiles and the Gentile Mission in Luke-Acts*. SNTSMS 23; Cambridge: Cambridge University, 1973.
Wilson, Walter T., 'Urban Legends: Acts 10:1-11:18 and the Strategies of Greco-Roman Fundation Narratives.' *JBL* 120/1 (2001) 77-99.
Winter, Bruce W., 'On Introducing Gods to Athens: An Alternative Reading of Acts 17:18-20.' *TynB* 47/1 (1996) 71-90.
Witherington III, Ben, 'Salvation and Health in Christian Antiquity: The Soteriology of Luke-Acts in Its First Century Setting' in I. Howard Marshall and David Peterson (eds.), *Witness to the Gospel*. Grand Rapids: Eerdmans, 1998, 145-66.
___. *The Acts of the Apostles: A Socio-Rhetorical Commentary*. Grand Rapids: Eerdmans, 1998.
Witherup, Ronald D., 'Cornelius Over and Over and Over again: "Functional Redundancy" in the Acts of the Apostles.' *JSNT* 49 (1993) 45-66.
___. 'Functional Redundancy in the Acts of the Apostles: A Case Study.' *JSNT* 48 (1992) 67-86.
Wordelman, Amy L., 'Cultural Divides and Dual Realities: A Greco-Roman Context for Acts 14' in Todd Penner and Caroline Vander Stichele (eds.), *Contextualizing Acts: Lukan Narrative and Greco-Roman Discourse*. SBLSS 20; Atlanta: Society of Biblical Literature, 2003, 205-32.
Wright, N. T., *Jesus and the Victory of God*. London: SPCK, 1996.
Zehnle, Richard F., *Peter's Pentecost Discourse*. Nashville: Abingdon Press, 1971.
Ziesler, J. A., 'The Name of Jesus in the Acts of the Apostles.' *JSNT* 4 (1979) 28-41.
Zweck, Dean, 'The *Exordium* of the Areopagus Speech.' *NTS* 35 (1989) 94-103.

Author Index

Abrahams, I. 53.
Abrams, M.H. 5, 9, 10, 14, 193.
Ådna, J. 166.
Agua, A.D. 197.
Aletti, J-N. 20, 22, 29, 32, 36, 183, 185, 208, 227.
Alexander, L.C.A. 1, 142, 219.
Allen, E.L. 211.
Allen, L.C. 102.
Alter, R. 11, 51, 132, 179, 181, 205.
Arnold, B.T. 53, 211.
Arrington, F.L. 1.
Assis, E. 11.
Aune, D.E. 136, 137, 139.
Avery-Peck, A.J. 79.
Balch, D.L. 110, 113, 114.
Baltzer, K. 102.
Bammel, E. 185.
Banks, R. 206.
Barclay, W. 151.
Barbi, A. 185.
Bar-Efrat, S. 4, 5, 6, 9, 10, 13, 14, 44, 81, 84, 98, 157, 191, 204, 214, 217, 218.
Barrett, C.K. 24, 25, 26, 27, 29, 46, 47, 48, 49, 50, 51, 52, 55, 56, 57, 58, 59, 60, 61, 62, 64, 65, 66, 67, 68, 69, 72, 74, 75, 76, 84, 87, 88, 89, 97, 98, 100, 101, 104, 105, 107, 108, 109, 110, 112, 113, 114, 115, 117, 120, 121, 122, 124, 126, 127, 128, 129, 130, 156, 162, 168, 169, 176, 180, 195, 196, 197, 202, 217, 232, 233.
Bassler, J.M. 77.
Bauckham, R. 87, 89, 91, 166, 167, 173, 185.
Bauer, W., Danker, F.W., Arndt, W.F., & Gingrich, F.W. (BDAG) 21, 48, 52, 59, 62, 75, 100, 102, 106, 109, 112, 113, 114, 115, 117, 122, 125, 129, 156, 158, 161, 164, 165, 171, 177, 178, 194, 196, 198, 202, 233, 234, 240, 242.
Bayer, H.F. 71.
Béchard, D.P. 107, 217.
Beck, N.A. 127.
Berlin, A. 5, 6, 7, 8, 9, 10, 11, 106, 108, 155.

Betz, O. 98, 211.
Bibb, C.W. 191, 224, 226.
Bietenhard, H. 57, 64.
Bimson, J.J. 219, 248.
Bock, D.L. 3, 51, 53, 56, 60, 63, 102, 103.
Bockmuehl, M. 167.
Boer, M.C. 175.
Bolt, P.G. 21, 204.
Bovon, F. 228.
Bowker, J.W. 94.
Brawley, R.L. 2, 99, 185, 197, 219, 222.
Brooks, J.A. & Winbery, C.L. 22, 114.
Bruce, F.F. 38, 46, 47, 50, 52, 60, 61, 62, 65, 69, 79, 87, 96, 97, 98, 100, 101, 105, 106, 108, 109, 110, 113, 114, 115, 118, 121, 122, 126, 129, 164, 165, 166, 177, 181, 183, 197, 217.
Büchsel, H. 79.
Buckwalter, H.D. 27, 29, 32, 33, 35, 50, 51, 52, 56, 57, 62, 70.
Burchard, C. 242.
Burnett, F.W. 224.
Cadbury, H.J. 193.
Callan, T. 167.
Caragounis, C.C. 197.
Carroll, J.T. 211.
Cassidy, R.J. 148, 210.
Charlesworth, J.H. 49, 60, 62.
Chatman, S. 8, 12, 14, 195.
Chen, D.G. 97, 101, 222.
Cheung, A.T.M. 146.
Childs, B.S. 102.
Clark, A.C. 84, 105, 172, 173, 208, 220.
Co, M.A. 193.
Collins, J.J. 62.
Conzelmann, H. 32, 59, 108, 110, 114, 115, 155, 158, 164, 165.
Cosgrove, C.H. 207, 208, 222.
Croatto, J.S. 211.
Croy, N.C. 118.
Culley, R.C. 192.
Culpepper, R.A. 4.
Culy, M.M. & Parsons, M.C. 23, 28, 109, 130.
Cunningham, S. 85, 148, 184, 185, 186, 209, 211, 212, 213.

Dahl, N.A. 99, 165.
Danove, P.L. 2, 192.
Darr, J.A. 6, 11, 13, 14, 183, 191, 199, 224.
Dawsey, J.M. 1.
Davidson, M.J. 40.
Dibelius, M. 110, 112, 113, 114.
Dillon, R.J. 209, 213.
Docherty, T. 11, 219.
Downing, F.G. 89, 136.
Dunn, J.D.G. 21, 23, 26, 27, 28, 29, 39, 47, 51, 52, 59, 61, 65, 66, 69, 70, 72, 76, 81, 83, 96, 106, 164, 166, 168, 176, 181, 195, 237.
Dupont, J. 135, 165, 173.
Egan, K. 9.
Elbert, P. 181.
Evans, C.F. 32.
Eynde, S. 61.
Feldman, L.H. 232.
Fiensy, D.A. 87.
Finn, T.M. 232.
Fitzmyer, J.A. 37, 49, 197, 205, 217, 242.
Flemming, D. 109.
Forster, E.M. 5, 6, 9, 204.
Foulkes, I.W. 57, 64.
Franklin, E. 32, 56, 62.
Frein, B.C. 211.
Funk, R.W. 11, 192.
Gager, J.G. 232.
Garrett, S.R. 136, 138, 141, 146.
Gärtner, B. 110, 112, 113, 114, 115, 118.
Garvey, J. 6, 7.
Gasque, W.W. 135, 151, 222.
Gaventa, B.R. 43, 81, 121, 125, 126, 130, 138, 139, 140, 172, 180, 207, 208, 210, 221, 227, 242.
Geller, S.A. 2.
Gempf, C. 115, 139, 232.
Genette, G. 3.
Giles, K.N. 121.
Gordon, R.P. 97.
Goulder, M.D. 208.
Gowler, D.B. 193.
Green, J.B. 35, 65, 70, 208, 222.
Green, W.S. 82.

Green, W.S. & Silverstain, J. 82, 83.
Guthrie, D. 21, 33, 35, 36, 38.
Haenchen, E. 24, 26, 27, 29, 47, 51, 56, 57, 58, 59, 61, 64, 65, 66, 69, 75, 81, 87, 96, 97, 103, 106, 108, 110, 112, 113, 114, 115, 119, 126, 130, 138, 154, 155, 164, 196, 217, 227, 240, 242.
Hamm, D. 126, 159, 211.
Hansen, W. 93, 94, 132.
Harris, M.J. 119, 121.
Hartman, L. 50.
Harvey, A.E. 101.
Harvey, W.J. 5, 6, 7, 82, 84, 144, 153, 175.
Hemer, C.J. 115, 232.
Hengel, M. 87, 89.
Hill, C.C. 87, 159, 170.
Hochman, B. 6.
Holmås, G.O. 176.
Horbury, W. 50.
Horst, P.W. 108, 116.
House, H.W. 217.
House, P.R. 213.
Hultgren, A.J. 127.
Hur, J. 25, 26, 28, 29, 31, 35, 36, 37, 38, 41.
Hurtado, L.W. 35, 52, 56.
Jacobson, G.R. 209.
Jervell, J. 34, 38, 39, 42, 50, 65, 93, 121, 136, 142, 150, 175, 205, 219, 225.
Johnson, A. 86, 225.
Johnson, L.T. 23, 27, 33, 47, 49, 56, 59, 70, 86, 96, 97, 98, 100, 106, 108, 109, 113, 121, 125, 129, 130, 138, 139, 157, 164, 165, 166, 170, 172, 178, 181, 183, 185, 196, 209, 211, 240.
Kahl, W. 139.
Kaiser, W.C. 166.
Karris, R.J. 2.
Kaufmann, Y. 90.
Kee, H.C. 136, 137, 208.
Kennedy, G.A. 95, 109, 116.
Kesich, V. 76, 174.

Kilgallen, J.J. 102, 104, 147, 148, 160, 185, 209.
Klauck, H.-J. 137, 138, 139, 140, 141, 142, 146, 152.
Klinghardt, M. 167.
Klutz, T.E. 82, 89, 140, 141.
Kodell, J. 201, 203.
Koet, B.J. 207.
Kolenkow, A.B. 211.
Kollmann, B. 154, 172.
Kraabel, A.T. 232.
Kurz, W.S. 4, 124, 132, 177.
Lampe, G.W.H. 32, 38, 206.
Lanser, S.S. 12.
Larkin, W.J. 33, 43, 66.
Latourelle, R. 91, 207.
Léonas, A. 61.
Levinskaya, I. 179.
Litwak, K.D. 110, 211.
Long, W.R. 125.
Longenecker, B.W. 183, 185, 217.
Longenecker, R.N. 101.
Lotman, J.M. 8, 222.
Louw, J.P. & Nida, E.A. (L&N) 21, 23, 24, 27, 36, 47, 48, 49, 50, 52, 58, 59, 62, 64, 66, 69, 70, 72, 74, 75, 80, 87, 96, 97, 100, 102, 103, 104, 106, 109, 111, 112, 113, 115, 117, 121, 125, 127, 129, 156, 157, 158, 161, 165, 167, 177, 178, 179, 194, 196, 197, 201, 202, 233, 234, 240, 242.
Lövestam, E. 94, 98, 99, 100, 101, 102, 103.
Lyons, W.J. 183.
MacRae, G.W. 32.
Maddox, R. 1, 32, 197.
Mair, L. 137.
Malina, B.J. & Neyrey, J.H. 242.
Maloney, L.M. 71, 81, 247.
Marcus, J. 118.
Marguerat, D. & Bourquin, Y. 4, 5, 9.
Marguerat, D. 26, 31, 38, 39, 41, 42, 45, 63, 82, 83, 91, 94, 124, 125, 127, 129, 130, 131, 136, 138, 139, 140, 180, 182, 183, 206, 219, 222, 227, 228.

Marshall, I.H. 23, 24, 25, 26, 27, 32, 33, 34, 35, 46, 47, 49, 50, 51, 56, 57, 58, 59, 61, 62, 64, 65, 69, 70, 72, 75, 76, 84, 87, 88, 89, 93, 97, 98, 99, 100, 101, 102, 104, 106, 107, 108, 110, 112, 113, 114, 115, 117, 121, 122, 124, 126, 128, 130, 138, 156, 157, 159, 164, 165, 166, 168, 173, 194, 195, 196, 197, 205, 217, 240, 242.
Martens, K. 97.
Martin-Asensio, G. 48, 53, 93, 98, 100, 118, 160, 170.
Mattill, A.J. 206, 207, 209.
McBride, D. 78, 79, 86, 90, 185, 211.
Mealand, D.L. 219.
Ménard, J. 56.
Menzies, R.P. 38, 211.
Merenlahti, P. & Hakola, R. 4.
Metzger, Bruce M. 69, 97, 101, 121.
Michaelis, W. 202.
Miller, J.B.F. 135.
Minear, P.S. 202, 212, 213.
Mittelstadt, M.W. 160, 170, 212, 213, 216.
Moessner, D.P. 207, 209, 210, 212.
Morris, L. 34, 35.
Motyer, J.A. 102.
Moule, C.F.D. 32, 87, 101.
Moulton, J.H. 114.
Moulton, J.H. & Howard, W.F. 97.
Mowery, R.L. 29, 33, 34, 36, 41, 76.
Muhlack, G. 207.
Murphy-O'Connor, J. 232.
Nave, G.D. 183.
Neagoe, A. 132, 142, 159, 160, 169, 216.
Neirynck, F. 208.
Neudorfer, H.-W. 161.
Newman, B.M. & Nida, E.A. 23, 97, 114, 121.
Nock, A.D. 137.
Nodet, E. & Taylor, J. 167.
Nolland, J. 76, 197.
O'Neill, J.C. 27, 53.

O'Reilly, L. 38, 79, 83, 91, 201, 202, 203, 208, 210, 211.
Osborne, G.R. 199.
Oswalt, J.N. 102.
O'Toole, R.F. 25, 32, 49, 66, 87, 131, 172, 180, 197, 207, 209, 211.
Overman, J.A. 232.
Owen, H.P. 113, 115.
Pao, D.W. 202, 203, 242, 243.
Parsons, M.C. 22, 23, 28, 32, 109, 130, 219.
Pathrapankal, J. 242.
Pervo, R.I. 1.
Pesch, R. 23, 28, 87, 101, 113, 138.
Petersen, N.R. 2.
Peterson, D. 57, 63, 197, 205.
Phelan, J. 13, 192.
Pillai, C.A. 94, 95, 98, 99.
Plevnik, J. 131.
Plunkett, M.A. 75, 205.
Polhill, J.B. 21, 22, 28, 85, 109, 110, 114, 115, 116, 118, 122, 138, 140, 142, 143, 146, 196, 197, 242.
Porter, S.E. 53, 93, 94, 95, 96, 107, 108, 113, 115, 123.
Powell, M.A. 2, 3, 5, 10, 32, 34, 35, 185, 205.
Praeder, S.M. 1, 207.
Radl, W. 207, 209, 212.
Rakotoharintsifa, A. 184.
Rapske, B. 71, 140, 185, 209.
Rasmussen, C.G. 172.
Read-Heimerdinger, J. 172.
Reasoner, M. 2, 205, 210, 211.
Reimer, A.M. 82, 137, 140.
Reimer, I.R. 181.
Rese, M. 101.
Richard, E. 32, 157, 215.
Rimmon-Kenan, S. 11.
Robbins, V.K. 218.
Robertson, A.T. 106, 240.
Rosenblatt, M.-E. 124, 219.
Rosner, B.S. 117, 193, 197, 219.
Rowe, C.K. 70.
Salmeier, M.A. 35, 39, 52, 197, 205, 207, 218, 226.
Sanders, J.T. 93, 175, 185.
Sandnes, K.O. 117.
Sandt, H. 51, 101, 102, 103, 104, 162, 166.
Savran, G.W. 4, 192, 195.
Schiffman, L.H. 49, 58, 60, 62.
Schneider, Von G. 25, 27, 29, 74, 81, 83, 87, 93, 102, 121, 123, 237.
Scholes, R. & Kellogg, R. 4, 7, 9, 30, 44, 205, 219.
Schubert, P. 109, 111, 114, 117, 118.
Schwartz, D.R. 22.
Schweizer, E. 47, 93, 101.
Seccombe, D. 162.
Segal, A.F. 136, 137.
Shauf, S. 141, 207.
Sheeley, S.M. 191, 213, 222.
Shelton, J.B. 36.
Shepherd, W.H. 11, 31, 74, 191, 119, 224.
Sieber, J.H. 39.
Skinner, M.L. 209, 229.
Soards, M.L. 21, 22, 47, 61, 64, 65, 66, 69, 71, 74, 95, 96, 98, 99, 100, 101, 114, 116, 117, 122, 123, 129, 131, 158, 164, 165, 166, 169, 170, 222, 241.
Spencer, F.S. 21, 140, 155, 170, 171, 172, 180, 197.
Spitaler, P. 24.
Squires, J.T. 35, 96, 103, 104, 117, 129, 157, 205.
Stählin, G. 38.
Stanzel, F.K. 5, 10.
Stenschke, C.W. 175.
Sternberg, M. 19, 42, 43, 124, 132, 177, 193, 204, 221, 227.
Strauss, M.L. 94, 101, 102, 103, 146, 147.
Strelan, R. 139, 141, 142, 170.
Stronstad, R. 212.
Sylva, D.D. 159, 160, 162.
Tajra, H.W. 127, 130, 132.
Talbert, C.H. 191, 208, 210, 213, 215, 217, 219.
Tannehill, R.C. 48, 65, 77, 84, 85, 88, 147, 160, 166, 170, 172, 180, 191, 214.

Author Index

Tannenbaum, R.F. 232.
Taylor, J. 167.
Taylor, N.H. 159.
Thompson, M.M. 2, 194.
Tolmie, D.F. 2.
Tomson, P.J. 183.
Trebilco, P.R. 140.
Trites, A.A. 42, 210.
Tuckett, C.M. 34, 51, 69.
Turner, M. 29, 32, 36, 37, 38, 39, 52, 203, 211.
Tyson, J.B. 147, 185, 228.
Uspensky, B. 7, 8.
Veltman, F. 93.
Vos, C.S. 138, 141.
Wallace, D.B. 46, 48, 69, 109, 111, 114, 116, 119, 120, 183, 196, 240.
Walsh, R. 4, 5, 10.
Walton, S. 121, 156, 205.
Walworth, A.J. 4, 6, 14, 184, 185, 191.
Warrington, K. 32.
Watson, D.F. 119, 121.
Watts, J.W. 2.
Weissenrieder, A. 142.
Westcott, B.F. & Hort, F.J.A. 101.
Westermann, C. 102.
Whitsett, C.G. 98, 101, 102.
Wiarda, T. 167.
Wilckens, U. 99.
Wilcox, M. 61, 98, 232.
Wilk, F. 75, 224.
Willimon, W.H. 202.
Wilson, S.G. 105, 110, 111, 112, 113, 115, 116, 117, 125, 126, 151, 167.
Wilson, W.T. 179.
Winter, B.W. 109, 115.
Witherington III, B. 2, 47, 49, 57, 58, 65, 72, 95, 100, 105, 108, 109, 112, 113, 114, 121, 122, 126, 130, 131, 146, 149, 155, 157, 162, 164, 166, 172, 181, 196, 216, 222, 242.
Witherup, R.D. 124, 131, 132, 177, 179, 205.
Wordelman, A.L. 139.
Wright, N.T. 50.

Zehnle, R.F. 45, 47, 51, 54.
Ziesler, J.A. 32, 35, 50, 57.
Zweck, D. 108, 109, 111, 116.

Scripture Index

Genesis (Gen)
1-2   195
1:1   110
1:22   201
1:27   113
1:28   113, 201
2:4   110
2:13   172
3:9-19   19
6:13-7:4   19
8:17   201
9:1   201
9:1-17   19
9:7   201
12:1-3   19
12:3   61
14:19   110, 195
14:22   110
15:13-14   161
16:7   26
17:10-13   162
17:20   201
21:17   26
22:11   26
22:18   61
28:3   201
28:12   26
28:15   23
35:11   201
47:27   201
48:4   201

Exodus (Exod)
1:7   201
3:2   26
3:12   23, 162
3:4-22   19
5:1   23
6:7   23
12:3   161
14:19   26
19:5   23, 165
19:18   168
20:1-17   19
20:11   110, 195
25-30   161
31:17   110
32:34   26

Leviticus (Lev)
17-18   167
23:29   60
26:9   201

Numbers (Num)
22:31   26

Deuteronomy (Deut)
7:6   165
14:2   165
18   60
18:15   60
18:18-19   60
23:1   180
31:23   23

Joshua (Josh)
1:9   23

Judges (Jdg)
2:1   26
3:9   98
3:15   98
5:23   26
13:6   26

1 Samuel (1 Sam)
8:7-9   19
8:20   98
10:18   19
13:14   98

2 Samuel (2 Sam)
7   102
7:12-16   49, 98, 101
24:16   26

1 Kings (1 Kgs)
17:8-9   170
18-21   170
18:46   170
19:7   26

2 Kings (2 Kgs)
1:3   26
2:11   170
19:15   110, 195

1 Chronicles (1 Chr)
21:12   26

2 Chronicles (2 Chr)
2:12   110

Nehemiah (Neh)
9:6   110, 195

Psalms (Ps)
2   98
2:1-2   156
2:7   101, 103
2:34   51
16:8-11   49, 51
16:10   102, 103
42:11   80
43:5   80
89   102
89:21   98
107:20   69
110:1   50, 51
115:15   110
118:22   64
121:2   110
124:8   110
134:3   110
135:4-6   195
146:6   110

Isaiah (Isa)
6:1-10   125
6:4   168
35   79
37:16   110, 195
37:36   26
41:10   23
42:5   110
43:21   165
43-45   19
44:28   98
45:18   110
45:21   166
51:13   110
52:7   69
52:13   56
53:7-8   180

55:3   102, 103
56:3-5   180
66:1-2   162

Jeremiah (Jer)
1:8   23
2:5   106
3:16   201
7:23   23
11:4   23
12:15   166
23:3   201
24:7   23
31:31-37   19
31:35   195
39:17   110

Ezekiel (Ezek)
11:20   23
30:3   58
36:22-37   19
36:28   23

Daniel (Dan)
4:37   110

Hosea (Hos)
11:1-11   19

Joel (Joel)
1:15   58
2:23   48
2:25-28   51
2:28-31   19
2:28-32   47, 51
2:31-32   58

Amos (Amos)
5:25-27   161
8:10   58
9:11-12   166
9:11-15   58

Micah (Mic)
4:1   58
4:6   58

Habakkuk (Hab)
1:5   104
1:5-11   104

Zephaniah (Zeph)
1:14-18   58

Zechariah (Zech)
1:12   26
3:6   26
10:6-12   19

Malachi (Mal)
3:1   19
4:1-3   58

Matthew (Mt)
3:11   21
3:17   19
7:21   231
10:32   231
10:33   231
11:2-5   79
12:50   231
15:13   231
16:17   231
17:5   19
18:10   231
18:19   231
18:35   231
21:25-26   99

Mark (Mk)
1:8   21
1:11   19
9:7   19
11:30-32   99
14:33   44

Luke (Lk)
1:11   52
1:35   32
1:74   162
2:49   231
3:16   21
3:22   19, 32
4:1   32
4:14-15   32
7:20-22   79
8:51   44
9:20   44
9:22   209
9:26   231
9:28   44
9:33   44
9:35   19

10:1   154
10:17-19   141
10:21   231
10:22   231
11:2   231
11:13   21, 231
12:30   231
12:32   231
12:41   45
13:33   209
19:28   45
17:25   209
17:33   121
20:4-6   99
20:42   52
21:12-19   210, 212
22:8   45
22:22   114
22:29   231
22:30   45, 79
22:31   45
22:37   209
22:42   231
22:69   52
23:33   52
23:34   231
23:46   231
24:7   209
24:26   209
24:34   45
24:44   209, 210
24:49   21, 231

John (Jn)
2:16   231
5:17   231
5:43   231
6:32   231
6:40   231
7:31   79
12:28   19
20:30-31   79

Acts
1   168,
1-2   215, 244
1-5   168
1-7   237
1-12   214, 215
1:1   32
1:1-2   31
1:1-3   193, 197, 235

Scripture Index

1:1-6:7 215
1:2 37
1:3 21, 22, 28, 31, 197, 221
1:3-11 100
1:4 21, 79, 194, 231, 244
1:4-5 32, 231
1:4-8 20, 30, 31, 41
1:4-15 235
1:5 21, 73
1:5-6 79
1:6 22, 238
1:7 21, 22, 194, 231
1:8 21, 22, 25, 28, 32, 36, 39, 70, 73, 171, 206, 219, 231, 244
1:9-11 78, 86
1:10 26, 27
1:10-11 28
1:11 28, 33, 40, 41
1:12 192
1:14 86, 184, 244
1:15 244
1:15-26 86
1:16 23, 36, 212, 241
1:16-22 235
1:16-32 45
1:21 86, 238
1:21-22 79, 105
1:22 49
1:23 172
1:23-26 235
1:24 194, 238, 240
1:24-25 155
1:24-26 244
2 63, 65, 222
2-3 82, 83
2-4 37, 45
2:1-4 36, 41, 86
2:1-11 37, 73
2:1-13 235
2:2-3 36
2:2-4 32
2:4 32, 36, 78, 206, 208
2:5 113, 175, 233
2:5-13 82
2:6-12 91
2:11 52, 168, 195, 198
2:12-13 82
2:14 46, 47, 65, 86, 242
2:14-15 45, 47
2:14-36 46, 79, 83, 168, 196, 235
2:14-39 92, 244
2:14-40 45
2:14-41 86
2:15 46
2:15-16 46
2:16 46
2:16-21 36, 47, 79
2:16-36 45
2:17 48, 67, 77
2:17-18 37, 46, 47, 53
2:17-21 46, 51, 52
2:18 48
2:19-20 46
2:20-21 51, 194
2:20 58, 236, 238
2:21 46, 47, 50, 51, 52, 53, 60, 67, 69, 71, 77, 78, 80, 85, 91, 92, 210, 236, 238
2:22 33, 34, 46, 47, 48, 53, 211
2:22-24 46
2:22-32 48
2:22-36 52
2:22-37 80
2:23 34, 46, 48, 53, 114, 198, 211
2:23-24 48, 77
2:24 33, 34, 46, 47, 48, 49, 101
2:25 51, 52, 236, 238
2:25-28 47, 49
2:27 49, 51, 53, 102
2:29 47
2:29-31 47, 49, 51
2:30 49
2:30-31 34, 49, 101, 210
2:30-36 77
2:31 49, 51
2:31-33 54
2:32 33, 34, 47, 48, 49, 53, 66, 78, 101
2:33 32, 33, 35, 36, 38, 41, 46, 50, 52, 53, 66, 194, 195, 231, 236
2:33-35 50
2:33-36 50
2:34 51, 52, 53, 101, 236, 238
2:34-35 50
2:36 29, 34, 46, 48, 50, 51, 52, 53, 60, 69, 70, 78, 80, 85, 91, 158, 208, 222, 238
2:36-39 35
2:37 46, 47, 66
2:37-39 66, 83
2:37-42 235
2:38 35, 50, 51, 59, 66, 70, 71, 75, 77, 78, 85, 91, 92, 104
2:38-42 180
2:39 29, 36, 51, 66, 67, 74, 92, 194, 236, 238
2:40 50
2:40-47 244
2:41 46, 52, 63, 83, 86, 151
2:41-42 83
2:42 86, 168
2:42-43 207
2:42-47 168, 235, 243
2:43 52, 79, 82, 86, 168, 207, 244
2:43-47 11, 193
2:44 168, 184
2:46 168
2:47 52, 83, 84, 168, 185, 236, 238
3 2, 63, 65, 244
3-4 215, 244
3-5 216
3:1-10 82, 168, 207
3:1-11 235
3:1-26 86, 168
3:5 57
3:6 57, 208
3:6-7 91
3:7 79
3:10 36
3:10-11 82
3:11-12 65
3:12 54, 55, 82
3:12-18 54
3:12-26 45, 54, 79, 92, 196, 235
3:13 33, 34, 55, 56, 61, 62, 194, 195, 202, 203, 236
3:13-14 54, 55, 56
3:13-15 55
3:13-18 55

3:14 49, 55, 56, 62, 126
3:14-15 77
3:15 27, 33, 34, 55, 56, 61, 62, 66, 78, 80, 104, 175
3:15-16 54, 56
3:16 22, 35, 55, 56, 64, 66, 77, 83, 85, 92, 168, 244
3:17 55, 57, 61
3:17-18 55, 57
3:18 33, 34, 37, 57, 60, 61, 77, 210, 212
3:19 58, 59, 66, 71
3:19-21 55, 58, 59, 60
3:19-24 55, 58
3:19-26 54
3:20 34, 59, 236, 238
3:20-21 33, 59
3:20-22 194
3:21 58, 59, 60, 61, 69
3:21-24 77
3:22 61, 101, 210, 236, 238
3:22-23 60, 71
3:22-24 55, 58, 60, 78
3:23 60
3:24 37, 58, 60, 61
3:25 34, 48, 55, 58, 60, 61, 67, 69, 77, 92
3:25-26 71
3:26 33, 34, 43, 48, 55, 58, 60, 61, 66, 69, 74, 91, 101, 202
3:30-31 65
4 244
4:1-2 185
4:1-3 64, 84
4:1-7 235
4:2 64
4:4 54, 63, 83, 86, 151, 196, 200, 244
4:5-6 64
4:5-7 82
4:5-35 151
4:7 64
4:7-8 65
4:8 36, 38, 41, 85, 203, 206, 208
4:8-12 32, 45, 63, 64, 86, 92, 235
4:9 84, 216, 244
4:9-12 196
4:9-14 84
4:10 33, 34, 64, 77, 85
4:11 64
4:11-12 64
4:12 35, 60, 64, 67, 71, 77, 78, 79, 80, 85, 91, 92, 203
4:13-23 235
4:16 209
4:16-17 84
4:17 216
4:18 85
4:18-19 33
4:18-22 244
4:19 65, 80, 85, 92
4:19-20 45, 63, 64, 65, 84, 92
4:20 65, 66
4:21 84, 203
4:23-31 86
4:24 109, 110, 156, 157, 158, 184, 194, 195, 236
4:24-25 156
4:24-28 156
4;24-30 155, 168
4:25 36, 37, 156, 157, 211, 236
4:25-26 156, 157, 158
4:25-28 156
4:26 194, 238
4:27 33, 62, 156, 157
4:27-28 156, 157, 158
4:28 156, 157, 158
4:29 29, 156, 157, 158, 194, 196, 200, 236, 238
4:29-30 138, 156
4:30 33, 35, 156, 157, 158
4:31 36, 38, 41, 157, 196, 200, 203
4:32 168, 184
4:32-35 11, 168, 193, 235, 243, 244
4:33 29, 86, 168, 211, 238
4:35 86
4:36-37 154, 173, 192
4:37 11, 86
5:1-10 207
5:1-11 80, 86, 184, 216
5:1-28 235

5:1-6:7 215, 245
5:3 36, 221
5:3-4 39, 45, 86
5:5 79, 86, 87, 245
5:8-9 45
5:9 27, 238
5:10 79, 86, 245
5:11 87
5:12 65, 168
5:12-13 83, 207
5:12-14 87
5:12-16 67, 80, 82, 86, 168, 207, 245
5:12-18 84
5:13 82
5:14 83, 84, 168, 237, 238
5:15-16 79, 83, 207
5:16 207
5:17 36, 185
5:17-18 65, 185
5:17-28 82
5:19 27, 40, 79, 80, 194, 206, 209, 236, 238, 245
5:19-20 31, 41, 85, 216
5:19-26 151
5:20 26, 27, 28, 104, 175, 242
5:25 245
5:27-28 85
5:27-32 185
5:28 65, 85, 216
5:28-29 33
5:29 12, 28, 65, 80, 85, 86, 92
5:29-31 80
5:29-32 45, 63, 65, 85, 86, 92, 196, 235, 245
5:30 33, 34, 65, 66, 67, 194, 195, 236
5:30-32 66, 77
5:31 33, 34, 39, 52, 61, 66, 67, 71, 74, 78, 80, 91, 104, 222
5:31-32 75
5:32 37, 38, 66, 67, 78, 203, 242
5:33 85, 185, 245
5:33-34 235
5:34-40 85, 245
5:35-39 183, 235
5:36-37 245

Scripture Index

5:38 183
5:38-39 85
5:39 183
5:40-42 235
5:41 209
5:41-42 85
5:42 245
6-8 80, 216
6-9 216
6:1 87, 245
6:1-2 169
6:1-4 184
6:1-6 216, 235
6:1-7 219
6:2 86, 196, 202
6:2-4 45
6:2-6 87
6:3 36, 38, 170, 208
6:4 196, 202
6:5 36, 38, 154, 170, 206, 245
6:5-6 170
6:7 11, 87, 193, 196, 201, 202, 203, 216, 235, 245
6:8 36, 38
6:8-10 207, 245
6:8-15 169, 235
6:8-7:60 245
6:8-8:3 203
6:8-8:40 215, 245
6:8-12:25 215
6:9-14 185
6:10 36, 38, 41
6:11 159, 242
6:12 185
6:13 159, 161, 242
6:14 159, 161
7 88, 96
7:1 235
7:2 169, 236, 240
7:2-5 159
7:2-8 159, 160
7:2-53 155, 159, 235
7:3 161
7:4 159, 161
7:5 162
7:6 97
7:6-8 159
7:7 159, 161, 162
7:8 162
7:9 160

7:9-10 159
7:9-16 159
7:9-36 160
7:11-16 159
7:17 163
7:17-22 159
7:17-43 159
7:18 102
7:23-29 159, 164
7:25-28 160
7:30 40
7:30-31 26
7:30-37 159
7:31 236, 238
7:31-32 194
7:32 194, 236
7:32-33 161
7:33 238
7:33-34 194
7:34 163
7:35 40, 48
7:37 101, 102, 210
7:38-43 159
7:39-40 160
7:40 160
7:41-43 160
7:41-50 159
7:42 161
7:42-43 161
7:43 161, 195
7:44 161
7:44-45 161
7:44-47 159
7:44-53 159
7:45 162
7:46 162
7:48 159, 163, 194, 236
7:48-50 159, 162, 169, 194
7:49 238
7:51 39, 160, 163
7:51-53 159, 161
7:52 126, 169, 211
7:52-53 163
7:53 40
7:54-60 235
7:55 33, 36, 38, 41, 52, 195
7:55-56 21, 32, 169
7:56 35, 52, 195
7:57-60 185
7:59 238

7:60 144, 170, 238, 245, 246
8 88, 171, 218, 235
8-11 80, 127, 216
8-12 217
8:1 88, 169, 170, 171, 185, 192, 216, 246
8:1-40 218, 235
8:2 175, 233
8:3 144
8:4 169, 196, 200
8:4-40 245
8:5 170, 192, 211
8:5-7 207
8:5-8 88, 245
8:5-13 170, 171
8:6 170
8:6-7 170
8:9-13 171
8:9-24 136
8:10 195
8:10-11 171
8:12 31, 155, 197, 221
8:14 86, 196, 200
8:14-17 80, 88
8;14-24 171
8:15 36
8:15-17 37
8:16 238
8:17 36, 37, 41, 208
8:18-23 88
8:20 198
8:20-23 45
8:22 237, 238
8:24 237, 238
8:25 89, 196, 200, 237, 238
8:26 24, 26, 27, 28, 40, 41, 170, 171, 172, 194, 206, 236, 238
8:26-39 88
8:26-40 170
8:27 170, 180
8:27-28 175, 179
8:29 24, 36, 37, 38, 40, 41, 73, 170, 171, 180, 206
8:30 172
8:31 180
8:34 180
8:35 180
8:36 180

8:39 27, 36, 41, 171, 180, 194, 206, 236, 238
8:39-40 170
8:40 154, 172
9 105, 124, 125, 127, 216, 237
9:1 129, 238, 246
9:1-2 144
9:1-30 235, 245, 246
9:1-11:18 215, 246
9:2 198, 242
9:3 22, 125
9:3-6 32
9:3-18 135
9:3-19 144
9:4-16 20, 22, 31, 35
9:5 212, 238
9:6 23, 130
9:10 126, 238
9:10-16 33, 172
9:10-17 154
9:11 238
9:13 238
9:14-16 41
9:15 22, 25, 33, 146, 147, 148, 238
9:15-16 22, 149, 206, 209
9:16 33, 144, 151, 210
9:17 22, 36, 38, 154, 238
9:18 22
9:19 145
9:20 34, 145, 154, 192, 198, 211
9:22 38, 145
9:22-24 147
9:22-25 151
9:23-24 145
9:23-25 144
9:26-28 145
9:27 173, 238, 245
9:28 238
9:29 145, 147, 151, 185
9:30 145
9:31 41, 89, 193, 235, 237, 238
9:31-43 246
9:32-34 207
9:32-42 80, 207
9:32-43 89, 235
9:34 45, 79

9:35 89, 106, 237, 238, 240
9:36-41 207
9:40 45, 79
9:42 89, 238
10 72, 246
10-11 206
10:1-33 235
10:2 68, 175, 176, 233, 234
10:3 25, 27, 39, 89, 195
10:3-6 40, 41, 206
10:4 29, 176, 177, 178, 237
10:4-6 26, 28, 29
10:5 177, 179
10:7 175, 233
10:7-8 179
10:9-16 172, 206
10:9-20 91
10:9-43 80
10:9-48 89
10:10-16 72
10:11 72
10:11-16 67, 79
10:13 89
10:13-14 89
10:13-15 28
10:14 45, 72, 237
10:15 72, 75, 89
10:17 72, 179
10:19 36, 73
10:19-20 24, 28, 31, 37, 38, 39, 40, 41, 72, 79, 89, 206
10:20 25, 29, 43, 72
10:22 175, 176, 233
10:23 70
10:25-48 177
10:26-29 45
10:28 67, 68
10:29 179
10:30 27, 177
10:30-31 68
10:30-33 68
10:30-48 89
10:31 177, 178
10:31-33 67, 73
10:32 177, 179
10:33 179, 194, 238
10:34 28, 43, 68, 74, 236
10:34-35 68, 77, 92

10:34-43 45, 67, 68, 79, 92, 179, 196, 235
10:35 68, 113, 175, 177, 233
10:36 33, 34, 43, 68, 69, 70, 75, 196, 200, 202, 238
10:36-38 211
10:36-43 35, 68
10:37 68, 69, 242
10:38 33, 34, 37, 43, 68, 69, 202, 211
10:39 68, 70, 78, 86
10:40 33, 34, 68, 70
10:40-41 104
10:41 68, 70
10:41-42 78
10:42 22, 34, 68, 70, 71, 77, 78, 114, 117
10:42-43 68
10:43 68, 70, 71, 74, 75, 77, 78, 91, 92, 104, 210
10:43-44 75
10:44 36, 37, 71, 73, 196, 200, 203, 206, 242
10:44-45 41
10:44-48 73, 80, 235
10:45 37
10:47 36, 37, 45, 77
10:47-48 179
11 72, 74, 77, 154, 179, 216
11:1 196, 200
11:1-3 235
11:1-18 80, 90, 184, 246
11:2-3 71
11:4-17 67, 74, 235
11:5 72
11:5-10 72
11:5-12 71
11:5-15 77
11:5-17 45, 71, 78, 92
11:5-18 80
11:8 72
11:9 72, 75
11:11-12 72
11:12 25, 38, 72, 73
11:12-18 40
11:13 73
11:13-14 71, 73
11:14 73, 242,
11:15 36, 37, 73, 77,

Scripture Index

11:15-17 71, 73, 77
11:16 24, 73, 238
11:17 28, 74, 75, 77, 78, 91, 92, 198, 238
11:18 71, 74, 203, 237
11:18-30 235
11:19 196, 200, 246
11:19-20 216
11:19-21 169
11:19-26 170, 218
11:19-12:25 215, 246
11:20 238
11:20-21 25
11:20-22 169
11:21 106, 170, 237, 238, 240
11:22 105, 173
11:23 198, 237, 238
11:24 11, 36, 38, 237, 238
11:25-26 145, 173
11:25-30 173, 245
11:27-30 216
11:27-12:25 217
11:28 36, 38, 41
11:29 173, 204, 217
11:30 145, 173, 204, 217
12 2, 45, 216, 217, 237
12:1 173
12:1-2 186
12:1-6 80, 87
12:1-23 235
12:3 217
12:3-17 86
12:4-11 27
12:5 81, 88, 173
12:6 27
12:7 81, 194, 238
12:7-8 26, 27, 28
12:7-11 31, 40, 41, 79, 206
12:7-23 81
12:9 27
12:11 45, 81, 194, 217, 238
12:12 154
12:15 88
12:15-16 27
12:17 27, 154, 173, 194, 238
12:19 204, 217
12:22 195

12:23 40, 41, 81, 186, 194, 238
12:24 11, 88, 193, 196, 201, 202, 203, 216, 235, 247
12:25 154, 204, 217, 235, 245
12:25-15:39 173
12:25-28:31 245
13 96, 154, 222, 233
13-14 215, 247
13-19 217
13-28 214, 215, 217
13:1 145
13:1-15 235
13:2 24, 25, 31, 36, 37, 38, 41, 73, 135, 151, 206, 217, 239, 247
13:2-3 145, 155
13:3 105, 173
13:4-5 247
13:5 137, 140, 147, 196, 200
13:6 138
13:6-11 136, 147
13:6-12 137, 207, 247
13:7 140, 196, 200
13:7-8 138
13:7-12 149
13:9 36, 138, 146, 206, 208
13:9-11 38
13:10 138, 139, 237, 239
13:11 136, 138, 194, 239
13:11-12 20
13:12 136, 138, 140, 151, 239
13:13 245, 247
13:14 147
13:14-52 247
13:15 94
13:16 94, 95, 99, 175, 232, 233
13:16-17 96
13:16-25 95, 96
13:16-41 93, 94, 95, 133, 150, 196, 235
13:17 96, 97, 195, 236
13:17-20 95, 98
13:17-22 96, 104
13:17-23 99, 198
13:17-25 94, 95

13:18 96, 97
13:19 97
13:20 96, 97
13:20-22 95, 98
13:21 96
13:22 96, 98, 103
13:23 34, 35, 39, 98, 100, 101, 103, 133, 222
13:23-25 95, 96, 104
13:24-25 99
13:26 27, 35, 43, 94, 95, 99, 101, 103, 140, 175, 196, 198, 200, 232, 233
13:26-37 94, 95, 96, 99, 104
13:26-40 99
13:27 100
13:27-28 99, 100
13:27-29 95, 210
13:27-31 99
13:27-37 95, 99
13:29 100
13:30 33, 34, 100
13:30-31 95
13:31 99, 100, 103
13:32 99, 100, 103
13:32-33 101
13:32-37 95, 99, 103
13:33 33, 34, 100, 101, 103
13:33-34 100
13:33-35 100
13:34 33, 34, 103
13:34-35 103
13:34-37 102
13:35 100, 102, 103
13:36 103
13:36-37 102
13:37 33, 34, 99
13:38 94, 104
13:38-41 94, 95, 96, 104
13:38-39 95, 104
13:39 22, 104, 133, 135
13:40 94
13:40-41 95
13:42 242
13:42-52 235
13:43 99, 147, 151, 175, 198, 232, 233
13:44 140, 196, 200, 237, 239
13:45 36, 149, 185

13:46 94, 104, 140, 196, 200, 213
13:46-47 104, 147, 150
13:46-48 138, 139
13:46-51 147
13:47 194, 236, 239
13:48 140, 148, 196, 202, 203, 237, 239
13:49 140, 196, 200, 237, 239
13:50 147, 148, 151, 175, 186, 233
13:51 151, 247
13:52 36, 38, 41, 146
14 2, 118
14:1 138, 146, 147, 151
14:1-3 138
14:1-4 247
14:1-13 235
14:2 148, 186
14:3 122, 136, 138, 140, 143, 194, 196, 239
14:4 105
14:5 139, 148, 151
14:5-7 247
14:8-10 136, 138, 207
14:8-13 105, 136
14:8-18 150
14:8-23 247
14:9 139
14:9-10 139
14:11 151
14:11-13 106, 148
14:11-18 139
14:14 105
14:14-17 235
14:15 105, 106, 107, 110, 112, 195, 236, 240
14:15-17 93, 105, 106, 133, 150, 155
14:16-17 107
14:17 112
14:18-28 235
14:19 139, 148, 151, 185, 186
14:21 146
14:21-23 146
14:22 93, 197
14:23 203, 239
14:24-26 247
14:25 196, 200
14:26 198

14:26-28 146
14:27 205
15 69, 74, 77, 81, 88, 146, 179, 215, 216, 247
15:1-2 74, 164
15:1-5 147
15:1-6 235
15:1-11 80
15:1-21 146, 184
15:1-29 148
15:4 205
15:5 74, 75
15:6 74
15:6-11 90
15:7 25, 41, 75, 164, 196, 200, 203
15:7-8 166
15:7-9 75, 165, 173
15:7-11 39, 45, 67, 74, 75, 78, 92, 164, 235
15:7-12 166
15:7-21 246
15:8 28, 37, 38, 75, 76, 236, 240
15:8-9 77
15:8-11 92
15:9 72, 75, 76, 78, 165, 166
15:10 75, 76, 77, 78, 92, 167
15:11 75, 76, 77, 91, 203, 239
15:12 151, 173, 205
15:12-13 235
15:13 155, 173
15:13-18 164
15:13-21 155, 164
15:14 23, 164, 165, 198, 203
15:14-18 39, 173
15:14-21 76, 235
15:15 166
15:16-17 166, 241
15:17 194, 236, 239, 241
15:17-18 166
15:18 241
15:19 106, 167, 240
15:19-21 77, 164
15:20 167
15:22 154, 235
15:23-29 235
15:25-26 146

15:26 239
15:28 39
15:30-41 235
15:35 196, 200, 237, 239
15:35-40 146
15:36 196, 200, 237, 239
15:36-41 245
15:40 154, 237, 239
15:41 146
16-20 215, 248
16:1-3 154
16:1-4 235
16:1-5 248
16:3 154
16:4-5 146
16:5 193, 235
16:6 41, 196, 200, 203
16:6-7 25, 36, 38, 73, 151, 206, 217
16:6-10 135, 181, 248
16:6-12 248
16:6-40 235
16:7 33, 41
16:9 206
16:9-10 207
16:10 205
16:10-17 218
16:13 181
16:13-40 248
16:13-17:12 248
16:14 57, 175, 181, 233, 237, 239
16:15 146, 148, 239
16:16 237
16:16-18 136, 139, 207
16:16-24 136
16:17 140, 194, 195
16:18 35, 93, 140, 141, 208
16:19 149, 237
16:19-23 148
16:19-24 140, 149, 186
16:22 151
16:22-23 149, 151
16:25-26 136
16:25-30 140
16:25-34 136, 149, 207
16:26 209
16:30 140, 237
16:31 93, 140, 141, 239
16:31-34 146
16:32 196, 200, 237, 239

Scripture Index

16:34 140, 148
16:35 149
16:40 182
17 2
17:1 248
17:1-3 147
17:1-21 235
17:2-3 213
17:2-9 248
17:3 23, 141, 192, 211, 233
17:4 147, 148, 151, 175, 233
17:5 148, 149, 186
17:4-7 141
17:5 151, 185
17:7 149
17:10 146, 147, 248
17:11 196, 200
17:11-12 248
17:12 146, 147
17:13 148, 186, 196, 200
17:13-15 147, 248
17:14 146
17:16 107, 116, 117
17:16-34 248
17:16-18:11 248
17:17 175, 232, 233
17:17-18 107
17:18 107, 109, 117, 118, 141
17:18-19 136
17:18-21 148
17:19-20 107
17:22-23 108
17:22-24 108
17:22-31 93, 107, 133, 150, 235
17:23 109, 111, 116
17:24 108, 109, 111, 112, 116, 118, 194, 195, 236, 239
17:24-25 111, 112
17:24-27 111
17:24-29 108, 109, 111
17:24-31 111
17:25 108, 109, 111, 112, 115, 116, 118
17:25-26 115
17:25-28 21
17:26 112, 113, 115
17:26-27 108, 111
17:26-29 111, 112

17:27 113, 114, 116
17:28 113, 115
17:28-29 108, 111, 116
17:29 113, 116, 118, 195
17:30 108, 133
17:30-31 108, 111, 112, 116
17:31 33, 34, 108, 113, 114, 117, 118, 133
17:32 118, 134
17:32-34 235
17:34 146, 148
18 2, 235, 237
18-20 237
18:1 248
18:1-28 235
18:2-17 248
18:5 141, 196, 202
18:6 147, 213
18:6-7 93
18:7 175, 233
18:8 22, 146, 151, 239
18:9 23, 33, 239
18:10 29, 33
18:9-10 20, 22, 28, 33, 35, 41, 43, 135, 151, 152, 206, 217
18:11 43, 196, 200
18:12 151
18:12-17 149, 186
18:13 233
18:14-15 149, 152
18:18-23 248
18:19 147
18:22 146
18:23 146
18:24-28 218
18:24-19:41 248
18:25 239, 242
18:26 198, 242
19:1-6 141
19:1-7 89
19:1-19 235
19:1-20 248
19:2 36
19:2-4 93
19:2-6 37
19:5 239
19:6 36, 41, 141, 208
19:8 31, 147, 197, 221
19:8-9 147
19:8-10 141

19:9 146, 198, 204, 242
19:10 196, 200, 237, 239
19:10-12 136, 207
19:10-20 151
19:11 205
19:11-12 136, 141, 143, 207
19:13 141, 147, 204, 239
19:13-17 136
19:15-17 141
19:17 239
19:18 142
19:18-20 142
19:19 141
19:20 11, 193, 196, 201, 202, 218, 235, 239, 248
19:21-41 235, 248
19:23 198, 242
19:23-32 148
19:23-34 204
19:23-41 149
19:24-27 149, 186
19:27 233
19:29 36
19:29-31 151
19:30-31 146
19:35-41 186
19:37 149
19:40 149
20 204, 222
20-28 218
20:1-2 118
20:1-6 248
20:1-17 235
20:1-35 146
20:1-38 248
20:5-15 218
20:7-12 248
20:9-12 136, 141, 207
20:10 141
20:13-16 248
20:17 118
20:17-38 248
20:18-19 119
20:18-21 119
20:18-24 120
20:18-27 123
20:18-35 93, 118, 133, 150, 235
20:19 120, 122, 239
20:20-21 119

20:21 121, 122, 123, 131, 133, 134, 239
20:22 119
20:22-23 119
20:22-24 119
20:23 36, 38, 41, 122, 123, 135, 219
20:23-24 218
20:24 119, 120, 121, 122, 123, 133, 134, 196, 198, 203, 239
20:25 31, 119, 121, 197, 221
20:25-31 119, 120
20:25-27 119
20:27 121, 122, 133, 134, 198
20:28 36, 119, 121, 122, 123, 198
20:28-31 119
20:28-35 123
20:29-30 119
20:30 119
20:31 119
20:32 119, 120, 122, 123, 130, 133, 196, 202, 203
20:32-35 120
20:33-35 120
20:34 120
20:35 239
20:36-38 235
21-28 204, 215, 248
21:1-14 146
21:1-18 218
21:1-40 235
21:4 36, 38, 41, 135, 218
21:8 170
21:8-9 170
21:11 36, 38, 41, 135
21:12-13 218
21:13 239
21:14 237, 239
21:18 155, 173
21:18-22 184
21:19 205
21:19-26 146
21:20 203
21:20-22 247
21:20-25 148
21:21-25 147
21:27-30 123
21:27-31 148
21:28 124, 125
21:31 185
21:31-32 152
21:31-34 149, 151
21:31-36 142, 149, 151, 186
21:40 123
22 105, 124, 127, 131, 132, 143
22-27 2
22:1 123
22:1-21 93, 133, 150, 235
22:3 124, 125, 195
22:3-21 23, 124, 135
22:4 124, 129, 198, 242
22:6 125
22:6-11 124
22:8 239
22:9 125
22:10 126, 130, 239
22:11 125
22:12 126, 175, 233
22:14 22, 125, 126, 194, 210, 236
22:14-15 125, 127, 134
22:14-16 124
22:15 126, 131, 134
22:16 35
22:17 125
22:17-21 33, 124, 125, 207
22:18 126
22:19 239
22:19-20 126
22:21 126, 130, 134, 147, 206
22:22 126, 149
22:22-30 235
22:29 149
22:30 126, 148
23 2
23:1 22, 126
23:1-24 235
23:4 195
23:6 23, 148
23:6-7 134
23:6-8 127
23:11 20, 23, 28, 33, 35, 40, 41, 135, 149, 151, 152, 206, 219, 239
23:12 185
23:12-14 148
23:12-24 142, 152
23:13-15 149
23:16-24 186
23:25-30 235
23:27 149
23:29 149
23:31-35 235
24 132, 143
24:1-2 235
24:1-9 148
24:1-21 148
24:3-21 235
24:5 127
24:6 127
24:10 123
24:10-21 93, 123, 127, 133, 150
24:14 127, 134, 195, 198, 236, 242, 248
24:14-15 127
24:14-16 134
24:15 127
24:16 22, 128
24:21 128, 134
24:22 186, 198, 242
24:22-27 235
24:27 149, 186
25 2
25:1-5 142
25:1-7 148
25:1-13 235
25:2-3 149
25:9 149, 186
25:14-21 235
25:18-19 149
25:19 185
25:22-23 235
25:24 128
25:24-27 186, 235
25:25 128
25:26 237
26 105, 124, 125, 131, 132, 143
26:1 123
26:1-23 148, 235
26:2-23 93, 123, 128, 133, 135, 150
26:4-5 128
26:5 125
26:6 128, 129

Scripture Index

26:6-7 129
26:6-8 128, 129
26:6-23 128
26:7 129
26:7-8 128
26:8 129, 134
26:9 130
26:9-11 128
26:9-12 128, 129
26:10-11 129
26:11-12 128
26:13 131
26:13-15 128, 130
26:13-18 128, 129, 130
26:14 130
26:15 239
26:16 130
26:16-17 130
26:16-18 128, 129, 130, 131
26:17 130, 147
26:18 106, 130, 131, 134, 221, 240
26:19 22, 129
26:19-20 128
26:19-21 134
26:19-22 41, 128, 129, 134
26:19-23 149, 209
26:20 106, 129, 240
26:21 22, 129
26:21-22 128
26:22 128, 129, 130, 131
26:22-23 33, 128, 129, 210, 213
26:23 128, 129, 130, 131
26:24-32 235
26:29 93
26:31 149
27 2, 235
27-28 142
27:1-28:16 218
27:21-26 93
27:21-28:6 142
27:23 27, 40, 195
27:23-24 26, 28, 29, 41, 135, 152, 206
27:24 23, 28, 29, 43
27:25 28, 29
27:43 152, 186
28 124, 143
28:1-16 235
28:3-6 136
28:3-9 143
28:5-9 136
28:5-10 141
28:6 148
28:7-9 142
28:8-9 208
28:17-20 123
28:17-22 235
28:23 31, 197, 221
28:23-24 235
28:25 36, 37, 211, 212, 241
28:25-29 93, 235
28:26-28 213
28:28 147, 198
28:30-31 193, 235
28:31 25, 31, 142, 197, 219, 221, 239

Romans (Rom)
1-11 162
1:4 102
1:19 105
1:21 106
12:1 162
15:6 156
16:7 105

1 Corinthians (1 Cor)
2:3 23

2 Corinthians (2 Cor)
12:1-10 33

Galatians (Gal)
2:12 173

1 Timothy (1 Tim)
3:13 121

2 Peter (2 Pet)
1:1 164

Revelation (Rev)
10:6 110
14:7 110

Paternoster Biblical Monographs

(All titles uniform with this volume)
Dates in bold are of projected publication.
Condensed details are given for volumes published before 2004.

Joseph Abraham
Eve: Accused or Acquitted?
A Reconsideration of Feminist Readings of the Creation Narrative Texts in Genesis 1–3
'A perceptive exploration of modern feminist readings', Gordon McConville.
2002 / 978-0-85364-971-7 / xxiv + 272pp

Kevin L. Anderson,
'But God Raised Him from the Dead'
The Theology of Jesus' Resurrection in Luke-Acts
This first full-scale study of the resurrection of Jesus in Luke-Acts argues that the resurrection of Jesus constitutes the focus of the Lukan message of salvation. It situates Luke's perspective on resurrection amongst Jewish and Hellenistic conceptions of the afterlife, and within the complex of Luke's theology, christology, ecclesiology, and eschatology.
Kevin L. Anderson is an Assistant Professor of Bible and Theology at Asbury College, Wilmore, Kentucky, USA.
2006 / 978-1-84227-339-5 / xx + 354pp

Octavian D. Baban
On the Road Encounters in Luke-Acts
Hellenistic Mimesis and Luke's Theology of the Way
The book argues on theological and literary (mimetic) grounds that Luke's on-the-road encounters, especially those belonging to the post-Easter period, are part of his complex theology of the Way. Jesus' teaching and that of the apostles is presented by Luke as a challenging answer to the Hellenistic reader's thirst for adventure, good literature, and existential paradigms.
Octavian D. Baban is New Testament and New Testament Greek Lecturer at the Bucharest State University and at the Bucharest Baptist Theological Centre, Bucharest, Romania.
2006 / 978-1-84227-253-4 / xviii + 332pp

Paul Barker
The Triumph of Grace in Deuteronomy
This book is a textual and theological analysis of the interaction between the sin and faithlessness of Israel and the grace of Yahweh in response, looking especially at Deuteronomy chapters 1–3, 8–10 and 29–30. The author argues that the grace of Yahweh is determinative for the ongoing relationship between Yahweh and Israel and that Deuteronomy anticipates and fully expects Israel to be faithless.
Paul Barker is Visiting Lecturer in Old Testament, Ridley College, Melbourne, and Vicar, Holy Trinity Doncaster, Victoria, Australia.
2004 / 978-1-84227-226-8 / xxii + 270pp

Jonathan F. Bayes
The Weakness of the Law
God's Law and the Christian in New Testament Perspective
'Will provoke wide-ranging and stimulating debate', William S. Campbell.
2000 / 978-0-85364-957-1 / xii + 244pp

Michael F. Bird
The Saving Righteousness of God
Studies on Paul, Justification and the New Perspective
This book presents a series of studies on contentious aspects of Paul's doctrine of justification including the meaning of 'righteousness', the question of imputation, the role of resurrection in justification, an evaluation of the New Perspective, the soteriological and ecclesiological significance of justification, justification by faith with judgment according to works, and debates over the orthodoxy of N.T. Wright. The burden of the volume is to demonstrate that reformed and 'new' readings of Paul are indispensable to attaining a full understanding of Paul's soteriology.

Michael F. Bird is New Testament Lecturer, Highland Theological College, Dingwall, Scotland, UK.

2007 / 978-1-84227-465-1 / xviii + 230pp

David Bostock
A Portrayal of Trust
The Theme of Faith in the Hezekiah Narratives
This study provides detailed and sensitive readings of the Hezekiah narratives (2 Kings 18–20 and Isaiah 36–39) from a theological perspective. It concentrates on the theme of faith, using narrative criticism as its methodology. Attention is paid especially to setting, plot, point of view and characterization within the narratives. A largely positive portrayal of Hezekiah emerges that underlines the importance and relevance of scripture.

David Bostock is a teaching fellow in Old Testament at the University of St Andrews, Scotland, UK.

2006 / 978-1-84227-314-2 / xx + 252pp

Mark Bredin
Jesus, Revolutionary of Peace
A Non-violent Christology in the Book of Revelation
'Bold and engaging', Richard Bauckham.

2003 / 978-1-84227-153-7 / xviii + 262pp

Robinson Butarbutar
Paul and Conflict Resolution
An Exegetical Study of Paul's Apostolic Paradigm in 1 Corinthians 9
The author sees the apostolic paradigm in 1 Corinthians 9 as part of Paul's unified arguments in 1 Corinthians 8–10 in which he seeks to mediate in the dispute over the issue of food offered to idols. The book also sees its relevance for dispute-resolution today, taking the conflict within the author's church as an example.

Robinson Butarbutar has served as a minister, theological lecturer and mission organizer in his homeland of Indonesia.

2007 / 978-1-84227-315-9 / xviii + 276pp

Daniel J-S Chae
Paul as Apostle to the Gentiles
His Apostolic Self-awareness and its Influence on the Soteriological Argument in Romans
'An outstanding piece of work', I. Howard Marshall.

1997 / 978-0-85364-829-1 / xiv + 378pp

Ling Cheng
The Characterisation of God in Acts
The Indirect Portrayal of an Invisible Character
Based on the plot-oriented nature of the Acts narrative, Dr Cheng shows that God's supreme saving will and mission plan determine the development of human history as well as the narrative, and his sovereign authority and power governs the movement of characters and the development of events and thus assures the fulfilment of his salvific plan. From the carrying out of the divine redemptive plan emerges a God who is invisible-yet-perceivable, dominant-yet-cogent, and continuous-yet-changing.

Ling Cheng teaches New Testament Studies at Taiwan Theological Seminary.

2009 / 978–1–84227–628–0 / approx. 300pp

Luke L. Cheung
The Genre, Composition and Hermeneutics of the Epistle of James
'A masterly study', Richard Bauckham.
2003 / 978-1-84227-062-2 / xvi + 372pp

Youngmo Cho
Spirit and Kingdom in the Writings of Luke and Paul
An Attempt to Reconcile these Concepts
The relationship between Spirit and kingdom is a relatively unexplored area in Lukan and Pauline studies. This book offers a fresh perspective of two biblical writers on the subject. It explores the difference between Luke's and Paul's understanding of the Spirit by examining the specific question of the relationship of the concept of the Spirit to the concept of the kingdom of God in each writer.

Youngmo Cho is Assistant Professor of New Testament Studies, Asia LIFE University, Daejon, South Korea.

2005 / 978-1-84227-316-6 / xviii + 228pp

Andrew C. Clark
Parallel Lives
The Relation of Paul to the Apostles in the Lucan Perspective
'Crisp and methodological elucidation of the issues', Max Turner.
2001 / 978-1-84227-035-6 / xviii + 386pp

Andrew D. Clarke
Secular and Christian Leadership in Corinth
A Socio-Historical and Exegetical Study of 1 Corinthians 1–6
This volume is an investigation into the leadership structures and dynamics of first-century Roman Corinth. These are compared with the practice of leadership in the Corinthian Christian community which are reflected in 1 Corinthians 1–6, and contrasted with Paul's own principles of Christian leadership.

Andrew D. Clarke is Senior Lecturer in New Testament, Department of Divinity with Religious Studies, University of Aberdeen, Scotland, UK.

2006^2 / 978-1-84227-229-9 / 206pp

Victor Copan
Saint Paul as Spiritual Director
An Analysis of the Imitation of Paul with Implications and Applications to the Practice of Spiritual Direction

In recent years much has been written on spiritual direction. However, confusion and at times outright contradiction exists between the aims and methodologies of various models of Christian spiritual direction. In order to develop solid criteria for evaluating and critiquing these models it is necessary to root the practice of spiritual direction in the biblical record. The intention of this study is to provide such biblical moorings by examining the Apostle Paul as a case study in his function as a spiritual director—with respect to his aims and praxis of spiritually forming the members of the congregations he founded.

Victor Copan is Associate Professor of Ministry, Palm Beach Atlantic University, Florida, USA.

2007 / 978-1-84227-367-8 / xxvi + 296pp

John C. Crutchfield
Psalms in Their Context
An Interpretation of Psalms 107–118

Psalms in their Context employs a canonical methodology to interpret Psalms 107-118. This methodology begins with a study of each poem as a separate work, but also includes consideration of each psalm in its various literary contexts, including its relation to adjacent psalms, its Psalter context, and its canonical context. The author suggests that each psalm should be understood in light of the Psalter's three-fold themes of wisdom, eschatology and worship. An Appendix reviews selected evidence from the Dead Sea Scrolls on when and how the Psalter may have been put together.

John C. Crutchfield is Associate Professor of Biblical Studies, Columbia International University, Columbia, South Carolina, USA.

2011 / 978-1-84227-396-5 / approx. 240pp

Audrey Dawson
Healing, Weakness and Power
Perspectives on Healing in the Writings of Mark, Luke and Paul

As Mark, Luke and Paul reveal major differences in their emphases and theological presentations of divine healing, the evidence for, and causes of, these variations are analysed in relation to their views of Jesus' power and weakness, and the legacy of Jesus' healing is considered briefly over the subsequent few centuries.

Audrey Dawson was a consultant physician (clinical haematologist) and senior lecturer in the University of Aberdeen, becoming OBE for services to medicine. On retirement she completed her PhD at Aberdeen on which this book is based.

2008 / 978-1-84227-524-5 / xviii + 302pp

Havilah Dharamraj
A Prophet Like Moses?
A Narrative-Theological Reading of the Elijah Stories

In evaluating Elijah as a prophet after the Mosaic paradigm, this work proposes a radically different schema for interpreting what is one of the most dramatic and difficult texts in the Old Testament, namely, the earthquake-wind-and-fire theophany at Horeb.

Havilah Dharamraj is Assistant Professor, Department of Old Testament, South Asia Institute of Advanced Christian Studies, Bangalore, India.

2011 / 978-1-84227-533-7 / approx. 300pp

Stephen Finamore
God, Order and Chaos
René Girard and the Apocalypse

Readers are often disturbed by the images of destruction in the book of Revelation and unsure why they are unleashed after the exaltation of Jesus. This book examines past approaches to these texts and uses René Girard's theories to revive some old ideas and propose some new ones.

Stephen Finamore is Principal of Bristol Baptist College, UK.

2009 / 978-1-84227-197-1 / xxviii + 290pp

David G. Firth
Surrendering Retribution in the Psalms
Responses to Violence in the Individual Complaints

Firth examines the ways the book of Psalms inculcates a model response to violence through the repetition of standard patterns of prayer. Rather than seeking justification for retributive violence, it encourages not only a surrender of the right of retribution to Yahweh, but also sets limits on the retribution that can be sought.

David G. Firth is Tutor in Old Testament, Cliff College, Calver, UK.

2005 / 978-1-84227-337-1 / xviii + 154pp

William A. Ford
God, Pharaoh and Moses
Explaining God's Actions in the Exodus Plagues Narrative

The story of the Exodus from Egypt is of fundamental importance, both in the Old Testament and beyond. However, it also contains issues that are theologically problematic for readers, especially concerning the actions of God. Why does God send a series of plagues on Egypt? How do we understand the hardening of Pharaoh's heart? What do the answers to these questions say about the character of God? Ford addresses these questions, taking a narrative theological approach, reading the story as story. He concentrates on the passages within the story that appear to present rationales for God's actions, reading these 'explanations' in their context, paying attention to speaker, addressee, purpose, and reception. The picture that emerges is of God as responsive, speaking and acting to challenge the hearer to make the appropriate response to him.

William A. Ford is a Visiting Lecturer in Hebrew and Old Testament at All Nations Christian College, Ware, and previously studied at Durham and Oxford.

2006 / 978-1-84227-420-0 / xx + 248pp

Kabiro wa Gatumu
The Pauline Concept of 'Supernatural Powers'
A Reading from an African Worldview

The study of supernatural powers is fraught with hermeneutical challenges, which increase further in the African context. While Western anthropology tends to discount the idea of supernatural powers by attempting to 'explain them away', Western biblical scholarship has mainly worked from the premise of 'demythologizing' them. But none of these approaches make sense to African scholars for whom supernatural powers constitute an integral component of the spiritual psyche. This book, based on the examination of over a thousand documentary sources (both ancient and modern), attempts to address the issue of interpreting supernatural powers from an African worldview. The author analyses, identifies, and critiques major hermeneutical errors and offers a 'bridging hermeneutic' using the method of reader-response criticism.

Kabiro wa Gatumu is Lecturer in New Testament Studies, New Testament Greek and African Biblical Hermeneutics at St Paul's University, Limuru, Kenya.

2008 / 978-1-84227-532-0 / xxvi + 300pp

Scott J. Hafemann
Paul, Moses and the History of Israel
The Letter/Spirit Contrast and the Argument from Scripture in 2 Corinthians 3
An exegetical study of the call of Moses, the second giving of the Law (Exodus 32–34), the new covenant, and the prophetic understanding of the history of Israel in 2 Corinthians 3. Hafemann demonstrates Paul's contextual use of the Old Testament and the essential unity between the Law and the Gospel within the context of the distinctive ministries of Moses and Paul.
Scott J. Hafemann is the Mary F. Rockefeller Distinguished Professor of New Testament at Gordon-Conwell Theological Seminary, South Hamilton, Massachusetts, USA.
2005 [1995] / 978-1-84227-317-3 / xii + 498pp

Scott J. Hafemann
Suffering and Ministry in the Spirit
Paul's Defence of His Ministry in II Corinthians 2:14–3:3
'A book of persuasive power', Jerome Murphy O'Connor.
2000 [1990] / 978-0-85364-967-0 / xvi + 262pp

Paul M. Hoskins
Jesus as the Fulfillment of the Temple in the Gospel of John
Interpreters often associate John 1:14, 1:51, 2:18-22 and 4:20-24 with Jesus' replacement of the Temple. Based on these texts, one can already begin to see that he fulfills and replaces the Temple in that he is the new locus of God's presence, glory, revelation, and abundant provision for his people. In particular, John 2:18-22 clearly associates Jesus' role as the Temple with his death and resurrection.
Paul M. Hoskins is Assistant Professor of New Testament, Southwestern Baptist Theological Seminary, Fort Worth, Texas, USA.
2006 / 978-1-84227-360-9 / xvi + 266pp

Barry C. Joslin
Hebrews, Christ, and the Law
The Theology of the Mosaic Law in Hebrews 7:1–10:18
Joslin seeks to fill a lacuna in studies of Hebrews, namely, the writer's theology of the Mosaic Law, which is seen most clearly in the doctrinal centre of the book, 7:1–10:18. He concludes that for the writer the work of Christ has *transformed* the Law, and that this involves both its fulfillment and internalization in the New Covenant; the Law has forever been affected christologically. As such, there are continuous and discontinuous aspects of the Law that hinge on Christ, the writer's chief 'hermeneutical principle'.
Barry C. Joslin is Assistant Professor of Christian Theology, Boyce College, The Southern Baptist Theological Seminary, Louisville, KY, USA.
2008 / 978-1-84227-530-6 / xx + 334pp

Mark Keown
Congregational Evangelism in Philippians
The Centrality of an Appeal for Gospel Proclamation to the Fabric of Philippians
Did Paul want his congregations to pick up the ministry of evangelism or did he envisage himself and other 'specialist' proclaimers continuing the ministry of the gospel? Dr Keown argues that one essential element of the rhetorical appeal of the letter is an injunction to the Philippians to continue to preach the gospel with renewed unity in the face of pagan opposition. He suggests Paul envisaged 'specialist proclaimers' leading the evangelistic mission and equipping 'general believers' to share the gospel as one dimension of living in the world.
Mark J. Keown is Lecturer in New Testament at Laidlaw College, Auckland, New Zealand.
2008 / 978-1-84227-510-8 / xxii + 360pp

Roger A. Latham
Christian Scripture and Postmodernity
Toward a Confessional Hermeneutic in Postmodern Biblical Studies
This book engages in depth with the work of pioneering postmodern scholars to explore the strongly ideological character of much postmodern biblical scholarship, and explains the failure of some confessional approaches to respond adequately to the new environment. Christian interpretation has a valid role to play as a distinct ideological perspective within the spectrum of academic approaches in Biblical Studies, and Latham proposes a multidisciplinary model for confessional interpreters which, along with a distinctively Christian ethics of interpretation, will enable Christian scholars to engage constructively with those whose methods, values and ideologies differ from theirs.
Roger Latham is a Team Vicar on the Cartmel Peninsula in the Diocese of Carlisle.
2010-11 / 978–1–84227–631–0 / approx. 300pp

Nicholas P. Lunn
Word-Order Variation in Biblical Hebrew Poetry
Differentiating Pragmatic Poetics
This study tackles the neglected subject of word order in biblical Hebrew poetry. The fact that the order of clause constituents frequently differs from that found in prose has often been noted, but no systematic attempt has been offered by way of explanation. Here two separate factors are taken into consideration: that of purely poetic variation (defamiliarisation), and that of pragmatic markedness. This work offers a new approach to the poetry of the Old Testament that will aid towards more accurate translation, exegesis, and discourse analysis of poetic texts.
Nicholas P. Lunn is a Senior Translation Consultant with Wycliffe Bible Translators, UK.
2006 / 978-1-84227-423-1 / xxii + 374pp

Douglas S. McComiskey
Lukan Theology in the Light of the Gospel's Literary Structure
Luke's Gospel was purposefully written with theology embedded in its patterned literary structure. A critical analysis of this cyclical structure provides new windows into Luke's interpretation of the individual pericopes comprising the Gospel and illuminates several of his theological interests.
Douglas S. McComiskey is Professor of New Testament, Ridley College, Melbourne, Australia.
2004 / 978-1-84227-148-3 / xviii + 388pp

Martin Mosse
The Three Gospels
New Testament History Introduced by the Synoptic Problem
Mosse combines a relentlessly logical assault on the Synoptic Problem with a radical treatment of New Testament history and chronology. Arguing for early dates and traditional authorship of the Synoptics, and against the redundant hypothesis of Q, he tackles also the major cruces in early church history, including the later career of Paul.
Martin Mosse holds degrees in classics, mathematics and theology. He currently runs a think tank called BRAINWAVES.
2007 / 978-1-84227-520-7 / xxxii + 364pp

Stephen Motyer
Your Father the Devil?
A New Approach to John and 'The Jews'
'This elegantly-written book breaks fresh ground', Graham Stanton.
1997 / 978-0-85364-832-1 / xiv + 260pp

Esther Ng
Reconstructing Christian Origins?
The Feminist Theology of Elizabeth Schüssler Fiorenza: An Evaluation
'Strongly challenges Fiorenza's rather rosy picture of egalitarianism', Ruth B. Edwards.
2002 / 978-1-84227-055-4 / xxiv + 468pp

Robin Parry
Old Testament Story and Christian Ethics
The Rape of Dinah as a Case Study
What is the role of story in ethics and, more particularly, what is the role of Old Testament story in Christian ethics? This book, drawing on the work of contemporary philosophers, argues that narrative is crucial in the ethical shaping of people and, drawing on the work of contemporary Old Testament scholars, that story plays a key role in Old Testament ethics. Parry then argues that when situated in canonical context Old Testament stories can be reappropriated by Christian readers in their own ethical formation. The shocking story of the rape of Dinah and the massacre of the Shechemites provides a fascinating case study for exploring the parameters within which Christian ethical appropriations of Old Testament stories can live.
Robin Parry is Commissioning Editor for Paternoster, UK.
2004 / 978-1-84227-210-7 / xx + 350pp

Robert L. Plummer
Paul's Understanding of the Church's Mission
Did the Apostle Paul Expect the Early Christian Communities to Evangelize?
This book engages in a careful study of Paul's letters to determine if the apostle expected the communities to which he wrote to engage in missionary activity. It helpfully summarizes the discussion on this debated issue, judiciously handling contested texts, and provides a way forward in addressing this critical question. While admitting that Paul rarely explicitly commands the communities he founded to evangelize, Plummer amasses significant incidental data to provide a convincing case that Paul did indeed expect his churches to engage in mission activity. Throughout the study, Plummer progressively builds a theological basis for the church's mission that is both distinctively Pauline and compelling.
Robert L. Plummer is Assistant Professor of New Testament Interpretation, The Southern Baptist Theological Seminary, Louisville, Kentucky, USA.
2006 / 978-1-84227-333-3 / xviii + 190pp

David Powys
'Hell': A Hard Look at a Hard Question
The Fate of the Unrighteous in New Testament Thought
'This book is an impressive and thorough discussion of a thorny question', Graham Stanton.
1997 / 978-0-85364-831-4 / xxii + 478pp

Ian E. Rock
Paul's Letter to the Romans and Roman Imperialism
An Ideological Analysis of the Exordium (Romans 1:1-17)
This book argues that Romans may be seen as an attempt by a subordinated group to redress both actual and potential issues of confrontation, and to offer hope, even in the face of death. An analysis of the exordium in Romans 1:1-17 demonstrates that the letter is focused on strengthening the faith of the Roman Christians in the lordship of Jesus Christ, whose universal rule stands in contrast to the claims of the Roman Empire.
Ian E. Rock is Principal of Codrington College, St John, Barbados, West Indies.
978-1-84227-458-3 / approx. 300pp

Sorin Sabou
Between Horror and Hope
Paul's Metaphorical Language of Death in Romans 6.1-11
This book argues that Paul's metaphorical language of death in Romans 6.1-11 conveys two aspects: horror and hope. The 'horror' aspect is conveyed by the 'crucifixion' language, and the 'hope' aspect by 'burial' language. The life of the Christian believer is understood, as relationship with sin is concerned ('death to sin'), between these two realities: horror and hope.
Sorin Sabou is Lecturer at Bucharest Baptist Seminary and Senior Pastor of the Romanian Baptist Church, Brasov, Romania.
2005 / 978-1-84227-322-7 / xvi + 160pp

Rosalind Selby
The Comical Doctrine
The Epistemology of New Testament Hermeneutics
This book argues that the gospel breaks through postmodernity's critique of truth and the referential possibilities of textuality with its gift of grace. With a rigorous, philosophical challenge to modernist and postmodernist assumptions, Selby offers an alternative epistemology to all who would still read with faith *and* with academic credibility.
Rosalind Selby is a lay preacher in the United Reformed Church and completed her doctorate at the University of Aberdeen, UK.
2006 / 978-1-84227-212-1 / xvi + 282pp

Kiwoong Son
Zion Symbolism in Hebrews
Hebrews 12.18-24 as a Hermeneutical Key to the Epistle
This book challenges the general tendency of understanding the Epistle to the Hebrews against a Hellenistic background and suggests that the Epistle should be understood in the light of the Jewish apocalyptic tradition. The author especially argues for the importance of the theological symbolism of Sinai and Zion (Heb. 12.18-24) as it provides the Epistle's theological background as well as the rhetorical basis of the superiority motif of Jesus throughout the Epistle.
Kiwoong Son completed his doctorate at London School of Theology and has served as a chaplain to Korean and Asian students at Royal Holloway College, University of London, UK.
2005 / 978-1-84227-368-5 / xviii + 248pp

Kevin Walton
Thou Traveller Unknown
The Presence and Absence of God in the Jacob Narrative
'A lucid and perceptive interpretation of the Jacob narratives', Gordon McConville.
2003 / 978-1-84227-059-2 / xvi + 238pp

Jason A. Whitlark
Enabling Fidelity to God
Perseverance in Hebrews in Light of Reciprocity Systems of the Ancient Mediterranean World
The primary focus of this book is to demonstrate how Hebrews represents, in view of its historical and religious context, human fidelity to God. In order to provide a fresh perspective on this issue it examines Hebrews' understanding of fidelity from the perspective of Hebrews' authorial audience. Its conclusions have far reaching implications for the soteriology of Hebrews, the author's and the auditors' presumed experience of salvation in Jesus Christ, and how the message of the supremacy of Jesus Christ was heard in the context Hebrews presupposes.

Jason A. Whitlark is a Professor in Religion, Baylor University, Waco, Texas, USA.

2008 / 978-1-84227-573-3 / xviii + 226pp

George M. Wieland
The Significance of Salvation
A Study of Salvation Language in the Pastoral Epistles
The language and ideas of salvation pervade the three Pastoral Epistles. This study offers a close examination of their soteriological statements. In all three letters the idea of salvation is found to play a vital paraenetic role, but each also exhibits distinctive soteriological emphases. The results challenge common assumptions about the Pastoral Epistles as a corpus.

George M. Wieland is Lecturer in New Testament, Carey Baptist College and Auckland University, New Zealand.

2006 / 978-1-84227-257-2 / xxii + 344pp

Alistair Wilson
When Will These Things Happen?
A Study of Jesus as Judge in Matthew 21–25
This study seeks to allow Matthew's carefully constructed presentation of Jesus to be given full weight in the modern evaluation of Jesus' eschatology. Careful analysis of the text of Matthew 21–25 reveals Jesus to be standing firmly in the Jewish prophetic and wisdom traditions as he proclaims and enacts imminent judgement on the Jewish authorities then boldly claims the central role in the final and universal judgement.

Alistair Wilson is Principal of Dumisani Theological Institute, and Extraordinary Associate Professor of New Testament, North-West University, South Africa.

2004 / 978-1-84227-146-9 / xxii + 272pp

Lindsay Wilson
Joseph Wise and Otherwise
The Intersection of Covenant and Wisdom in Genesis 37–50
This book offers a careful literary reading of Genesis 37–50 that argues that the Joseph story contains both strong covenant themes and many wisdom-like elements. The connections between the two helps to explore how covenant and wisdom might intersect in an integrated biblical theology.

Lindsay Wilson is Vice Principal and Lecturer in Old Testament, Ridley College, University of Melbourne, Australia.

2004 / 978-1-84227-140-7 / xvi + 340pp

Stephen I. Wright
The Voice of Jesus
Studies in the Interpretation of Six Gospel Parables
'A book which genuinely has something fresh to offer', I. Howard Marshall.
2000 / 978-0-85364-975-5 / xiv + 280pp

New and unscheduled titles:

Mark Bonnington
The Antioch Episode of Galatians 2:11-14 in Historical and Cultural Context
The Antioch 'incident' over table-fellowship suggests significant disagreement between the leading apostles. This book analyses its background by locating the incident within the dynamics of social interaction between Jews and Gentiles, proposing a new way of understanding the relationship between the individuals and issues involved.
978-1-84227-050-9 / approx. 300pp

Stefan Kürle
The Appeal of Exodus
The Characters of God, Moses and Israel in the Rhetoric of the Book of Exodus
978-1-84227-657-0 / approx. 300pp

Daniel W. MacDougall
The Authenticity of 2 Thessalonians
978-1-84227-433-0 / approx. 300pp

John E. Morgan-Wynne
The Cross in the Johannine Writings
978-1-84227-658-7 / approx. 300pp

Ester Petrenko
Created in Christ Jesus for Good Works
The Integration of Soteriology and Ethics in Ephesians
978-1-84227-636-5 / approx. 300pp

Jennifer M. Shepherd
Exorcising a Dead Sea Scroll
A Contextual Reading of 11QapocryphalPsalms in the Shadow of Psalm 91 and Cave 11
978-1-84227-653-2 / approx. 300pp

Lawson Stone
Holy War and Holy Hero
978-1-84227-400-2 / approx. 300pp

Paternoster Theological Monographs

(All titles uniform with this volume)
Dates in bold are of projected publication.
Condensed details are given for volumes published before 2004.

James N. Anderson
Paradox in Christian Theology
An Analysis of the Presence, Character, and Epistemic Status of Paradoxical Christian Doctrines

Dr Anderson develops and defends a model of understanding paradoxical Christian doctrines according to which the presence of such doctrines is unsurprising and adherence to paradoxical doctrines can be entirely reasonable. As such, the phenomenon of theological paradox cannot be considered as a serious intellectual obstacle to belief in Christianity. The case presented in this book has significant implications for the practice of systematic theology, biblical exegesis, and Christian apologetics.

James N. Anderson is a Research Fellow of the University of Edinburgh, Scotland, UK.

2007 / 978-1-84227-462-0 / xvi + 328pp

Emil Bartos
Deification in Eastern Orthodox Theology
An Evaluation and Critique of the Theology of Dumitru Staniloae

'This book deals with a major topic of importance—Staniloae is the greatest Romanian theologian of the twentieth century', Kallistos Ware.

1999 / 978-0-85364-956-4 / xii + 370pp

Paul H. Brazier
Barth and Dostoevsky
A Study of the Influence of Fyodor Dostoevsky on the Development of Karl Barth (1915–1922)

A work of historic and systematic theology *Barth and Dostoevsky* examines the influence of Dostoevksy on Barth. It demonstrates that the writings of Dostoevsky effected the development of Barth's theology. This influence was mediated by his friend and colleague Eduard Thurneysen and was in the form of a key element of Barth's thought: his understanding of sin and grace. This study, therefore, explicates: first, the reading of Dostoevsky by Barth 1915–16, and the influence on his understanding of sin and grace; second, a study of Thurneysen in so far as his life and work complements and influences Barth; third, Barth's illustrative use of Dostoevsky, around 1918–21, the period of the rewriting of his seminal commentary on Romans.

Paul H. Brazier originally trained in the fine arts. He holds degrees from King's College, London, where he completed his PhD on which this book is based.

2007 / 978-1-84227-563-4 / xxiv + 246pp

Graham Buxton
The Trinity, Creation and Pastoral Ministry
Imaging the Perichoretic God

In this book the author proposes a three-way conversation between theology, science and pastoral ministry. His approach draws on a Trinitarian understanding of God as a relational being of love, whose life 'spills over' into all created reality, human and non-human. By locating human meaning and purpose within God's 'creation-community' this book offers the possibility of a transforming engagement between those in pastoral ministry and the scientific community.

Graham Buxton is Director of Postgraduate Studies in Ministry and Theology, Tabor College, Adelaide, Australia.

2005 / 978-1-84227-369-2 / xviii + 310pp

Iain D. Campbell
Fixing the Indemnity
The Life and Work of George Adam Smith

When Old Testament scholar George Adam Smith (1856–1942) delivered the Lyman Beecher lectures at Yale University in 1899, he confidently declared that 'modern criticism has won its war against traditional theories. It only remains to fix the amount of the indemnity.' In this biography, Iain D. Campbell assesses Smith's critical approach to the Old Testament and evaluates its consequences, showing that Smith's life and work still raises questions about the relationship between biblical scholarship and evangelical faith.

Iain D. Campbell is Minister of Back Free Church of Scotland, Isle of Lewis, Scotland, UK.

2004 / 978-1-84227-228-2 / xx + 256pp

Daniel Castelo
The Apathetic God
Exploring the Contemporary Relevance of Divine Impassibility

This book attempts a view of God and suffering that takes the testimony of the early church seriously while also considering with equal vigour the contemporary climate. It emphasizes divine impassibility because a balance between impassibility and passibility requires establishing space within a contemporary climate that all too easily assumes passibility.

Daniel Castelo is Assistant Professor of Theology, School of Theology, Seattle Pacific University, Washington, USA.

2009 / 978-1-84227-536-8 / xvi + 152pp

Tim Chester
Mission and the Coming of God
Eschatology, the Trinity and Mission in the Theology of Jürgen Moltmann

This book explores the theology and missiology of the influential contemporary theologian, Jürgen Moltmann. It highlights the important contribution Moltmann has made while offering a critique of his thought from an evangelical perspective. In so doing, it touches on pertinent issues for evangelical missiology. The conclusion takes Calvin as a starting point, proposing 'an eschatology of the cross' which offers a critique of the over-realised eschatologies in liberation theology and certain forms of evangelicalism.

Tim Chester is part of a church planting initiative in Sheffield and was previously Research and Policy Director for Tearfund and visiting lecturer in Christian Community Development at Redcliffe College, Gloucester, UK.

2006 / 978-1-84227-320-3 / xviii + 264pp

Sylvia Wilkey Collinson
Making Disciples
The Significance of Jesus' Educational Strategy for Today's Church

This study examines the biblical practice of discipling, formulates a definition, and makes comparisons with modern models of education. A recommendation is made for greater attention to its practice today.

Sylvia Wilkey Collinson is a Visiting Lecturer, Morling College, Sydney, Australia.

2004 / 978-1-84227-116-2 / xiv + 278pp

Darrell Cosden
A Theology of Work
Work and the New Creation
Through dialogue with Moltmann, Pope John Paul II and others, this book develops a genitive 'theology of work', presenting a theological definition of work and a model for a theological ethics of work that shows work's nature, value and meaning now and eschatologically. Work is shown to be a transformative activity consisting of three dynamically inter-related dimensions: the instrumental, relational and ontological.
Darrell Cosden is Lecturer in Theology and Ethics at the International Christian College, Glasgow, Scotland, UK.
2005 / 978-1-84227-332-6 / xvi + 208pp

Oliver Crisp
An American Augustinian
Sin and Salvation in the Dogmatic Theology of William G.T. Shedd
Shedd's theology is arguably one of the richest resources in the American Reformed tradition yet it has not received the attention it deserves. Shedd was a theologian unafraid to think for himself, even if this meant he ended up with views that were not held by others with whom he had a natural affinity. His theology of sin and salvation illustrate well this creative innovation within a tradition. Crisp explores the relationship between sin and salvation in Shedd's theology, with an eye to both its philosophical and dogmatic significance for contemporary theology.
Oliver Crisp is Lecturer in Theology, University of Bristol, UK.
2007 / 978-1-84227-526-9 / xvi + 184pp

Garry J. Deverell
The Bonds of Freedom
Vows, Sacraments and the Formation of the Christian Self
This book proposes that Christian worship is a key source for any theology seeking to understand the covenant between God and human beings in the Christian tradition. Through a detailed examination of phenomenological, biblical and theological sources, the author seeks to write a theology in which the selfhood of God and human beings is seen as essentially 'vowed' or 'covenantal'. This claim is then explored through a detailed examination of eucharistic and baptismal practices within the worship life of the church. Eucharistic worship is understood as a 'non-identical performance' of the covenant established between God and human beings in baptism. Here, then, is a theology that understands Christian worship not simply as 'form' or 'event' but, more radically, as a mutual act of promising and commitment between God and human beings.
Garry J. Deverell is a minister of the Uniting Church in Australia and an Honorary Research Associate, Centre for Studies in Religion and Theology, Monash University, Victoria, Australia.
2008 / 978-1-84227-527-6 / xvi + 214pp

Paul G. Doerksen
Beyond Suspicion
Post-Christendom Protestant Political Theology in John Howard Yoder and Oliver O'Donovan
By pursuing a critical comparison of the political theologies of John Howard Yoder and Oliver O'Donovan, the present work shows how post-Christendom Protestant political theology has attempted to move beyond the suspicion that politicians corrupt morality, and that politics is corrupted by theology without putting forward some hidden attempt to reassert a contemporary version of Christendom.
Paul G. Doerksen teaches Christian Theology and Ethics in Winnipeg, Manitoba, Canada.
2009 / 978-1-84227-634-1 / approx. 300pp

Stephen M. Dunning
The Crisis and the Quest
A Kierkegaardian Reading of Charles Williams
'An invaluable contribution to our understanding of this extraordinary man', Glen Cavaliero.
2000 / 978-0-85364-985-4 / xxiv + 254pp

Keith Ferdinando
The Triumph of Christ in African Perspective
A Study of Demonology and Redemption in the African Context
'I am excited by this book', R.T. France.
1999 / 978-0-85364-830-7 / xviii + 450pp

Craig Gardiner
Melodies of Community
Christian Community through the Metaphor of Music, with Dietrich Bonhoeffer and the Iona Community

Gardiner adopts the musical metaphor of polyphony to articulate a new paradigm for exploring the nature of Christ and argues that the church can still affirm ecumenical unity while celebrating the diverse patterns of practice and belief. He weaves together Bonhoeffer, the Iona Community and a rich variety of further metaphors to suggest a 'Discipline of Counterpoint' with which the Christian community might perform divine melodies such as worship, healing, ecumenism, peace, justice and ecology.

Craig Gardiner is pastor of Calvary Baptist Church, Cardiff, a member of the Council of the Baptist Union of Great Britain and serves on its Faith and Unity Executive.
2010 / 978-1-84227-564-1 / approx. 300pp

Richard Gibb
Grace and Global Justice
The Socio-Political Mission of the Church in an Age of Globalization

What does it mean for the twenty-first-century church to conceive of itself as a community defined by the covenant of grace? *Grace and Global Justice* explores the ramifications of this central Christian doctrine for the holistic mission of the church in the context of a globalized world.

Richard Gibb is Assistant Minister of Charlotte Chapel, Edinburgh, UK.
2006 / 978-1-84227-459-0 / xviii + 248pp

Andrew Goddard
Living the Word, Resisting the World
The Life and Thought of Jacques Ellul
'The best introduction to Ellul's thought currently available', Alister E. McGrath.
2002 / 978-1-84227-053-0 / xxiv + 378pp

Andrew Hartropp
Economic Justice
Biblical and Secular Perspectives Contrasted

This book argues that a biblically-rooted account of justice in economic life has three great strengths as opposed to the confusing disarray of views evident in the secular world: it is harmonious; it is substantial; and it is contemporary. It indicates how a biblical understanding of production and exchange ('free trade' versus 'fair trade' and equality versus freedom) applies to contemporary topics such as the relationships between borrowers and lenders, and the use of monopoly power.

Andrew Hartropp has lectured in economics at Brunel University and is currently a Church of England Curate in Watford, Hertfordshire, UK.
2007 / 978-1-84227-434-7 / xvi + 222pp

Sharon E. Heaney
Contextual Theology for Latin America
Liberation Themes in Evangelical Perspective
In the context of Latin America, the theology of liberation is both dominant and world renowned. However, this context and the pursuit of theological relevance belong also to other voices. In this book, Sharon Heaney examines and systematises the thought of five evangelical theologians striving for liberation in Latin America.

Sharon E. Heaney teaches Religious Studies at Bloxham School, Oxfordshire, having completed her doctorate at Queens University, Belfast, Northern Ireland, UK.

2008 / 978-1-84227-515-3 / xx + 292pp

Timothy D. Herbert
Kenosis and Priesthood
Towards a Protestant Re-Evaluation of the Ordained Ministry
Herbert argues it is possible to re-imagine priesthood so that it becomes a useful way to understand the nature and importance of ordained ministry without undervaluing or negating the priesthood of all believers.

Timothy D. Herbert is Principal of the Carlisle and Blackburn Diocesan Training Institute, Carlisle, UK.

2008 / 978-1-84227-565-8 / xxii + 300pp

Roger Hitching
The Church and Deaf People
A Study of Identity, Communication and Relationships with Special Reference to the Ecclesiology of Jürgen Moltmann
'An excellent book', Jürgen Moltmann.

2003 / 978-1-84227-222-0 / xxii + 236pp

Mark F.W. Lovatt
Confronting the Will-to-Power
A Reconsideration of the Theology of Reinhold Niebuhr
'A constructive evaluation', Anthony C. Thiselton.

2001 / 978-1-84227-054-7 / xviii + 216pp

Neil B. MacDonald
Karl Barth and the Strange New World within the Bible
Barth, Wittgenstein, and the Metadilemmas of the Enlightenment (Revised Edition)
'Brilliant and nuanced', Christopher R. Seitz.

2001^2 / 978-0-85364-970-0 / xxvi + 404pp

Neil B. MacDonald and Carl R. Trueman (eds)
Barth, Calvin, and Reformed Theology
Barth and Calvin belong to the first rank of great theologians of the Church. Historically, Calvin's influence on Reformed doctrine has been much greater than that of Barth's. In contrast, Barth's Reformed credentials have been questioned—not least in his understanding of election and atonement. The question is: who should be of greater importance for the Reformed church in the twenty-first century in the light of recent academic research into the Bible? Who has the better arguments on the Bible? Barth or Calvin: who should carry the mantle of Reformed theology in the future? Doctrinal areas of focus are the nature of the atonement, scripture, and the sacraments.

Neil B. MacDonald is Senior Lecturer in Theology, University of Surrey Roehampton, London, UK.

Carl R. Trueman is Professor of Church History, Westminster Theological Seminary, Philadelphia, USA.

2008 / 978-1-84227-567-2 / xiv + 182pp

Keith A. Mascord
Alvin Plantinga and Christian Apologetics
This book draws together the contributions of the philosopher Alvin Plantinga to the major contemporary challenges to Christian belief, highlighting in particular his ground-breaking work in epistemology and the problem of evil. Plantinga's theory that both theistic and Christian belief is warrantedly basic is explored and critiqued, and an assessment offered as to the significance of his work for apologetic theory and practice.
Keith A. Mascord lectures in Philosophy at Moore Theological College, Sydney, Australia.
2006 / 978-1-84227-256-5 / xvi + 236pp

Gillian McCulloch
The Deconstruction of Dualism in Theology
With Reference to Ecofeminist Theology and New Age Spirituality
'McCulloch's informed and timely book fills an important gap', Christopher Partridge.
2002 / 978-1-84227-044-8 / xii + 282pp

Leslie McCurdy
Attributes and Atonement
The Holy Love of God in the Theology of P.T. Forsyth
'Skilful and nuanced', Trevor Hart.
1999 / 978-0-85364-833-8 / xiv + 328pp

David H. McIlroy
A Trinitarian Theology of Law
In Conversation with Jürgen Moltmann, Oliver O'Donovan and Thomas Aquinas
This book explores the neglected significance of the doctrine of the Trinity for the understanding of human law. Through interaction with the thought of Moltmann, O'Donovan and Aquinas, it argues that human law is called to play a positive but limited role in maintaining 'shallow justice' and relative peace. Human law is overshadowed by the work of the Son, included in the purposes of the Father, and used as an instrument by the Holy Spirit. However, the Spirit works in those who are in Christ to effect 'deep justice', a work of sanctification which culminates in glorification – the experience of perfect, free, willing obedience in heaven.
David H. McIlroy is a practising barrister and a theologian and an Associate Research Fellow of Spurgeon's College, London, UK.
2009 / 978-1-84227-627-3 / xxii + 262pp

John E. McKinley
Tempted for Us
Theological Models and the Practical Relevance of the Impeccability and Temptation of Christ
How could Christ be tempted to sin despite his divine impeccability? How could Christ experience temptation in a way that makes him truly empathetic for others who are not impeccable as he is? How could Christ resist temptation in a way that others can reasonably follow his human example? Historical theology yields several models for working out the apparent dilemmas that follow from the traditional affirmations about Jesus' temptation. In response, McKinley explores the biblical and theological evidence for Christ's impeccability and temptation with the goal of formulating a contemporary model. Doing this clarifies both the full humanity of Christ and the true relevance and implications of his earthly life for Christian sanctification in conformity to Christ.
John E. McKinley is Assistant Professor of Systematic Theology, Biola University, La Mirada, California, USA.
2009 / 978-1-84227-537-5 / xxii + 346pp

Nozomu Miyahira
Towards a Theology of the Concord of God
A Japanese Perspective on the Trinity
'A profound contribution to East–West dialogue', John Macquarrie.
2000 / 978-0-85364-863-5 / xiv + 256pp

Eddy José Muskus
The Origins and Early Development of Liberation Theology in Latin America
With Particular Reference to Gustavo Gutiérrez
'Fills a crucial gap', D. Eryl Davies.
2002 / 978-0-85364-974-8 / xiv + 296pp

Jim Purves
The Triune God and the Charismatic Movement
A Critical Appraisal from a Scottish Perspective
All emotion and no theology? Or a fundamental challenge to reappraise and realign our trinitarian theology in the light of Christian experience? This study of charismatic renewal as it found expression within Scotland at the end of the twentieth century evaluates the use of Patristic, Reformed and contemporary models of the Trinity in explaining the workings of the Holy Spirit.
Jim Purves is pastor of Bristo Baptist Church, Edinburgh, and serves on the Baptist Union of Scotland's national leadership team.
2004 / 978-1-84227-321-0 / xxiv + 246pp

Anna Robbins
Methods in the Madness
Diversity in Twentieth-Century Christian Social Ethics
The author compares the ethical methods of Walter Rauschenbusch, Reinhold Niebuhr and others. She argues that unless Christians are clear about the ways that theology and philosophy are expressed practically they may lose the ability to discuss social ethics across contexts, let alone reach effective agreements.
Anna Robbins is Lecturer in Theology and Contemporary Culture and Director of Training at the London School of Theology, UK.
2004 / 978-1-84227-211-4 / xx + 294pp

Ed Rybarczyk
Beyond Salvation
Eastern Orthodoxy and Classical Pentecostalism on Becoming Like Christ
At first glance eastern Orthodoxy and classical Pentecostalism seem quite distinct. This ground-breaking study shows they share much in common, especially as it concerns the experiential elements of following Christ. Both traditions assert that authentic Christianity transcends the wooden categories of modernism.
Ed Rybarczyk is Assistant Professor of Systematic Theology, Vanguard University, California, USA.
2004 / 978-1-84227-144-5 / xii + 356pp

Signe Sandsmark
Is World View Neutral Education Possible and Desirable?
A Christian Response to Liberal Arguments
(Published jointly with The Stapleford Centre)
'Bold, balanced and sensitive', Andrew Wright.
2000 / 978-0-85364-973-1 / xiv + 182pp

Alison Searle
'The Eyes of your Heart'
Literary and Theological Trajectories of Imagining Biblically

This book develops a theory of imagining biblically that explores the contributions scripture can make to new ways of thinking about creativity, reading, interpretation and criticism. The methodology employed in order to demonstrate this thesis consists of a theoretical exploration of current theological understandings of the 'imagination' and their implications within the field of literary studies. The biblical text locates the function generally defined as 'imagination' in the heart ('the eyes of the heart', Ephesians 1:18). This book assesses what the biblical text as a literary and religious document contributes to the concept of 'imagination'.

Alison Searle is a postdoctoral research associate on the James Shirley Project at Anglia Ruskin University, Cambridge, UK.

2008 / 978-1-84227-627-3 / xviii + 232pp

Andrew Sloane
On Being a Christian in the Academy
Nicholas Wolterstorff and the Practice of Christian Scholarship

'Accurate, meticulously researched, lucidly presented and critically sympathetic', Nicholas Wolterstorff.

2003 / 978-1-84227-058-5 / xvi + 274pp

Damon W.K. So
Jesus' Revelation of His Father
A Narrative-Conceptual Study of the Trinity with Special Reference to Karl Barth

This book explores the trinitarian dynamics in the context of Jesus' revelation of his Father in his earthly ministry with references to key passages in Matthew's Gospel. It develops from the exegeses of these passages a non-linear concept of revelation which links Jesus' communion with his Father to his revelatory words and actions through a nuanced understanding of the Holy Spirit, with references to K. Barth, G.W.H. Lampe, J.D.G. Dunn and E. Irving.

Damon W.K. So serves as an adviser of the Oxford Chinese Christian Church having studied at London Bible College and the University of Oxford, UK.

2006 / 978-1-84227-323-4 / xviii + 348pp

Daniel Strange
The Possibility of Salvation Among the Unevangelised
An Analysis of Inclusivism in Recent Evangelical Theology

'One of the best comprehensive surveys of this debate', Gavin D'Costa.

2002 / 978-1-84227-047-9 / xviii + 362pp

Scott Swain
God According to the Gospel
Biblical Narrative and the Identity of God in the Theology of Robert W. Jenson

Robert W. Jenson is one of the leading voices in contemporary Trinitarian theology. His boldest contribution in this area lies in his use of the Bible's narrative structure both to ground and explicate a panentheistic doctrine of the Trinity. *God According to the Gospel* critically examines Jenson's proposal and, through an engagement with canon and creed, outlines an alternative way of reading the biblical characterization of the Trinity.

Scott Swain teaches Theology and Biblical Interpretation at Southwestern Baptist Theological Seminary, Fort Worth, Texas, USA.

2010 / 978-1-84227-258-9 / approx. 300pp

Justyn Terry
The Justifying Judgement of God
A Reassessment of the Place of Judgement in the Saving Work of Christ

Terry's argument is that judgement, understood as the whole process of bringing justice, is the primary metaphor of atonement, with others – victory, redemption and sacrifice – subordinate to it. Judgement also provides the proper context for understanding penal substitution and the call to repentance, baptism, eucharist and holiness.

Justyn Terry teaches at the Trinity Episcopal School for Ministry, Ambridge, PA, USA.

2007 / 978-1-84227-370-8 / xvi + 228pp

Graham Tomlin
The Power of the Cross
Theology and the Death of Christ in Paul, Luther and Pascal

'Here is the groundwork of constructive theology at its best', Stephen Williams.

1999 / 978-0-85364-984-7 / xiv + 344pp

Steven Tsoukalas
Krsna and Christ
Body-Divine Relation in the Thought of Sankara, Ramanuja and Classical Christian Orthodoxy

This work compares the Krsnavatara (Krsna in his *avatara* state) doctrines of Sankara and Ramanuja and the incarnation of Christ as represented by classical Christian orthodoxy, and draws out comparative theological and soteriological implications. The result is a demonstration that many of the popularly held similarities between *avatara* and incarnation are superficial, and that therefore careful consideration of epistemologies and ontologies should be undertaken when comparing theologies and soteriologies pertinent to *avatara* and incarnation.

Steven Tsoukalas is Adjunct Professor of Comparative Religion and Theology, Wesley Biblical Seminary, Jackson, Mississippi, USA.

2006 / 978-1-84227-435-4 / xvi + 310pp

Adonis Vidu
Postliberal Theological Method
A Critical Study

The postliberal theology of Frei, Lindbeck, Thiemann, Milbank and others is one of the more influential contemporary options. Vidu focuses on several aspects pertaining to its theological method, specifically its understanding of background, hermeneutics, epistemic justification, ontology, the nature of doctrine and christological method.

Adonis Vidu is Associate Professor of Theology, Gordon-Conwell Theological Seminary, South Hamilton, Massachusetts, USA.

2005 / 978-1-84227-395-1 / xiv + 270pp

Adonis Vidu
Theology after Neo-Pragmatism

How are theological claims justified? What is the meaning of Christian talk about the non-empirical and the transcendent? Should Evangelical theology continue to hitch a ride with realism? These important contemporary issues are approached by way of a theological conversation with neo-pragmatic philosophers such as Davidson, Rorty, Putnam, McDowell, and others. This is an introduction to an influential philosophical trend and a critical and constructive theological proposal, at once scriptural and historicist, pragmatic and realist.

Adonis Vidu is Associate Professor of Theology, Gordon-Conwell Theological Seminary, South Hamilton, Massachusetts, USA.

2008 / 978-1-84227-460-6 / xx + 308pp

Graham J. Watts
Revelation and the Spirit
A Comparative Study of the Relationship between the Doctrine of Revelation and Pneumatology in the Theology of Eberhard Jüngel and of Wolfhart Pannenberg

The relationship between revelation and pneumatology is relatively unexplored. This approach offers a fresh angle on two important twentieth-century theologians and raises pneumatological questions which are theologically crucial and relevant to mission in a postmodern culture.

Graham J. Watts is Minister of Albany Road Baptist Church, Cardiff, Wales, UK.

2005 / 978-1-84227-104-9 / xx + 230pp

Nicholas J. Wood
Faiths and Faithfulness
Pluralism, Dialogue and Mission in the Work of Kenneth Cragg and Lesslie Newbigin

Wood offers a critical account of two key twentieth-century missionary-theologians who addressed the issue of pluralism within a confessional framework. He argues for a reconsideration of the biblical themes of fullness and fulfilment, which may offer a way of holding together the traditions of continuity, which Cragg shows can never be total, and of discontinuity, which Newbigin argues can never be absolute. He contributes to the development of an appropriate missiological approach to inter-faith issues which takes people of faith seriously while allowing faithfulness to the Christian gospel.

Nicholas J. Wood is Fellow in Religion and Culture, and Director of the Oxford Centre for Christianity and Culture at Regent's Park College, University of Oxford. He is a member of the Faculty of Faculty in the University of Oxford and a President of the National Christian Muslim Forum.

2009 / 978-1-84227-371-5 / xviii + 220pp

Nigel G. Wright
Disavowing Constantine
Mission, Church and the Social Order in the Theologies of John Howard Yoder and Jürgen Moltmann

'A strong-minded, original contribution', Alan Kreider.

2000 / 978-0-85364-978-6 / xvi + 252pp

Terry J. Wright
Providence Made Flesh
Divine Presence as a Framework for a Theology of Providence

Traditional discussions of the Christian doctrine of providence often centre on the relation between divine agency and human freedom, seeking to offer an account of the extent to which a person is free before God, the first cause of all things. Terry J. Wright argues that such riddles of causation cannot determine the content of providence, and suggests a unique and alternative framework that depicts God's providential activity in terms of divine faithfulness to that which God has made. Providence is not God as first cause acting through creaturely secondary causation, rather providence is God's sovereign mediation of the divine presence across the whole world, achieved through creaturely faithfulness made possible and guaranteed by his own faithful action in Jesus Christ.

Terry J. Wright is an Associate Research Fellow at Spurgeon's College, London, UK.

2009 / 978-1-84227-632-7 / approx. 300pp

Theodore Zachariades
The Omnipresence of Jesus Christ
A Neglected Aspect of Evangelical Christology
Omnipresence is the key to unlock the kenosis question. The popular view of the incarnation whereby Christ possesses but does not independently exercise divine relative attributes is shown to be problematic and cannot be maintained with Christ's omnipresence, which by definition demands possession and use. Drawing on historical studies from the early church and John Calvin's christological exposition utilizing such concepts as *communicatio idiomatum* and *extra calvinisticum*, this work argues for a robust Chalcedonian incarnational christology that avoids all forms of kenotic thought.

Theodore Zachariades is founding pastor of Sovereign Grace Baptist Fellowship, Tullahoma, Tennessee, and teaches for Luther Rice University's distance learning program, Lithonia, Georgia, USA.

2010–11 / 978-1-84227-531-3 / approx. 300pp

New and unscheduled titles:

Nicholas John Ansell
The Annihilation of Hell
Universal Salvation and the Redemption of Time in the Eschatology of Jürgen Moltmann
978-1-84227-525-2 / approx. 300pp

Laurence M. Blanchard
Will God Save Us All? [Provisional title]
An Assessment of the Historical Development and Contemporary Expression of Universalism in Western Theology
978-1-84227-638-7 / approx. 300pp

David Hilborn
The Words of our Lips
Language-Use in Free Church Worship
Studies of liturgical language have tended to focus on the written canons of Roman Catholic and Anglican communities. By contrast, David Hilborn analyses the more extemporary approach of English Nonconformity. Drawing on recent developments in linguistic pragmatics, he explores similarities and differences between 'fixed' and 'free' worship, and argues for the interdependence of each.
978-0-85364-977-9 / approx. 300pp

John G. Kelly
One God, One People
The Differentiated Unity of the People of God in the Theology of Jürgen Moltmann
The author expounds and critiques Moltmann's doctrine of God and highlights the systematic connections between it and Moltmann's influential discussion of Israel. He then proposes a fresh approach to Jewish–Christian relations building on Moltmann's work using insights from Habermas and Rawls.
978-0-85346-969-4 / approx. 300pp

Robert Knowles
Anthony C. Thiselton and the Grammar of Hermeneutics
The Search for a Unified Theory
978-1-84227-637-2 / approx. 300pp

Esther L. Meek
Contact with Reality
An Examination of Realism in the Thought of Michael Polanyi
978-1-84227-622-8 / approx. 300pp

Myron B. Penner
Subjectivity and Knowledge
Self and Being in Kierkegaard's Thought
978-1-84227-406-6 / approx. 300pp

Hazel Sherman
Reading Zechariah
The Allegorical Tradition of Biblical Interpretation through the Commentary of Didymus the Blind and Theodore of Mopsuestia
A close reading of the commentary on Zechariah by Didymus the Blind alongside that of Theodore of Mopsuestia suggests that popular categorising of Antiochene and Alexandrian biblical exegesis as 'historical' or 'allegorical' is inadequate and misleading.
978-1-84227-213-8 / approx. 300pp

www.ingramcontent.com/pod-product-compliance
Lightning Source LLC
Chambersburg PA
CBHW052052300426
44117CB00012B/2087